Women and the Transmission of Religious Knowledge in Islam

Asma Sayeed's book explores the history of women as religious scholars from the first decades of Islam through the early Ottoman period (seventh to the seventeenth centuries). Focusing on women's engagement with *ḥadīth*, this book analyzes dramatic chronological patterns in women's *ḥadīth* participation in terms of developments in Muslim social, intellectual, and legal history. Drawing on primary and secondary sources, this work uncovers the historical forces that shaped Muslim women's public participation in religious learning. In the process, it challenges two opposing views: that Muslim women have been historically marginalized in religious education, and alternately that they have been consistently empowered thanks to early role models such as 'Ā'isha bint Abī Bakr, the wife of Prophet Muḥammad. This book is a must-read for those interested in the history of Muslim women as well as in debates about their rights in the modern world. The intersections of this history with topics in Muslim education, the development of Sunnī orthodoxies, Islamic law, and *ḥadīth* studies make this work an important contribution to Muslim social and intellectual history of the early and classical eras.

Asma Sayeed is Assistant Professor of Islamic Studies in the Department of Near Eastern Languages and Cultures at the University of California, Los Angeles. She has published articles in *Studia Islamica* and *Islamic Law and Society* and has contributed a number of encyclopedia articles on women's history in early and classical Islam.

For Rashid, Sulaiman, and Yusuf

Cambridge Studies in Islamic Civilization

Women and the Transmission of Religious Knowledge in Islam

ASMA SAYEED
University of California, Los Angeles

CAMBRIDGE
UNIVERSITY PRESS

CAMBRIDGE
UNIVERSITY PRESS

32 Avenue of the Americas, New York NY 10013-2473, USA

Cambridge University Press is part of the University of Cambridge.

It furthers the University's mission by disseminating knowledge in the pursuit of education, learning and research at the highest international levels of excellence.

www.cambridge.org
Information on this title: www.cambridge.org/9781107529816

First published 2013
First paperback edition 2015

A catalogue record for this publication is available from the British Library

Library of Congress Cataloguing in Publication data
Sayeed, Asma.
Women and the transmission of religious knowledge in Islam / Asma Sayeed.
pages ; cm – (Cambridge studies in Islamic civilization)
ISBN 978-1-107-03158-6
1. Women in Islam – History. 2. Women scholars – Islamic Empire. 3. Muhammad, Prophet, d. 632 – Companions. I. Title.
BP173.4.S33 2013
297.082–dc23 2012043744

ISBN 978-1-107-03158-6 Hardback
ISBN 978-1-107-52981-6 Paperback

Contents

Acknowledgments

I have accumulated countless debts as this project evolved from an idea into a book. I'd like to acknowledge just a few here with apologies for my omissions. Years ago, a conversation with Khaled Abou El Fadl about female jurists in early Islam sparked my interest, leading me to the world of women's *ḥadīth* transmission. I conducted my first research on *muḥadditha*s at SUNY-Binghamton under the exacting guidance of Akbar Muhammad, whose passion for Muslim social history was infectious and inspiring. At Princeton, Hossein Modarressi's patient mentoring, profound knowledge, and insightful comments on drafts of my dissertation have enriched the project and contributed to my growth as a scholar in critical ways. I also owe a special debt to Michael Cook. His meticulous review of the dissertation and subsequently the book manuscript has been invaluable. More importantly, his exemplary scholarship and his encouragement and support of my work have been formative throughout my career.

Colleagues and friends contributed to the project in many ways. Qasim Zaman, Issam Eido, and Martin Nguyen read selected chapters and provided valuable comments. Racha el Omari was always willing to help with many, sundry questions on Arabic translation and transliteration. My conversations with Shahab Ahmed have helped me hone a number of key points. Hanna Siurua's careful copyediting saved me from many errors and helped improve the work. Intisar Rabb provided thoughtful feedback on the introduction as well as on some central themes in the book, and her friendship over the years has provided comfort, humor, and inspiration.

My parents, Fatima and Zafar Sayeed, and my siblings, Sarah, Nadiyah, Mujahid, Salihah, and Muhasin, have supported me and made themselves available whenever I needed them. My mother especially has bolstered me with her love and unflagging energy. I've also been fortified by the good-humored support of my in-laws Mark Deevey, Shazia Khan, and the Alvis. Our Princeton clan, Faria Abedin, Simin Syed, Sofia Dasti, and their families, have been a source of comfort, strength, and community. My sons, Sulaiman and Yusuf, alternately tolerated my long library hours and battled my single-minded focus on my book. In the process, they have enriched my life beyond measure. My greatest debt is to my husband, Rashid Alvi, for reading more drafts than he cares to remember. He has been a true partner in this endeavor, and his belief in Muslim women's education is indelibly imprinted here.

Finally, I am grateful to the anonymous reviewers for their extensive, thoughtful comments and to Marigold Acland, Sarika Narula, and the team at Cambridge University Press for helping bring this manuscript to press.

Introduction

On the authority of Rā'iṭa, one of Muḥammad's Companions:

> I said to 'Abd Allāh b. Mas'ūd [her husband], "you and your children have kept me so busy that I can't give charity (*ṣadaqa*). I am unable to give anything as *ṣadaqa* because of [what I spend on] you." Ibn Mas'ūd said to her, "By God, I don't want you to do this if you don't get a reward for it." So she went to the Prophet and said, "O Messenger of God, I am a woman who is skilled in the work of my hands and [I] sell what I make. My children, my husband, and I have no income other than that. And they've kept me so busy that I can't give *ṣadaqa*.... Do I get a reward for what I spend?" [T]he Prophet of God said to her, "Spend on them and you will be compensated accordingly."
>
> Ibn Ḥanbal (d. 241/855)[1]

> Zaynab bint al-Kamāl was born in 646 [AH]. In [6]48, she was brought to Ḥabība bint Abī 'Umar. She heard [*ḥadīth*] from Muḥammad b. 'Abd al-Hādī, Ibrāhīm b. Khalīl, and Khaṭīb Marda.... Al-Dhahabī said, "[S]he transmitted a great deal [of religious knowledge]. Students would crowd around her and read lengthy books to her. She was kind in her manners, generous in her spirit; it may well be that they had her listen to their readings for most of the day... She was afflicted with opthalmia in her youth and never married. She died on 19th Jumādā al-Ūlā in the year 740, having passed 90 years of age. Great numbers of people turned out for her funeral. She had a camel-load of *ḥadīth* [compilations]. She was the last in the world to transmit from Sibṭ al-Silafī and other scholars by virtue of her *ijāza*s [i.e., certificates] from them.
>
> Ibn Ḥajar al-'Asqalānī (d. 852/1449)[2]

[1] Aḥmad b. Ḥanbal, *Musnad* (Beirut: al-Maktab al-Islāmī, 1993), 3:660–61.

[2] Ibn Ḥajar al-'Asqalānī, *al-Durar al-Kāmina fī A'yān al-Mi'a al-Thāmina* (Cairo: Dār al-Kutub al-Ḥadītha, 1966), 2:209–10. Her full name is given at the beginning of this entry as Zaynab bint Aḥmad b. 'Abd al-Raḥīm b. 'Abd al-Wāḥid b. Aḥmad al-Maqdisiyya. I have shortened Ibn

These two accounts bookend several centuries of the history of Muslim women as transmitters of religious knowledge. Even stripped of context, they evoke women's spiritual aspirations and authority in disparate settings. Rā'iṭa, the speaker in first report, is the sole earner of her household. Worried that her expenditures on her family prevent her from gaining the heavenly rewards for charitable spending, she takes her concern directly to Muḥammad. His reassurance and her transmission of it are preserved in Muslim tradition not merely as a historical artifact. Rather, her narration conveys an authoritative legal precedent to all Muslims about charity. The second account encapsulates Zaynab bint al-Kamāl's educational career, which spanned nine decades. She was taken in her infancy to acquire certification for religious texts that she taught later in her life, apparently undeterred by her opthalmia, an eye disease. In her seniority, she attracted large numbers of male and female students eager to partake of her knowledge.

These intriguing descriptions whet our curiosity about Muslim women's religious learning. What else did Rā'iṭa transmit? Where does she stand with respect to other Companions who also narrated reports? Did Muslims contest her authority, or Zaynab's? What does it mean for a two-year-old girl to be brought to teachers, and how does she then go on to transmit that knowledge as a ninety-year-old woman? How did women's religious learning change during the centuries separating Rā'iṭa and Zaynab and thereafter? And what do women's intellectual endeavors tell us about their times?

This book, inspired by such questions, uncovers a surprising history, and in the process unsettles two well-known and opposing narratives about Muslim women's religious education. One view, projecting backward from contemporary news reports about the repression of Muslim women by extremists, reads similar oppression into most of Muslim history. The second, extrapolating from the impressive achievements of well-known early women such as Prophet Muḥammad's wife 'Ā'isha bint Abī Bakr (d. 58/678), promotes an unfailingly positive account of educational access and opportunities for Muslim women throughout history.

My analysis highlights the fluctuating fortunes of Sunnī female religious scholars across nearly ten centuries (seventh–sixteenth centuries) and nuances monochromatic views about their education. These shifting, uneven patterns of women's transmission of religious knowledge (specifically *ḥadīth*) structure the narrative of this book. My central thesis is that

Ḥajar's biography of Zaynab in this excerpt to emphasize a few salient characteristics of women's *ḥadīth* transmission in her time.

women's initial participation – a largely ad hoc, unregulated enterprise – was sharply curtailed by the professionalization of this field in the early second/eighth century, only to be resuscitated in the mid-fourth/tenth century as "traditionism" and "traditionalism" became prevalent expressions of Sunnī Islam.[3]

Ḥadīth transmission emerged early on as the principal arena for Muslim women's religious education. Conveying Muḥammad's words, decisions, and actions on innumerable matters, *ḥadīth* constitute the bulk of normative religious knowledge transmitted from the earliest decades of Islam. They are vital as sources of law, second only to the Qur'ān, and as records of the early Islamic past. After the death of Muḥammad, his Companions (those Muslims who had actually met him) became valued sources about the practice of the new faith. Men and women participated in a free, unregulated exchange of information. This matrix produced the tradition of the female *ḥadīth* transmitter and provided a template that would be revisited and refashioned to accommodate the needs and visions of subsequent generations of Muslims.

Over the course of ten centuries, women's participation in *ḥadīth* transmission rose and abated in four distinct phases. In Chapter 1, I treat the earliest decades of Islamic history, when many female Companions shared their firsthand knowledge of the Prophet. The communal memory of Muslims preserves not just numerous sayings from 'Ā'isha bint Abī Bakr, but also the few words of more obscure women such as al-Jahdama, known to us only because she reported seeing Muḥammad with *henna* in his hair. Further, some women of this first generation are portrayed as interpreting the legal significance of reports with a view to guiding and shaping Muslim practice. As may be expected, several of the Prophet's wives are prominent transmitters during this period.

This early acceptance of women as authoritative sources for information about Muḥammad quickly faded – a development that I analyze in Chapter 2. By the end of the first century, these sayings were increasingly deployed to serve political, legal, sectarian, and theological agendas. Forgery became rampant, prompting widespread calls for professionalization and more stringent criteria for determining valid transmission. Legal

[3] I use traditionism to refer to the view that upheld the importance of *ḥadīth* reports in deriving Islamic law and that promoted this view through accurate transmission of them. Traditionalism, on the other hand, references a broader outlook and implicates not just the derivation of Islamic law but also approaches to understanding Muslim history and to mitigating inter-*madhhab* division among Sunnīs. I discuss my usage of this term later in this introduction and provide a more detailed analysis of its historical dimensions in Chapter 4.

acumen, linguistic training, direct (face-to-face) contact with teachers, and an ability to undertake long, arduous, solitary journeys in order to acquire even a single report became a sine qua non for accomplished transmitters. Most women could not compete in this environment, and their participation dropped precipitously, remaining negligible for the next two and a half centuries.

Remarkably, in the mid-fourth century of Islamic history, women reemerged as trustworthy *shaykhas* coveted for their religious learning and revered for their piety. In Chapter 3, I assess how new developments, among them the canonization of *ḥadīth* collections, the growing acceptance of written (as opposed to oral) transmission, and the increased incidence of kinship-based groupings within the scholarly class (*'ulamā'*), created favorable conditions for this trend. The revival drew strength from precedents of the female Companions whose contributions as transmitters of reports were recalled in modeling feminine piety and religious learning. Chapter 4 explores how the ascendancy of Sunnī traditionalism as an orthodoxy provided the final impetus for a full-scale mobilization of women in this arena from the sixth/twelfth to the ninth/fifteenth century. My narrative ends with another sharp contraction in female participation in *ḥadīth* transmission in the late Mamlūk and early Ottoman period (tenth/sixteenth century). Here, the trajectory of women's religious education takes a different turn as attested by scattered references in the contemporary literature to their legal training and increasing involvement with organized Ṣūfism. This latter period of decline is therefore substantively different from the one that occurred during the second/eighth and third/ninth centuries.

To make sense of how trends in women's education are intertwined with a host of social, intellectual, and political factors, I draw on interdisciplinary theoretical insights. Studies on the sociology of education, for example, have highlighted the multiple social uses of knowledge.[4] In this vein, the history of women as *ḥadīth* transmitters affirms that evolving social uses of religious knowledge (specifically *ḥadīth*) shaped women's educational access and participation. Pierre Bourdieu's work on the different forms of capital is helpful in understanding the trend in the classical

[4] For an introduction to this field (in contexts other than the Islamic one studied here), see Alan R. Sadovnik (ed.), *Sociology of Education* (New York: Routledge, 2007). See also Volker Meja and Nico Stehr (eds.), *The Sociology of Knowledge*, 2 vols. (Northampton: Edward Elgar, 1999), for seminal articles in the field and an overview of its development.

period when women reemerged as celebrated teachers of *ḥadīth*.[5] Bourdieu has prompted us to think of capital not just as accumulated material resources, but also as assets that can accrue in the form of social dispositions and cultural goods, which in turn confer coveted status and upward social mobility. Women's accumulation of *ḥadīth* learning during the classical period translated well into cultural capital and lent status to the scholarly families who supported their endeavors.[6]

Women's resounding successes from the fourth/tenth to the ninth/fifteenth century were built on two foundations. First, their participation was seen as a continuation of established tradition, based on the precedent of the prominent female transmitters of the Companion generation. However, notwithstanding the appearance of and claims to continuity, the roles of female Companions were distinct from those of women of the classical era. The former, as witnesses to Muḥammad's life, were authors of the accounts they narrated. Some of them were also sought out for their opinions on legal, ritual, and credal matters. In their time, the reports lacked the formal structure of *ḥadīth*, namely an *isnād* (chain of transmission) appended to a distinct *matn* (text). The formulaic accounts preserved in the collections of *ḥadīth* should not mask that their contribution lay in the very origination of these reports. By contrast, women of the classical period were honored primarily as faithful reproducers of *ḥadīth* proper, which by their time had been sifted and arranged and had generated extensive commentary. Additionally, women of the later eras are praised in the historical literature for embodying feminine piety by espousing asceticism and engaging with *ḥadīth* transmission from the cradle to the grave. Talal Asad has distilled the theoretical underpinning of such reworking of past models in his outline of an Islamic discursive tradition, thereby providing a framework for analyzing evolutions in the forms and contents of women's *ḥadīth* transmission. Asad states:

> A tradition consists essentially of discourses that seek to instruct practitioners regarding the correct form and purpose of a given practice that, precisely because it is established, has a history. These discourses relate conceptually to *a past* (when the practice was instituted, and from which the knowledge of its point and proper

5 Pierre Bourdieu, "The Forms of Capital," trans. Richard Nice, in *Handbook of Theory and Research for the Sociology of Education*, ed. John G. Richardson, 241–58 (New York: Greenwood Press, 1986).

6 Michael Chamberlain has also applied Bourdieu's ideas to his analysis of practices associated with religious learning in classical Muslim societies. See his *Knowledge and Social Practice in Medieval Damascus, 1190–1350* (New York: Cambridge University Press, 1994).

performance has been transmitted) and *a future* (how the point of the practice can best be secured in the short or long term, or why it should be modified or abandoned), through *a present* (how it is linked to other practices, institutions, and social conditions).[7]

Tradition and its maintenance are valuable not because "traditional practices" are blind imitations of past practices. Rather, discursive traditions enable stable evolution by orienting practices to the past while allowing for modification of original models. Asad conceives broadly of an "Islamic discursive tradition" to address shortcomings in previous anthropological approaches to Islam. Qasim Zaman, in his study of contemporary South Asian *'ulamā'*, draws out the utility of applying Asad's model to multiple discourses *within* Islam: the *Sharī'a*, classical Islamic historiography, and Ṣūfism are other such examples that Zaman notes.[8] I extend Asad's model to understand evolutions in the arena of *ḥadīth* transmission. In Chapters 3 and 4, I cast the revival of female *ḥadīth* transmission as exemplifying a discursive tradition in which the *'ulamā'* as a social class responded to profound changes in the field of *ḥadīth* studies (such as the canonization of *ḥadīth* literature and the acceptance of written transmission) and reintegrated women into this arena of Islamic learning. This reintegration, in turn, facilitated adaptation by the *'ulamā'* to changing political and social orders that accompanied the dissolution of central 'Abbāsid power and the rise of autonomous dynasties.

A second and related foundation for women's success was that the collective gatekeepers of tradition embraced and sanctioned their accomplishments. Here too Talal Asad's theoretical insights and conceptual model of "orthodoxy" are instructive. Critiquing the prevalent definition of Muslim orthodoxy as "a specific set of doctrines at the heart of Islam," Asad defines orthodoxy not as "a mere body of opinion, but a distinctive relationship – a relationship of power." He continues: "[W]herever Muslims have the power to regulate, uphold, require, or adjust *correct* practices, and to condemn, exclude, undermine, or replace *incorrect* ones,

[7] Talal Asad, "The Idea of an Anthropology of Islam," *Occasional Papers Series*, Center for Contemporary Arab Studies, Georgetown University (1986), 14–15. In developing his outline of tradition, Asad credits the influential works of Alasdair MacIntyre, in particular his *After Virtue* (Notre Dame: University of Notre Dame Press, 1984). See also MacIntyre, *Whose Justice? Which Rationality?* (Notre Dame: University of Notre Dame Press, 1988) for further development of his ideas on tradition.

[8] Muhammad Qasim Zaman, *'Ulamā' in Contemporary Islam: Custodians of Change* (Princeton: Princeton University Press, 2002), 4–7.

there is the domain of orthodoxy."[9] Asad's assertion that orthodoxy exists *wherever* Muslims exercise such power is balanced by his emphasis that the Islamic discursive tradition maintains the centrality of foundational texts (the Qur'ān and *ḥadīth*). By retaining the referents of foundational texts while accounting for localized interpretations of doctrine and practices, Asad advocates a view that acknowledges the existence of multiple orthodoxies synchronically and diachronically.

Traditionalism was one of several Muslim orthodoxies that existed between the early Islamic centuries and the late classical period. The term "traditionalism," one of academic coinage, is contested and its connotations vary depending on historical context.[10] I have incorporated it here to evoke a particular set of characteristics that are important for understanding the history of women's religious education. My own usage is broad and references a worldview inspired by the following beliefs: that *ḥadīth* reports are of primary importance in interpreting the Qur'ān and in deriving Islamic law; that consensus (*ijmā'*) is an important guarantor of the righteousness of the Muslim community; and that the pious early ancestors (*salaf*), irrespective of their political affiliations and other differences, are exemplary for all future generations. Traditionalists also tend to either avoid speculative theology altogether or strive to mitigate its influence in their religious discourse.[11] This is the worldview that Marshall Hodgson has famously called Jamā'ī Sunnism. For him, the defining characteristics include a collective interest in minimizing division among

[9] Asad, "Anthropology of Islam," 15. By comparison, the prevailing definition of orthodoxy is "correct or sound belief according to an authoritative norm"; see *Encyclopedia of Religion*, 2nd edition, s.v. "Orthodoxy and Heterodoxy." Asad's conceptualization is more complete because it integrates the ideas of correct doctrine and correct practice while evoking the contestations that occur to establish and maintain orthodoxy.

[10] For discussions about the use of the word "traditionalism," see Benyamin Abrahamov, *Islamic Theology: Traditionalism and Rationalism* (Edinburgh: Edinburgh University Press, 1998), especially Introduction and chapter 1; William Graham, "Traditionalism in Islam: An Essay in Interpretation," *Journal of Interdisciplinary History* 23, no. 3 (Winter 1993): 495–522; George Makdisi, "Ash'arī and the Ash'arites in Islamic Religious History II," *Studia Islamica* 18 (1963): 48–52; Marshall Hodgson, *The Venture of Islam* (Chicago: University of Chicago Press, 1974), 1: 64–66, for an analysis of the problems associated with the use of "tradition" and "traditionalism"; and Sherman Jackson, *On the Boundaries of Theological Tolerance in Islam* (New York: Oxford University Press, 2002), 16–29, for a keen critique of shortcomings in the usage of the terms "traditionalism" and "rationalism."

[11] In contrast to my own broad usage, some scholars use the term to signify only Ḥanbalī theologians and their followers during the classical period. See, for example, Richard Martin and Mark Woodward, *Defenders of Reason in Islam* (Oxford: Oneworld, 1997), 10–15.

the four major Sunnī schools of law and an understanding that theological reasoning within acceptable boundaries was permissible.[12]

As an orthodoxy, traditionalism enjoyed tremendous success and exercised pervasive influence in the central Islamic lands from approximately the sixth/twelfth to the tenth/sixteenth century. Women were able to promote this orthodoxy because those who articulated its social vision *upheld* the tradition of female transmission of religious knowledge, as originally instituted by the Companion generation, and *adjusted* the practice in accordance with their needs in the classical era. The accomplishment of traditionalism in including women comes into sharper focus in comparison with Mu'tazilism, a rationalist orthodoxy that enjoyed success primarily among the ruling and intellectual elites in the second/eighth and third/ninth centuries. Unlike traditionalists, Mu'tazilīs appear to have eschewed women's active participation in the promulgation of their ideology, and we find few records of accomplished female Mu'tazilī theologians in the annals of Islamic history. This pattern will appear counterintuitive from our modernist perspective, which conditions us to think of rationalist ideologies as more amenable to women's empowerment and participation and traditionalist ones as being inimical to their interests. Asad's theoretical contribution sensitizes us to the dynamics of inclusion and exclusion that underpin different orthodoxies, which in turn profoundly impact women's involvement.

SOURCES AND METHODOLOGICAL ISSUES

Given the centrality of *ḥadīth* to Muslim life, the traditions and their transmitters were subject to scholarly scrutiny. While women's lives are largely overlooked in the male-authored annals of Islamic history, their participation in the field of *ḥadīth* was more diligently documented. As a result, this is one of the few areas of premodern Muslim women's history for which we have considerable source material. Arabic biographical dictionaries and chronicles are among the most important sources for reconstructing women's *ḥadīth* participation. These include compilations arranged according to generations of scholars and noteworthy persons, such as the *Ṭabaqāt* of Ibn Sa'd (d. 230/845) and the *Siyar A'lām al-Nubalā'* of al-Dhahabī (d. 748/1348), as well as centenary dictionaries, such as *al-Durar al-Kāmina fī*

[12] Marshall Hodgson, *Venture of Islam*, 1:276–79 for an introduction to his use of the term Jamā'ī Sunnism. See also *Venture of Islam*, vol. 2 (passim), where he describes the spread of this understanding of Sunnism across the Muslim world during the classical eras.

A'yān al-Mi'a al-Thāmina of Ibn Ḥajar al-'Asqalānī (d. 852/1449) and *al-Ḍaw' al-Lāmi' fī A'yān al-Qarn al-Tāsi'* of al-Sakhāwī (d. 902/1497). Such works amply attest women's activities and the widespread acceptance of their participation in religious education.

The abundance of data, however, should not blind us to its inherent limitations. First, these sources were composed by men, and we have few self-narratives of women's experiences in this arena. Second, most entries on women in biographical compendia are formulaic and frugal, hindering our ability to compose a nuanced history. Lineages, death dates, teacher-student networks, and remarks on the moral character and personal piety of various women comprise the bulk of what early and classical biographers preserved for posterity. Such information goes only so far in our attempts at historical reconstruction. Needless to say, classical Muslim biographers were not interested in issues of women's empowerment or the role of gender in determining women's educational access. Questions about women's concerns, their daily lives, and their routines can only be answered inferentially, sometimes by reading into the silences of our sources.

Two other sources of more limited utility that contain scattered references to women's narration of reports are legal compendia and manuals on the sciences of *ḥadīth* transmission. The prescriptive nature of both genres dictates a different methodological approach. For example, *al-Kifāya fī 'Ilm al-Riwāya*, the *ḥadīth* manual of al-Khaṭīb al-Baghdādī (d. 463/1071), prescribes a curriculum for study and the appropriate etiquette for teachers and students. We cannot, of course, assume that students maintained these standards. In fact, the presumption is often that if authorities repeatedly insist on a protocol, it is because that protocol is being violated. In general, the extent to which individual men and women adhered to the standards enunciated by leading scholars must be gleaned from other sources related directly to the individual in question. Similarly, legal manuals present historical evidence only to the extent necessary to substantiate or undermine the claims of jurists. On the topic of women's access to public space such as mosques (popular sites for religious instruction), *ḥadīth* reports are presented selectively to support a juristic prescription. Nevertheless, judicious use of these sources can help us recreate some of the historical circumstances affecting women's participation in the transmission of religious knowledge.

For the earliest decades of Islamic history, we can look to the individual *ḥadīth* credited to female narrators. The chains of transmission (*isnād*s) appended to these reports can augment our knowledge of the teacher-student networks of the women who appear in them. An analysis of the *ḥadīth* texts (*matn*) themselves reveals the subjects about which women imparted knowledge. Finally, because the Companions are portrayed as the first authors of the texts they convey, various narrative elements can at times be used to reconstruct the circumstances of women's participation and their own perceptions of their roles.

Use of *ḥadīth* and historical reports from the earliest decades of Islam, however, requires grappling with debates about the authenticity of this material. The most comprehensive early collections of *ḥadīth* from which it is possible to draw data for this study date to the latter part of the second/eighth century.[13] The first extensive biographical work, the *Ṭabaqāt* of Ibn Sa'd, dates to the beginning of the third/ninth century. We are therefore confronted with one of the enduring debates of early Islamic historiography: the use of *ḥadīth* as primary sources, especially for the first decades of Islam. The literature on this issue is extensive. Here I present only the contours of the debate and the position I take in this study.

It is a cornerstone of faith for many Muslims that authenticated *ḥadīth* convey the sayings and actions of Muḥammad as reported by his Companions.[14] Some modern scholars of Islamic history also maintain that these traditions form a relatively accurate record of the rise of Islam and the formation of the first Muslim polity, as well as Muḥammad's ritualistic practices and injunctions.[15] At the opposite end of the spectrum, other scholars hold that the *ḥadīth* are primarily fabrications and cannot

[13] While there are earlier collections, comprised of notes (*ṣuḥuf*) compiled by second-century authors, the *Muwaṭṭa'* of Mālik b. Anas (d. 179/796) is one of the earliest surviving substantial collections containing traditions attributed to female Companions.

[14] It is important to point out here that in the derivation of law, Muslims themselves aspire not to absolute certainty about the authenticity of a *ḥadīth* but rather to a high degree of probability that a particular report accurately conveys Muḥammad's views. For an exposition of this view, see Wael Hallaq, "Authenticity of Prophetic *Ḥadīth*: A Pseudo-Problem," *Studia Islamica* 89 (1999): 75–90.

[15] See, for example, Nabia Abbott, *Studies in Arabic Literary Papyri*, vol. 1, *Historical Texts* (Chicago: University of Chicago Press, 1957–72), and Fuat Sezgin, *Ta'rīkh al-Turāth al-'Arabī*, vol. 1, *'Ulūm al-Qur'ān wa'l-Ḥadīth* (Riyad: Wizārat al-Ta'līm al-'Ālī, 1991). See also Fred Donner, *Narratives of Islamic Origins: The Beginnings of Islamic Historical Writing* (Princeton: Princeton University Press, 1998). In the introduction to this work, Donner provides a more detailed presentation of the debate than I have given here. It is also worth noting that the use of *ḥadīth* in Muslim historical writing is secondary to the use of *akhbār* (historical reports other than those ascribed to Muḥammad). The latter form an important basis for works on Muḥammad's life (*sīra*) and the military conquests of the early community (*maghāzī*). See the works of Tarif Khalidi, *Arabic Historical Thought in the Classical Period* (New York: Cambridge University Press, 1994) and Chase Robinson, *Islamic Historiography* (New York: Cambridge University Press, 2003) for their analyses of developments in historical writing in early and classical Islam.

be utilized for meaningful historical inquiry into the first century of Islam.[16]

Scholars have articulated diverse approaches to testing the authenticity of Muslim tradition. These include assessments of patterns in the provenance and regional circulation of *ḥadīth*, quantitative analyses of transmission patterns, and investigations into the social and historical developments that gave rise to particular traditions.[17] These methods have yielded varying results, with a few studies convincingly dating selected traditions to the first decades of Islam.[18] Several scholars have concluded that there is a "genuine core" to which much of Muslim tradition belongs.[19] Others have maintained, however, that overlays of forgeries and tampering with the "core" make it difficult, if not impossible, to distinguish the real from the forged.

My own view is that judicious use of *ḥadīth* can yield valuable insights into a range of issues in early Islamic history. Accordingly, I analyze the reports ascribed to early Muslim women to understand the Muslim communal memory of the role of women as transmitters.[20] As such, I am not concerned with decisively establishing whether the women to whom the reports are ascribed actually uttered them. Because the authoritative

16 Two landmark Western studies that are critical of the authenticity of *ḥadīth* literature are Ignaz Goldziher, *Muslim Studies*, translated by C. R. Barber and S. M. Stern (Chicago: Aldine, 1968), vol. 2, and Joseph Schacht, *Origins of Muhammadan Jurisprudence* (Oxford: Clarendon, 1959). See also Harald Motzki (ed.), *Ḥadīth: Origins and Developments* (Burlington: Ashgate Variorum, 2004) for a valuable collection of formative articles in Western *ḥadīth* studies.

17 A few such studies are as follows: G. H. A. Juynboll, *Muslim Tradition: Studies in Chronology, Provenance, and Authorship of Early Ḥadīth* (New York: Cambridge University Press, 1983); Michael Cook, "Eschatology and the Dating of Traditions," *Princeton Papers in Near Eastern Studies* 1 (1992): 23–47; and Herbert Berg, *The Development of Exegesis in Early Islam: The Authenticity of Muslim Literature from the Formative Period* (Richmond: Curzon, 2000).

18 See, for example, Harald Motzki's articles "*Muṣannaf* of 'Abd al-Razzāq al-Ṣan'ānī as a Source of Authentic *Aḥādīth* of the First Century A.H.," *Journal of Near Eastern Studies* 50, no. 1 (1990): 1–21, and "The Prophet and the Cat: On Dating Mālik's *Muwaṭṭa'* and Legal Traditions," *Jerusalem Studies in Arabic and Islam* 22 (1998): 18–83.

19 For example, Donner in *Narratives of Islamic Origins* presents an extensive and plausible argument for this view.

20 A similar methodology has been effectively adapted in other recent studies of early female personalities. See, for example, Jamal Elias, "The *Ḥadīth* Traditions of 'Ā'isha as Prototypes of Self-Narrative," *Edebiyāt* 7 (1997): 215–33; Franz Rosenthal, "Muslim Social Values and Literary Criticism: Reflections on the Ḥadīth of Umm Zar'," *Oriens* 34 (1994): 31–56; Denise A. Spellberg, *Politics, Gender, and the Islamic Past* (New York: Columbia University Press, 1994); and Denise Soufi, "The Image of Fāṭima in Classical Muslim Thought" (PhD diss., Princeton University, 1997).

ḥadīth collections date from the late second/eighth to the late third/ninth century, we can at the very least use them to explore what was ascribed to women and in circulation about them in the period contemporary to the compilers of these collections. Through these *ḥadīth* and the associated biographical literature, we can also extract the profiles of the women who were portrayed as narrating the *ḥadīth*. Thus our historical evidence permits us to address several questions: Were the female narrators remembered as scholars or more as purveyors of oral tradition acquired through happenstance? To what extent does the portrayal of the narration activity of the female Companions resemble that of women of the Seljūq, Ayyūbid, and Mamlūk periods? And how did Muslim women who were culturally and religiously restricted in their interactions with men negotiate a field of learning that placed a premium on direct contact and oral transmission between students and teachers? Even though we cannot decisively answer the question of the authenticity of any of the *ḥadīth* ascribed to women of the earliest generations, we can certainly arrive at conclusions about the perceptions that later generations had regarding female participation in the transmission of religious knowledge.

A final methodological comment concerns the type of *ḥadīth* that I use for this study. The first two chapters, focusing on early *ḥadīth* transmission, draw data from the six authoritative collections (*al-kutub al-sitta*)[21] as well as from the *Muwaṭṭa'* of Mālik b. Anas (d. 179/796); the *Musnad* collections by al-Ḥumaydī (d. 219/834), Ibn Ḥanbal (d. 241/855), ʻAbd b. Ḥumayd al-Kissī (d. 249/863), and al-Dārimī (d. 255/869); and the *Ṣaḥīḥ* of Ibn Khuzayma (d. 311/924).[22] There are other important Sunnī

[21] The six collections are as follows: the *Ṣaḥīḥ* collections of al-Bukhārī (d. 256/870) and Muslim (d. 261/875) and the *Sunan*s of Ibn Māja (d. 273/887), Abū Dāwūd (d. 275/889), al-Tirmidhī (d. 279/892), and al-Nasā'ī (d. 303/915).

[22] All of the previously named collections have been indexed in a *musnad* fashion (i.e., according to the Companion narrating the reports) by al-Mizzī (d. 742/1341) in his *Tuḥfat al-Ashrāf bi-Maʻrifat al-Aṭrāf*, 13 vols. (Beirut: Dār al-Gharb al-Islāmī, 1999), and also in the modern compilation *al-Musnad al-Jāmiʻ*, compiled by Bashshār ʻAwwād Maʻrūf et al., 22 vols. (Beirut: Dār al-Jīl, 1993). In general, the traditions ascribed to female Companions in these two index compilations do not differ much from those in other indices drawn from other collections. A comparison of traditions ascribed to women in these indices with those in Ibn Ḥajar al-ʻAsqalānī's *Taʻjīl al-Manfaʻa bi-Zawā'id Rijāl al-A'imma al-Arbaʻa* (Beirut: Dār al-Kutub al-ʻIlmiyya, 1996) reveals uniformity in terms of overall content and subject matter attributed to female Companions. The differences lie primarily in the numbers of traditions ascribed to each woman in different compilations. To a much lesser extent, there are differences in terms of the Successors to which the female Companions narrate. The *Taʻjīl al-Manfaʻa* lists the narrators who do not appear in one of the four canonical works, namely the *Ṣaḥīḥ*s of al-Bukhārī and Muslim and the *Sunan*s of al-Tirmidhī and al-Nasā'ī (i.e., the *zawā'id rijāl al-a'imma al-arbaʻa*), but who do appear

compilations not accounted for here. My selection, which includes the six most authoritative works and other widely circulated ones, provides a representative sample of the *ḥadīth* narrated by women.[23] For the most part, the traditions analyzed here are classified by *ḥadīth* critics and scholars as *muttaṣil* and *marfūʿ*. That is to say, they are distinguished by an uninterrupted (*muttaṣil*) chain of transmission (*isnād*) that goes back to Muḥammad himself (*marfūʿ*).[24] The traditional Muslim approach has deemed such chains of transmission to be the most trustworthy and most valid for legal discourse. Conversely, these are precisely the *isnād*s most stringently questioned by those who doubt the authenticity of Muslim tradition.[25] In such circles, they are regarded as patently forged chains attached to fabricated texts; both the *isnād*s and their texts have been "perfected" in order to enhance their status as legal proofs. In addition, the *ḥadīth* narrated by women tend to carry another type of chain, namely a family *isnād*, in which members of one family narrate to each other or in which a client (*mawlā*) narrates from his/her master or patron.

in the following collections: the *Muwaṭṭaʾ* of Mālik; the *Musnad* of al-Shāfiʿī (d. 204/820); the *Musnad* of Ibn Ḥanbal; the *Sunan* of al-Dārimī; the *Muntaqā* of Ibn al-Jārūd (d. 307/920); the *Ṣaḥīḥ* of Ibn Khuzayma; the *Mustakhraj* of Abū ʿAwāna (d. 316/928); the *Sharḥ Maʿānī al-Āthār* of al-Ṭaḥāwī (d. 321/933); the *Ṣaḥīḥ* of Ibn Ḥibbān (d. 354/965); the *Sunan* of al-Dāraquṭnī (d. 385/995); and the *Mustadrak* of al-Ḥākim al-Naysābūrī (d. 405/1014).

23 For example, I have not thoroughly analyzed the *Muṣannaf*s of ʿAbd al-Razzāq al-Ṣanʿānī (d. 211/827) or Ibn Abī Shayba (d. 235/849), which contain traditions narrated by women that do not always report sayings or actions of the Prophet. However, I have compared the women listed in the indices of these collections with the ones in my database. The representation of women in these two works is limited in comparison with the collections chosen for closer analysis for this study. (The indices of both of these works contain sections that group the traditions according the narrators who appear in their *isnād*s. See Muḥammad Salīm Ibrāhīm Samāra et al. [eds.], *Fihris Aḥādīth wa-Āthār al-Muṣannaf li'l-Ḥāfiẓ al-Kabīr Abī Bakr ʿAbd al-Razzāq b. Hammām al-Ṣanʿānī*, vols. 3–4 [Beirut: ʿĀlam al-Kutub, 1988]; and Muḥammad Salīm Ibrāhīm Samāra et al. [eds.], *Fihris Aḥādīth wa-Āthār al-Muṣannaf li'l-Imām al-Ḥāfiẓ ʿAbd Allāh b. Muḥammad b. Abī Shayba*, vols. 3–4 [Beirut: ʿĀlam al-Kutub, 1989].)

24 This is as opposed to *isnād*s appearing in many works of *sīra*, *maghāzī*, and in some of the early legal works such as the *Muṣannaf* of ʿAbd al-Razzāq al-Ṣanʿānī. The *isnād*s in the aforementioned genres are often of the following varieties deemed weaker as legal proofs by *ḥadīth* critics and jurists: *mursal* (*isnād* in which a Companion is "missing," i.e., a Successor appears to narrate directly from Muḥammad); *munqaṭiʿ* (*isnād* that is interrupted at any point in the chain); or *mawqūf* (*isnād* that claims a Companion as the final authority). Explanations for the classifications of *isnād*s and their ranking as legal proofs can be found in Ibn al-Ṣalāḥ (d. 643/1245), *Muqaddima fī ʿUlūm al-Ḥadīth* (Beirut: Dār al-Kutub al-ʿIlmiyya, 1995), 39–58.

25 See, for example, Schacht, *Origins*, 163–75.

Transmissions of this type have been deemed particularly suspect as chains fabricated to withstand the scrutiny of *ḥadīth* critics.[26]

Because the aforementioned chains of transmission have come under heavy criticism, it is important to discuss their utility for this study. The collections chosen for this study, in particular the six authoritative Sunnī collections, are largely composed of traditions that were utilized in legal discussions on matters related to creed and practice. As John Burton writes in his *Introduction to the Ḥadīth*, these traditions and their implications for religious practice were not taken lightly by *ḥadīth* scholars and jurists.[27] The premise in this study is that since these *ḥadīth* were often considered viable proofs for legal discourse, they had to be transmitted and/or crafted with both credible *isnād*s and credible narratives.[28] In other words, these *ḥadīth* could not violate with abandon the perceptions that Muslims of later generations had about their predecessors. To succeed within the domain of legal discussion, both the *isnād* and the *matn* of a tradition had to appeal to, or resonate in some way with, the collective memory of Muslims of the second/eighth and third/ninth centuries. Thus whether or not these *isnād*s preserve an actual chain of transmission, they undoubtedly conform to an envisaged portrait of transmission. Even if they are wholesale forgeries, they are still valuable because they reveal the perceptions that Muslims had of the early female narrators as dependable transmitters. Although conclusive comment on the authenticity of individual *ḥadīth* is not possible, my analysis of chronological trends nevertheless leads to a hypothesis proposing the early dating of traditions ascribed to many of the female Companions. I outline this hypothesis in the conclusion to the book and present a potentially fruitful avenue for future research into early Islamic social history.

Though the source material at hand is rich and varied, women's engagement with *ḥadīth* across Islamic history remains understudied. More than

26 Schacht, *Origins*, 170; G. H. A. Juynboll, "Early Islamic Society as Reflected in its Use of *Isnāds*," in *Studies on the Origins and Uses of Islamic Ḥadīth* (Brookfield: Ashgate Variorum, 1996), 171–79.

27 In explaining the exegetical activity of the early scholars, John Burton emphasizes the seriousness of their task and notes that "To the Muslim scholar, every detail, however minute, might make the difference between eternal life and death"; see John Burton, *Introduction to the Ḥadīth* (Edinburgh: Edinburgh University Press, 1994), xvii.

28 Reports in the *faḍā'il* (exemplary characteristics) and *fitan* (trials and tribulations) categories were not subject to the same scrutiny by *ḥadīth* critics as those in categories such as *ṭahāra* (i.e., ritual purity), *ṣalāt*, or *ḥajj*. Because the former were not commonly utilized for legal applications and often had other didactic purposes, there was more leeway among *ḥadīth* critics in accepting or rejecting them.

a century ago, Ignaz Goldziher appended a brief, anecdotal summary of the topic to his *Muslim Studies*.[29] Since then, there have been a handful of articles and chapter-length contributions such as those of Jonathan Berkey and Omaima Abou-Bakr on women in the Mamlūk period (thirteenth to sixteenth centuries), and that of Richard Bulliet on Iranian elite women in the pre-Mongol period (eleventh and twelfth centuries).[30] More recently, Muhammad Akram Nadwi has authored a detailed overview of female *ḥadīth* transmission as an introduction to his forthcoming Arabic biographical dictionary of female *ḥadīth* scholars.[31] While Nadwi collates valuable information about the range of women's participation, he does not aim to provide historical synthesis and analysis.[32] Similarly, a number of Arabic biographical dictionaries and monographs relevant to this topic offer a wealth of intriguing anecdotes but do not advance broader historical or conceptual conclusions.[33] My book is thus the first detailed investigation of female *ḥadīth* transmission that employs a rigorous historical

[29] Goldziher, *Muslim Studies*, 2:366–68.

[30] Jonathan Berkey, *The Transmission of Knowledge in Medieval Cairo* (Princeton: Princeton University Press, 1992), 161–81; Omaima Abou-Bakr, "Teaching the Words of the Prophet: Women Instructors of the *Ḥadīth* (Fourteenth and Fifteenth Centuries)," *Hawwa* 1, no. 3 (2003): 306–28; Richard Bulliet, "Women and the Urban Religious Elite in the Pre-Mongol Period," in *Women in Iran from the Rise of Islam to 1800*, ed. Guity Nashat and Lois Beck, 68–79 (Urbana: University of Illinois Press, 2003).

[31] Mohammad Akram Nadwi, *al-Muhaddithat: The Women Scholars in Islam* (London: Interface, 2007), xi. Nadwi's Arabic biographical compendium (forthcoming), numbering fifty-seven volumes, brings together numerous references to female *ḥadīth* transmitters from the rise of Islam to the present. His efforts in this regard were highlighted by Carla Powers in her article "A Secret History," *New York Times*, February 25, 2007, bringing the research into the mainstream.

[32] Nadwi characterizes his contribution as follows: "That material is, though arranged and organized, a *listing*; it is, by analogy with a word dictionary, much nearer to 'words' than 'sentences', and far from 'paragraphs' linked into an 'essay'." *al-Muhaddithat*, xi.

[33] Arabic works devoted specifically to women and religious learning in classical Islam include: ʿAbd al-ʿAzīz Sayyid al-Ahl, *Ṭabaqāt al-Nisā' al-Muḥaddithāt: Min al-Ṭabaqa al-Ūlā ilā al-Ṭabaqa al-Sādisa* (Cairo: n.p., 1981); Ṣāliḥ Maʿtūq, *Juhūd al-Mar'a fī Riwāyat al-Ḥadīth: al-Qarn al-Thāmin al-Hijrī* (Beirut: Dār al-Bashā'ir al-Islāmiyya, 1997); Mashhūr Salmān, *'Ināyat al-Nisā' bi'l-Ḥadīth al-Nabawī, Ṣafaḥāt Muḍī'a min Ḥayāt al-Muḥaddithāt ḥattā al-Qarn al-Thālith 'Ashar al-Hijrī* (Beirut: Dār Ibn Ḥazm, 1994). Also, mention should be made here of Nājiya Ibrāhīm's study of Shuhda al-Kātiba, a sixth/twelfth-century scholar. The monograph is unusual in that it synthesizes anecdotal information into a cohesive biographical study (see *Musnidat al-'Irāq: Shuhda al-Kātiba* [Amman: Mu'assasat al-Balsam, 1996]). There are also two examples of published compilations of *ḥadīth* narrated by women: Shuhda al-Kātiba, *al-'Umda min al-Fawā'id wa'l-Āthār al-Ṣiḥāḥ wa'l-Gharā'ib fī Mashyakhat Shuhda* (Cairo: Maktabat al-Khānjī, 1994) and *Juz' Bībā bint 'Abd al-Ṣamad al-Harthamiyya* (d. 477/1084) (Kuwait: Maktabat al-Khulafā', 198-). The biographical dictionary by ʿUmar Riḍā Kaḥḥāla, *A'lām al-Nisā'*, 5 vols. (Damascus: al-Maṭbaʿa al-Hāshimiyya bi-Dimashq, 1959) is not solely devoted to

methodology to explain patterns in women's activity from Egypt to Iran over the course of nearly ten centuries in the context of broader currents in Sunnī Muslim intellectual and social history.

My analysis bears out the view that major developments in Muslim history cannot be fully grasped without an inquiry into the dynamics of gender relations. The emergence of the *'ulamā'* as a social class and their increasing use of *ḥadīth* transmission to forge communal identity has been highlighted by Richard Bulliet, Jonathan Berkey, and Michael Chamberlain.[34] My work complements their studies with a thorough investigation of how women's educational activities perpetuated scholarly networks across time and place. I also draw on the insights of George Makdisi and William Graham who, among others, have elucidated the doctrinal history of Sunnī traditionalism.[35] I extend the purview to consider the social construction of orthodoxies as a process implicating women as well as men.

The demands of manageability circumscribe the scope of my study in three respects. First, my selection of *ḥadīth* compilations means that I focus on women's transmission of religious knowledge that was deemed authoritative in the context of the broader legal project of systematically articulating Sunnī law and normative practices. Women who transmitted other types of reports, such as *akhbār*, are not represented.[36] Second, I do not analyze *ḥadīth* in which women or issues related to them are mentioned but for which the ascribed authorities (after Muḥammad) are all male. The latter would entail a separate study on broader issues of the social

female *ḥadīth* transmitters but contains numerous entries about them and provides valuable references to archival material as well.

[34] Richard Bulliet, *The Patricians of Nishapur* (Cambridge, MA: Harvard University Press, 1972); Bulliet, *Islam: A View from the Edge* (New York: Columbia University Press, 1994); Berkey, *Transmission of Knowledge in Medieval Cairo*; Berkey, *The Formation of Islam* (New York: Cambridge University Press, 2003), 149–51, 224–30; and Chamberlain, *Knowledge and Social Practice in Medieval Damascus.*

[35] George Makdisi, "The Sunni Revival," reprinted in *History and Politics in Eleventh Century Baghdad* (Aldershot: Ashgate Variorum, 1991). William A. Graham, "Traditionalism in Islam."

[36] As mentioned earlier, *akhbār* are distinct from *ḥadīth* in that their ultimate source is someone other than Muḥammad (e.g., a Companion). Moreover, *akhbār* often have *isnāds* that are deemed unsound in the world of *ḥadīth* transmission; that is, they often carry interrupted chains featuring weak transmitters. For a discussion of these reports, the disparate projects represented by *ḥadīth* and *akhbār* (*sīra-maghāzī*), and their value as historical sources, see Shahab Ahmed, "The Satanic Verses Incident in the Memory of the Early Muslim Community: An Analysis of the Early *Riwāyah*s and their *Isnād*s" (PhD diss., Princeton University, 1999), 14–30.

perceptions and roles of women in early Islam in general. Finally, I limit my analysis to Sunnī Islam and do not include women's religious learning in other sectarian contexts.[37] The sources that inform this study document women who were active in the urban centers of the Ḥijāz, Khurāsān, Syria, and Egypt, areas with vastly different geographies and their own political, social, and intellectual histories. In presenting case studies, I contextualize the activities of women in terms of the local variables that shaped their careers. The wide-ranging scope of my work permits a greater understanding of the factors that unified women's educational experiences in spite of the diversity of their specific historical contexts. I have also encountered records of women similarly engaged in far-flung regions including al-Andalus, North and West Africa, the Caucasus, Anatolia, China, and South Asia. I hope that this work will inspire future studies on women's religious education in other geographical and historical contexts.

Although this book spans the first ten centuries of Islamic history, its relevance extends beyond an understanding of early and classical female *ḥadīth* transmission. My study also contributes to the critical project of historicizing women's religious activism in the modern period, a prevalent phenomenon in Muslim countries from Morocco to Indonesia. For example, the Qubaysiyyāt, a conservative, Ṣūfistic women's organization originating in Syria, has intrigued both academics and the Western media due to its members' assiduous and secretive pursuit of Islamic learning.[38] Another prominent example is Farhat Hashemi, who, from her base in Pakistan, has drawn legions of upper-class Muslim women globally into the orbit of traditional Muslim learning.[39] Saba Mahmood's landmark study of Egyptian women's religious revival has prompted critical reflection on how Western feminist ideals relate to such contemporary pietistic

[37] I analyze representations of Imāmī women's *ḥadīth* transmission in my article, "Women in Imāmī Biographical Collections," in *Law and Tradition in Classical Islamic Thought*, ed. Michael Cook et al., 81–98 (New York: Palgrave, 2013). See also Mirjam Künkler and Roja Fazaeli, "The Life of Two *Mujtahidahs*: Female Religious Authority in 20th Century Iran," in *Women, Leadership and Mosques: Contemporary Islamic Authority*, ed. Masooda Bano and Hilary Kalmbach, 127–60 (Leiden: Brill, 2011).

[38] For a study of the spread of Qubaysiyyāt ideas to the West, see Sarah Islam, "Qubaysiyyāt: Growth of an International Muslim Women's Revivalist Movement in Syria and the United States, 1960–2008" (Master's thesis, Princeton University, 2010). See also Katherine Zoepf, "Islamic Revival in Syria Is Led by Women," *New York Times*, August 29, 2006.

[39] For an introductory essay on Farhat Hashemi's organization, see Khanum Shaikh, "New Expressions of Religiosity: Al-Huda International and the Expansion of Islamic Education for Pakistani Muslim Women," in *Women and Islam*, ed. Zayn Qassam, 163–84 (Santa Barbara: Praeger, 2010).

movements.[40] Yet, the dearth of rigorous analyses on women's religious participation in early and classical Islam hinders our appreciation of the way in which the activities of modern Muslim women relate to and draw on the past. My own work complements scholarship on contemporary women's Islamic activism and elucidates continuities and ruptures.

The history of women as *ḥadīth* transmitters in early and classical Islam has mixed implications for contemporary feminist discourse about Muslim women's agency and empowerment. In interpreting the significance of gender in premodern eras, leading historians such as Joan Scott and Caroline Bynum have cautioned that questions borne of feminist concerns run the risk of producing anachronistic analyses.[41] Mindful of this danger, I aim to represent women's commitments in terms of the historical contexts that produced them. To understand the fluctuating trends of Muslim women's participation in early and classical Islam, we must avoid reading into our texts either misogyny or alternatively explicit desires to empower women. As I show in Chapters 3 and 4, women's agency expressed by a subversion of patriarchal norms is not a theme in the dramatic increase of Muslim women's pious activism in the classical era. Rather, what was at stake was the faithful preservation of Muḥammad's legacy, an endeavor intended in no small part to counter deleterious factors such as the perceived corruption of the times and the ever-increasing temporal distance from the life of the Prophet. The mass reproduction and consumption of traditionalist literature and the promotion of short chains of transmission (*isnād* [pl. *asānīd*] *'ālī*) back to Muḥammad were measures taken to mitigate this damage. These impulses rendered women authoritative in limited contexts. It would stretch our imaginations as well as the historical realities conditioning these women's actions to view them as reflections of the concerns that animate contemporary feminist discourses. The ranges of action of classical Muslim women were constrained by the norms of their communities, which channeled their intellectual potential toward *ḥadīth* transmission rather than law or theology. It is through embracing and upholding those norms, not subverting them, that they acquired stature and, in all likelihood, personal fulfillment.

[40] Saba Mahmood, *Politics of Piety: The Islamic Revival and the Feminist Subject* (Princeton: Princeton University Press, 2005).

[41] Joan Scott "Gender: A Useful Category for Historical Analysis," *American Historical Review* 91, no. 5 (1986): 1055; and Caroline Bynum, *Holy Feast and Holy Fast* (Los Angeles: University of California Press, 1987), 8–9 and epilogue. For an articulation of similar concerns for the field of medieval Muslim women, see Julie Scott Meisami, "Writing Medieval Women: Representations and Misrepresentations," in *Writing and Representation in Medieval Islam*, ed. Julia Bray, 47–87 (New York: Routledge, 2006), 74.

CHAPTER 1

A Tradition Invented: The Female Companions

> Abū ʿAbd Allāh Sālim Sabalān, whose honesty pleased ʿĀʾisha and whom she used to employ, said that she showed him how the Prophet used to perform the ablution. "She rinsed her mouth three times and washed her face three times. She then washed her right hand thrice then her left hand thrice. She placed her hand toward the front of her head and passed it to the back once. Then she cleaned her ears and passed her hands over her sides."
>
> Sālim said, "I used to go to her as a contracted slave; she did not veil herself from me. I would sit in front of her, and she would speak with me. Until one day, I went to her and said, 'Invoke blessings for me, O Mother of the Believers.' She said, 'For what?' I said, 'Allāh has freed me.' She replied, 'May Allāh bless you,' and drew the partition (*ḥijāb*) in front of me. I did not see her again after that day."[1]

For Muslim jurists, this report answers a rather prosaic question: how should a woman wipe her head for ablution? For social historians, it's a gem of a different sort. Traditions that so clearly evoke the milieu of the first decades of *ḥadīth* transmission and capture the complexities of male-female interaction are not common. While Sālim was a slave, ʿĀʾisha had used his help and admitted him into her company. In the process, he became a repository for her teaching. The authoritativeness of Sālim's report derives from his eyewitness encounter: he actually *saw* ʿĀʾisha performing the ablution. Attentive to protocol, Sālim clarifies that his direct access to ʿĀʾisha was terminated upon his manumission. With its

[1] Aḥmad b. Shuʿayb al-Nasāʾī, *Sunan* (Beirut: Dār al-Kutub al-ʿIlmiyya, n.d.), 1:72–73. For the biography of Sālim, see Yūsuf b. ʿAbd al-Raḥmān al-Mizzī, *Tahdhīb al-Kamāl fī Asmāʾ al-Rijāl* (Beirut: Muʾassasat al-Risāla, 1992), 10:154–56.

wealth of explicit details and subtexts, this report is an invaluable resource that extends our understanding of early *ḥadīth* transmission beyond the often sparse, formulaic data provided in Arabic biographical dictionaries and chronicles.

Combining information from the available sources yields a panoramic view of female *ḥadīth* participation. This chapter focuses on the female Companions, the most influential women of early Islam. Their lives constitute the templates upon which successive generations of Muslim women modeled their piety and service to Islam. Muḥammad's decisions in their cases are the basis for myriad rulings. The female Companions are remarkable in yet another respect. In shaping the narrative of *ḥadīth* reports, they author texts that eventually become secondary scriptures for Muslims.[2] While both male and female Companions narrate *ḥadīth*, women's contributions are especially noteworthy because their voices are comparatively muted in early and classical Muslim legal discussions. In speaking of authorship of *ḥadīth* by the Companions, I draw on Muslim collective memory and communal understanding of their roles. The historicity and authenticity of attribution of individual narratives are of secondary importance to the fact that Muslim tradition itself assigns these roles to the Companions and in so doing creates an extraordinary space for women's public religious participation.

Two examples elucidate how women's authorial voices function in *ḥadīth* reports. In the first, the narrator simply repeats words attributed to Muḥammad:

> Salmā Umm Rāfi' said, "The Messenger of God said, 'A house without dates is like a house without food.'"[3]

In the second, the narrator may weave the dramatic backdrop for her story for a strikingly different effect.

> Khawla bint Tha'laba said, "I swear by God, that He, most High and Majestic, revealed the beginning of *Sūrat al-Mujādila* with respect to me and Aws b. Ṣāmit. I was with him, and he was an old man who had become ill-tempered and easily vexed. He came to me one day, and we argued about something. He got angry and said, "You are to me like my mother's back" [i.e., he forswore sexual relations with her]. He went off and spent some time with his people.
>
> Then he came back and wanted to be intimate with me. I said, "No way. By God, in whom I put all my trust, you will not come to me after what you said until and

[2] For a more detailed discussion of the scriptural value of *ḥadīth*, see Aisha Musa, *Ḥadīth as Scripture* (New York: Palgrave, 2008).

[3] Muḥammad b. Yazīd b. Māja, *Sunan* (Cairo: Dār al-Ḥadīth, 1994), 2:1105, #3328.

unless God and His Prophet rule in our case." He jumped on me, and I defended myself and overpowered him the way a woman can overpower a weak, old man.

I went to one of my neighbors and borrowed some of her clothes. Then I made my way to the Prophet and sat in front of him and told him about what had happened to me and lodged my complaints about what I had to deal with of Aws's ill nature. The Prophet said, "Khawla, your cousin is an old man; fear God in your dealings with him."

I said, "By God, I will not be reassured till I get a Qur'ānic revelation about this matter." That which used to overcome the Prophet overcame him, and then it was lifted from him. And he said to me, "Khuwayla, God has revealed [verses] concerning you and your husband."

He recited to me, "Indeed God has heard the statement of the woman who disputes with you concerning her husband and who complains to God. And God hears the argument between you both. Verily, God is All-Hearer, All-Seer." [He recited] until the verse, "And for the disbelievers, there is a painful doom."[4]

Then the Prophet of God said to me, "Ask him [Aws] to free a slave." I said, "By God, O Prophet, he doesn't have one to free." Then he said, "Let him fast two consecutive months." I said, "By God, O Prophet, he's an old man; he doesn't have it in him to fast." Then he said, "Let him feed sixty poor people with a camel-load (*wasq*) of dates." I said, "He doesn't have that either." The Prophet said, "We'll help him out with a measure of dates." And I said, "And I, O Prophet, will help him with the other one."[5] He said, "You've spoken well, and you've done the right thing. Go and give charity on his behalf, and I entrust you to be good to your cousin." And I did [what the Prophet had advised]. . . ."[6]

According to mainstream Muslim tradition, the didactic core of a *ḥadīth* preserves the pronouncement of Muḥammad. Yet as the second example illustrates, a report can contain much more than just Muḥammad's words. The narrating Companion is viewed as supplying the details that contextualize the report and enliven its message. Storytelling is necessarily implicated in such an act, and in this regard, the Companions are unlike the narrators of subsequent generations, who are primarily charged with faithfully reproducing the traditions.[7] To fully comprehend the role of

[4] Qur'ān, 58:1–4 (*Sūrat al-Mujādila*).

[5] The term used for this measure is *'araq* defined variously as fifteen or thirty times as much as the measure *ṣā'*, which itself was defined differently across various regional centers of the Muslim world.

[6] Ibn Ḥanbal, *Musnad*, 6:459, #27309.

[7] This is notwithstanding the instances in which narrators in post-Companion generations supply their own commentary. Such instances are uncommon and do not compromise the general rule that the Companions are seen as the primary composers of the *ḥadīth* narratives. For more detailed analyses of how storytelling functions in *ḥadīth* texts, see Sebastian Günther, "Fictional Narration and Imagination within an Authoritative Framework, Towards a New Understanding of *Ḥadīth*," in *Story-Telling in the Framework of Non-Fictional Arabic Literature*, ed. Stefan Leder, 433–71(Wiesbaden: Harrassowitz, 1998), and Suhair Calamawy, "Narrative Element in *Ḥadīth* Literature,"

the Companions, it is vital to distinguish the classical Sunnī orthodox position, which, after the fourth/tenth century, promoted the view that *ḥadīth* preserved the exact words of Muḥammad, from the more realistic concession of many earlier transmitters and *ḥadīth* critics who appreciated the futility of trying to reproduce Muḥammad's words verbatim.[8] In the earliest decades of transmission, the concern was more with accurately preserving meaning (*riwāya bi'l-ma'nā*) rather than the exact words of Muḥammad's pronouncements (*riwāya bi'l-lafẓ*).[9] This historical perspective permits a deeper appreciation of the extent to which men and women of the earliest generations were engaged in crafting the historical memory of Muḥammad and his community. For this chapter, I draw on the biographies of 112 female Companions and the traditions ascribed to them.[10] Each woman's contribution to the *ḥadīth* corpus is in some way linked to her personal experience in the first Muslim community (*umma*). Some of the women are prolific, and biographers dwell on their celebrated roles. Others are more obscure and recognized only through their narration of one or two traditions. When evidence from *ḥadīth* narratives and

in *Arabic Literature to the End of the Umayyad Period*, ed. A. F. L. Beeston et al., 308–16 (New York: Cambridge University Press, 1983).

8 Al-Ḥasan b. 'Abd al-Raḥmān al-Rāmahurmuzī (d. 360/971) provides an overview of this discussion among early authorities and summarizes the views of leading scholars with respect to the importance of conveying the meaning of a report (irrespective of whether the transmission was verbatim). He reports that al-Shāfi'ī (d. 204/820), for example, accepted the non-verbatim transmissions of those who were learned in Arabic and had legal understanding (*fiqh*) because he was confident that they could convey the meaning with fidelity. He adds that this tended to be the majority view among early scholars as well as among several Companions. See *al-Muḥaddith al-Fāṣil bayna al-Rāwī wa'l-Wā'ī* (Beirut: Dār al-Fikr, 1971), 530–31.

9 See also Jonathan Brown, *Hadith: Muḥammad's Legacy in the Medieval and Modern World* (Oxford: Oneworld, 2009), 23, for similar observations about the aims of early *ḥadīth* transmission.

10 Although there is no definitive list of Companions, male or female, there have been attempts by classical Muslim authors and contemporary academics to compile a count. Ibn Ḥajar recorded the names of 1,545 women out of a total of 12,304 Companions. This number reflects the editor's enumeration in the 1977 edition of Ibn Ḥajar's *al-Iṣāba fī Tamyīz al-Ṣaḥāba*, ed. Ṭāhā Muḥammad al-Zaynī (Cairo: Maktabat al-Kulliyāt al-Azhariyya, 1977), vols. 12–13. Ruth Roded in her modern study of women in Muslim biographical collections arrived at the number 1,232 after sifting through Ibn Sa'd's *al-Ṭabaqāt*, Ibn 'Abd al-Barr's (d. 463/1071) *al-Istī'āb fī Ma'rifat al-Aṣḥāb*, and Ibn Ḥajar's *al-Iṣāba* (see *Women in Islamic Biographical Collections* [Boulder: Lynne Rienner Publishers, 1994], 19, footnote 22). Not all of those named in these lists are known for transmitting *ḥadīth*. As outlined in the introduction, this chapter deals with the controlled set of all female Companions who narrate in the canonical six Sunnī collections and selected works attributed to their authors as well as women who narrate in the *Muwaṭṭa'* of Mālik b. Anas, the *musnad* collections of al-Ḥumaydī and Aḥmad b. Ḥanbal, the *Sunan* of al-Dārimī, and the *Ṣaḥīḥ* of Ibn Khuzayma.

additional historical sources is combined, the following features appear as salient characteristics:

1. Irrespective of the gender of the narrator, an eyewitness encounter with Muḥammad was the only prerequisite for a Companion to narrate reports. That is, the narrations of women were not considered less reliable than those of men. Considerations of whether the narrator was versed in the Qur'ān and its sciences or in Arabic grammar, or whether she even possessed basic literacy, were immaterial. Given the rudimentary state of Muslim education after Muḥammad's death, it is anachronistic to conceive of standardized criteria that may have qualified a man or woman to transmit reports. Indeed, we cannot even assert the existence of a field of *ḥadīth* transmission proper during these early decades.[11] Only in the second century do we see fledgling efforts by scholars to elaborate on the qualifications of a *ḥadīth* transmitter.[12]
2. Women's relaying of reports about Muḥammad's actions and speech was in large part an ad hoc enterprise. While some male Companions are reported to have taught in study circles, this is seldom true of women.[13] Rather, female Companions transmitted knowledge in response to specific inquiries about diverse matters from ritual obligations to marriage and divorce, and the virtues of Muḥammad and his family.
3. Female Companions typically transmitted within localized kinship and clientage (*mawlā*) networks.[14] This is as opposed to transmitters (male and female) of later generations whose networks were

[11] Studies of education in early Islam concur that pedagogy took place in study circles (*ḥalaqa*s) in mosques, homes, and public spaces and that recitation and memorization of the Qur'ān was central to these circles. Small schools (*kuttāb*s) devoted to the study of the Qur'ān were among the first institutions specifically devoted to pedagogy. For a general introduction to Muslim education in early and classical Islam, see Jeffrey Burke, "Education," in *The Islamic World*, ed. Andrew Rippin, 305–17 (New York: Routledge, 2008); Aḥmad Shalabī, *Ta'rīkh al-Tarbiya al-Islāmiyya* (Cairo: Maktabat al-Nahḍa al-Miṣriyya, 1966), 44–136; and Sebastian Günther, "Be Masters in that You Teach and Continue to Learn," in *Islam and Education*, ed. Wadad Kadi and Victor Billeh, 61–82 (Chicago: University of Chicago Press, 2007).

[12] For a succinct overview of the development of early Sunnī *ḥadīth* criticism, see Brown, *Hadith*, 77–86.

[13] Muhammad Mustafa Azami, *Studies in Early Hadith Literature* (Indianapolis: American Trust Publications, 1992), 183–99.

[14] The term *mawlā* in the context of this chapter generally signifies a patron-client relationship. In early Islam, such bonds, contracted between Muslim Arabs and non-Arabs and between freed slaves and their prior owners, facilitated the management of relationships in

more geographically dispersed due to the popularity of journeys to collect *ḥadīth* (*riḥla*s).

In this chapter, I group the female Companions into three types: (1) Muḥammad's wives, (2) his female kin, and (3) other women whose participation merited the attention of legal scholars and historians, either because they sought *fatwā*s that became legal precedents or because their participation in battles and in other aspects of the life of the early community was noteworthy.[15] I round out the analysis with a consideration of the transmission activity of more obscure women.

THE WIVES OF MUḤAMMAD

Muḥammad's wives are distinct among the female Companion-Narrators.[16] The Qur'ān refers to them as the Mothers of the Believers (*ummahāt al-mu'minīn*) and states that they are unlike other women of the community in terms of duties and privileges.[17] Elevated as unrivaled models for the Muslim community, the wives represent a different paradigm from that of other women. It is not only through transmitting Muḥammad's traditions that they participate in shaping religious knowledge. Their own actions and preferences are part of the *sunna* that was scrutinized by later generations for legally significant precedents.[18] In addition, the Prophet's behavior with them concerning conjugal or domestic matters was the focus for believers wishing to execute the minutiae of daily life according to the Prophet's model.

Paradoxically, even as Muḥammad's wives were repositories for information about him, divine command restricted their interaction with male tradition-seekers. One Qur'ānic verse enjoins the wives to "stay quietly in your homes and do not flaunt your charms as they used to flaunt them in

a predominantly tribal society. For a more detailed explanation and historical overview, see EI^2, s.v. "*mawlā*."

15 I provide the names of all these women and brief biographies for them in Appendices A-1 and A-2 of my dissertation "Shifting Fortunes" (PhD diss., Princeton University, 2005).

16 While there is disagreement over the number of women Muḥammad is said to have married, the general consensus is that he was survived by nine wives.

17 The most direct Qur'ānic reference is *Sūrat al-Aḥzāb*, 6:28–34. A fuller treatment of the position of the wives of the Prophet as set forth in the Qur'ān may be found in Barbara Stowasser, *Women in the Qur'an, Traditions, and Interpretation* (New York: Oxford University Press, 1994), 85–103.

18 I use the term *sunna* to refer to the normative behavior of the Prophet and members of his community who were deemed exemplars for later Muslims.

the days of pagan ignorance (*jāhiliyya*)."[19] Other verses mandated a physical separation (*ḥijāb*) between Muḥammad's wives and men who did not fall into one of the following categories: their fathers, sons, brothers, brothers' sons, sisters' sons, and their own slaves.[20] The Qur'ānic vision can be construed as limiting the extent to which the wives could have participated in the process of direct, face-to-face, oral transmission of *ḥadīth*.

However, not all the wives understood the verses as mandating strict seclusion and restricting contact between themselves and seekers of religious knowledge. In particular, the sheer quantity of *ḥadīth* ascribed to 'Ā'isha and Umm Salama (d. ca. 59/679) and their extensive narration networks composed of kin and non-kin men and women reveal that these two women were regularly consulted on a host of legal and ritual matters. Compilers have enumerated between 1,500 and 2,400 *ḥadīth* for which 'Ā'isha is the first authority.[21] Umm Salama, though a distant second, contributed between 175 and 375 reports. The other seven wives trail behind but are nonetheless counted among trustworthy conveyors of Muḥammad's practice.[22] The analysis that follows accordingly focuses foremost on 'Ā'isha and her role and then turns to Umm Salama. The other co-wives will be discussed together because of their comparatively limited roles.

19 Qur'ān, 33:33.

20 Qur'ān, 33:53, 33:55. There is general agreement among exegetes of the Qur'ān that the verses mandating seclusion of Muḥammad's wives were revealed soon after his marriage to Zaynab bint Jaḥsh in 5 AH. This was due to the excessive lingering of some of the male wedding guests in Zaynab's quarters; see, for example, Muḥammad b. Jarīr al-Ṭabarī (d. 310/923), *al-Jāmi' al-Bayān* (Beirut: Dār al-Shāmiyya, 1997), 6:220–22; and Maḥmūd b. 'Umar al-Zamakhsharī (d. 538/1144), *al-Kashshāf* (Cairo: Maktabat Muṣṭafā al-Bābī al-Ḥalabī, 1966), 3:271–72. It is open to interpretation whether or not these restrictions regarding the mobility of the wives were in force only while Muḥammad was living. As I discuss in greater detail later in the chapter, 'Ā'isha's active participation in the life of the community after Muḥammad's death suggests that her own understanding was that the strictures were loosened after his death.

21 The discrepancies in the counts are generally a result of differences in how compilers distinguish between the numerous *isnāds* and textual variants in different traditions. Al-Mizzī, collecting *isnāds* from the six authoritative collections as well as some other minor works, attributes 2,093 *ḥadīth* to her in *Tuḥfa*, 11:130–896. *Al-Musnad al-Jāmi'* provides 1,357 *ḥadīth* collated from a range of canonical and noncanonical collections as described in the introduction (for the *musnad* of 'Ā'isha's traditions in this compilation, see *al-Musnad al-Jāmi'*, 19:241–852 and 20:5–434).

22 The remaining seven wives are Zaynab bint Jaḥsh (d. 20/641), Ramla bint Abī Sufyān (d. 44/664), Ḥafṣa bint 'Umar (d. 45/665), Ṣafiyya bint Ḥuyayy (d. 52/672), Sawda bint Zam'a (d. 54/674), Juwayriya bint al-Ḥārith (d. 56/676), and Maymūna bint al-Ḥārith (d. 61/681). A breakdown of the numbers of their traditions is provided in the section on their contributions.

ʿĀʾISHA

ʿĀʾisha's status as the favorite wife of Muḥammad undoubtedly contributed greatly to her authority as a transmitter of his preferences and opinions. She was also the daughter of Abū Bakr (d. 13/634), one of Muḥammad's closest associates and his successor. Her love of poetry as well as her extensive knowledge of genealogy, tribal lore, and accounts of the battles fought by Muslims is traced to her father.[23] The combination of privileged kinship and marriage uniquely qualified ʿĀʾisha as the locus for numerous reports on the early Muslim community. ʿĀʾisha's role as the maternal aunt and teacher of ʿUrwa b. al-Zubayr (d. 93/711f.), an outstanding early scholar, further amplified her reputation. Muslim historians credit much of his knowledge and authority in *ḥadīth* transmission to ʿĀʾisha.[24] Ultimately, ʿUrwa's scholarly achievements as her student enhanced her stature as a teacher.

Biographers have paid varying levels of attention to ʿĀʾisha's role as a transmitter of religious knowledge.[25] They agree that she surpassed most of her contemporaries because she related Muḥammad's traditions with a critical sense for their meanings and an understanding (*fiqh*) of their legal implications. Ibn Saʿd foreshadows the growth of ʿĀʾisha's reputation as a legal expert (*faqīha*). He cites an exchange in which Masrūq (d. 63/683) was asked whether ʿĀʾisha was well versed in the laws of inheritance and distributive shares (*al-farāʾiḍ*).[26] Masrūq swears by God that indeed she

[23] In a tradition cited by Abū Nuʿaym al-Iṣbahānī (d. 430/1038), ʿUrwa quizzes her as to the source of her knowledge of medicine. He says that he does not marvel at her knowledge of *fiqh*, as he can trace that to the fact that she was the wife of the Prophet and the daughter of Abū Bakr. Similarly, her knowledge of poetry and battle lore (*ayyām*) can be traced to Abū Bakr. However, he cannot understand how she became an expert in medical treatments as well. ʿĀʾisha replies that her skills in this area derive from her ministrations to the Prophet during his final illness. See Abū Nuʿaym al-Iṣbahānī, *Ḥilyat al-Awliyāʾ* (Cairo: Maktabat al-Khānjī, 1932), 2:50.

[24] See, for example, his biography in Ibn Ḥajar, *Tahdhīb al-Tahdhīb* (Beirut: Dār al-Kutub al-ʿIlmiyya, 1994), 7:160.

[25] Her reputation as an outstanding woman in various regards has been well documented in the biographical works and in secondary literature. Here I focus only on depictions of her as a *ḥadīth* transmitter and a legal expert. For fuller treatment of ʿĀʾisha's biography and historical roles, see Nabia Abbott's *Aishah: The Beloved of Muhammad* (1942; repr., London: al-Saqi Books, 1985). A more recent study of her legacy is Spellberg's *Politics, Gender, and the Islamic Past.*

[26] Stowasser has translated "*farāʾiḍ*" in the more general sense of "religious obligations" (see Stowasser, *Women in the Qurʾan*, 117, footnote 57). It is more likely that Ibn Saʿd used the term in its technical sense to refer to the law of inheritance and the distribution of shares of inheritance.

was knowledgeable in this matter and that the older Companions referred to her as an authority.[27] Given the complex nature of Muslim inheritance regulations, 'Ā'isha's proficiency in this area indicates her advanced abilities in mathematics.

Whereas Ibn Sa'd makes only passing reference to her intellect and focuses more on her relationship with Muḥammad and her often stormy interactions with her co-wives, biographers from the fifth/eleventh century onward devote steadily increasing attention to her legal expertise. Ibn 'Abd al-Barr expands on evidence of 'Ā'isha's intellect by citing the Masrūq tradition mentioned earlier, as well as others related by early luminaries, among them 'Aṭā' b. Abī Rabāḥ (d. 114/732f.) and 'Urwa, who asserts, "I have not seen anyone more knowledgeable in matters of *fiqh*, medicine, and poetry than 'Ā'isha." He also includes the assessment of the famed scholar al-Zuhrī (d. 124/742) that "if the knowledge of 'Ā'isha were to be weighed against that of all the wives and the other women combined, the knowledge of 'Ā'isha would be greater." Ibn 'Abd al-Barr's representation of 'Ā'isha's intellectual contributions is elaborated upon by his successors, including al-Mizzī and Ibn Ḥajar.[28] The trend culminates with Kaḥḥāla in the modern period. He begins his biography with superlative praise of her as "the greatest *muḥadditha* of her age, distinguished by her intelligence, fluency, and eloquence, who had a profound influence in the dissemination of knowledge from the Prophet."[29] She is also the only woman of the early Islamic period whose legal thinking has been documented and analyzed in a modern compilation of *fiqh*.[30]

The evolution of 'Ā'isha's intellectual biography, through which she becomes the *muḥadditha* and *faqīha* par excellence of Muslim history, was in large part a by-product of the efforts of *ḥadīth* compilers who, from the late second/eighth century to the end of the third/ninth century, produced a large corpus of authoritative collections. Aḥmad b. Ḥanbal, for example, enumerates approximately 2,400 *ḥadīth* on her authority.[31] 'Ā'isha does

[27] Muḥammad b. Sa'd, *al-Ṭabaqāt* (Leiden: E. J. Brill, 1904–18), 8:45.

[28] Yūsuf b. 'Abd Allāh b. 'Abd al-Barr, *al-Istī'āb fī Ma'rifat al-Aṣḥāb* (Cairo: Maktabat Nahḍat Miṣr, 196–), 4:1881–85; al-Mizzī, *Tahdhīb al-Kamāl*, 35:227–36; Ibn Ḥajar, *al-Iṣāba*, 13:38–42.

[29] Kaḥḥāla, *A'lām al-Nisā'*, 3:9–131.

[30] See Sa'īd Fāyiz Dukhayyil, *Mawsū'at Fiqh 'Ā'isha Umm al-Mu'minīn: Ḥayātuhā wa-Fiqhuhā* (Beirut: Dār al-Nafā'is, 1989).

[31] Ibn Ḥanbal, *Musnad*, 6:37–319. See Scott Lucas, *Constructive Critics, Ḥadīth Literature, and the Articulation of Sunnī Islam* (Leiden: Brill, 2004), for a detailed analysis of how the efforts of scholars such as Ibn Sa'd, Ibn Ma'īn (d. 233/848), and Ibn Ḥanbal were critical to the project of fashioning Sunnī orthodoxy.

not just narrate about conjugal relations, ritual purity, and the supererogatory devotions that Muḥammad performed at home, topics on which we expect her to be authoritative. Her voice is also evident in traditions on fasting, pilgrimage, inheritance, and eschatology, among other subjects. Biographers, assessing the contributions of various Companions, male and female, and those of traditionists of subsequent generations, explained the numerical and qualitative disparity between ʿĀʾisha and her contemporaries through reference to her superior intellect.[32]

The narrative details in her reports give us frequent glimpses of a woman who was quick to correct erroneous traditions and anxious to check impulses of the community that she felt were not in tune with the Prophet's legacy. Al-Zarkashī's (d. 794/1392) medieval compilation, *al-Ijāba li-Īrād mā Istadrakathu ʿĀʾisha ʿalā al-Ṣaḥāba*, is a unique testament to ʿĀʾisha's historical presence as a critic of reports who also displayed legal discernment.[33] Al-Zarkashī documents numerous instances in which she is said to have corrected or contradicted traditions and rulings of other Companions and Successors, many of them of considerable stature such as ʿUmar b. al-Khaṭṭāb (d. 23/644), ʿAbd Allāh b. ʿAbbās (d. 68/687f.), and ʿAbd Allāh b. ʿUmar (d. 73/693). In the traditions collected by al-Zarkashī, her forceful personality is amply evidenced. For example, she frequently corrects the traditions narrated by the prolific Abū Hurayra (d. 58/677f.). The following incident demonstrates well the tension between them:

> ʿAlqama b. Qays reported, "We were with ʿĀʾisha, and Abū Hurayra was also there. ʿĀʾisha asked him, 'O Abū Hurayra, are you the one who narrates from the Prophet about the woman tormented [in Hell] because she did not give food or drink to her cat [leaving it hungry and thirsty] and did not let it out to feed on small creatures until it died?'
>
> Abū Hurayra said, 'I heard it from the Prophet.'
>
> ʿĀʾisha responded, 'A believer is too dear to God that he/she be tormented on account of a cat. On account of this, it must have been that the woman was a disbeliever. O Abū Hurayra, when you relate traditions from the Prophet, be careful of what you say!'"[34]

[32] She generally ranks among the top five narrators of Muḥammad's traditions. See, for example, the list in Muḥammad Z. Ṣiddīqī's work *Ḥadīth Literature: Its Origin, Development and Special Features*, rev. ed. (Cambridge: Islamic Texts Society, 1993), 15–18.

[33] Muḥammad b. Bahādur al-Zarkashī, *al-Ijāba li-Īrād mā Istadrakathu ʿĀʾisha ʿalā al-Ṣaḥāba* (Beirut: al-Maktab al-Islāmī, 1970).

[34] al-Zarkashī, *al-Ijāba*, 118.

In yet another interaction, 'Ā'isha asserts the Prophet's precedent in the face of collective memory loss. Members of the community had denied her request that the funerary bier of Sa'd b. Abī Waqqāṣ be brought through the *masjid* so that she could pray for him. Upon hearing that they feel it is prohibited to bring the bier into the mosque, she replies, "How quick people are to forget. It was within the *masjid* that the Prophet himself performed the *janāza* for Suhayl b. Bayḍā'."[35] Thus, 'Ā'isha's memory serves to steer the community back to the Prophet's model in the face of aberrant tendencies. These two examples illustrate well the tenor of 'Ā'isha's interactions. More than just a trustworthy eyewitness to the Prophet's life, she functions as an exegete and a critical traditionist.

'Ā'isha's traditions, taken together, reveal her profound involvement in the daily life of her community. Her commentary found its way into seemingly mundane aspects of a Muslim's life. A topic that occurs in several traditions concerns the diligence due in washing clothes that have traces of ritual impurity: does one immerse them fully in water or simply wash the part that is unclean?[36] In one rather interesting version of these reports, 'Abd Allāh b. Shihāb al-Khawlānī states that on one occasion when he was 'Ā'isha's guest, he happened to have an erotic dream.[37] Upon waking, he fully immersed his clothes in water. A servant girl reported this to 'Ā'isha, who interrogated him and ascertained that it had not been a wet dream; therefore no ritual impurity had resulted from it. Had it been a wet dream, she explained, he would only have needed to remove the traces of the impurity (by rubbing it when it dried out, for instance) rather than washing the entire garment. Numerous other instances in which 'Ā'isha answered questions on matters commonly deemed private underscore that while she was an esteemed wife of the Prophet, she was not above discussing matters intimate or sexual, even with men.

An element of dissuading believers from engaging in overly puritanical behavior occurs often in 'Ā'isha's *ḥadīth*, and in this she may be seen as a counterbalance to pious excesses evidenced in other Companions, among them 'Abd Allāh b. 'Umar. In a well-circulated *ḥadīth*, she censures Ibn

35 al-Zarkashī, *al-Ijāba*, 162. In another version, the wives collectively ask that the bier be brought to the *masjid*. They are denied the request, and when 'Ā'isha hears of this, she issues a condemnation of the ruling. In both versions, the import is the same. Sa'd b. Abī Waqqāṣ's death date is somewhere between 50 and 58/670–78.

36 See, for example, the following traditions in *al-Musnad al-Jāmi'*, 19:298–307, #16075–86. I generally cite the original collections of *ḥadīth* except in cases where I cite a cluster of traditions or the *musnad* (collection of traditions attributed to a specific narrator).

37 Muslim, *Ṣaḥīḥ* (Beirut: Dār al-Fikr, 1995), 2:1:16 (vol. 2, part 1, 16).

'Umar for ordering women to undo their braids before performing the major ritual ablution (*ghusl*), presumably so that their hair would be thoroughly cleaned.[38] To this she responds derisively, "How strange that Ibn 'Umar orders women to loosen their hair when performing *ghusl*. Why doesn't he just order them to shave their heads? The Prophet and I used to wash using the same vessel, and I would pour no more than three handfuls of water on my hair."

In another example, Shayba b. 'Uthmān (d. 59/679) seeks her counsel on the matter of disposing of material used to cover the Ka'ba. Shayba reports to her that the material was being buried so that ritually unclean people would not fashion garments from the sacred cloth. Pragmatically, 'Ā'isha points out that it is more profitable to sell the covering and give the proceeds as alms for the poor. As she reasons, once the material is removed from the Ka'ba, there should be no problem if menstruating women or otherwise ritually impure people wear it.[39]

'Ā'isha also stands out as a female Companion who derived legal rulings from Muḥammad's precedents. While her reasoning was not universally accepted, her presence was such that other Companions and Successors had to contend with her views. There are several instances in which 'Ā'isha is said to have stood apart from prominent Companions in her legal deductions. They include the following opinions ascribed to her: she permitted those who had been born out of wedlock (*walad al-zinā*) to lead prayers as long as they were qualified; she permitted women to travel for the Ḥajj without a *maḥram* (male guardian according to Islamic legal guidelines) as long as they could be assured of their safety; and she permitted *maḥram* bonds to be established between adults through a practice known as *riḍā' al-kabīr*.[40] While the first two opinions concurred with those of a few other early *fuqahā'*, the third was a more isolated view. Literally translated as "adult nursing," *riḍā' al-kabīr* referred to expressing breast milk and giving it to another person in a container.[41] In her ruling

38 Ibn Ḥanbal, *Musnad*, 6:52, #24153; Ibn Māja, *Sunan*, 1:198; and al-Nasā'ī, *Sunan*, 1:203.

39 al-Zarkashī, *al-Ijāba*, 149. For Shayba b. 'Uthmān's biography, see Ibn Ḥajar, *Tahdhīb al-Tahdhīb*, 4:342.

40 See Dukhayyil, *Mawsū'at Fiqh 'Ā'isha*, 531–52, for a discussion of these and other issues on which she issued opinions different from those of prominent Companions. Additional reports of her opinion on *riḍā' al-kabīr* occur in Ibn Sa'd, *al-Ṭabaqāt*, 8:339 (in the biography of Umm Kulthūm bint Abī Bakr), and Mālik b. Anas, *al-Muwaṭṭa'* (Beirut: Dār al-Gharb al-Islāmī, 1996), 2:123–26. The issue of *maḥram* bonds is discussed further later in the chapter.

41 While the literal translation of *riḍā'* is nursing, I translate the term as "to give milk to" in the context of a woman giving her breast milk to an adult male. It is clear from the classical

that *riḍā' al-kabīr* was a valid means for creating *maḥram* relations, 'Ā'isha was opposed not only by prominent men such as 'Umar, 'Alī b. Abī Ṭālib (d. 40/661), and 'Abd Allāh b. Mas'ūd (d. 32/653), but also rather emphatically by the other wives of Muḥammad.

'Ā'isha's role in the early debate on *riḍā' al-kabīr* centers on a question that eventually became marginal in the legal discourse on nursing: can women utilize the Prophet's *ḥadīth* on this topic to circumvent strictures imposed on male-female interactions? The following section provides a brief background as to the legal complexities associated with "adult nursing." The debate is an extensive one, and the overview that follows is purely for the purpose of providing a context for 'Ā'isha's view.[42] The Qur'ān decrees that certain categories of women are prohibited to men in marriage and specifies among them "mothers and sisters through nursing."[43] That is to say, if a woman has served as a wet nurse for a boy, she, her daughters, and any other girls that she may have nursed cannot have lawful sexual relations with him. In Arabian culture, wet nursing was a widespread practice. As a result, the determination of "lawful" candidates for sexual relations could pose a variety of challenges.

While nursing within the naturally determined time period (i.e., within the first two or three years of life) created a host of legal dilemmas, the issue of giving breast milk to adults appears to have wreaked havoc on the conceptualization of licit and illicit relationships in terms of marriage and social interaction.[44] The Prophet's endorsement of giving breast milk to an adult is found in a report in which Muḥammad allowed a

Arabic sources that nursing (requiring intimate contact between a man and a woman) is not what the jurists had in mind when discussing this issue.

42 For a more detailed discussion of nursing in the medieval Muslim world, see Avner Giladi, *Infants, Parents, and Wet Nurses: Medieval Islamic Views on Breastfeeding and Their Social Implications* (Leiden: Brill, 1999).

43 Qur'ān, 4:23.

44 As is apparent from various *ḥadīth*, the prohibition on "mothers and sisters through nursing" extends to women who could be taken as concubines as well as spouses. The following two traditions appearing in Mālik's *al-Muwaṭṭa'* exemplify the confusion stemming from the *riḍā' al-kabīr* debate. In one, 'Abd Allāh b. 'Umar reports on a man who complained to 'Umar b. al-Khaṭṭāb that his wife fed some of her breast milk to his concubine, thereby hoping to render the concubine in the category of *maḥram* for her husband. 'Umar advised the man to beat his wife and continue his relationship with the concubine as kinship could only be established through suckling of infants and young children (*riḍā' al-ṣaghīr*). In another, a man seeks Abū Mūsā al-Ash'arī's (d. 42/662f.) counsel because he has accidentally imbibed his wife's breast milk. Abū Mūsā confirms the man's fears saying, "I cannot but think that she is forbidden (*ḥarām*) for you." At this point Ibn Mas'ūd interjects and rules that kinship is only established by suckling in the first two years. Abū Mūsā defers to Ibn Mas'ūd's authority and the man's marriage is saved (see Mālik, *al-Muwaṭṭa'*, 2:125–26). These traditions reveal an early ambiguity regarding the

woman named Sahla bint Suhayl to give her breast milk to Sālim, her adopted son, who had already reached adulthood. Muḥammad is said to have allowed this because Sahla sensed some discomfort on the part of her husband when Sālim visited their home. Variants of the tradition explain that Sahla's husband felt uneasy about Sālim's visits to their home after the revelation of the Qur'ānic verse 33:4, which emphasized that adopted sons are not like real sons in terms of regulations pertaining to marriage.[45] However, by giving him a requisite amount of her breast milk, she could render him among the men forbidden to her for marriage, and he would be able to visit her freely.

Given the indicators from the Qur'ān and *ḥadīth*, Muslim jurists immersed themselves in the intricacies of this rather complex conundrum.[46] Much ink was spilled over questions such as: How much milk must be transferred before the bond is established? Does the testimony of one woman suffice to establish that nursing occurred between a woman and a boy (who was not her son by birth)? Does the transfer of breast milk that is not for the purpose of nourishment establish foster kinship? Resolving these questions was crucial for Muslim cultures in which daily interactions were regulated and circumscribed according to kinship networks, those established by blood relations as well as foster parentage.

After the death of Muḥammad, 'Ā'isha understood the Sahla *ḥadīth* to be a general one applicable to her as well as to the other wives. Through *riḍā' al-kabīr*, she reasoned, men could be transferred to the *maḥram* category and permitted to visit women with whom they had established foster kinship through nursing. Several reports suggest that 'Ā'isha, being in high demand for her religious knowledge, used the Sahla tradition as a

validity of *riḍā' al-kabīr*. It appears that a consensus that *riḍā' al-kabīr* does not establish *maḥram* bonds was reached in the early stages of legal development. Ibn Ḥazm (d. 456/1064) is among the few classical jurists who argue for the practice as a legitimate means for creating foster relationships: see 'Alī b. Aḥmad b. Ḥazm, *al-Muḥallā* (Beirut: Dār al-Kutub al-'Ilmiyya), 10:202–12. For the consensus, see Mālik, *al-Muwaṭṭa'*, 2:123–26; al-Shāfi'ī, *Kitāb al-Umm* (Beirut: Dār al-Kutub al-'Ilmiyya, 1993), 5:47–49; and 'Abd Allāh b. Aḥmad b. Qudāma (d. 620/1223), *al-Mughnī* (Beirut: Dār al-Kutub al-'Ilmiyya, 1994), 6:401–2. This practice drew renewed attention when a modern Egyptian *muftī* issued a ruling that *riḍā' al-kabīr* could be used to mitigate discomfort from male-female interactions in the workplace. For a contemporary Western perspective on this incident, see the article by Michael Slackman, "A Compass That Can Clash with Modern Life," *New York Times*, June 12, 2007. The modern Egyptian ruling was widely decried and, as such, lacks currency.

45 See, for example, Mālik, *al-Muwaṭṭa'*, 2:123–24, for a report connecting the Prophet's *fatwā* in Sahla's case to the revelation of Qur'ān, 33:4.

46 See Ibn Qudāma, *al-Mughnī*, 6:357–75, for a thorough discussion of issues related to nursing.

precedent to permit men who wanted to hear her *ḥadīth* into her company.[47] She would ask one of her sisters to give a requisite amount of breast milk to the visitor. This practice would establish a foster bond between ʿĀ'isha and the visitor in question, and he would be permitted to interact with her. Umm Salama and the other wives, however, disdained allowing men to visit them by this method.[48] One report attributes the following conversation to them:

> Umm Salama said to ʿĀ'isha, "You admit [to your presence] a young boy nearing puberty (*al-ghulām al-ayfaʿ*) whom I would not like to admit to mine." ʿĀ'isha responded, "Do you not find a model [worthy of emulation] in the Prophet?" She continued, "The wife of Abū Hudhayfa [i.e., Sahla bint Suhayl] said to the Prophet, 'O Messenger of God, Sālim enters my home though he is a grown man. [I fear that] Abū Hudhayfa feels some discomfort on account of him.' The Prophet said, 'Give him breast milk so that he can visit you.'"[49]

Through this interaction, ʿĀ'isha is represented as upholding Muḥammad's precedent even in the face of overwhelming consensus against her. Aside from displaying ʿĀ'isha's legal reasoning, the debate on *riḍāʿ al-kabīr* allows us to extrapolate that Muḥammad's other wives

47 The most direct statement of this is in Mālik, *al-Muwaṭṭa'*, 2:123, #1775. There are also other traditions in Mālik's *al-Muwaṭṭa'* about ʿĀ'isha's practice in this regard. She is said, for example, to have allowed those to whom her sisters and the daughters of her brother had given a requisite amount of breast milk to see her. In contrast, she did not permit those who had not established such *maḥram* bonds to see her (Mālik, *al-Muwaṭṭa'*, 2:122, #1770). Another tradition in the *Muwaṭṭa'* relates a failed attempt at establishing *maḥram* bonds. Yaḥyā related from Mālik who related from Nāfiʿ that Sālim b. ʿAbd Allāh b. ʿUmar informed him that ʿĀ'isha sent him away to be given the breast milk of her sister Umm Kulthūm bint Abī Bakr al-Ṣiddīq. She said, "Give him milk ten times so that he can come in to see me." Sālim said, "Umm Kulthūm gave me milk three times and then fell ill. . . . I could not go in to see ʿĀ'isha because Umm Kulthūm did not finish for me the ten times" (Mālik, *al-Muwaṭṭa'*, 2:121–22, #1768). This tradition is interesting because it portrays ʿĀ'isha as stringent in the application of rules regarding *riḍāʿ al-kabīr*, namely that the requisite amount of milk had to be transferred. Thus, even as she is depicted as contravening consensus, she is simultaneously portrayed as doing so within guidelines set by the Prophet's precedent.

48 Interestingly, there is one unusual tradition, cited in *al-Muwaṭṭa'*, that Ḥafṣa bint ʿUmar allowed ʿĀṣim b. ʿAbd Allāh b. Saʿd to go to her sister, Fāṭima bint ʿUmar, so that he could be given breast milk and consequently permitted in her company. While the tradition states that ʿĀṣim at the time was still young, it is interesting as another explicit case of a wife of Muḥammad adopting this practice as a means for allowing access to males who would otherwise not be permitted to see them (Mālik, *al-Muwaṭṭa'*, 2:122, #1769). This underscores the point that the contentious issue was the age at which such foster bonds could be established and not whether the transfer of breast milk could be used to circumvent restrictions on male visitors who were not *maḥram*. For the report regarding the consensus of the wives against *riḍāʿ al-kabīr*, see Mālik, *al-Muwaṭṭa'*, 2:123–24, #1775.

49 Muslim, *Ṣaḥīḥ*, 5:2:29, and al-Nasā'ī, *Sunan*, 6:104.

played more circumscribed roles in the transmission of reports because they did not readily permit non-*maḥram* visitors into their company.

The portrait of 'Ā'isha that emerges from her narrations as well as legal commentary on her opinions is of a woman extraordinarily engaged not just in the transmission of Muḥammad's sayings but also in shaping the meaning that Muḥammad's practice would have for later generations. Although dicta ascribed to her were discarded or adapted according to the needs of later *fuqahā'*, it is clear that she was a rare female voice with which they would have to contend in their legal discourse.[50]

UMM SALAMA

Hind bint Abī Umayya, better known by her *kunya* Umm Salama, ranks second to 'Ā'isha in female *ḥadīth* transmission.[51] Whereas 'Ā'isha's position in the community was in no small part attributable to being Abū Bakr's daughter, Umm Salama's prestige derived partly from her membership in the influential Makhzūmī clan of Quraysh. Her first marriage was to Abū Salama (d. 4/625), a well-known Companion of Muḥammad and his foster-brother.[52] He is said to have been among the earliest converts to Islam, and Umm Salama followed him in conversion. The two performed the migration to Abyssinia together, and Umm Salama's account of her experiences on this *hijra* as well as in the abode of the Negus of Abyssinia figures prominently in the earliest biographies of Muḥammad.[53] After Abū Salama's death from a wound received during the Battle of Uḥud (3/625),

[50] Al-Zarkashī's work offers many examples of how later jurists grappled with traditions reported on 'Ā'isha's authority. In cases where 'Ā'isha's views clearly contravene later consensus, al-Zarkashī himself takes pains to reconcile these reported views with those that contradict them (see, for example, al-Zarkashī, *al-Ijāba*, 126–28 and 137–39). Dukhayyil also devotes a section to issues on which 'Ā'isha disagreed with other prominent Companions (*Mawsū'at Fiqh 'Ā'isha*, 531–52).

[51] Biographical references for her are available in the following sources: Ibn Sa'd, *al-Ṭabaqāt*, 8:660–67; Abū Nu'aym al-Iṣbahānī, *Ma'rifat al-Ṣaḥāba* (Riyad: Dār al-Waṭan li'l-Nashr, 1998), 6:3218–22; Ibn 'Abd al-Barr, *al-Istī'āb*, 4:1920–22; al-Mizzī, *Tahdhīb*, 35:317–20; Ibn Ḥajar, *al-Iṣāba*, 13:161–63; and Kaḥḥāla, *A'lām al-Nisā'*, 5:221–27.

[52] His full name is Abū 'Abd Allāh b. 'Abd al-Asad b. Hilāl. He and Muḥammad were both nursed by a woman named Thuwayba. For his biography, see Ibn Sa'd, *al-Ṭabaqāt*, 3:170–72. See also the following more detailed studies about Umm Salama: Amīna al-Ḥasanī, *Umm Salama Umm al-Mu'minīn*, 2 vols. (Rabat: Wizārat al-Awqāf wa'l-Shu'ūn al-Islāmiyya, 1998), and Yasmin Amin, "Umm Salama and her *Ḥadīth*" (Master's thesis, American University in Cairo, 2011).

[53] See 'Abd al-Malik b. Hishām (d. 218/833), *al-Sīra al-Nabawiyya* (Beirut: al-Maktaba al-'Aṣriyya, 1994), 1:249–54.

Abū Bakr and then 'Umar proposed to her, but she refused them both. The Prophet followed with his own proposal. Her hesitation in accepting is elaborated upon in her biographies as well as in traditions narrated on her authority. The triple obstacles of native jealousy, old age, and the responsibilities of raising four children from her previous marriage prevented Umm Salama from embracing Muḥammad's invitation. However, after some persuasion, she joined the ranks of his co-wives.

Umm Salama's position in Muḥammad's household also contributes to her prestige as a source for reports. She was the leader of one "camp" of co-wives comprising Zaynab bint Jaḥsh, Ramla bint Abī Sufyān, Juwayriya bint al-Ḥārith, and Maymūna bint al-Ḥārith.[54] In this capacity, she carried a complaint to the Prophet regarding the preferential treatment of 'Ā'isha.[55] In the various versions of this tradition, the wives were offended that the Anṣār always sent their gifts to Muḥammad on 'Ā'isha's allotted day. They too were fond of presents and wanted gifts to be sent on a more equitable basis. While these efforts to persuade Muḥammad were to no avail as he defended his relationship with 'Ā'isha, it is telling that Umm Salama was chosen to represent the disheartened wives.[56] They clearly viewed her as an assertive wife who had some influence with the Prophet. Taken together, biographical sources, *ḥadīth* narratives, and accounts from the *sīra* portray Umm Salama as an influential woman who offset 'Ā'isha in her temperament and her position in the Prophet's household. In a similar vein, Shī'īs view Umm Salama, and not 'Ā'isha, as the most revered wife after Khadīja, Muḥammad's first and only wife until her death.[57]

[54] This division of ranks is referred to in Ibn Ḥanbal, *Musnad*, 6:333, #26505–6. Al-Ḥasanī explains this divide between the wives in greater detail (see al-Ḥasanī, *Umm Salama*, 142–63).

[55] Other versions of this tradition have Fāṭima or Zaynab beseeching the Prophet on behalf of the wives (see al-Bukhārī, *Ṣaḥīḥ* [Beirut: Dār al-Qalam, 1987], 3–4:316–17). In this edition of Bukhārī's *Ṣaḥīḥ*, different volumes are bound together, and their pages numbered sequentially.

[56] The theme of Umm Salama as a representative of women's concerns is taken up again in traditions that specify her inquiries as the cause for revelation of Qur'ānic verses pertaining to the equality of male and female believers before God (Qur'ān, 33:35). See, for example, Ibn Ḥanbal, *Musnad*, 6:346, #26595. For other versions of this tradition, see *al-Musnad al-Jāmi'*, 20:680–82, #17638–40.

[57] There are many Shī'ī biographies extolling the virtues of Umm Salama, particularly in comparison with 'Ā'isha. A contemporary Twelver Shī'ī view of Umm Salama is given in Sayyid Muḥsin al-Amīn al-'Āmilī, *A'yān al-Shī'a* (Beirut: Dār al-Ta'āruf, 1986), 10:272. Spellberg explores the Shī'ī representations of 'Ā'isha in greater detail throughout her work *Politics, Gender, and the Islamic Past*.

The number and content of Umm Salama's reports reveal the esteem accorded her by Companions and Successors. Including repetitions, she is credited with 175 traditions.[58] While these span a wide range of subjects, most of her *ḥadīth* occur in the categories of ritual purity (*ṭahāra*), prayer (*ṣalāt*), marriage (*nikāḥ*), and trials and tribulations (*fitan*). A major distinction between 'Ā'isha and Umm Salama is that the latter's reports overlap to a greater extent. For example, one-fourth of Umm Salama's thirty-two traditions on prayer relate to the occasion on which she saw the Prophet performing additional cycles of prayer after the 'Aṣr prayer. Similarly, seven of the nine traditions she narrates on funerary matters (*janā'iz*) relate to the death of her first husband, Abū Salama. While 'Ā'isha's traditions also overlap and contain repetitions, she is considered an authority on many more subjects than Umm Salama.

Nonetheless, Umm Salama's testimony was actively sought and considered decisive on several issues. In one account, a woman named Mussa al-Azdiyya relates that after she performed the Ḥajj, she visited Umm Salama and sought her advice on a matter of ritual practice.[59] Mussa remarked to Umm Salama that Samura b. Jundab had told the women to make up the prayers they missed during their menstrual periods. In response, Umm Salama ruled against Samura and analogized the issue to that of postpartum women who, during the time of the Prophet, would abstain from prayer for forty days without making up the missed prayers. In another well-attested *ḥadīth*, a difference of opinion occurred between 'Abd Allāh b. 'Abbās and Abū Salama b. 'Abd al-Raḥmān b. 'Awf (d. 94/712) over the period that a woman who has given birth soon after the death of her husband must wait before remarrying.[60] Abū Hurayra joined the debate on the side of

[58] *Al-Musnad al-Jāmi'*, 20:569–706. These *ḥadīth* are related to approximately 140 different matters. Some traditions are repeated with variant narratives or related by different Successors.

[59] Abū Dāwūd, *Sunan* (Beirut: Maktaba al-'Aṣriyya, n.d.), 1:83–84. This type of narrative setting occurs frequently in women's traditions, indicating that the Ḥajj provided an ideal time for garnering traditions and information from well-known authorities, among them Muḥammad's wives.

[60] *'Idda* is the technical term for this waiting period. This tradition appears in the following collections: Mālik, *al-Muwaṭṭa'*, 2:105–6; Muslim, *Ṣaḥīḥ*, 5:2:90; al-Tirmidhī, *Sunan* (Beirut: Dār al-Fikr, 1994), 2:406; and al-Nasā'ī, *Sunan*, 6:192–93. In debating this issue, jurists were at odds over the interpretation of two apparently conflicting verses on the waiting period of a widow. In the Qur'ān, 2:234, the waiting period is designated as four months and ten days, and in verse 65:4, the waiting period for a pregnant (divorced) woman is until she gives birth. See also Ibn Qudāma, *al-Mughnī*, 7:315–20, for an overview of the legal discussion on the waiting period of widows.

Abū Salama, who said that the requisite waiting period is over once the woman has given birth. The three sent Kurayb, a client (*mawlā*) of Ibn ʿAbbās, to Umm Salama for the decisive word. She confirmed Abū Salama's view, citing the Prophet's ruling in a similar case: Subayʿa al-Aslamiyya had given birth a few days after her husband died, and the Prophet permitted her to remarry according to her wishes without observing the Qur'ānically mandated waiting period of four months and ten days.

The fact that contradictory traditions were ascribed to Umm Salama further strengthens the point that her testimony carried legal weight. The controversy over whether ablution is necessary after consuming cooked food (*wuḍū' mim-mā massat al-nār*) illustrates how ascriptions to Umm Salama strengthened one's case.[61] In the anti-ablution cluster of traditions, Umm Salama relates that the Prophet had once eaten cooked meat in her quarters and gone out to pray without performing ablution. In a more detailed narrative from this cluster, ʿAbd Allāh b. Shaddād (d. 81/700f.) relates the exchange he had with Marwān b. al-Ḥakam (d. 65/685) on this topic.

> I heard Abū Hurayra say, "'*wuḍū'* is obligatory from [i.e., after eating] that which has been touched by fire." This was mentioned to Marwān. He [Marwān] said, "I don't know whom to ask about this."
>
> [I said,] "How can that be when the wives of the Prophet are amongst us?" So he sent me to Umm Salama, who told me that the Prophet went out to pray after eating the meat from a bone. He prayed without performing the ablution.[62]

In direct contradiction with this testimony is another report cited by the pro-ablution camp, reported by Muḥammad b. Ṭalḥa:

> I said to Abū Salama, "Your foster-son Sālim does not perform ablution after eating cooked food." He [Abū Salama] struck Sālim on his chest and declared, "I swear on the authority of Umm Salama, the wife of the Prophet, that she used to testify on the authority of the Prophet that he used to perform *wuḍū'* from cooked food."[63]

Thus, the authority of Umm Salama is invoked to support opposing camps on this issue of ritual purity. While this is one way in which her legacy was

[61] For an examination of the legal controversy on *wuḍū'* from cooked food and its implications for ritual purity law, see Marion Katz, *Body of Text* (Albany: SUNY Press, 2002), 101–23. In her analysis, Katz asserts that the Arabic phrase "*mā massat al-nār*" was likely to have referred to cooked food and not only that which was literally touched by fire. In this vein, foods such as bread (which was baked) and cheese (which was boiled) were also included under the rubric of "foods touched by fire" (see Katz, *Body of Text*, 102–3).

[62] Ibn Māja, *Sunan*, 1:165; and al-Nasā'ī, *Sunan*, 1:107–8.

[63] Ibn Ḥanbal, *Musnad*, 3:362, #26717.

utilized in legal debates, there are several instances in which the reports of Umm Salama show no contradictions in and of themselves, but rather are used to oppose the traditions attributed to ʿĀʾisha.

This depiction recurs both in the biographical literature and in individual traditions ascribed to the two women. We encountered earlier the idea of Umm Salama as a foil for ʿĀʾisha through her leadership of a camp of co-wives distinct in their interests from the group headed by ʿĀʾisha. The greatest divide between the two women arose after the death of Muḥammad and was centered on their factional loyalties. ʿĀʾisha, in her leadership role in the Battle of the Camel (36/656), was allied with Ṭalḥa b. ʿUbayd Allāh (d. 36/656) and al-Zubayr b. al-ʿAwwām (d. 36/656).[64] Umm Salama, on the other hand, supported the faction of ʿAlī.[65] She also opposed ʿĀʾisha's participation in the Battle of the Camel and is said to have articulated this in an eloquent dispatch.[66] In contrast to some of ʿĀʾisha's anti-ʿAlid traditions, Umm Salama is credited with several reports in which the Prophet expresses his preference for ʿAlī and Fāṭima, and their offspring.[67] One tradition goes so far as to include her in the category of Muḥammad's closest kin (*ahl al-bayt*), a category revered by Shīʿites in particular.[68]

Although Umm Salama was not as prolific as ʿĀʾisha, a significant niche was carved out for her in what would evolve to become the field of *ḥadīth* transmission. Her prestige as an early convert and a prominent wife is reflected in her status among the Companions. Like ʿĀʾisha, she was a coveted legal authority. Yet she is not portrayed as being involved in the day-to-day concerns of the community. Rather, she was available for consultation on a more selective basis, generally to prominent men of the community and to women who may have sought her guidance. In this, Umm Salama's profile resembles that of the wives of Muḥammad other than ʿĀʾisha. Umm Salama's case suggests that although Muḥammad's wives were perceived as valuable authorities for traditions about him, the strictures imposed by their seclusion overrode the community's desire to utilize them fully in this regard.

64 For a closer analysis of her role in this incident, see Spellberg, *Politics*, 101–49.

65 Umm Salama's stance during this political crisis is examined in detail by al-Ḥasanī, *Umm Salama*, 2:357–87.

66 Spellberg, *Politics*, 132–38, and al-Ḥasanī, *Umm Salama*, 1:371–90.

67 Ibn Ḥanbal, *Musnad*, 6:340, #26557; 6:338, #26542; and 6:364–65, #26739; al-Tirmidhī, *Sunan*, 5:466.

68 Ibn Ḥanbal, *Musnad*, 6:338, #26542.

Wife	# *Ḥadīth*
Zaynab bint Jaḥsh (d. 20/641)	7
Ramla bint Abī Sufyān (Umm Ḥabība) (d. 44/664)	22
Ḥafṣa bint ʿUmar (d. 45/665)	25
Ṣafiyya bint Ḥuyayy (d. 52/672)	8
Sawda bint Zamʿa (d. 54/674)	4
Juwayriya bint al-Ḥārith (d. 56/676)	6
Maymūna bint al-Ḥārith (d. 61/681)[69]	37

FIGURE 1: Chart of the Numbers of *Ḥadīth* Narrated by the Seven Co-Wives

OTHER CO-WIVES

Figure 1 above illustrates the comparatively restricted participation of Muḥammad's remaining seven wives.[70]

Three salient characteristics of the narration of the co-wives suggest that their roles were subordinate and complementary to those of ʿĀʾisha and Umm Salama. First, notwithstanding the range of their traditions, these are still heavily concentrated in a few topics such as ritual purity (*ṭahāra*), prayer (*ṣalāt*), and tribulations (*fitan*). For the most part, their reports corroborate those of ʿĀʾisha and Umm Salama rather than adding new information about Muḥammad's practices. Second, the autobiographical component so pronounced in the narratives of the two leading co-wives is rarer with respect to the seven other wives.[71] In general, there is little intersection between the issues that are important in the individual biographies of these women and the traditions that they narrate. For example,

[69] For the sake of consistency, and because *al-Musnad al-Jāmiʿ* includes more *ḥadīth* collections than al-Mizzī's work (*Tuḥfa*), I have provided the numbers from the former rather than from the latter. With respect to the wives of Muḥammad, the numerical discrepancies between the *Tuḥfat al-Ashrāf* and *al-Musnad al-Jāmiʿ* are minor and do not alter the conclusions regarding the transmissions of the wives of the Prophet.

[70] Maymūna's number is slightly higher than those of the others primarily because of repetitions of certain traditions with minor variations either in the narrative or in the second link of the *isnād*. She actually narrates on twenty-eight issues as nine of her *ḥadīth* are repetitions. The other six wives' *musnads* do not contain as many repetitions.

[71] For autobiographical narratives in the *ḥadīth* of ʿĀʾisha, see *al-Musnad al-Jāmiʿ*, 19:784–816. See also Elias, "The *Ḥadīth* Traditions of ʿĀʾisha" on the autobiographical element in her reports. For Umm Salama's autobiographical narratives, see *al-Musnad al-Jāmiʿ*, 20:604–8, #17546–52, and 20:632–37, #17583–84.

Zaynab bint Jaḥsh's biographies are replete with accounts of her divorce from Zayd b. Ḥāritha, the Prophet's adopted son, and her subsequent divinely ordained marriage to Muḥammad. Two occasions of revelation are linked to the Prophet's relationship with her.[72] Yet none of her traditions touches on these matters.[73] Finally, there are fewer explicit indications that these seven wives were consulted by those outside of their kin and clientage circles.[74] Reports frequently depict Companions such as Abū Hurayra or Marwān dispatching messengers to 'Ā'isha and Umm Salama with questions on the Prophet's *sunna*. When the other wives are sought out, it is usually by their male relatives or by other women.[75] In general, the traditions of these seven wives are presented as relatively brief pronouncements without an elaborate narrative structure to situate the encounter. Ramla bint Abī Sufyān's narrations reinforce the point that the wives were available for direct consultation primarily to members of their families and client groups and to other women. In *isnād*s from the *Tuḥfat al-Ashrāf* and *al-Musnad al-Jāmi'*, Ramla is credited with narrating to eighteen men and women. Ten of these are women or men in her kinship and clientage circle. The remaining eight are men who do not belong to these categories.[76] The narratives preserved by the Sunnī compilers contain details of the encounters in cases where related men or women narrate from her. Thus, we have her brother Mu'āwiya saying, "I asked Umm Ḥabība, the wife of the

[72] These two revelations concern her divorce from Zayd and her marriage to Muḥammad (Qur'ān, 33:37–38, 40, 53), and the *ḥijāb* regulations (Qur'ān, 33:53–55).

[73] Another such example is Maymūna, whose biographers focus on whether the Prophet married her while he was in *iḥrām* during the *'umra* performed in 7 AH. Over half of Ibn Sa'd's entry for Maymūna is devoted to traditions on this issue (see Ibn Sa'd, *al-Ṭabaqāt*, 8:94–100). Yet only one of her *ḥadīth* relates to this topic; see Ibn Ḥanbal, *Musnad*, 6:374, #26808, and Ibn Māja, *Sunan*, 1:632.

[74] It is noteworthy that the canonical collections do not generally include *isnād*s in which the narrator reporting on the authority of one of these seven co-wives is not her kin or client or is not especially prominent. Rather, such *isnād*s occur in works such as the *Musnad* of Ibn Ḥanbal, which is reputed to contain some weak traditions. It is premature to assert a causal connection at this point since there may have been other reasons why compilers such as al-Bukhārī and Muslim rejected *isnād*s wherein there is no family connection.

[75] For example, Mu'āwiya, Ramla's brother, seeks her out (Ibn Māja, *Sunan*, 1:209). Similarly, Maymūna's *maḥram* appear with frequency in her *isnād*s. They include her nephew, 'Abd Allāh b. 'Abbās, and her grandson, 'Ubayd Allāh b. 'Abd Allāh b. 'Abbās (see, for example, *al-Musnad al-Jāmi'*, 20:518–21, #17441–43; 20:531, #17455; and 20:533, #17458).

[76] The *isnād*s with these eight men are not cited in the *Ṣaḥīḥ* collections of al-Bukhārī and Muslim. Most of them appear only in the *Musnad* of Ibn Ḥanbal. However, as stated earlier, al-Bukhārī and Muslim may have rejected these *isnād*s for reasons aside from the fact that they are narrated by non-kin of Ramla.

Prophet, 'did the Messenger of God pray in the clothes in which he had had intercourse?'"[77] The words "*sa'altu-hā*" (I asked her) used in this tradition suggest direct contact and only occur in traditions in which *maḥram* men or women narrate from her. In another tradition, Abū Sufyān b. Sa'īd b. al-Akhnas b. Sharīq relates, "I entered the quarters of Umm Ḥabība," at which point the subnarrator interjects, "she was his maternal aunt."[78] The account then continues with a description of how Ramla (Umm Ḥabība) poured some water for him and encouraged him to perform ablution because the Prophet had done so after eating cooked food. Interestingly, such narrative detail that situates the encounter is generally absent from reports in which the wives are narrating to non-kin or non-client males. In the case of Ramla and her *ḥadīth* transmission to eight non-*maḥram* men, we are left to wonder about the circumstances of the encounter between them. It may well be that, like 'Ā'isha, Ramla was indeed available for broader consultation on matters of religious practice. The texts of the reports and supplementary historical sources, however, provide little indication that this was the case.

The picture of transmission networks that emerges from the *isnād*s of the seven co-wives satisfies expectations of their social interaction given the rulings on *ḥijāb* and the seclusion of Muḥammad's wives after his death.[79] It is said that Sawda bint Zam'a and Zaynab bint Jaḥsh were particularly observant of the strictures. Sawda assiduously observed the Qur'ānic commandment that the wives should stay at home and even refused to perform pilgrimage with the other co-wives irrespective of permission to do so from 'Uthmān (r. 23–35/644–55), the third caliph.[80] In this light, it makes sense that Sawda, though she outlived many of the wives, is known for only four traditions.[81]

Though the protocols of seclusion and *ḥijāb* are maintained with fidelity in the narratives of the seven co-wives, such is not the case with 'Ā'isha and Umm Salama. Al-Mizzī lists approximately 200 narrators from 'Ā'isha, primarily from the *isnād*s of the six canonical collections. Her network includes numerous men who are not directly related to her nor were they known to be her clients. Likewise, of the approximately eighty men who

77 Ibn Māja, *Sunan*, 1:209.

78 See, for example, al-Nasā'ī, *Sunan*, 1:107.

79 Ibn Sa'd, *al-Ṭabaqāt*, 8:124–28, 150–53. See also Stowasser, *Women in the Qur'an*, 115–17, for a discussion of the wives' seclusion during Muḥammad's life and after his death.

80 The relevant verse is Qur'ān, 33:33. For Sawda's refusal to perform pilgrimages, see Ibn Sa'd, *al-Ṭabaqāt*, 8:150.

81 See *al-Musnad al-Jāmi'*, 19:217–19.

are listed as narrating from Umm Salama, the majority do not belong to her kinship or clientage circles.[82] In several instances when messengers were sent to ʿĀ'isha and Umm Salama, the phrase "I entered the quarters of" (*dakhaltu ʿalā*) is used. Whether or not there was a physical barrier (*ḥijāb*) between ʿĀ'isha or Umm Salama and the messenger (a detail not regularly provided in such narratives), it is noteworthy that the broader community of men and women frequented the quarters of these two wives seeking religious knowledge – an accessibility not characteristic of the other wives.

ʿĀ'isha's narratives, in particular, vividly convey her expansive interpretations of the *ḥijāb* rulings. In a variant of the aforementioned report in which a servant girl is the intermediary between ʿĀ'isha and Ibn Shihāb al-Khawlānī, ʿĀ'isha directly advises a visitor about how to deal with traces of ritual impurity on his clothes. The Arabic wording speaks of a more informal exchange in which ʿĀ'isha herself observes a visitor washing his clothes and advises him on the proper behavior to ensure ritual purity (*ʿan ʿAlqama wa'l-Aswad anna rajulan nazala bi-ʿĀ'isha fa-aṣbaḥa yaghsilu thawba-hu*...).[83] She assures him that rather than washing the entire garment, he could have just cleansed the specific spot where he observed the impurity or sprinkled water around the area if he just suspected impurity but did not actually see it. The reference to ʿĀ'isha's visitor is best understood in conjunction with Ibn Saʿd's description of the dwellings of Muḥammad's wives, each of which bordered the mosque and had its own entrance onto the communal gathering area of the mosque.[84] In this context, we can envision a fluid situation where those staying in the mosque may have been observed by the wives, and as the report above suggests, their interactions could serve as a medium for transmitting religious knowledge.

Another tradition concerns ʿĀ'isha's contact with the blind poet Ḥassān b. Thābit (d. 54/674).[85] Masrūq goes to visit her and finds Ḥassān reciting poetry in her presence. He wants to know why she allows him to

[82] For a list of those who narrated from ʿĀ'isha, see her biography in al-Mizzī, *Tahdhīb*, 35:227–36; for those who narrated from Umm Salama, see al-Mizzī, *Tahdhīb*, 35:317–20.

[83] Muslim, *Ṣaḥīḥ*, 2:1:159–60.

[84] See Ibn Saʿd, *al-Ṭabaqāt*, 8:117–20. Stowasser also notes that the wives' dwellings served as a physical extension of the mosque space where many members of the community would congregate. See Stowasser, *Women in the Qur'an*, 91.

[85] al-Bukhārī, *Ṣaḥīḥ*, 5–6:468–69. Al-Mizzī provides additional versions in *Tuḥfa*, 11:740. See also Spellberg, *Politics*, 70–73 and 94–95 for further discussion of Ḥassān's role during the incident.

enter, even though the Qur'ān condemns his behavior in the "Affair of the Slander" (*ḥadīth al-ifk*), during which 'Ā'isha was falsely accused of adultery and then divinely vindicated in verses that harshly censure those who spread rumors about innocent women.[86] Ḥassān b. Thābit was reportedly among those who had propagated the false reports about her. 'Ā'isha defends him saying that blindness is his punishment and that Ḥassān used to defend the Prophet by reciting poetry on his behalf. In this report, the fact that he is not *maḥram* is not even an issue, and neither Masrūq nor 'Ā'isha refer to Ḥassān's blindness as an exception allowing face-to-face contact.

'Ā'isha's interaction with Ḥassān, however, contradicts the precedent derived from a different incident related by Umm Salama about Ibn Umm Maktūm's visit.[87] According to Umm Salama, this blind Companion visited her and Maymūna after the revelation of the *ḥijāb* verse. Muḥammad ordered his wives to observe seclusion, even though Ibn Umm Maktūm could not see them. The Prophet explained that they (the wives) could see him and so should observe the *ḥijāb*. Abū Dāwūd in his *Sunan* comments that this ruling must have been specific to Muḥammad's wives, as he had ruled in another case that Fāṭima bint Qays, a divorced woman, could observe her waiting period in the home of Ibn Umm Maktūm. In the latter case, Muḥammad had specified that it would be better for Fāṭima to spend her days with him *because* he was blind and would not see her dressing and undressing. With Muḥammad's wives, the *ḥijāb* was not only intended to preserve them from the male gaze but also to prevent them from seeing non-*maḥram* men.

The range of behavior with respect to seclusion by the wives is fascinating *not* because it reveals the submission of some of them to the rulings as opposed to the rebellion of others. On the contrary, this diversity of approaches highlights the right of interpretation that the wives exercised even when confronted with what appears to us as a highly restrictive ruling. Some wives, such as Sawda, opted for the least lenient interpretation and as such refused to go out even to perform the Ḥajj. At the other end of the spectrum, 'Ā'isha did not view the *ḥijāb* rulings as unilaterally confining her to her home. When she chose to follow her understanding, she was criticized on the basis of her discernment and her understanding of Muḥammad's precedent but was not branded as someone who had rebelled against it.

[86] Qur'ān, 24:11–17.
[87] Abū Dāwūd, *Sunan*, 4:63–64.

Curiously, Muslim jurists in subsequent generations did not unanimously agree that 'Ā'isha's behavior, though grounded in her legal reasoning, was exemplary. The efforts of some classical scholars to come to terms with her leadership in the Battle of the Camel reveal their discomfort with her sociopolitical decisions. In other respects as well, there was ambivalence as to whether she represented a role model for the common Muslim woman, or whether in her position as a "super-wife," she transcended limitations placed on other women within the Prophet's household and in the community at large. For example, al-Zarkashī reports that when Abū Ḥanīfa (d. 150/767f.) was asked about 'Ā'isha's travels without a *maḥram*, he responded that everyone was *maḥram* for her because she was "the Mother of the Believers." He argued that not all women are equal to her in this respect, and therefore her example does not serve as a valid precedent.[88] Similarly, jurists may have reasoned that 'Ā'isha's expertise justified a relaxation of *ḥijāb* restrictions. As historical patterns in women's transmission after the Companion generation suggest, it did indeed take centuries for the memory of 'Ā'isha as *muḥadditha* and *faqīha* to gain traction in the Muslim tradition as truly exemplary for all women.

The discrepant applications of *ḥijāb* and seclusion on the part of 'Ā'isha, Umm Salama, and the other wives aside, it is important to bear in mind that the lower participation of most of Muḥammad's wives reflects more than stringent isolation on their part. The quantity and quality of their *ḥadīth* are also a by-product of how their reports were culled and recorded. The reports detailing how to clean ritual impurities, how long women can mourn for the dead, or how many cycles Muḥammad prayed voluntarily are answers to specific questions raised by Muslims after the death of the Prophet. For private matters or issues relating specifically to women, it was natural that Muḥammad's wives would have some answers.[89] Yet the needs of Sunnī compilers for such reports were filled largely by the narrations of 'Ā'isha and Umm Salama. This imbalance compounds the impression of the more marginal participation of the seven co-wives in *ḥadīth* learning.

[88] al-Zarkashī, *al-Ijāba*, 132. Another example of a jurist grappling with 'Ā'isha's legacy is to be found in Ibn Ḥazm, who argues against her *ijtihād* (independent legal reasoning) that the Prophet would have forbidden women from going to mosques if he had seen the corruption that prevailed after him. Ibn Ḥazm argues that 'Ā'isha's *ijtihād* cannot overturn clear *sunna* from the Prophet (see *al-Muḥallā*, 3:112–16).

[89] See John Burton, *An Introduction to the Ḥadīth* for his view that early *ḥadīth* were essentially exegetical and intended to clarify points left vague in the Qur'ān.

If Muḥammad's wives primarily served to provide testimony on his private actions, what were the roles of other female Companions? These other women would not have had free access to many private aspects of his behavior. Thus, they were on a par with male Companions, who were primarily witnesses to Muḥammad's actions in the public arena. Nevertheless, a number of these other female Companions were repositories of information about him.

OTHER FEMALE RELATIVES

In addition to Muḥammad's wives, there are women who were accorded privileged status as members of his kin group. Of his four daughters, only one, Fāṭima (d. 11/632), survived him, and only by a few months. In *al-Musnad al-Jāmi'*, she is credited with seven *ḥadīth*.[90] Most of these relate to the virtues (*faḍā'il*) of Muḥammad and his family. Al-Suyūṭī (d. 911/1505) lists additional traditions associated with her in his *Musnad Fāṭima*, but not all of these are direct narrations from Muḥammad.[91] Four of his female paternal cousins are also credited with traditions in the collections analyzed here: Fākhita bint Abī Ṭālib (28 *ḥadīth*); Dhubā'a bint al-Zubayr (5 *ḥadīth*); Durra bint Abī Lahab (1 *ḥadīth*); and Umm al-Ḥakam bint al-Zubayr (1*ḥadīth*). In addition, Umm al-Mundhir bint Qays, Muḥammad's maternal aunt, is credited with one tradition. Three of his granddaughters are said to have survived him, but none are credited with participation in the transmission of reports.[92] While they may have been too young in his lifetime to narrate directly from him, they could have

90 See her *musnad* in *al-Musnad al-Jāmi'*, 20:459–62. An obvious explanation for the low number of traditions ascribed to her is that she died soon after Muḥammad. Her biographies and hagiographies are far more developed in Shī'ī literature. See Soufi, "The Image of Fāṭima in Classical Muslim Thought" for a detailed examination of her legacy and the hagiography surrounding her. Fāṭima's biographies are available in the following sources: Ibn Sa'd, *al-Ṭabaqāt*, 8:11–20; al-Mizzī, *Tahdhīb*, 35:247–54; Ibn Ḥajar, *al-Iṣāba*, 13:71–77; and Kaḥḥāla, *A'lām al-Nisā'*, 4:108–32. Also see Hossein Modarressi, *Tradition and Survival* (Oxford: Oneworld, 2003), 17–22, for a list of compilations of traditions on the authority of Fāṭima as well as those about her life and virtues.

91 al-Suyūṭī, *Musnad Fāṭima al-Zahrā'* (Beirut: Mu'assassat al-Kutub al-Thaqāfiyya, 1993). In addition to Fāṭima, Muḥammad's female relatives include three granddaughters, five paternal aunts, one maternal aunt, and eighteen female cousins. Because biographers do not always provide death dates for his female relations, it is difficult to ascertain how many of them are believed to have survived Muḥammad. The eighth volume of Ibn Sa'd's *al-Ṭabaqāt* contains separate sections devoted to his female kin (Ibn Sa'd, *al-Ṭabaqāt*, 8:11–35).

92 They are Umāma bint Abī al-'Āṣ, Zaynab bint 'Alī, and Umm Kulthūm bint 'Alī. For their biographies, see Ibn Sa'd, *al-Ṭabaqāt*, 8:168–69, 8:341, and 8:339–41, respectively.

participated in transmitting through his wives. However, no such endeavors are recorded in the Sunnī collections analyzed here.

Another striking absence in the selected *ḥadīth* compilations is that of Muḥammad's paternal aunt, Ṣafiyya bint ʿAbd al-Muṭṭalib, who died during the caliphate of ʿUmar (r. 13–23/634–44).[93] She is celebrated in the sources for her valor during the Battle of Uḥud. There, brandishing a spear, she ridiculed the deserters and did not shudder at the sight of her brother Ḥamza dying on the battlefield (Ḥamza is reported to have had his liver torn out and eaten by Hind bint Umayya after his death on the battlefield). She is also commended for killing a prowler near the fortress sheltering the women and children.[94] In biographical accounts, her bravery is juxtaposed with the cowardice of Ḥassān b. Thābit, who had been left to protect the women and children but who refused to attack the intruder. Ṣafiyya is said to have lived for approximately a decade after Muḥammad's death, providing ample opportunity for *ḥadīth* enthusiasts to collect and record her memories. Ibn Saʿd and Ibn Ḥajar both assert that she narrated traditions. None of these, however, appear in any of the collections included in this study.[95]

The most prolific female narrator of Muḥammad's agnatic clan is Fākhita bint Abī Ṭālib, the sister of ʿAlī b. Abī Ṭālib.[96] She is better known by her *kunya*, Umm Hāniʾ. Credited with twenty-eight traditions on thirteen different matters, Umm Hāniʾ is the preferred female source of the Prophet's clan.[97] Her biographers describe her first and foremost as a woman whom Muḥammad wanted to marry but who was denied to him, first by her father, who wanted to marry her to a suitor of her own

93 Ibn Saʿd, *al-Ṭabaqāt*, 8:27–28; Abū Nuʿaym al-Iṣbahānī, *Maʿrifat al-Ṣaḥāba*, 6:3377–78; ʿIzz al-Dīn ʿAlī b. Muḥammad b. al-Athīr (d. 630/1233), *Usd al-Ghāba fī Maʿrifat al-Ṣaḥāba* (Tehran: al-Maktaba al-Islāmiyya, 1958), 5:492–93; Ibn ʿAbd al-Barr, *al-Istīʿāb*, 4:1873; Ibn Ḥajar, *Tahdhīb*, 12:19–20. Ibn Saʿd, Abū Nuʿaym, and Ibn Ḥajar do not assign a specific death date to her within this time period. Ibn al-Athīr and Ibn ʿAbd al-Barr, however, write that she died in 20 AH at the age of seventy or seventy-three, respectively.

94 This incident occurred when Muḥammad left Medina for a battle. It is disputed whether this was during the Battle of Uḥud (as Ibn Saʿd writes) or during the Battle of the Khandaq (as Ibn al-Athīr maintains).

95 Ibn Ḥajar alludes to her transmission of reports in *al-Iṣāba*, 12:20. It may be that her words were incorporated into traditions narrated on the authority of other Companions or that they appear in collections other than the selected ones.

96 Her biography is available in the following sources: Ibn Saʿd, *al-Ṭabaqāt*, 8:32, 8:108–9; al-Mizzī, *Tahdhīb*, 35:389–90; Ibn Ḥajar, *al-Iṣāba*, 13:300–1; and Kaḥḥāla, *Aʿlām al-Nisāʾ*, 4:14–16.

97 See *al-Musnad al-Jāmiʿ*, 20:437–58.

socioeconomic status, and then by a divine command that placed her in one of the unlawful categories.[98] She was among the converts who remained in Mecca and did not see the Prophet between the time of his migration and the conquest of Mecca. The majority of her traditions relate to one or two encounters in which Muḥammad is said to have visited her in her home on the day of the conquest of Mecca.[99] The narrative of many of her traditions, therefore, situates her in a privileged position as a witness to actions of Muḥammad that no one else saw. In this way, her function as a narrator is very similar to that of Muḥammad's wives: she is privy to acts few others could have seen because they were performed in her home. This is reflected in the tradition of ʿAbd Allāh b. al-Ḥārith b. Nawfal, who relates, "I asked around and searched eagerly to find someone who could tell me that the Prophet prayed a voluntary prayer after sunrise and before noon (*ṣalāt al-ḍuḥā*).[100] I could not find a soul to do so until Umm Hāniʾ reported to me that the Prophet came [to her home] after daybreak on the day of the Conquest." The remainder of the tradition details how Muḥammad prayed the *ṣalāt al-ḍuḥā* in her home.

Umm Hāniʾ's other traditions indicate that her qualifications as a narrator arise almost exclusively from her encounter with Muḥammad in Mecca after the conquest. Her reports relating to the Prophet's advice on voluntary fasting and invocations (*dhikr*) are also set within the framework of this meeting. As the sister of ʿAlī, her pedigree may have boosted her repute as a source for religious knowledge. However, she does not appear to have served as a locus for large numbers of traditions, particularly of the pro-ʿAlid variety. Overall, the low incidence of narration by female members of the Prophet's clan and the absence of his granddaughters as transmitters indicates that kinship alone did not determine a woman's reputation or the extent of her participation as a narrator.

OTHER WOMEN PROMINENT IN THE LIFE OF THE FIRST MUSLIM COMMUNITY

In addition to Muḥammad's wives and kin, there were others who were conspicuously engaged in the life of the early Muslim community. These women were later sought out as authorities for the Prophet's conduct as

[98] Qurʾān, 33:50. This verse allowed Muḥammad to marry only those of his female cousins who had emigrated with him to Medina, and she was not among them.
[99] See, for example, Ibn Ḥanbal, *Musnad*, 6:386, #26894, and 6:385, #26886.
[100] Ibn Ḥanbal, *Musnad*, 6:386, #26894, and Ibn Māja, *Sunan*, 1:439. The *ṣalāt al-ḍuḥā* is a voluntary prayer said to have been performed after sunrise and before noon.

well as for their own experiences. The following characteristics predominate in historical descriptions of these women:

1. They claimed precedence (*sābiqa*) as early converts to Islam and were especially esteemed by Muḥammad for their service to his cause.
2. They participated in battles as fighters and as nurses tending to the dead and the wounded.
3. They pledged allegiance to the Prophet in a pact known as the "pledge of women" (*bay'at al-nisā'*).
4. They were subjects of legal decisions (*fatwā*s) issued by Muḥammad that would become the focus of later juristic debates.

Numerically, this group consists of fifty-three women. The sections that follow highlight how some of them acquired prestige in the historical sources.

EARLY CONVERTS AND THOSE RECOGNIZED FOR SERVICE TO MUḤAMMAD AND HIS HOUSEHOLD

The early converts in this group are conspicuous for the degree of their familial intimacy with Muḥammad. I examine the following three in greater detail: Asmā' bint Abī Bakr (55 *ḥadīth*), Lubāba bint al-Ḥārith (12 *ḥadīth*), and Umm Ayman, also known as Baraka (2 *ḥadīth*).

Asmā' (d. 73/692) stands out as a woman whose profile combines the benefits of kinship ties to Muḥammad's inner circle with the prestige of service to Islam. She was the sister of 'Ā'isha, the daughter of Abū Bakr, and the wife of al-Zubayr b. al-'Awwām, a close Companion of Muḥammad.[101] Moreover, her two sons, 'Abd Allāh b. al-Zubayr (d. 73/692) and 'Urwa, were illustrious in their own right.[102] An episode that took place before the *hijra* is often used to illustrate her loyalty to Muḥammad and Abū Bakr. Biographers and several of her reports state that she provisioned the Prophet and her father before their migration to Medina. She tore her sash in half in order to tie up the rations of the two

[101] Her biography is available in the following sources: Ibn Sa'd, *al-Ṭabaqāt*, 8:182–86; al-Mizzī, *Tahdhīb*, 35:123–25; Ibn Ḥajar, *al-Iṣāba*, 12:114–15; and Kaḥḥāla, *A'lām al-Nisā'*, 1:36–43.

[102] 'Abd Allāh b. al-Zubayr is best known for his bid for leadership of the *umma*. He established a counter-caliphate in Medina (ca. 64–73/684–92) in opposition to the Umayyads' caliphate in Damascus. Her second son, 'Urwa, acquired a reputation as a *ḥadīth* scholar, jurist, and advisor to the political elite.

men, thereby earning the honorific "*Dhāt al-niṭāqayn*" (she of the two belts). Her proximity to the Prophet, through 'Ā'isha, Abū Bakr, and al-Zubayr, made her a perfect focus for later seekers of traditions.

Asmā' ranks as the third most prolific female Companion-Transmitter after 'Ā'isha and Umm Salama. She narrates on several subjects and her authority is not confined to one or two encounters with Muḥammad. Her biographers present her life in colorful detail, giving us a clear impression of her personality and position in the early community. She lived to the ripe old age of a hundred, making her one of the longest-surviving female Companions.[103] Asmā''s biographies focus on four aspects of her life: her preparation of the provisions for the migration of Muḥammad and Abū Bakr to Medina; her marital relationship with al-Zubayr, who was known for his harshness toward her; her refusal to accept her pagan mother, Qutayla bint 'Abd al-'Uzzā, as a visitor until the Prophet explicitly allowed her to do so; and her vigorous defense of her son 'Abd Allāh, whose beheaded corpse was displayed on a gibbet as a warning to all rebels by al-Ḥajjāj b. Yūsuf (d. 95/714), the Umayyad governor responsible for suppressing his revolt.[104]

Lauding her conduct in these incidents, biographers portray her as a devout, ascetic, long-suffering woman. Her conjugal relationship was far from harmonious or easy; she mainly occupied herself with tending to al-Zubayr's meager parcel of land, his horse, and his camel. In one account, she tells how she used to carry heavy loads of date-stones from al-Zubayr's land to their home (a distance of approximately two miles). Muḥammad happened upon her once as she was making her way home and offered her a ride behind him. She declined out of fear of al-Zubayr's jealousy. When she reported this encounter to her husband, he relented, saying it was harder for him to hear of her labors than to have her share Muḥammad's mount.[105] In another anecdote, Muḥammad passes his hand over a swelling she has on her neck and asks God to heal and pardon her.[106] We can glean from this incident and others like it that the Prophet

[103] Abū Nu'aym al-Iṣbahānī, *Ma'rifat al-Ṣaḥāba*, 6:3253. See also Juynboll's article on the utility of very old Companions in the process of *ḥadīth* transmission: "The Role of the *Mu'ammarūn* in the Early Development of the *Isnād*," in *Studies on the Origins and Uses of Islamic Ḥadīth*, 155–75.

[104] The incident between Asmā' and her mother, and the Prophet's subsequent *fatwā*, are said to have occasioned the revelation of the Qur'ānic verses 60:8–9 (*Sūrat al-Mumtaḥana*). These express divine sanction for continuing relationships and dealing justly and kindly with non-Muslims who do not actively fight the believers.

[105] Ibn Sa'd, *al-Ṭabaqāt*, 8:183.

[106] Ibn Sa'd, *al-Ṭabaqāt*, 8:183.

regarded her with a degree of familial intimacy.[107] Al-Mizzī mentions that she grew blind with age, yet did not suffer any impairment of her mental faculties.[108] In this frail, aged condition, she confronted al-Ḥajjāj to demand that her son be lowered from the gibbet and given a proper burial. After his body was sent to Mecca, she provided the funeral bier and offered the *janāza* for him.[109] She herself died a few days after her son's death.

Asmā''s reports reveal that she was, in fact, deemed a reliable source of information on various topics. She is credited with fifty-five *ḥadīth*, the subjects of which include ritual purity (*ṭahāra*), prayer (*ṣalāt*), and charity (*zakāt*).[110] The following themes recur in more than one tradition: Muḥammad's prayer during the solar eclipse that she is said to have witnessed, his encouragement of giving generously in charity, and her own denunciation of al-Ḥajjāj's treatment of her son 'Abd Allāh.[111] The narratives accompanying the incident of the Prophet's prayer marking the solar eclipse (*ṣalāt khusūf al-shams*) are of varying lengths and stress different aspects of the incident. One brief tradition simply reports that Muḥammad ordered slaves to be emancipated at the time of the solar eclipse.[112] Several provide lengthier narratives, describing Asmā''s happening upon the congregation and joining the lengthy prayer. The emphasis in these traditions is on the unusual length of the prayer followed by a sermon in which Muḥammad cautioned his followers about the Day of Judgment.[113] Others focus on aspects of the sermon without mentioning the prayer.[114]

This cluster illustrates well how collective memory is utilized in *ḥadīth* narratives. The core of the *ṣalāt khusūf al-shams* cluster has three common

107 The Prophet would be classified as among her *maḥram* because she was 'Ā'isha's half-sister.

108 al-Mizzī, *Tahdhīb*, 35:125.

109 Kaḥḥāla, *A'lām al-Nisā'*, 4:42.

110 This is the number of traditions ascribed to her in *al-Musnad al-Jāmi'*. Al-Mizzī's *Tuḥfat al-Ashrāf* ascribes forty-two traditions to her (see *Tuḥfa*, 11:5–25). The discrepancy arises primarily from the *musnad* works included in *al-Musnad al-Jāmi'* but not in the *Tuḥfat al-Ashrāf*.

111 For the cluster of traditions concerning the prayer for the solar eclipse, see *al-Musnad al-Jāmi'*, 19:10–16, #15737–41, and for that concerning her denunciation of al-Ḥajjāj, see 19:51–54, #15780–88.

112 Ibn Ḥanbal, *Musnad*, 6:389, #26918, and al-Bukhārī, *Ṣaḥīḥ*, 1–2:471.

113 al-Bukhārī, *Ṣaḥīḥ*, 1–2:470; and Mālik, *al-Muwaṭṭa'*, 1:263.

114 al-Nasā'ī, *Sunan*, 4:103–4. The sociocultural ramifications of the solar eclipse traditions are very interesting. As a whole, the *ḥadīth* aim at situating within an Islamic framework a natural phenomenon that had various meanings in the pagan Arab culture as well as in the Zoroastrian and Byzantine traditions of the lands conquered by Muslims.

denominators: that Asmā' was there, that the prayer was long, and that Muḥammad gave a sermon after the prayer. Beyond this, the cluster undergoes permutations, each of which stresses different didactic elements.[115] The point of one tradition is to convey Muḥammad's order to emancipate slaves. Another version states that Muḥammad warned of the trials of the grave in which souls would be tormented (*fitnat 'adhāb al-qabr*). A third version appears more concerned with the fate of a woman whom Muḥammad saw in a vision of Hell during the prayer. The woman was being violently scratched by her cat, which she had neglected during her time on earth.[116] Those holding the view that the traditions are authentic could explain these differences by arguing that Asmā' narrated the traditions to different people and that she herself placed emphasis on disparate elements. Those who are more skeptical would maintain that the discrepancies are indications of their status as forgeries ascribed to Asmā' to give them greater credence. In either case, the traditions coalesce to authenticate a collective memory of Asmā''s presence at this incident.

A second point of relevance to this cluster is that the prayer for the solar eclipse is said to have occurred in a large group. It is, therefore, an instance in which a woman's testimony is accepted for an occasion that both men and women attended.[117] This is a different scenario for women's transmission from that represented by Umm Hāni' earlier where she is a solitary witness to Muḥammad's *ṣalāt al-ḍuḥā*. Asmā' bint Abī Bakr is not the only female Companion to narrate traditions regarding an occasion that both men and women witnessed. Ṣafiyya bint Shayba and Umm al-Ḥusayn al-Aḥmasiyya also relate what they witnessed of the Prophet's actions and

115 As mentioned before, some traditions rooted in this incident are shortened to maxims such as "The Prophet ordered emancipation [of slaves] on the day of the eclipse" (see *al-Musnad al-Jāmi'*, 19:10, #15737). There are even more variations on the theme if we take into account the *ḥadīth* of other Companions on this topic. This phenomenon of variations on a core theme is by no means particular to the traditions of women. Rather, it is widespread in the *ḥadīth* corpus. Contradictions that occur between the versions have generally provided fuel for those who question the authenticity of the traditions. The traditional Muslim approach has been to evaluate the traditions based on their *isnād*s, and when contradictions remain after the culling process, there has been a tendency to reconcile or explain them rather than reject one version as false.

116 This tradition is similar to the one narrated by Abū Hurayra in the section on 'Ā'isha above.

117 There are other *ṣalāt khusūf al-shams* traditions that are narrated by male authorities, indicating that Asmā''s testimony was accepted on a par with that of men. See, for example, al-Bukhārī, *Ṣaḥīḥ*, 1–2:464, #974; 1–2:465, #977; and 1–2:469, #984–85.

speech during his Farewell Pilgrimage.[118] These examples, however, are not characteristic of the majority of women's traditions, which recount personal encounters with the Prophet. That Asmā' was not alone in narrating the solar eclipse traditions reveals that female Companions did not have to claim the privilege of an exclusive encounter with Muḥammad in order to serve as an authority on that encounter.

Like the *ṣalāt khusūf al-shams* cluster, the traditions in which Asmā' denounces al-Ḥajjāj evince a core narrative with embellishments. The background to the tradition is the suppression of 'Abd Allāh b. al-Zubayr's revolt during the reign of the fifth Umayyad caliph 'Abd al-Malik b. Marwān (r. 65–86/685–705) and his subsequent killing by the governor al-Ḥajjāj. In the four traditions that Asmā' narrates on this topic, the common element is her confrontation with al-Ḥajjāj, in which she informs him that Muḥammad predicted that a liar and a tyrant would emerge from the tribe of Thaqīf. The tyrant is none other than al-Ḥajjāj. In all the versions, al-Ḥajjāj is rendered powerless to defend himself in the face of her verbal assault. Asmā' uses her close association with the Prophet to counter al-Ḥajjāj's political and worldly authority. The contradictions and mutations in this core occur in the details of her confrontation with al-Ḥajjāj. In one version, after Ibn al-Zubayr's death, al-Ḥajjāj summons Asmā' to come to him. She refuses, and ultimately he is forced to go to her to express his disgust with her son.[119] In another narrative, she goes with her servant girl (because she herself is blind) to reproach al-Ḥajjāj while he is preaching from the *minbar*. In front of the entire congregation, she brands him as the tyrant about whom Muḥammad had warned in his *ḥadīth*. As in the case of the solar eclipse traditions, one can come to divergent conclusions about the contradictions in these versions depending on one's stance in the authenticity debate. In most scenarios, however, there would be agreement that a common perception of Asmā' as an assertive, courageous woman underlies the traditions. It is this communal memory of Asmā' that allowed her to serve as an acceptable authority figure for the Prophet's traditions on a variety of subjects.

Despite Asmā''s reputation, there are limits to her authority. Asmā' rarely functions as a mediator for legal disputes, and her narration network is

[118] For Ṣafiyya bint Shayba, see *al-Musnad al-Jāmi'*, 19:232–33, #15979–80. For Umm al-Ḥusayn, see *al-Musnad al-Jāmi'*, 20:722–24, #17680–87.

[119] Muslim, *Ṣaḥīḥ*, 8:2:85–86.

primarily within her kinship and clientage circle.[120] Fāṭima bint al-Mundhir, her daughter-in-law, and 'Urwa, her son, are cited most often as the Successors who narrate her traditions. In this, she is similar to the wives of the Prophet other than 'Ā'isha and Umm Salama.

A woman whose historical profile is parallel to that of Asmā' is Lubāba bint al-Ḥārith.[121] She was the wife of 'Abbās b. 'Abd al-Muṭṭalib (d. 32/653), the Prophet's uncle; the mother of 'Abd Allāh b. 'Abbās, a preeminent scholar of the early Muslim community; and the sister of Maymūna, the Prophet's wife. She is acclaimed as the first woman to accept Islam after Khadīja.[122] Ibn Sa'd notes that she had six children, the likes of whom the world had never seen. So great was the regard for her progeny that poets lauded her as being among the *munjibāt* (women who beget nobility). Further adding to her repute was her position as the wet nurse of the Prophet's grandsons, Ḥasan and Ḥusayn. Biographers point out that after the advent of Islam, she was the only woman whom Muḥammad visited regularly. She deloused him and applied kohl to his eyes. That this level of closeness between Muḥammad and a woman to whom he was not wed may have been discomfiting for biographers is apparent from Ibn Sa'd onward. Her biographers are careful to note that she is the only non-*maḥram* woman with whom the Prophet was allowed this intimacy after the advent of Islam. In citing this privilege, the biographers seem to have forgotten their own accounts of Umm Sulaym bint Milḥān.[123] The mother of Anas b. Mālik (d. 91/709f.), an honored Companion and a prolific narrator of Prophetic traditions, Umm Sulaym is also said to have accepted him as a visitor to her home.[124]

120 In one case, Ibn 'Abbās and her son, 'Abd Allāh b. al-Zubayr, disagreed on a matter related to pilgrimage rituals, and Ibn 'Abbās suggested that they refer the matter to Asmā'. Ibn Ḥanbal, *Musnad*, 6:388.

121 Her biographies are available in the following sources: Ibn Sa'd, *al-Ṭabaqāt*, 8:202–4 (s.v. "Umm al-Faḍl"); al-Mizzī, *Tahdhīb*, 35:297–98; Ibn Ḥajar, *al-Iṣāba*, 13:265–66 (s.v. "Umm al-Faḍl"); and Kaḥḥāla, *A'lām al-Nisā'*, 4:272–73.

122 This biographical summary is derived from Ibn Sa'd, *al-Ṭabaqāt*, 8:202–4.

123 For her biography, see Ibn Sa'd, *al-Ṭabaqāt*, 8:310–18; for mention of Muḥammad's visits, see Ibn Sa'd, *al-Ṭabaqāt*, 8:312–13.

124 Similar reports of Muḥammad's visitations are recorded about Umm Ḥarām bint Milḥān, the maternal aunt of Anas b. Mālik. See, for example, her biographies in the compilations of Ibn Ḥajar (*al-Iṣāba*, 13:193) and Ibn 'Abd al-Barr (*al-Istī'āb*, 4:1931). The modern editor of Ibn 'Abd al-Barr's *al-Istī'āb* carefully notes that Umm Ḥarām was within the "permitted degrees of kinship" as she was Muḥammad's aunt through a foster relationship (see *al-Istī'āb*, 4:1931, note 1). Given that Umm Ḥarām and Umm Sulaym were sisters, there may be some confusion among the biographers as to the identities of these women and the roles they played.

Lubāba, credited with twelve *ḥadīth* on seven topics, was not an authority on a wide range of issues.[125] Her narrations, furthermore, are about isolated incidents that cannot be considered as precedents for major points of creed or ritual practice. One tradition, narrated in at least three versions, concerns Muḥammad's reaction when his grandson Ḥasan urinated on him.[126] The Prophet simply sprinkled some water on the spot and declared that this measure was sufficient to restore ritual purity in the case of a boy's urine. In the case of a girl's, however, the garment had to be washed (thoroughly). These traditions are not well attested in the canonical sources, indicating that the compilers did not set too much stock by them. Another tradition, also narrated in at least three versions, asserts that Lubāba heard the Prophet recite *Sūrat al-Mursalāt* in the last prayer that he led in congregation before his death.[127] She has only two widely cited traditions that have implications for practice. One concerns her testimony that the Prophet did not fast on the Day of 'Arafa.[128] The other reports the Prophet's *fatwā* in the case of a man who complained that his first wife fed his second wife (whom he had recently married) some of her breast milk.[129] The man was worried that this rendered his second wife unlawful for him. The Prophet judged that the transfer of such small amounts of breast milk did not put the second wife in the forbidden category. Lubāba also has a restricted narration network, and several of her traditions are passed on to her son, 'Abd Allāh b. 'Abbās.[130]

Umm Ayman, the final example in this group, was a servant in Muḥammad's household. He had inherited her as a slave from his father, and though he freed her upon his marriage to Khadīja, she remained to care for their children. Muḥammad is said to have felt great affection for her, calling her "my mother" on occasion, and included her among his

125 *al-Musnad al-Jāmi'*, 20:501–10.

126 Ibn Māja, *Sunan*, 1:174, and Abū Dāwūd, *Sunan*, 1:102.

127 The better attested of these versions occurs in Mālik, *al-Muwaṭṭa'*, 1:128; Ibn Ḥanbal, *Musnad*, 6:383, #26873; al-Bukhārī, *Ṣaḥīḥ*, 1–2:363; Muslim, *Ṣaḥīḥ*, 2:2:150; Ibn Māja, *Sunan*, 1:272; al-Tirmidhī, *Sunan*, 1:332; and al-Nasā'ī, *Sunan*, 2:168.

128 See, for example, this tradition as cited in the following collections: Mālik, *al-Muwaṭṭa'*, 1:503; Ibn Ḥanbal, *Musnad*, 6:381–82, #26861, #26864; al-Bukhārī, *Ṣaḥīḥ*, 3–4:95; Muslim, *Ṣaḥīḥ*, 4:2:3–4; and Abū Dāwūd, *Sunan*, 2:326.

129 See Ibn Ḥanbal, *Musnad*, 6:382, #26865; Muslim, *Ṣaḥīḥ*, 5:2:25–26; Ibn Māja, *Sunan*, 1:624; and al-Nasā'ī, *Sunan*, 6:100.

130 She also narrates one tradition each to Tammām b. al-'Abbās, her stepson, and to 'Umayr b. 'Abd Allāh, her client. For biographical information on Tammām, see Muḥammad b. 'Alī al-Ḥusaynī, *Kitāb al-Tadhkira* (Cairo: Maṭba'at al-Madanī, 1997), 1:202; on 'Umayr, see Ibn Ḥajar, *Tahdhīb*, 8:126.

family members.[131] Ibn Sa'd mentions her clumsy tongue and her malapropisms. For example, she would mistakenly greet others with "*salām lā 'alaykum*" [Peace *not* be upon you] until Muḥammad allowed her to make do with "*salām*." As with Lubāba, the Prophet visited her frequently. She is also known for participating in the battles of Uḥud and Khaybar (7/628), during which she provided water for the Muslim warriors and cared for the wounded. Umm Ayman's two traditions, however, give no indication of her status in the early Muslim community. One concerns the generic topic of the Prophet's exhortations to be steadfast in prayer.[132] Another describes her preparation of some food for Muḥammad.[133] In spite of her proximity to the Prophet, she was clearly not regarded as a good vehicle for conveying his *sunna*.

FEMALE PARTICIPANTS IN BATTLES

The participation of women on the battlefield as nurses or as fighters boosted the reputation of some female Companions as traditionists.[134] Umm Ayman, discussed earlier, is one such example. Biographers also laud Nusayba bint Ka'b for taking part in several raids and minor battles (*ghazawāt*) with Muḥammad.[135] Ibn Sa'd reports that she was present at the momentous occasions of Uḥud, al-Ḥudaybiyya (6/628), the expedition to Khaybar, the first completed *'umra* (7/628), and the battles of Ḥunayn (8/630) and Yamāma (11/632). At Uḥud, she courageously defended Muḥammad while others around him fled. And at Yamāma, she persevered in fighting even after losing her hand in combat.[136] Yet only one of Nusayba bint Ka'b's twenty traditions pertains to her military efforts. Instead, her *ḥadīth* mostly touch on ritual purity and the pledge of

131 Her life is the subject of a monograph by Muḥammad Riḍā 'Abd al-Amīr al-Anṣārī, *Wafā' al-Imā'* (Beirut: Majma' al-Buḥūth al-Islāmiyya, 1996).

132 Ibn Ḥanbal, *Musnad*, 6:469, #26353.

133 Ibn Māja, *Sunan*, 2:1107.

134 For a more detailed study of this topic, see Ilse Lichtenstadter, *Women in the Aiyām al-'Arab* (London: Royal Asiatic Society, 1935).

135 For her biographies, see Ibn Sa'd, *al-Ṭabaqāt*, 8:301–4; Abū Nu'aym al-Iṣbahānī, *Ma'rifat al-Ṣaḥāba*, 6:3455–56; and Ibn Ḥajar, *al-Iṣāba*, 13:257–58. Her life is also the subject of a monograph by Amīna 'Umar al-Kharrāṭ, *Umm 'Imāra* (Damascus: Dār al-Qalam, 1998).

136 Ibn Sa'd, *al-Ṭabaqāt*, 8:301–4. The biographical accounts of Nusayba's participation in battles are unusually detailed and provide rich source material for research on women's participation in the battlefield in early Islam. In particular, the reports of her brave defense of Muḥammad at Uḥud clearly captured the imagination of her biographers, who dwell on this episode.

women, discussed below. Nevertheless, biographers focus on her military achievements perhaps as a means to enhance her reputation as a *ḥadīth* transmitter.

WOMEN'S PLEDGE OF ALLEGIANCE (BAY'AT AL-NISĀ')

A recurrent theme in the biographies of female Companions is the formal pledge of allegiance to the Prophet. The following Qur'ānic verse outlines the prerequisites for women desiring to convert to Islam:

> O Prophet! If believing women come unto you, taking pledge of allegiance unto you that they will ascribe nothing as partner unto God, and will neither steal nor commit adultery nor kill their children, nor produce any lie that they have devised by their own effort [lit. between their hands and feet], nor disobey you in what is right, then accept their allegiance and ask God to forgive them. Lo! God is Forgiving, Merciful.[137]

Ibn Sa'd begins his section on the biographies of women with an excursus on the topic of their pledge of allegiance to the Prophet. While the accounts indicate that on at least one occasion, the Prophet entered into a formal covenant with women after the *hijra*, there is no consensus as to who may have been present for the pact(s). It may also have been that such pacts were a routine in which Muḥammad outlined the demands of the new religion to women and offered them a chance to accept it. The specific circumstances of these pledges aside, later biographers viewed reports of pledging as a mark of distinction.[138] Many of the women included in this study are said to have offered allegiance to the Prophet. For some women, it is their only claim to fame. Salmā bint Qays, for example, is known for only one tradition, in which she seeks clarification from Muḥammad on a stipulation of the pledge: that women should not

[137] Qur'ān, 60:12. It is not clear whether the Qur'ānic injunction regarding the pledge of allegiance was intended for every woman who wished to accept Islam or limited only to those who accepted Islam against the wishes of their families and fled to Medina after the Pact of al-Ḥudaybiyya (6 AH). See also Asma Afsaruddin, "Reconstituting Women's Lives: Gender and the Poetics of Narrative in Medieval Biographical Collections," *Muslim World* 92, no. 3/4 (2002): 461–80, for Afsaruddin's interpretation of the evolving treatments of the women's pledge of allegiance in classical Muslim literature.

[138] It is not clear what, if any, practical differences in terms of social status existed between women who did not take part in a formal pledge and those who did.

mislead their husbands.[139] Similarly, Umayma bint Ruqayqa has two traditions attributed to her. The better-attested one repeats the Qur'ānic framework for women's pledges: that women are asked to disavow polytheism, stealing, fornication, infanticide (*lā naqtulu awlādanā*), falsely attributing paternity in cases of adultery, and disobedience (to the Prophet).[140]

SEEKERS AND SUBJECTS OF *FATWĀS*

A final category of women in this group comprises seekers or subjects of *fatwā*s from the Prophet that would later have legal significance in communal debates. In biographical sources, these women are sometimes recognized or deemed prominent for reasons other than the legal rulings associated with them. However, in the *ḥadīth* compilations, their utility rests primarily on a single incident in their lives that comes under the scrutiny of later generations of Muslims. One example is Barīra, a slave freed by 'Ā'isha bint Abī Bakr, who was a notably influential, strong-willed woman. Ibn Sa'd cites Ibn 'Abbās's report:

> When Barīra was given the choice of staying with her husband, he was a slave of the Banū Mughīra. He was called Mughīth Aswad. I happened upon him in the streets of Medina trailing her and trying to please her; the tears flowed upon his beard, and she was saying, "I have no need of you."[141]

Choosing independence, she resisted all of Mughīth's entreaties. In addition to this account of her strong personality, a report that the Umayyad leader 'Abd al-Malik b. Marwān sought her company highlights her status as a respected Companion.[142]

Barīra narrates only one tradition. Yet its influence in legal discourse is considerable.[143] Her report recounts three of Muḥammad's *fatwā*s: that

[139] The Prophet responds that this means that women should not give away their husbands' property without their permission. For her biography, see Ibn 'Abd al-Barr, *al-Istī'āb*, 4:1861–62, and for her *ḥadīth*, see Ibn Ḥanbal, *Musnad*, 6:471, #27364.

[140] See Mālik, *al-Muwaṭṭa'*, 2:578–79. For other versions of this report, see Ibn Ḥanbal, *Musnad*, 6:401; Ibn Māja, *Sunan*, 2:959; al-Nasā'ī, *Sunan*, 7:148–49; and al-Tirmidhī, *Sunan*, 3:219–20. The second tradition relates that the Prophet had a vessel that he kept under his bed to relieve himself at night (see Abū Dāwūd, *Sunan*, 1:7, and al-Nasā'ī, *Sunan*, 1:31).

[141] Ibn Sa'd, *al-Ṭabaqāt*, 8:190.

[142] As mentioned earlier, 'Abd al-Malik b. Marwān was the fifth Umayyad caliph. It is not clear whether he sought Barīra's advice during his caliphate or before it. For the report about her interaction with 'Abd al-Malik, see Ibn Ḥajar, *al-Iṣāba*, 12:156–57.

[143] al-Nasā'ī, *Sunan al-Kubrā* (Beirut: Mu'assasat al-Risāla, 2001), 5:49–50.

the loyalty of a freed slave belongs to the one who freed him/her; that once a married female slave has been freed, she has the liberty to terminate her marriage;[144] and that charity (*ṣadaqa*) that she received and then passed on to a member of Muḥammad's household was deemed a gift (and not charity) from her. Ibn Ḥajar asserts that scholars have enumerated more than 300 rulings based on her tradition, indicating its importance for legal discussions.[145] However, *ḥadīth* compilers distinguish between the importance of Barīra's historical role and her narrative authority. The version in which she narrates her story directly on the authority of Muḥammad is only attested in the *Sunan al-Kubrā* of al-Nasā'ī. On the other hand, al-Bukhārī, Muslim, Abū Dāwūd, and Ibn Māja favor *isnād*s in which 'Ā'isha narrates the story of Barīra. Their selection further emphasizes the narrative authority of 'Ā'isha over and above that of other women.[146]

Fāṭima bint Qays al-Fihriyya is also best known for a *fatwā* the Prophet issued in her case.[147] While two of Fāṭima's fourteen traditions relate to *zakāt* and *fitna*, twelve of them describe her divorce from Abū 'Amr b. Ḥafṣ b. al-Mughīra, who irrevocably divorced her while he was away on a military campaign.[148] In Fāṭima's account, she complains to Muḥammad that Abū 'Amr's family in Medina has refused to provide maintenance or lodging for her. Muḥammad, however, confirms that she is not entitled to such support. He then allows her to move to the home of the blind man, Ibn Umm Maktūm, to observe her waiting period. This ruling established a precedent for denying economic support to an irrevocably divorced woman.

After Muḥammad's death, Fāṭima asserted her experience as valid precedent in spite of vociferous opposition.[149] A number of prominent

[144] Jurists disagreed about whether or not Barīra's husband had been a slave at the time of her manumission; this would also have had implications in the derivation of laws based on her precedent. Ibn Sa'd, *al-Ṭabaqāt*, 8:187–89.

[145] Ibn Ḥajar, *al-Iṣāba*, 12:157.

[146] See al-Bukhārī, *Ṣaḥīḥ*, 3–4:300; Muslim, *Ṣaḥīḥ*, 5:2:114; Abū Dāwūd, *Sunan*, 2:270; Ibn Māja, *Sunan*, 1:670. Al-Nasā'ī, in *Sunan*, 5:107–8, also includes the *isnād* narrated on the authority of 'Ā'isha.

[147] Biographies of Fāṭima bint Qays may be found in Ibn Sa'd, *al-Ṭabaqāt*, 8:200–2, and in Ibn Ḥajar, *Tahdhīb*, 12:393–94. For her traditions, see *al-Musnad al-Jāmi'*, 20:466–88. The compilers of *al-Musnad al-Jāmi'* have combined various versions of Fāṭima's *ḥadīth* into twelve different ones. Al-Mizzī cites sixteen different versions of the tradition (see al-Mizzī, *Tuḥfa*, 12:19–30).

[148] *al-Musnad al-Jāmi'*, 20:466–87, #17397–408. For a biography of Abū 'Amr, see Ibn Ḥajar, *Tahdhīb*, 12:159–60.

[149] This issue has considerable legal significance in the area of marriage and divorce; as such, it is the subject of extensive Muslim legal discussion. These discussions in turn have provoked the interest of Western scholars. See, for example, Joseph Schacht, *Origins*, 225–26; G. R. Hawting, "The Role of the Qur'ān and *Ḥadīth* in the Legal Controversy

Companions differed over whether divorced women should observe their waiting periods in their husbands' homes or whether they should move back to their family residences. 'Umar and 'Ā'isha, for example, held that triply divorced women were entitled to lodging and maintenance during their waiting periods.[150] Further, a Qur'ānic verse forbade men from evicting women who were observing these periods.[151] Thus, the weight of divine command as well as the opinion of respected authorities dictated that Fāṭima's case could not be considered a general ruling.

Nonetheless, Fāṭima staunchly asserted that her precedent was broadly applicable. According to one tradition, she took the initiative of transferring her niece who had been irrevocably divorced to her own home.[152] Marwān b. al-Ḥakam, the governor of Medina at the time, sent a messenger to Fāṭima to ask her why she had not allowed her niece to observe her waiting period in her husband's home. Fāṭima sent the messenger back with her own argument citing other Qur'ānic verses in favor of her position. She is credited with saying, "I will debate you on the basis of the Book of God," before laying out her case and augmenting it by citing Muḥammad's *fatwā* in her own case.[153] Marwān, however, was not persuaded by her logic. She had met with similar failure in asserting her case before 'Umar.[154] Irrespective of the disapproval of Companions, Fāṭima is portrayed as a woman who was cognizant of the importance of her case and who presented her precedent in the hopes of influencing the outcome of legal debates. The portraits of women such as Fāṭima and

about the Rights of a Divorced Woman during her 'Waiting Period' (*'Idda*)," *Bulletin of the School of Oriental and African Studies* 52 (1989): 430–45; and Scott Lucas, "Divorce, *Ḥadīth*-Scholar Style: From al-Dārimī to al-Tirmidhī," *Journal of Islamic Studies* 19, no. 3 (2008): 333–37.

150 The term "triply divorced" is a technical one referring to cases wherein the intent to divorce has been articulated thrice by the husband. According to majority juristic opinion, this triple pronouncement of divorce renders it irrevocable and the spouses cannot remarry unless and until the wife marries someone else and that marriage is dissolved. For an analysis of this practice in the Mamlūk period, see Yossef Rapoport, *Marriage, Money and Divorce in Medieval Islamic Society* (Cambridge: Cambridge University Press, 2005), 69–110.

151 Qur'ān, 65:6.

152 Ibn Ḥanbal, *Musnad*, 6:463, #27329. A version with similar import is found in Ibn Ḥanbal, *Musnad*, 6:463, #27327, and Muslim, *Ṣaḥīḥ*, 5:2:83.

153 Fāṭima is said to have cited Qur'ān 65:1 and argued that the wording of this verse limits the obligation of providing maintenance and lodging only to cases of divorce that are not final, in which it is possible that something new (i.e., reconciliation) will come about.

154 I have analyzed the significance of the early rejection of Fāṭima's *ḥadīth* in "Gender and Legal Authority: An Examination of Early Juristic Opposition to Women's *Ḥadīth* Transmission," *Islamic Law and Society* 16, no. 2 (2009):115–50.

Barīra, described earlier, confirm a collective memory that some women of the first generation participated in shaping legal discussions. This scenario becomes rarer in the second/eighth and third/ninth centuries, during which women were marginalized in both *ḥadīth* and legal circles – a development that will be taken up in Chapter 2.

LESS KNOWN WOMEN

This final category comprises forty-four Companion-Traditionists whose lives are shrouded in obscurity. Most of the women in this group narrate a single *ḥadīth* each. Biographers know no more about these women than can be learned from the tradition(s) with which they are associated. In a few instances the name of a spouse or a few circumstantial details regarding the *ḥadīth* are added. In some cases, such as those of al-Jahdama and Sawda, there is disagreement as to whether the woman is a Companion or a Successor.[155] The subject matter covered by these women's traditions is diverse and includes ritual purity, the Ḥajj, and eschatology. In most cases these women are credited with brief pronouncements concerning what they witnessed of the Prophet's behavior. For example, al-Jahdama, as mentioned earlier, simply reports that she saw the Prophet emerging from his home with traces of *henna* in his hair.[156] In some instances, women of this group are the subjects of Muḥammad's *fatwā*s. However, such cases are much rarer than in the previous categories.[157] The inclusion of these women's traditions signals the relevance of these *ḥadīth* for later legal discourses and indicates that women who are remembered as transmitters did not necessarily have a high profile in the life of the early community.

155 For the biography of al-Jahdama, see Ibn Ḥajar, *al-Iṣāba*, 12:182; and for that of Sawda, see Ibn Ḥajar, *al-Iṣāba*, 12:237–38.

156 Although al-Jahdama's identity is obscure, her tradition probably played some part in the legal discussion regarding the use of dyes. See Ibn Ḥajar, *al-Iṣāba*, 12:182. For further reading on the authenticity of traditions surrounding the use of *henna* and dyes, see G. H. A. Juynboll, "Dyeing the Hair and Beard in Early Islam: A Ḥadīth-Analytical Study," *Arabica* 33 (1986): 49–75.

157 This is a logical outcome of the complementary tasks of the *ḥadīth* compilers and the authors of the *rijāl* works (i.e., works that scrutinize the biographies and reports circulated about male and female transmitters to ascertain their reliability). The latter often served to explicate the background for individual *ḥadīth*, and this involved providing fuller information on the lives of the transmitters. If the Prophet had issued a *fatwā* that came to have legal significance, it would be more important to contextualize the injunction by offering further details on the woman's life.

CONCLUSION

Through the foregoing analysis, we obtain a picture of the transmission of religious knowledge of a range of women: Muḥammad's wives, his female kin, and other women who participated in the life of the early Muslim community in various ways. There is also a significant minority (a little over 25 percent of the women included in this study) who do not appear to have acquired any such prominence. This arena was thus a field open to women from various backgrounds. To some extent, it was the utility of the traditions for later legal discourses, rather than the prominence of the transmitters, that determined the inclusion of traditions in the *ḥadīth* compilations.

We also arrive at a clearer understanding of how Muḥammad's wives navigated the transmission of reports in spite of their divinely mandated seclusion. Most of them are not credited with numerous reports. Their networks are largely comprised of women and men belonging to their *maḥram* or clientage circles. The two exceptions are ʿĀ'isha and Umm Salama. ʿĀ'isha, the most prolific and prominent female Companion, was highly involved in the life of the community. An unrivaled source of information about Muḥammad's preferences and practices, she is depicted as a legal authority as well as a transmitter of reports. Umm Salama's profile is similar to that of ʿĀ'isha, except that she is more reserved in her role as a traditionist. The picture we gain of Muḥammad's wives, aside from ʿĀ'isha and Umm Salama, conforms to the ideal image of them as secluded from the society at large. There is some ambivalence as to how stringently ʿĀ'isha and, to a lesser extent, Umm Salama may have observed the *ḥijāb* strictures. The debate on *riḍāʿ al-kabīr* portrays Umm Salama as more concerned than ʿĀ'isha with observing seclusion. Reports that various Companions who were not their *maḥram* sought their advice in legal disputes do not provide clear indications as to whether *ḥijāb* rulings were strictly observed by ʿĀ'isha and Umm Salama. Further, reports ascribed to ʿĀ'isha, such as those in which she has direct contact with a blind man (Ḥassān b. Thābit) and a male slave belonging to someone else, reveal ambiguity in the sources about the extent of ʿĀ'isha's participation without *ḥijāb*. Finally, her position that *riḍāʿ al-kabīr* was a valid means for establishing *maḥram* relations suggests that she attempted to utilize one of Muḥammad's precedents to facilitate her function as a transmitter of religious knowledge, and beyond that, to be more engaged in the life of the *umma*.

Female Companions were credited with sayings on a large variety of subjects. While Muḥammad's wives were a popular locus for reports concerning ritual purity, marriage, or divorce, they did not narrate exclusively on these topics. Rather, a woman's traditions were often set in the context of her contact with Muḥammad, which in turn could give rise to reports on a host of topics.

Finally, there is no apparent concern among biographers for portraying these women as literate, educated, or scholarly. Because we know very little about literacy in the early Islamic period or about the extent of other religious knowledge that these women had, it is difficult to assess how learned they may have been. It is fair to say that there is very little evidence that literacy or legal acumen was a prerequisite for transmission of reports on the part of these female Companions.[158] 'Ā'isha's case appears exceptional as she was learned in poetry, medicine, mathematics, and genealogy. In general, the Companion-Traditionists were commemorated because they were contemporaries of Muḥammad, and as such their experiences were valid precedents subject to the scrutiny of later generations. This picture changes with later generations of female *ḥadīth* transmitters, whose careers and reputations were in fact based on their mental capacities, and in particular their retentive abilities. A corollary of the observation that the female Companion-Narrators were not always scholars is the fact that they do not appear to have been decisive authorities for legal disputes. In general, female Companions are not portrayed as *faqīha*s (those endowed with the requisite knowledge and acumen for legal discourse). This depiction confirms their limited roles as *rāwiya*s, that is, as narrators of reports that they passed on to future generations with no control over their use in legal discourse.

We may readily imagine that the female Companions served as role models for women of subsequent generations who wished to emulate their predecessors. However, an overview of the participation of women from the second/eighth to the fourth/tenth century reveals that this was not the case. The next chapter discusses the female Successors and the rapid demise of women as transmitters of religious knowledge.

[158] This observation pertains to the world of male traditionists as well because the transmission of reports, unlike law, was more open to the participation of lay classes of society who may have had little formal training in the religious sciences.

CHAPTER 2

The Successors

> Abū Hishām [Mughīra b. Miqsam (d. ca. 136/753)] reported, "They [i.e., scholars] used to dislike narration on the authority of women except the wives of Muḥammad."[1]
>
> Abū Bakr al-Hudhalī (d. 159/775f.) reported that al-Zuhrī asked, "O Hudhalī, do you like *ḥadīth*?" He said, "Yes," and continued, "the manliest of men enjoy it, and the effeminate among them dislike it."[2]

The second/eighth century witnessed a contraction in the heretofore unregulated arena of *ḥadīth* transmission. The first report in the chapter epigraph shows that some scholars came to favor Muḥammad's wives to the exclusion of other women as reliable transmitters. The mere fact of having seen the Prophet no longer conferred sufficient authority on all female Companions to transmit his *ḥadīth*. And the conversation between al-Zuhrī and al-Hudhalī in the second report expresses the gender associations that came to characterize this arena. Manly men mastered its challenges while effeminate ones shrank from its hardships.

Before women's widespread exclusion from this domain, however, a few female Successors (the generation immediately after the Companions)

1 Abū al-Qāsim 'Abd Allāh b. Aḥmad b. Maḥmūd al-Ka'bī al-Balkhī (d. 319/931), *Qabūl al-Akhbār wa-Ma'rifat al-Rijāl* (Beirut: Dār al-Kutub al-'Ilmiyya, 2000), 1:51. For a biography of Mughīra, see Ibn Ḥajar, *Tahdhīb*, 10:242–43.

2 al-Khaṭīb al-Baghdādī, *Sharaf Aṣḥāb al-Ḥadīth* (Ankara: Dār Iḥyā' al-Sunna al-Nabawiyya, 1971), 70. In this section, al-Khaṭīb al-Baghdādī cites a similar report according to which al-Zuhrī said, "Only the manliest men engage in seeking out *ḥadīth* (*ṭalab al-ḥadīth*) and the effeminate ones abstain in this regard" (see *Sharaf Aṣḥāb al-Ḥadīth*, 71). Al-Hudhalī is considered an unreliable transmitter. For his biography, see Khalīl b. Aybak al-Ṣafadī (d. 764/1363), *al-Wāfī bi'l-Wafayāt* (Beirut: Dār Iḥyā' al-Turāth al-'Arabī, 2000), 15:202.

left their mark as transmitters of reports. This chapter concerns itself with women's participation from the late first/seventh century until the early fourth/tenth century, a period culminating in the compilation of the major Sunnī *ḥadīth* collections. A survey of these centuries exposes the continuities and ruptures in relation to the era of the Companions. These transformations were largely a result of the growing role of Prophetic sayings in formulating Islamic law and theology. Not all Muslims agreed that these reports reliably preserved Muḥammad's teachings. Nor was there any unanimity about how to determine their authenticity. The resultant debates about the legal value of the reports gave rise, in turn, to criteria that were disproportionately onerous for women.

Many women of the Successor generation continued to learn reports about Muḥammad under ad hoc circumstances even in an increasingly regulatory environment. Through encounters with Companions, they actively sought instruction in how to practice their new religion. Karīma bint Hammām, for example, reports that she heard a woman asking 'Ā'isha bint Abī Bakr whether women were permitted to use *henna*. 'Ā'isha responded that it was not forbidden, but that she herself had refrained from it because the Prophet disliked its odor.[3] This is the only *ḥadīth* that Karīma narrates in the selected Sunnī compilations, and chroniclers and *ḥadīth* scholars do not deem her an accomplished transmitter.[4] A lengthier report describes how some other women acquired religious knowledge from the Companions. Ya'lā b. Ḥakīm (death date unknown) reported from Ṣuhayra bint Jayfar (of the Successor generation):

> We performed Ḥajj then went on to Medina. We went to visit Ṣafiyya bint Ḥuyayy and met a group of Kūfan women in her company. They said, "If you [i.e., the newcomers] want, you can ask [the questions] and we'll listen, or if you prefer, we'll ask and you can listen." We said, "You go ahead and ask." So they asked her about matters related to women and their husbands and about menstruation. Then they asked her about a beverage made of dates in clay vessels (*nabīdh al-jarr*).[5]

Like Sālim's narrative on learning ablution from 'Ā'isha, cited in Chapter 1, Ṣuhayra's account helps recreate the early environment for

[3] Abū Dāwūd, *Sunan*, 4:76, and al-Nasā'ī, *Sunan*, 8:142.
[4] Ibn Ḥajar, *Tahdhīb*, 12:398.
[5] Ibn Ḥanbal, *Musnad*, 6:380, #26857. Ibn Ḥanbal includes another, briefer version of this report transmitted via a slightly different *isnād* (see Ibn Ḥanbal, *Musnad*, 6:380, #26854). For the biography of Ya'lā b. Ḥakīm, see Ibn Ḥajar, *Tahdhīb*, 11:349. For that of Ṣuhayra, see al-Ḥusaynī, *Tadhkira*, 4:2243, #9926. Nadwi notes other similar encounters that took place when women undertook the Ḥajj; see *al-Muhaddithat*, 73–74.

the transmission of religious knowledge.[6] We can picture the fellow pilgrims in Medina stopping by the quarters of Ṣafiyya, one of Muḥammad's wives, to inquire about a host of practical feminine concerns. Ṣuhayra and her band are not alone. A group of Kūfan women have had the same idea. They listen to each other's questions and together benefit from Ṣafiyya's answers. The women, aside from Ṣuhayra and Ṣafiyya, are anonymous.[7]

Ṣuhayra's story is that of numerous women of the Successor generation, whether or not their pursuit of knowledge is documented in the *ḥadīth* collections. Most of them were not *ḥadīth* scholars gathering all the traditions known to the Companions they encountered. Nor did they demonstrate legal discernment or understanding of Arabic morphology and grammar – skills that came to distinguish more accomplished transmitters.[8] Rather, daily exigencies dictated their *ḥadīth* learning as they struggled to understand what was expected of them as Muslim women. Not all of their inquiries were about issues specific to women, such as menstruation, childbirth, or domestic concerns. As is clear from the distribution of the subjects of nearly 525 traditions that feature women of the Successor generation in the *isnād*s, women acquired knowledge on a range of issues, including prayer, fasting, pilgrimage, charity, and eschatology.[9]

Alongside this informal, unregulated transmission by women whose lives are not commemorated in any detail by historians, there are a handful of more accomplished women whose religious knowledge and exemplary

6 It is worth pointing out here that narrative of the type we encounter in Ṣuhayra's tradition is even rarer than the detailed accounts related by the Companions. As discussed earlier, Companions shaped the narrative structures of the reports and the task of subsequent generations was to memorize and faithfully reproduce these texts. Information about the circumstances under which Successors and subsequent generations of narrators heard the reports is usually not provided.

7 We can only speculate about whether other aspects of this encounter are relayed in reports other than this one wherein the encounter is explicitly described. In the selected compilations, Ṣafiyya is recorded as narrating two additional traditions to women. One of them is to a woman named Umm Ḥabība bint Dhu'ayb (see Abū Dāwūd, *Sunan*, 3:229). The second is to Shumaysa (alternatively known as Sumayya) about how she (i.e., Ṣafiyya), as a Jewish woman, was received among the wives of Muḥammad (see Ibn Ḥanbal, *Musnad*, 6:380, #26858). The texts of the traditions do not, however, specify whether these exchanges transpired in the context of the meeting mentioned earlier.

8 Ṣuhayra herself is described as "an unknown woman" (*imra'a majhūla*) in her biographical entry by al-Ḥusaynī in his *Tadhkira*. There is confusion over her name, and the absence of information about her life and her transmission network clearly indicates that she was not known for systematically collecting and teaching *ḥadīth*.

9 Of the nearly 525 *ḥadīth* transmitted by women of the Successor generation for which I recorded the primary subject matter, approximately 50 traditions are on topics related to ritual purity, 6 concern divorce, and only 3 are related to marriage.

piety attracted students and earned the admiration of chroniclers. In the decades after the Companions, a mere eight women are commemorated in the classical Sunnī collections for narrating more than just one or two *ḥadīth* and for doing so within a relatively broad transmission network. With the exception of Ṣafiyya bint Shayba (d. end of the 90s), these women fall into two categories: (1) those whose knowledge of *ḥadīth* is predominantly linked to a particular female Companion, and (2) those who gained renown as ascetics. The four women in the former category, Zaynab bint Abī Salama al-Makhzūmiyya (d. ca. 73/692), ʿAmra bint ʿAbd al-Raḥmān (d. 98/716), ʿĀʾisha bint Ṭalḥa (d. ca. 101/719), and Fāṭima bint al-Mundhir (death date unknown), followed closely in the footsteps of the female Companions in the nature of their transmission activity. Three others, Umm al-Dardāʾ al-Ṣughrā (d. ca. 81/700), Muʿādha bint ʿAbd Allāh (d. 83/702), and Ḥafṣa bint Sīrīn (d. after 100/718), represented new models of female learning and piety as teachers and leaders in the emergent ascetic movement.

Within this cohort, each woman's profile naturally differs because of a host of variables such as her network of teachers and students, her geographic location, and not least, her personality (a variable that is more difficult to ascertain). Here I discuss four of these women.[10] By highlighting features common to all of them as well as a few traits unique to some, I document how a few female Successors acquired exemplary reputations in this arena. Their stories, evincing some of the gender-based differentiation that came to characterize *ḥadīth* transmission, also set the stage for the stark decline and near disappearance of women from the historical records in the post-Companion generations up to the fourth/tenth century.

SUCCESSORS WITH KINSHIP-DERIVED PROMINENCE

The legal discernment and methodical collection of Prophetic reports evinced by ʿAmra bint ʿAbd al-Raḥmān distinguishes her among the women whose knowledge was kinship-based.[11] Credited with sixty-six reports on a broad range of topics, ʿAmra benefited from her special access to ʿĀʾisha bint

[10] My dissertation details the contributions of each of these eight women and their learning networks. See "Shifting Fortunes," 122–48.

[11] Her biography appears in the following sources: Ibn Saʿd, *al-Ṭabaqāt*, 8:353; Ibn Ḥibbān, *Kitāb al-Thiqāt* (Beirut: Dār al-Kutub al-ʿIlmiyya, 1998), 2:428; al-Mizzī, *Tahdhīb*, 35:241–43; al-Dhahabī, *Siyar Aʿlām al-Nubalāʾ* (Beirut: Muʾassasat al-Risāla, 1981), 4:507–8; and Kaḥḥāla, *Aʿlām al-Nisāʾ*, 3:356–57.

Abī Bakr, her paternal aunt in whose custody she was raised. Nearly all of 'Amra's *isnād*s in the compilations examined here are on 'Ā'isha's authority.[12] Additionally, al-Mizzī's notice for her lists Rāfi' b. Khudayj, 'Ubayd b. Rāfi' al-Zuraqī, and Marwān b. al-Ḥakam as non-kin men who transmitted to her, but these *isnād*s are not recorded in the collections examined for this study. In a pattern typical of most of the prolific female Successors, 'Amra's male kin, save for a few prominent exceptions such as al-Zuhrī and Yaḥyā b. Sa'īd al-Anṣārī (d. 143/760), are mentioned in her *isnād*s as authorities to whom she transmits.[13] Ibn Sa'd breaks with his customary reticence about women's intellectual accomplishments and refers to her as a learned woman (*'ālima*). He also cites 'Umar b. 'Abd al-Azīz's (d. 101/720) instructions to Abū Bakr b. Muḥammad b. Ḥazm (d. 120/738) to preserve the *ḥadīth* of the Prophet, the practices of previous generations (*sunna māḍiya*), and the *ḥadīth* of 'Amra, thereby confirming the centrality of her storehouse of knowledge.[14]

'Ā'isha's expertise on a wide range of Muḥammad's precedents was transferred to 'Amra to the extent that she was consulted on legal matters. For example, Abū Bakr b. Muḥammad b. Ḥazm, the governor of Medina, wrote to 'Amra seeking counsel on the punishment of a thief.[15] She replied on the basis of 'Ā'isha's report that the hand of a thief is to be cut off when the amount stolen exceeds one quarter of a *dīnār*. 'Amra is also known for relaying 'Ā'isha's view that the prevailing corruption after Muḥammad's death was sufficient cause to overturn his general ruling that women should not be prevented from going to mosques.[16] Ironically, 'Ā'isha's

12 Sixty-three of her traditions are on 'Ā'isha's authority. The remaining three are from Ḥamna bint Jaḥsh, the sister of Zaynab bint Jaḥsh; her own sister, Umm Hishām bint Ḥāritha; and from Ḥabība bint Sahl.

13 Male kin who transmit her traditions include her son Muḥammad b. 'Abd al-Raḥmān (death date unknown; for his biography, see Ibn Ḥajar, *Tahdhīb*, 9:255); her nephew 'Abd Allāh b. Abī Bakr b. 'Amr b. Ḥazm (d. ca.130/747; for his biography, see Ibn Ḥajar, *Tahdhīb*, 5:147); another nephew, Muḥammad b. 'Abd al-Raḥmān b. Sa'd b. Zurāra (d. ca. 124/741f.; for his biography, see Ibn Ḥajar, *Tahdhīb*, 9:256–57); and her grandson Ḥāritha b. Abī al-Rijāl (d. 148/765f.; for his biography, see Ibn Ḥajar, *Tahdhīb*, 2:153).

14 Ibn Sa'd, *al-Ṭabaqāt*, 8:353. It is said that 'Umar's orders arose from his concern about the loss of religious knowledge due to the passing away of earlier generations of scholars. The meaning of the term *sunna* in early historical and legal sources is debated. Here I have translated it as the practices of previous generations to distinguish it from the *ḥadīth* of the Prophet.

15 *al-Musnad al-Jāmi'*, 20:49, #16807. Muḥammad b. Abī Bakr b. Ḥazm was 'Amra's nephew.

16 There are two slightly differing versions of 'Ā'isha's ruling as transmitted by 'Amra. See, for example, al-Bukhārī, *Ṣaḥīḥ*, 1–2:407 and Abū Dāwūd, *Sunan*, 1:155–56 for one version, and for the second version, see Muslim, *Ṣaḥīḥ*, 2:2:137.

ijtihād on this matter was used to buttress early and classical rulings that deterred women from attending congregational prayers in mosques.[17]

That 'Amra's legal authority derives from her relationship with a single Companion should not detract from the fact that she commands it at all. She is among the rare women to whom classical biographers refer as a *faqīha* (i.e., one possessing the critical faculties for legal reasoning and judgments, and not just a vehicle for the transfer of knowledge).[18] 'Ā'isha's other female kin, such as her sister Umm Kulthūm, did not acquire the same status as 'Amra, nor did 'Amra's sisters, who were also said to have been in 'Ā'isha's care.[19] Therefore, 'Amra's reputation was based on a historical memory that she had an extraordinary ability to assimilate 'Ā'isha's traditions and disseminate them with an understanding of their practical and legal implications. It is in this light that *ḥadīth* critics praise her as one of the most trusted sources, along with 'Urwa b. al-Zubayr and Hishām b. 'Urwa, for 'Ā'isha's traditions.

'Amra's achievements can profitably be compared to those of 'Ā'isha bint Ṭalḥa b. 'Ubayd Allāh, another niece of 'Ā'isha bint Abī Bakr, who is credited with thirteen traditions.[20] Unlike 'Amra, the *'ālima* and *faqīha*, 'Ā'isha bint Ṭalḥa emerges primarily as a littérateur. Although biographers acknowledge that she was knowledgeable in the *ḥadīth* of her aunt, her attraction for historians and *ḥadīth* seekers alike lies in her knowledge of poetry, her literary talents, and, not least, her charisma and beauty. In this vein, Abū Zur'a al-Dimashqī (d. 280/893), the third-century *ḥadīth* critic, is reported to have made the following judgment: "People narrated from her due to her personal merits, and her urbanity and renown in literary circles (*li-faḍā'ilihā wa-adabihā*)."[21] Even though biographers

[17] For a summary of legal discourse on the topic of women going to congregational prayer in mosques, see 'Abd al-Karīm Zaydān, *Mufaṣṣal fī Aḥkām al-Mar'a wa'l-Bayt Muslim* (Beirut: Mu'assasat al-Risāla, 1994), 1:209–15.

[18] al-Dhahabī, *Siyar*, 4:507; Ibn al-'Imād (d. 1089/1679), *Shadharāt al-Dhahab* (Beirut: Dār Ibn Kathīr, 1986), 1:395.

[19] Ibn Sa'd, *al-Ṭabaqāt*, 8:353.

[20] The following sources contain her biographies: Ibn Sa'd, *al-Ṭabaqāt*, 8:342; Abū al-Faraj al-Iṣbahānī (d. 356/967), *Kitāb al-Aghānī* (Beirut: Dār al-Thaqāfa, 1990), 11:165–85; Ibn 'Asākir (d. 571/1176), *Ta'rīkh Dimashq* (Beirut: Dār al-Fikr, 1995), 69:248–60; al-Dhahabī, *Siyar*, 4:369–70; al-Ṣafadī, *al-Wāfī*, 16:343–45; al-Mizzī, *Tahdhīb*, 35:237–38; 'Abd Allāh b. As'ad al-Yāfi'ī (d. 768/1367), *Mir'āt al-Jinān wa-'Ibrat al-Yaqẓān* (Beirut: Mu'assasat al-A'lamī li'l-Maṭbū'āt, 1970), 1:211–12. 'Ā'isha bint Ṭalḥa was the daughter of Umm Kulthūm, the sister of 'Ā'isha bint Abī Bakr.

[21] al-Mizzī, *Tahdhīb*, 35:238. Ibn 'Asākir cites Abū Zur'a al-Dimashqī's appraisal in his *Ta'rīkh Dimashq*, 69:248. For an overview of the multiple connotations of *adab* from early Islamic history to the modern period, see *EI*^{2}, s.v. "Adab."

do not overtly speak of the literacy of these prolific female Successors, it is likely that as accomplished relatives of Muḥammad's wives, they did learn at least the rudiments of reading and writing. These skills in turn may have been a factor in their success.

'Ā'isha is reputed in the historical sources to have been more open in mixed company, disdaining to cover her face so that her beauty would not be hidden. Abū al-Faraj al-Iṣbahānī states that she freely kept company with men and allowed them in her presence as though she herself were a man.[22] One may expect that her intimate access to 'Ā'isha bint Abī Bakr combined with her readiness to mingle with men would have resulted in more prolific transmissions to a wider range of non-kin men. Yet, 'Ā'isha bint Ṭalḥa's network with respect to the transmission of religious knowledge consists mostly of male kin.[23] Moreover, 'Ā'isha bint Ṭalḥa is not remembered in any of the sources as a *faqīha*, and only a few men seem to have sought her reports.

'Ā'isha's profile signals a transitional milieu that afforded new opportunities for women's intellectual engagement. Her activities as a belletrist indicate that by the early second/eighth century, some elite women's education encompassed more than rudimentary religious learning. These developments are amply evidenced in the 'Abbāsid historiographical tradition and provide the backdrop for the rich lore related to caliphs such as Hārūn al-Rashīd (r. 170–93/786–809) and his court. What is striking about 'Ā'isha's record is that her influence extended beyond literary circles to encompass the transmission of reports. The discrepancy in the reputations of 'Amra and 'Ā'isha bint Ṭalḥa underscores that the women associated with 'Ā'isha bint Abī Bakr were not a monolithic group. Rather, each woman's unique characteristics and talents are reflected in their *ḥadīth* transmission activity as well as in other genres of historical writing.

22 Abū al-Faraj al-Iṣbahānī, *al-Aghānī*, 11:165. See also Ibn 'Asākir, *Ta'rīkh Dimashq*, 69:253. There are several such references in *al-Aghānī* and the *Ta'rīkh Dimashq* to her behavior with men.

23 Her nephews Ṭalḥa b. Yaḥyā b. Ṭalḥa (d. ca. 148/765f.; for his biography, see Ibn Ḥajar, *Tahdhīb*, 5:26–27) and Mu'āwiya b. Isḥāq b. Ṭalḥa (death date unknown; for his biography, see ibid., 10:184), predominate in her chains of transmission. Even the supplementary information from biographical collections does not significantly change the picture of her transmission activity. Al-Mizzī, for example, knows her as an authority only for 'Ā'isha bint Abī Bakr's traditions, and he adds two students to the list compiled from the *isnād*s. They are 'Abd Allāh b. Yasār (I could not identify the 'Abd Allāh b. Yasār to whom al-Mizzī is referring in 'Ā'isha bint Ṭalḥa's entry), and Yūsuf b. Māhak (d. ca. 113/731; for his biography, see Ibn Ḥajar, *Tahdhīb*, 11:368).

ASCETIC WOMEN

With their lives spanning the second half of the first century, Umm al-Dardā' and Ḥafṣa bint Sīrīn are pioneers in the history of female asceticism in Islam. Their biographies diverge considerably from those Successors discussed earlier in that their transmission of reports seems secondary to their accomplishments as ascetics.[24] Their activities are testament to an arena of female pious participation wherein gender boundaries appear less fixed than in other spheres of religious learning and where women could serve as teachers of law and *ḥadīth* as well as asceticism.

Umm al-Dardā' al-Ṣughrā, a wife of the Companion Abū al-Dardā' (d. 32/652), is credited with twenty-three traditions and ranks among the most prolific of the female Successors.[25] Ibn Ḥibbān (d. 354/965), Ibn 'Asākir (d. 571/1176), and Ibn al-Jawzī (d. 597/1201) remember Umm

[24] Several Western studies have examined the phenomenon of Muslim women's asceticism and mysticism. A well-known work, first published in the early twentieth century, is Margaret Smith's *Rabi'a, the Life and Works of Rabi'a and Other Women Mystics in Islam* (1928; repr., New York: Cambridge University Press, 1984). An overview of the early history of Muslim women's asceticism and mysticism is available in the biographical compilation of Abū 'Abd al-Raḥmān al-Sulamī (d. 412/1021) entitled, *Early Sufi Women: Dhikr an-Niswa al-Muta'abbidāt aṣ-Ṣūfiyyāt*, trans. and ed. Rkia E. Cornell (Louisville: Fons Vitae, 1999). Subsequent references to this work will be to "al-Sulamī, *Early Sufi Women*." See also Maria Dakake, "'Guest of the Inmost Heart': Conceptions of the Divine Beloved among Early Sufi Women," *Comparative Islamic Studies* 3, no. 1 (2007): 72–97, and Laury Silvers, "'God Loves Me': The Theological Content and Context of Early Pious and Sufi Women's Sayings on Love," *Journal for Islamic Studies* 30 (2010): 33–59.

[25] Her name is also given as Hujayma bint Ḥuyayy al-Waṣṣābiyya. Biographies of her are found in the following sources: Ibn Ḥibbān, *Kitāb al-Thiqāt*, 3:120; Ibn 'Asākir, *Ta'rīkh Dimashq*, 70:146–64; Ibn al-Jawzī, *Ṣifat al-Ṣafwa* (Beirut: Dār al-Kutub al-'Ilmiyya, 1989), 4:244–46; al-Dhahabī, *Siyar*, 4:277–79; al-Mizzī, *Tahdhīb*, 35:352–58; and Ibn Ḥajar, *al-Iṣāba*, 12:240–42. Her *nisba* alternately appears as al-Awṣābiyya, designating a Ḥimyaritic provenance; see Yāqūt al-Ḥamawī (d. 626/1229), *Mu'jam al-Buldān* (Beirut: Dār al-Kutub al-'Ilmiyya, 1990), 5:435, s.v. "Waṣṣāb." Biographers use *kunya*s to distinguish between her and an older wife of Abū al-Dardā', namely Khayra bint Abī Ḥadrad. The older wife is known as Umm al-Dardā' al-Kubrā and the younger one (Hujayma) as Umm al-Dardā' al-Ṣughrā. Earlier sources, such as Abū Nu'aym al-Iṣbahānī and Ibn 'Abd al-Barr, evince some confusion about the identities of the two women and whether they were actually one and the same. This confusion, however, is partly resolved by the late seventh/thirteenth century. Ibn al-Athīr (d. 630/1233), in his *Usd al-Ghāba*, acknowledges them as two different women, but confuses their characteristics and confers the fame and attributes of Umm al-Dardā' al-Ṣughrā on Umm al-Dardā' al-Kubrā; see Ibn al-Athīr, *Usd al-Ghāba*, 5:580–81. By the eighth/fourteenth century, the ambivalence is gone as Umm al-Dardā' al-Kubrā is commemorated as the less prolific older Companion who narrates one or two traditions, and Umm al-Dardā' al-Ṣughrā is celebrated as an influential female scholar and ascetic (see al-Dhahabī, *Siyar*, 4:277–79; al-Mizzī, *Tahdhīb*, 35:352–58; and Ibn Ḥajar, *al-Iṣāba*, 12:240–42).

al-Dardā' as one of the most respected ascetics of the late first/seventh century. Ibn Ḥibbān states that she used to divide her time between Jerusalem and Damascus, spending six months in each city, and that she was a pious, ascetic woman (*min al-'ābidāt*), whose reports circulated among the Syrian traditionists.

Ibn 'Asākir's detailed biography in his *Ta'rīkh Dimashq* sheds further light on her asceticism and transmission of religious knowledge. He praises her as proficient in the ways of pietistic self-denial and worship (*zāhida*) and knowledgeable in the legal applications of traditions (*faqīha*). Intriguing details of Umm al-Dardā''s interactions with influential men who sought her company further highlight her uniqueness.[26] The Umayyad caliph 'Abd al-Malik b. Marwān (d. 86/705) was among those who enjoyed her counsel. They would converse together at the entrance to the Dome of the Rock until the call to sunset prayer, upon which 'Abd al-Malik would extend his arm to Umm al-Dardā' and walk her to the women's section.

Umm al-Dardā' transcended gender boundaries in other striking ways that were not normative and may have caused discomfort. Ibn 'Asākir cites a report that Umm al-Dardā', dressed in the traditional robe of ascetics (*burnus*), frequented the mosque with Abū al-Dardā' and prayed in the men's row.[27] She also attended circles for Qur'ānic recitation and taught the Qur'ān until her husband ordered her to join the women's rows. However, her assemblies for male ascetics, dedicated to ritual devotions and the remembrance of God (*majlis al-dhikr*), do not appear to have been similarly curtailed by her husband.[28] These circles may well have provided a context for transmitting traditions on a wide range of topics that she learned from her husband and other Companions.

Owing to her fame and her public assemblies, Umm al-Dardā''s transmission network was far more extensive than that of the women examined

[26] One of these men was the Umayyad caliph Mu'āwiya b. Abī Sufyān (r. 41–60/661–80), who proposed marriage to her after the death of Abū al-Dardā'. She refused, claiming her undying loyalty to Abū al-Dardā', and cited a tradition in which Abū al-Dardā' related that one's final earthly spouse would be his/her spouse in heaven. This account is widely cited in her biographies (see Ibn 'Asākir, *Ta'rīkh Dimashq*, 70:151–55).

[27] The use of woolen cloaks among the ascetics of early Islam may be a borrowing from contemporary Christian ascetics; see Tor Andrae, *In the Garden of Myrtles*, trans. Brigitta Sharpe (Binghamton: SUNY Press, 1987), 10. Damascus and Baṣra were home to Christian female ascetics who could have influenced their Muslim counterparts. Studies of early Christian ascetics include Peter Brown, *Body and Society: Men, Women, and Sexual Renunciation in Early Christianity* (New York: Columbia University Press, 1988). See also *Holy Women of the Syrian Orient*, introd. and trans. Sebastian P. Brock and Susan Harvey (Berkeley: University of California Press, 1987).

[28] Ibn 'Asākir, *Ta'rīkh Dimashq*, 70:151, 156–57.

earlier. While many of her reports are on the authority of Abū al-Dardā', she also narrated from 'Ā'isha, Abū Hurayra, Salmān al-Fārisī, Faḍāla b. 'Ubayd al-Anṣārī, and Ka'b b. 'Āṣim al-Ash'arī.[29] In contrast to the female Successors examined earlier, Umm al-Dardā' transmitted her traditions to many more men, including a broader range who were not among her kin. Al-Mizzī, for example, lists a total of forty-one men who heard her reports.[30] No single narrator dominates in her *isnād*s as do the male kin of 'Amra and Zaynab in their *isnād*s. Finally, though her own ascetic practices and leadership of ascetic circles is a strong feature of her historical personality, her transmission was not just limited to this class.[31] Jurists such as Makḥūl al-Shāmī (d. 112/730) and Maymūn b. Mihrān (d. 117/735) also sought out her reports. Indeed, in the *isnād*s examined for this study, most of the men who narrate from her did not establish reputations as ascetics.

This composite portrait of Umm al-Dardā' highlights her unusual career and her prolific and methodical teaching, which surpasses even that of 'Amra bint 'Abd al-Raḥmān. A telling testimony to the historical memory of Umm al-Dardā' occurs in al-Dhahabī's *Tadhkirat al-Ḥuffāẓ*, which lists highly accomplished male and female *ḥadīth* transmitters. 'Ā'isha bint Abī Bakr is the sole woman listed in the Companion generation, and the only one among the Successors is Umm al-Dardā'.[32] Al-Dhahabī's inclusion of Umm al-Dardā', as well as the

[29] Details about her transmission network are drawn from *isnād* evidence as well as from her biographies. One of her *isnād*s records her transmitting *ḥadīth* to her brother, Sālim. She is not known to have had any surviving children who would have carried on her *ḥadīth* within a family network.

[30] al-Mizzī, *Tahdhīb*, 35:352–53. In the Sunnī compilations selected for this study, she narrates to twenty-two transmitters.

[31] A few men with reputations as ascetics do appear in her *isnād*s; these include Rajā' b. Ḥaywa b. Jarwal (d. 112/730); for his biography, see Ibn Ḥajar, *Tahdhīb* 3:236–37, and 'Awn b. 'Abd Allāh b. 'Utba (d. ca. 115/733); for his biography, see Ibn Ḥajar, *Tahdhīb* 8:147–48.

[32] al-Dhahabī, *Tadhkirat al-Ḥuffāẓ* (Beirut: Dār al-Kutub al-'Ilmiyya, 1998), 1:25, 1:44. The editor's introduction lists the following ranks and their definitions: *musnid*, one who narrates traditions in his possession with a sound *isnād*, and who may or may not have critical knowledge of the traditions; *muḥaddith*, one who is knowledgeable in the transmission of the *ḥadīth*, has critical knowledge of the text and traditionists, and has contact with and knowledge about the narrators of his own time; *ḥāfiẓ*, a rank above *muḥaddith* in terms of his narration and understanding of the traditions; *ḥujja*, one who has attained superior rank as a traditionist due to his precise and exacting knowledge of *isnād*s and their texts (classical scholars stipulated that a *ḥujja* had to memorize 300,000 traditions and have knowledge about their *isnād*s and *matns*); *ḥākim*, one who has mastered nearly all the known traditions; and *amīr al-mu'minīn fī al-ḥadīth*, the highest rank of achievement in *ḥadīth* studies reserved for scholars such as Sufyān al-Thawrī, Muslim, and al-Bukhārī. The editor notes that al-Dhahabī's *Tadkhirat al-Ḥuffāẓ* includes those in the *ḥujja* category and above (see the introduction by Zakariyyā 'Umayrāt in *Tadhkirat al-Ḥuffāẓ*, 1:3–4).

evidence from her *isnād*s and biographies, indicates that she conformed more closely to 'Ā'isha's model of religious authority than did most other women, including 'Ā'isha's own nieces, 'Amra bint 'Abd al-Raḥmān and 'Ā'isha bint Ṭalḥa. Even today, the memory of Umm al-Dardā' persists in the Damascene mosque housing the grave of Abū al-Dardā', where the couple is said to have taught and worshipped and which continues to be a site for women's educational assemblies.

Umm al-Dardā', while outstanding in her achievements, was not unique in combining exemplary piety with religious learning and legal aptitude. Ḥafṣa bint Sīrīn, credited with seventeen traditions, drew students in Baṣra who were attracted to her piety as well as her knowledge of traditions and their legal and practical relevance.[33] Ibn al-Jawzī reports that when her brother Muḥammad b. Sīrīn (d. 110/729), the famed scholar, could not answer a question regarding the Qur'ān, he would turn to Ḥafṣa for insight.[34] Biographers also laud her vigilance, constancy in prayer, and persistent fasting. Ibn Sa'd includes a brief anecdote from Bakkār b. Muḥammad that he saw a *masjid* of Ḥafṣa within their household (*fī dār Sīrīn*), which also contained the *masjid*s of Muḥammad b. Sīrīn and Anas. The reference to "*masjid* Ḥafṣa" is likely to a space reserved for each of their prayers and meditative practices within their home.[35] Reports of her lesser miracles further augmented her reputation among ascetics (*kānat ṣāḥibat āyāt wa-karāmāt*).[36]

Ḥafṣa is an authority for traditions on a broad range of subjects that she heard from a number of Companions. Like other well-known female Successors, her *isnād*s in the selected compilations indicate that she transmitted mostly from one or two individuals. In Ḥafṣa's case, she appears primarily in traditions on the authority of Rabāb bint Ṣulay' and Nusayba bint Ka'b.[37] As

33 Biographical notices for her are available in the following sources: Ibn Sa'd, *al-Ṭabaqāt*, 8:355–56; Ibn Ḥibbān, *Kitāb al-Thiqāt*, 2:112; al-Sulamī, *Early Sufi Women*, 123; Ibn al-Jawzī, *Ṣifat al-Ṣafwa*, 4:20–22; al-Mizzī, *Tahdhīb*, 35:151–53; al-Dhahabī, *Siyar*, 4:507; and Kaḥḥāla, *A'lām al-Nisā'*, 2:229–31.

34 For Ibn Sīrīn's biographical notices, see Ibn Sa'd, *al-Ṭabaqāt*, 7 (part 1):140–50, and Ibn Ḥajar, *Tahdhīb*, 9:184–86. He was among the outstanding scholars and ascetics of the Successor generation. He is acclaimed as a jurist, Qur'ān exegete, *ḥadīth* transmitter, and as someone skilled in the interpretation of dreams. Another of their siblings, Karīma bint Sīrīn, is also known as a devout ascetic. However, she did not acquire the same fame as Ḥafṣa. See Ibn al-Jawzī, *Ṣifat al-Ṣafwa*, 4:22.

35 Ibn Sa'd, *al-Ṭabaqāt*, 7 (part 1): 148.

36 al-Sulamī, *Early Sufi Women*, 123. Among them was that her lamp would continue to illuminate her room even after the fuel was expended.

37 For the biography of Rabāb bint Ṣulay' (death date unknown), see al-Mizzī, *Tahdhīb*, 35:171–72; and for that of Nusayba bint Ka'b (death date unknown), see al-Mizzī, *Tahdhīb*, 35:372.

for her students, a total of eleven men, ascetics as well as those with expertise in exegesis and law, are named in her *isnād*s and biographical sources.[38]

Ḥafṣa's renown is amplified over time in the historiographical tradition. Ibn Sa'd, in the third/ninth century, does not dwell on her virtues as a narrator or as an ascetic for that matter. Rather, he simply informs us of her genealogy and provides a few anecdotal reports about her.[39] But by the eighth/fourteenth century, following the revival of women's participation in *ḥadīth* transmission, she is commemorated as one of the most trusted Successors. For example, al-Mizzī cites a report that Iyās b. Mu'āwiya deemed Ḥafṣa more trustworthy than al-Ḥasan al-Baṣrī and her brother, Muḥammad b. Sīrīn. Al-Dhahabī bestowed on her the epithet *al-faqīha* (the jurist), and Ibn al-'Imād (d. 1089/1679) continued this tradition in her obituary notice.[40] As in the case of Umm al-Dardā', the use of *faqīha* for Ḥafṣa indicates that her scholarly reputation exceeded that of most of her female contemporaries. More recently, Rkia Cornell has concluded that Ḥafṣa's extensive influence suggests that she led her own school of female ascetics in Baṣra.[41]

The final transmitter presented here is the Meccan Ṣafiyya bint Shayba. She is a rare, if not unique, female Successor who established herself as a reliable traditionist without the benefits of kinship to a female Companion or connection to an ascetic network.[42] Credited with thirty-four reports on

38 For example, she is said to have transmitted to Iyās b. Mu'āwiya (d. 122/740), a *qāḍī* of Baṣra and a jurist, as well as Qatāda b. Di'āma (d. 118/736), known as an exegete and jurist (for their biographies, see Ibn Ḥajar, *Tahdhīb*, 1:354–55 and 8:306–8, respectively).

39 Ibn Sa'd, *al-Ṭabaqāt*, 8:355–56.

40 al-Dhahabī, *Siyar*, 4:507; and Ibn al-'Imād, *Shadharāt*, 2:12.

41 Cornell, introduction to al-Sulamī, *Early Sufi Women*, 62.

42 Biographical notices for her are available in the following sources: Ibn Sa'd, *al-Ṭabaqāt*, 8:344; Ibn Ḥibbān, *Kitāb al-Thiqāt*, 2:240–41; Abū Nu'aym al-Iṣbahānī, *Ma'rifat al-Ṣaḥāba*, 6:3378–79; Ibn 'Abd al-Barr, *al-Istī'āb*, 4:1873; Ibn al-Athīr, *Usd al-Ghāba*, 5:492; al-Mizzī, *Tahdhīb*, 35:211–12; al-Dhahabī, *Siyar*, 3:507–9; Ibn Ḥajar, *al-Iṣāba*, 12:18; and Kaḥḥāla, *A'lām al-Nisā'*, 2:338–39. Ibn Ḥibbān counts her among the traditionists of Medina (*Kitāb al-Thiqāt*, 2:240–41). It is probably more accurate to assign to her a Meccan provenance, as does al-Dhahabī, *Siyar*, 3:508. Like Zaynab bint Abī Salama, Ṣafiyya is listed among the Companions by some scholars and as a Successor by others. Her status is disputed since she would have been very young when Muḥammad died. At best, she would have seen him (*la-hā ru'ya*) but would not have reached the age of legal maturity before his death. Ibn Ḥajar records disagreement as to whether she actually saw Muḥammad (see Ibn Ḥajar, *al-Iṣāba*, 12:18). Ṣafiyya's status as a young Companion is conveyed in one *ḥadīth* which describes her direct encounter with Muḥammad during his Farewell Pilgrimage. This *ḥadīth* is at times classified as *mu'allaq* or *mursal*. Such traditions are not considered as strong as the *marfū'* traditions (those narrated with an uninterrupted chain from Muḥammad onward). In view of this debate regarding her Companion status and due to her reliability as a transmitter, al-Dhahabī labels her tradition from Muḥammad as "one of the strongest of the *mursal* traditions" (*min aqwā al-marāsīl*); see al-Dhahabī, *Siyar*, 3:508. I include her with the Successors due to her young

a range of topics in the selected compilations, Ṣafiyya is second only to ʿAmra bint ʿAbd al-Raḥmān in the number of *ḥadīth* narrated. Her reputation may partly derive from the fact that she was the daughter of Shayba b. ʿUthmān b. Abī Ṭalḥa (d. 59/679), whom Muḥammad entrusted with the keys to the Kaʿba.[43] Although she does not transmit traditions from her father, her reliability as a narrator may have been boosted by the honor due to her father's position. Her residence in Mecca certainly would have contributed to the breadth of her transmission circle, because pilgrims would have been likely to seek out her transmissions. While her son, Manṣūr b. ʿAbd al-Raḥmān al-Ḥajabī (d. ca. 137/754), often appears in her *isnād*s, she also appears to have transmitted to a large circle of non-kin males.[44]

Ibn Saʿd, departing from his usual silence on the scale of a woman's transmission, states that people narrated extensively from her. Muḥammad b. ʿUbayd b. Abī Ṣāliḥ traveled to Mecca with ʿAdī b. ʿAdī al-Kindī, who sent him to Ṣafiyya because she was known as an authority for ʿĀʾisha's traditions.[45] During this meeting, Muḥammad b. ʿUbayd learned the ruling that a divorce or the emancipation of a slave was not considered valid when enacted under duress. Ṣafiyya's biographers, with the exception of al-Dhahabī, do not, however, commemorate her as a *faqīha*.[46] Rather, she is praised as a trustworthy transmitter who narrated extensively from Muḥammad's wives and from other female Companions.[47]

The historical memory of Ṣafiyya bint Shayba as a reliable authority affirms that it was indeed possible for women to engage in more than merely incidental transmission of religious knowledge. It is likely that

age at the time of Muḥammad's death and the fact that biographers do not commonly classify her as a Companion.

43 For his biography, see Ibn Ḥajar, *Tahdhīb*, 4:342. Her *nisba*, "al-Ḥajabiyya," is a reference to this occupation.

44 Manṣūr was also entrusted with the keys to the Kaʿba. For his biographical notice, see Ibn Ḥajar, *Tahdhīb*, 10:277. Nineteen different narrators of her traditions are recorded in the selected collections, and al-Mizzī adds three names from other collections. Only four of these are men who were related to her. In addition to her son, Manṣūr, three of her nephews appear in her *isnād*s (al-Mizzī, *Tahdhīb*, 35:211–12).

45 One report explicitly states that she had memorized reports on ʿĀʾisha's authority; see Abū Dāwūd, *Sunan*, 2:258, #2193.

46 al-Dhahabī, *Siyar*, 3:508.

47 Nineteen of her thirty-two traditions are on the authority of ʿĀʾisha. Ṣafiyya narrates from a number of other women, including Umm Salama, Ramla bint Abī Sufyān, Asmāʾ bint Abī Bakr, and Ḥabība bint Abī Tajrā. She is also said to have transmitted from ʿAbd Allāh b. ʿUmar and ʿUthmān b. Ṭalḥa, though these transmissions are not recorded in the selected collections. Al-Mizzī, *Tahdhīb*, 35:211–12.

other female Successors resident in Mecca had traditions in their possession that could have been widely disseminated, especially during the Ḥajj season. However, Ṣafiyya is the only Meccan female Successor to have attained significant recognition in the sources studied. Her uniqueness reinforces the idea that the potential for female participation was rarely actualized and that women were marginal in this arena very soon after the Companion generation.

The following aspects of women's *ḥadīth* participation in the generation immediately after the Companions are worth highlighting. First, none of the women studied is known to have assiduously collected *ḥadīth* from a broad range of Companions in the manner of 'Urwa b. al-Zubayr or other prominent male Successors. Their authority is mostly based on their narrations from one or two Companions. Second, there is little evidence of an intergenerational female network of transmission after the Successors. These women narrate predominantly to male authorities. While all of them are likely to have passed some of their knowledge onto other women, such transmissions were not recorded as part of the arena that came to be defined as formal *ḥadīth* transmission. Rather, women's learning and teaching of reports was subsumed under other activities such as pious asceticism and popular preaching. A few women, such as 'Amra and Umm al-Dardā', were explicitly remembered for their legal discernment (*fiqh*), but it was more common for women to be remembered only as reliable traditionists who may not have had a command of the legal application of the sayings they were relating. Finally, the collective careers of all of the prominent Successor women end with the close of the first century. The accomplishments of women in this domain would not manifest themselves again for nearly 250 years.

THE DEMISE OF WOMEN'S PARTICIPATION

Although the decline in the quantity and quality of women's *ḥadīth* participation was profound and pervasive, it has not yet attracted sustained scholarly analysis. The inclusion of significant numbers of female Companions in *isnād*s and the historical evidence of prominent female *ḥadīth* scholars from the mid-fifth century onward has produced a mistaken assumption of women's participation on an uninterrupted continuum from the first century AH until well into the Mamlūk period (ca. 648–922/1250–1517). For example, M. Z. Ṣiddīqī asserts that "at every period in Muslim history, there lived numerous eminent women-traditionists, treated by their brethren with reverence and respect."[48] Similarly, Leila Ahmed, who takes a more critical view of women's participation in Muslim intellectual life than Ṣiddīqī, states that the female Companions' precedent as transmitters of Muḥammad's reports guaranteed that women could serve in this capacity throughout Muslim history. Hence, "women traditionists, usually taught by their fathers, were found in Muslim societies in all ages, including the 'Abbāsid."[49] A few scholars have remarked that women's participation decreased after the Companion generation without assessing the trend further.[50] Given the neglect of this critical issue, I will first substantiate that there was indeed a precipitous decline and then explain why.

The following points of clarification are necessary to understand the data drawn from the *isnād*s and the method of analysis. *Isnād*s generally record the intergenerational transfer of information, and each link in the chain theoretically moves the *ḥadīth* text (*matn*) forward in time. The chains under analysis here are classified as *marfū'* (i.e., going back to Muḥammad) and *muttaṣil* (with a continuous chain of transmission); the first link generally connects Muḥammad with a Companion, the second link connects the Companion to a Successor, and so on until the time of the compiler of each canonical work. There are, of course, instances of intra-generational transfer of information that do not conform to the ideal *marfū' muttaṣil isnād*. Bearing this in mind, we can still use the ideal type as a rough measure of women's participation in successive generations after the Companions.

Whereas there are approximately 2,065 *ḥadīth* in which a woman is listed as the *first* authority after the Prophet, there are approximately 525 *ḥadīth* in which a woman is listed as a *second or later* narrator in the *isnād*s of the major Sunnī collections.[51] The disparity between these

48 Ṣiddīqī, *Ḥadīth Literature*, 117.

49 Leila Ahmed, *Women and Gender in Islam: Historical Roots of a Modern Debate* (New Haven: Yale University Press, 1992), 74. Ahmed characterizes the 'Abbāsid period as one of the most misogynist and oppressive ages for Muslim women.

50 See, for example, Roded, *Women in Islamic Biographical Collections*, 66–67, and Sayyid al-Ahl, *Ṭabaqāt al-Nisā' al-Muḥaddithāt*, 83–85. Both authors note that women's participation diminishes after the Companions but do not substantiate their impressions, nor do they investigate the causes of this trend. Nadwi also notes that there was a decline, which he attributes primarily to the increased incidence of traveling in search of *ḥadīth*. He also notes that while women continued to receive knowledge in this period, they were not transmitting it to others. He does not discuss these issues in detail nor does he explore other possible causes for the decline (Nadwi, *al-Muḥaddithāt*, 249–53).

51 The number of *ḥadīth* cited is based on the classification by the editors of *al-Musnad al-Jāmi'*. As noted in Chapter 1, the number can vary, sometimes considerably, depending on how one chooses to distinguish between the various versions of any given *ḥadīth*.

numbers is due in part to *ḥadīth* credited to ʿĀ'isha, which number close to 1,370 and account for roughly 66 percent of all traditions narrated by female Companions. Umm Salama also narrates a disproportionately large number of traditions in relation to other female Companions; she is credited with 175 traditions in *al-Musnad al-Jāmiʿ*. Because ʿĀ'isha and Umm Salama are not representative of the scale of recorded female participation, it makes sense to consider the numbers if we exclude their traditions from our calculations. We are left then with approximately 520 traditions narrated by women in the Companion generation and approximately 525 traditions narrated by women in the subsequent *eleven* generations up to the end of the third/ninth century.[52]

A summary of the data on women's position in these *isnād*s is as follows. Depending on the date of a given *ḥadīth* compilation, there are generally between four and twelve narrators, or "links," in an *isnād* chain between the Companion and the compiler of the work.[53] There are 276 women who appear in *isnād*s as links two through four.[54] Of the 276 women in links two through four, 244, or roughly 88 percent, appear as link two. Of these 244, several are classified as Companions by one or

[52] Here I am using Ibn Ḥajar al-ʿAsqalānī's definition of generation (*ṭabaqa*), which established a standard measure for *ḥadīth* transmission. I will discuss his definition in more detail in a subsequent section of this chapter. It should be noted that if we remove the entire *isnād*s of ʿĀ'isha's and Umm Salama's traditions from our earlier count (rather than subtracting only instances in which ʿĀ'isha and Umm Salama narrate), we are left with only approximately 250 instances of narration by women in the post-Companion generations rather than the 525 instances mentioned previously (since in approximately 275 instances women in the post-Companion generations were narrating from either ʿĀ'isha or Umm Salama). Another way to gauge women's contributions is to compare the male-female ratio of narrators in the Companion generation with that of later generations. *Al-Musnad al-Jāmiʿ* enumerates approximately 17,800 traditions narrated by men and women. Female Companions narrate approximately 12 percent of *ḥadīth*. In all the subsequent generations combined, women narrate only 3 percent of the traditions. If we exclude the traditions of ʿĀ'isha and Umm Salama, we emerge with approximately 3 percent of traditions being narrated by female Companions and a little more than 1 percent for subsequent generations after the Companions up to the end of the third/ninth century.

[53] On average, Mālik's *al-Muwaṭṭa'*, as an early compilation, would have fewer links in its *isnād*s than a later compilation, such as the *Ṣaḥīḥ* of Ibn Khuzayma. I use the numbers four and twelve as rough estimates based on the period encompassed by the compilations.

[54] As mentioned earlier, the number of female narrators is drawn primarily from the *isnād*s in *al-Musnad al-Jāmiʿ* and from the notices on women that appear in al-Mizzī's *Tahdhīb* and al-Ḥusaynī's *Kitāb al-Tadhkira*. The final tally of female narrators does not include women who are listed simply as "a woman of Banū Sulaym" or "a woman of the Anṣār," as it is impossible to control repetitions in such cases. There are less than ten such instances, so excluding them does not alter my evaluation of female transmission.

more of the *ḥadīth* scholars.[55] In some cases, these women's *ḥadīth* represent intra-generational transmission (e.g., from 'Ā'isha to Umm Salama). Thirty women appear as link three. Only two women appear as link four.[56] There are no women who appear after link four. To summarize, female transmission is highest in the first two links of the *isnāds* in major canonical and non-canonical Sunnī compilations. There is a steep decline by the third link. In the fourth link, the numbers are negligible, and thereafter, women do not appear in the *isnāds* at all up to the time of the compilers of the works themselves.

There is no consistent chronological correspondence between link numbers and generations of transmitters. For example, 'Ā'isha bint Abī Bakr (d. 58) (link one) may transmit a tradition to Ramla bint Abī Sufyān (d. 44) (link two), who then transmits it to Zaynab bint Abī Salama (d. 73) (link three). These links cover a more compressed period in comparison with an *isnād* that goes from 'Ā'isha to Mu'ādha bint 'Abd Allāh (d. 83/702) and then to Qatāda (d. 118/736). Such chronological disparities in *isnāds* prevent us from precisely correlating "links" with specific periods or even generations.[57] Nevertheless, link classifications are relevant because they provide a rough chronological sketch. For example, Companions do not narrate in a link position after four. Similarly, a Successor is unlikely to appear as a seventh link.

We can also track the trend of declining female participation using classifications from the discipline of *ḥadīth* study (*'ulūm al-ḥadīth*). Categorization of transmitters according to their generations (*ṭabaqāt*)

55 Specifically, approximately forty women who appear as link two are covered in Ibn Ḥajar's *al-Iṣāba fī Tamyīz al-Ṣaḥāba*, which aims to sort out names, genealogies, and confusion over identities for all the Companions known to Ibn Ḥajar. However, because *isnāds* do not consistently provide full names for women, it is sometimes difficult to match names in *isnāds* with those in *al-Iṣāba*, particularly for women about whom little is known.

56 There are three cases in which the same woman appears in more than one link: (1) Zaynab bint Abī Salama (d. 73/692) appears as links two, three, or four depending on the tradition. I classified her as link two because in most of her traditions she narrates from a Companion (as link two) and because she is classified as a younger Companion whose life overlapped with that of many of the Successors. (2) Ḥafṣa bint Sīrīn (d. after 100/718) appears both as a second link and as a third. I included her among the second links as she is said to have lived until the beginning of the second century and is classified as a Successor. (3) Qurayba bint 'Abd Allāh appears as a third and fourth link. I classified her as a third link because Ibn Ḥajar classifies her as belonging to the Successor generation rather than the subsequent generation (Ibn Ḥajar, *Taqrīb al-Tahdhīb* [Beirut: Dār al-Kutub al-'Ilmiyya, 1993], 2:656). All subsequent references to the *Taqrīb*, unless otherwise noted, are to this 1993 Beirut edition.

57 Additionally, because we do not know death dates for most of the women in the *isnāds*, we cannot precisely trace the decline of women's participation as transmitters.

has been a traditional approach of *ḥadīth* scholars attempting to organize and evaluate the contributions of hundreds of transmitters throughout Muslim history.[58] The term *ṭabaqa* in the context of describing the inter-generational transfer of *ḥadīth* typically takes into account a variety of factors including the birth and death dates of a scholar and the teachers from whom he or she transmitted traditions. For the purposes of this study, the *ṭabaqa* structure employed by Ibn Ḥajar al-ʿAsqalānī is particularly useful as it classifies many (164 of a total of 276) of the women included in my data according to twelve *ṭabaqāt*.[59] Ibn Ḥajar's *ṭabaqa* structure is not entirely intuitive. He puts the Companions into one *ṭabaqa*, divides the Successors into five *ṭabaqāt*, and the two generations after the Successors into three groups (*ṭabaqāt*) each. These divisions, particularly the ones among the Successors, are based partially on groupings of the teachers of the Successors and also on whether the Successors in each group actually narrated from the Companions or only saw them. It is also important to clarify that the terms "Companions," "Successors," and "Successors to Successors" do not correspond narrowly to three distinct generations in early Islamic history. Each group may be further subdivided according to their ages. For example, Abū Bakr (d. 13/634) is among the eldest of the Companions; ʿĀʾisha (d. 58/678) falls in the subgeneration after him; and Zaynab bint Abī Salama (d. 73/692) is in the younger subset of Companions. These distinctions do not affect my own conclusions.[60] What is important is that Ibn Ḥajar's divisions are correlated with specific periods, allowing me to map trends in women's participation in concrete chronological terms, even though there are no death dates for most of the

[58] The use of *ṭabaqāt* as an organizing principle is observable in every field of learning throughout Muslim history. For an overview, see *EI*², s.v. "Ṭabaqāt," and Ibrahim Hafsi, "Recherches sur le genre *ṭabaqāt*," *Arabica* 23 (1976): 227–65 and *Arabica* 24 (1977): 1–41, 150–86.

[59] Ibn Ḥajar, *Taqrīb*, 1:24–26. I prefer to use Ibn Ḥajar's classification even though it is not as well known as that of al-Dhahabī. Al-Dhahabī employed the *ṭabaqa* structure in a number of his works including *Tadhkirat al-Ḥuffāẓ*, *al-Muʿīn fī Ṭabaqāt al-Muḥaddithīn*, and *Siyar Aʿlām al-Nubalāʾ*. For a more detailed discussion of al-Dhahabī's use of this organizing principle, see Scott Lucas, *Constructive Critics*, 40–112. There are two major differences between the *ṭabaqāt* delineated by al-Dhahabī in his *Muʿīn* and those of Ibn Ḥajar in his *Taqrīb*. First, al-Dhahabī begins his periodization with the eldest generation of Successors, whereas Ibn Ḥajar starts with the Companions. Second, al-Dhahabī classifies a few selected scholars from each generation up to his own in the early eighth/fourteenth century. Ibn Ḥajar, on the other hand, limits his work to twelve *ṭabaqāt*, from the Companions up to the generation of al-Nasāʾī (d. 303/915).

[60] For a more detailed explanation of Ibn Ḥajar's reasoning, see Muḥammad ʿAwwāma's introduction to Ibn Ḥajar's *Taqrīb al-Tahdhīb* (Aleppo: Dār al-Rashīd, 1991), 42–47.

women who appear in the *isnāds* studied here. Figure 2 charts the numbers of women in links two through four according to Ibn Ḥajar's *ṭabaqāt*. The first group (*Ṭabaqa* 1) consists of Companions who have narrated from other Companions and who therefore would be classified as "link two."

As for the 112 women who are not listed in the *Taqrīb al-Tahdhīb*, we can provide approximate classifications based on other sources or on their numerical position in *isnāds*.[61] Nine of them can be identified as Companions; ninety-six of them are second links who transmitted from Companions. According to Ibn Ḥajar's scheme, they may fall in a *ṭabaqa* between two and four because the fifth *ṭabaqa* designates those who narrated from Successors. A *terminus ante quem* for their transmission would thus be around the year 125. The remaining seven women are third links. Of these seven, two transmitted from Companions, which again places them in *ṭabaqa*s two through four. Five of them transmitted from Successors and we may locate them in *ṭabaqa*s five through nine. Their transmission may have occurred up to the early third/ninth century. Thus, this group of 112 shows a similar distribution across time to the group listed in the *Taqrīb* and confirms the original observation that women's transmission is seen primarily in the first 150 years of Islamic history and is negligible from the mid-second to the early fourth century.

In addition to the low numbers of women overall who participate in the centuries immediately following the post-Companion generation, another striking aspect of female narration up to the fourth/tenth century is its utterly restricted scope for individual women. Two hundred and twenty-three women, approximately 80 percent of our data set, appear in only one *isnād* in the collections studied. Fifty women narrate between two and fourteen traditions each. Five women – statistical outliers – narrate between twenty-one and sixty-six traditions each. Thirteen women are recorded as narrators in the *Tahdhīb al-Kamāl* of al-Mizzī and *Kitāb al-Tadhkira* of al-Ḥusaynī, but were not found in the *isnāds* checked for this study.[62] Judging by their entries in these two works, these

[61] For the most part, there is very little information about these 112 women in the biographical sources. *Ḥadīth* critics put such narrators in the category of *majhūlāt* (women about whom nothing is known) or write that they do not have enough information to assess a woman's status as a transmitter (*lā yuʿraf ḥālu-hā*). The latter phrase is employed in cases where minimal information is available about a narrator.

[62] Al-Mizzī's work provides entries only for the narrators found in the six canonical compilations and in some of the lesser compilations by the authors of these same six compilations. However, in composing the entries and lists of students and teachers, al-Mizzī drew on other sources in addition to the canonical works. The same is true of al-Ḥusaynī's *Kitāb al-Tadhkira*.

Ṭabaqa	Ibn Ḥajar's Description	Number of Women
I	Companions (*al-ṣaḥāba*) – all the Companions are placed together in one group	22
II (d. ca. 95/713)	The eldest of the Successors (*kibār al-tābiʿīn*) – contemporaries of Saʿīd b. al-Musayyab (13–94)	6
III (d. ca. 110/728)	The middle group of Successors (*al-ṭabaqa al-wusṭā min al-tābiʿīn*) – contemporaries of al-Ḥasan al-Baṣrī (21–110) and Muḥammad b. Sīrīn (33–110)	78
IV (d. ca. 125/742)	The generation of Successors after those in the third *ṭabaqa* who primarily narrated from the eldest of the Successors – contemporaries of Qatāda (61–118) and Ibn Shihāb al-Zuhrī (58–124)	28
V (d. ca. 150/767)	The youngest group of Successors who may have seen the Companions and the eldest of the Successors but did not transmit *ḥadīth* from the Companions – contemporaries of Sulaymān b. Mihrān al-Aʿmash (61–148)	7
VI (d. ca. 150/767)	Those who are close in age to the youngest group of Successors but did not meet any of the Companions – contemporaries of Ibn Jurayj (80–150) (*The distinction between narrators in groups V and VI is not based on death dates, but on the criterion of seeing or meeting with one of the Companions [a mark of prestige]. Neither group transmitted from the Companions.)	8
VII (d. ca. 180/796)	The eldest of the generation after the Successors (*kibār atbāʿ al-tābiʿīn*) – contemporaries of Sufyān al-Thawrī (97–161) and Mālik b. Anas (93–179)	15
VIII (d. ca. 200/815)	The middle group of the generation after the Successors – contemporaries of Ismāʿīl b. Ibrāhīm b. ʿUlayya (110–193) and Sufyān b. ʿUyayna (107–198)	0
IX (d. ca. 205/820)	The youngest of the generation after the Successors – contemporaries of al-Shāfiʿī (150–204)	0
X (d. ca. 240/854)	The eldest of the generation after the *atbāʿ al-tābiʿīn*, who did not meet any of the Successors (*kibār al-ākhidhīn ʿan tabaʿ al-atbāʿ*) – contemporaries of Aḥmad b. Ḥanbal (164–241)	0
XI (d. ca. 255/868)	The middle group of the above generation – contemporaries of al-Bukhārī (194–256)	0
XII (d. ca. 280/893)	The youngest of the above generation – contemporaries of al-Tirmidhī (206–279)	0

FIGURE 2: Chart of Number of Women in *Ṭabaqas* 1–12

thirteen women appear to have contributed only one or two traditions each. Figure 3 shows a graph of the numbers of traditions narrated by women in the selected compilations. It does not include the five women who are identified as statistical outliers; they would appear too far over to the right of the graph.

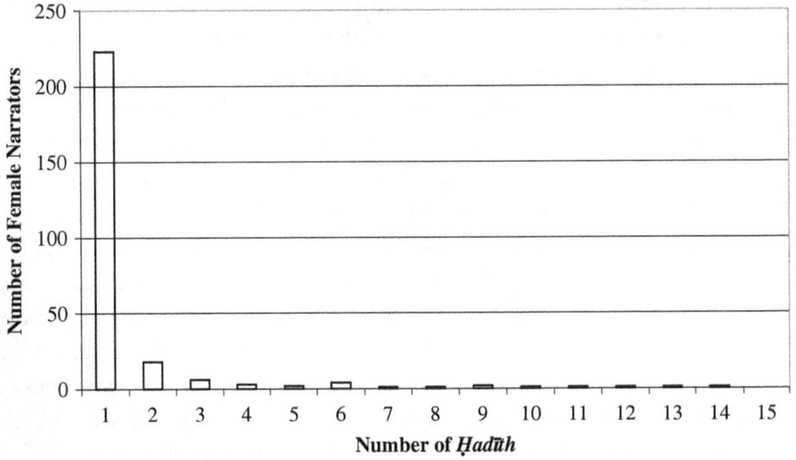

FIGURE 3: Graph of the Number of *Ḥadīth* Narrated by Women of Post-Companion Generations

As this figure reveals, the post-Companion generations can hardly be considered prolific transmitters. Only eight women, approximately 3 percent of the total, appear in the *isnād*s of more than ten *ḥadīth*.

This picture of the diminishing significance of female traditionists is further reinforced when we reconstruct the circumstances of their narration. Many of these women are identified in biographical sources only through mention of their reports or the remark, unhelpful for our purposes, that they narrated reports and were deemed acceptable narrators. In forty-four cases, women are identified only through a male relative, appearing as "sister of x" or "aunt of y." Given the paltry information on many women, it is difficult to ascertain what, if any, special qualifications they had as transmitters.

Whereas in the decades immediately after the Companions there are a handful of women who distinguish themselves as transmitters, the same is not true for the generations immediately after the Successors. In links three and four (roughly the period from 110/728 to 180/796), just before women's prolonged disappearance from the *ḥadīth* records, their activity is severely constrained. As mentioned previously, of the 276 women in our database, thirty are third links and only two are fourth links. The thirty women who narrate as third links contribute one tradition each in twenty-eight cases and two traditions in the remaining two cases. Half of them are doomed to anonymity in the *rijāl* works. In Ibn Ḥajar's *Taqrīb*, many of them are designated as women about whom no judgments can be made regarding reliability (*lā yu'raf ḥālu-hā*). Five of them were not found in the *rijāl* works but were located in the *isnād*s of one of the selected collections. As such, they cannot be considered to have left any meaningful impression as *ḥadīth* transmitters on biographers and *ḥadīth* critics. Of the women who feature as the third link and who are known as reliable transmitters, only two, Karīma bint al-Miqdād and Umm al-Aswad al-Khuzā'iyya, are deemed exceptionally reliable (*thiqa*). Five were placed in the less laudatory but acceptable category of *maqbūla*.[63] Similarly, the two women who figure as link four in the selected collections narrate only one report apiece. As for their renown as transmitters, Ibn Ḥajar can only conclude for both, *lā yu'raf ḥālu-hā*. Thus the activity that did occur on the part of women in the second/eighth century was not of great consequence to the *ḥadīth* collectors and scholars who documented and studied the transmitters. This remarkably low level of participation allows us to push back the date of significant female involvement in the transmission of religious knowledge to the end of the first/seventh century.

The collective portrait that emerges from the *isnād*s highlights the early gender-based differentiation in the careers of male and female transmitters during the period covered in this chapter. Relatively prolific women such as 'Amra bint 'Abd al-Raḥmān, Zaynab bint Abī Salama, and Umm al-Dardā' are anomalies in an overall picture of limited female participation. Even though these women were commemorated as exceptional female transmitters, their accomplishments do not approximate those of prominent men in the field. That these women do not appear to have circulated among male Companions to collect and record traditions is the first indication that women's presence in this domain was incidental. That they did not pass their authority to other women who would in turn have become prominent in the post-Successor generations suggests that female participation in *ḥadīth* transmission was either actively discouraged or not incorporated in a historically significant way.

The contrast with minimal common denominators in the biographies of prominent post-Companion male traditionists is striking. Acclaimed male authorities assiduously collect traditions from a number of authorities and, in turn, transmit these traditions to large numbers of students; their narration networks include both kin and non-kin authorities; they learn and

[63] For an elucidation of these terms, see Ibn Ḥajar, *Taqrīb*, 1:24–25. For biographies of Karīma bint al-Miqdād, see al-Mizzī, *Tahdhīb*, 35:293, and Ibn Ḥajar, *Taqrīb*, 2:657; and for those of Umm al-Aswad al-Khuzā'iyya, see al-Mizzī, *Tahdhīb*, 35:328, and Ibn Ḥajar, *Taqrīb*, 2:664.

transmit traditions on a wide range of subjects; and, finally, they are described in the biographical literature as discerning transmitters with knowledge of the legal relevance and application of traditions.[64]

The underrepresentation of ʻAlid women in the Sunnī *isnād*s is a final feature of the decline that merits mention here. It would not be unreasonable to expect that women descended from ʻAlī b. Abī Ṭālib would be well represented in the collections analyzed here. ʻAlī, the cousin of Muḥammad and the husband of his daughter Fāṭima, is a revered member of the Prophet's household in both the Shīʻī and Sunnī traditions. His descendants (ʻAlids) similarly were accorded a special status in both sects, albeit at a more exalted level in the Shīʻī one.[65] If there was one group of women among whom we would expect to find active and prolific female *ḥadīth* transmitters, it is among the ʻAlid women, who, by virtue of their relationship with ʻAlī, were members of the Prophet's extended household. In Shīʻī historical memory, some of these women are extolled for their roles in Ḥusayn's struggle for the caliphate and their participation in the Battle of Karbalāʼ (61/680).[66] A few of them are famed for eloquent verbal defenses of Ḥusayn and lamentations over the losses at Karbalāʼ.[67] Given their lineage and status, we might expect that they would participate in collecting and transmitting traditions from members of their own household as well as from other Companions.

[64] Examples of the most-celebrated men in early *ḥadīth* transmission include ʻUrwa b. al-Zubayr, al-Zuhrī, and Sufyān al-Thawrī. All of them earned superlative praise as *ḥadīth* scholars and jurists. Such was the reputation of these men that most other male transmitters did not approximate their fame. Men of lesser rank than these three who were nonetheless prominent and prolific *ḥadīth* authorities include Maymūn b. Mihrān, Nāfiʻ (the *mawlā* of ʻAbd Allāh b. ʻUmar, d. ca. 117/735), and Ibn Jurayj (d. 150/767). While these men differ from each other in the specifics of their recorded accomplishments and reputations, their biographies exhibit the previously outlined criteria for successful transmission. Biographical references for these scholars in Ibn Ḥajar's *Tahdhīb* are as follows: for ʻUrwa b. al-Zubayr, see 7:159–62; for al-Zuhrī, see 9:385–90; for Sufyān al-Thawrī, see 4:101–4; for Maymūn b. Mihrān, see 10:348–50; for Nāfiʻ, see 10:368–70; and for Ibn Jurayj, see 6:352–55.

[65] This undisputed fact of kinship gave rise to contested interpretations of religious authority and political succession in the Sunnī and Shīʻī traditions. For the purposes of our analysis, this schism should not obscure the consensus that members of the Prophet's household were granted an elevated status in the Sunnī tradition also.

[66] Several studies have examined the lives of these women. Contemporary Muslim scholars have been interested in them not only for their historical roles but as exemplars for modern Muslim women. One such example is Sukayna bint al-Ḥusayn, as discussed later in the chapter.

[67] See, for example, the speeches of Zaynab bint ʻAlī and Umm Kulthūm bint ʻAlī as recorded in Ibn Abī Ṭāhir al-Ṭayfūr (d. 280/893), *Balāghāt al-Nisāʼ* (Beirut: Dār al-Aḍwāʼ, 1999), 31–36.

Only two ʿAlid women, Fāṭima bint al-Ḥusayn b. ʿAlī b. Abī Ṭālib (d. 110/728) and Fāṭima bint ʿAlī b. Abī Ṭālib (d. 117/735) appear in the *isnād*s of the compilations studied here.[68] Fāṭima bint ʿAlī is credited with a scant two traditions and Fāṭima bint al-Ḥusayn with seven.[69] Surprisingly, Sukayna bint al-Ḥusayn (d. 117/735), Muḥammad's great-granddaughter who was among the most prominent women in the annals of early Islam, does not appear in the *isnād*s of any of the selected compilations. Celebrated in Sunnī and Shīʿī sources as an intelligent, articulate, and literary figure, Sukayna resembles ʿĀ'isha bint Ṭalḥa in many respects.[70] In his brief entry on her, Ibn Ḥibbān states that she transmitted from the people of her household to Kūfan traditionists. None of these transmissions is recorded in the major canonical Sunnī literature. The absence of these ʿAlid women from the *isnād*s examined here suggests that sectarian interests may have influenced the compilers of the selected collections, all of whom were Sunnī.[71]

[68] For the biography of Fāṭima bint al-Ḥusayn, see al-Mizzī, *Tahdhīb*, 35:254–40; and for that of Fāṭima bint ʿAlī, see al-Mizzī, *Tahdhīb*, 35:263. In a section entitled "A listing of women who did not narrate from the Prophet but from his wives and other women," Ibn Saʿd provides biographical entries for several female descendants of ʿAlī, including Umm Kulthūm and Zaynab, daughters of ʿAlī and Fāṭima. See Ibn Saʿd, *al-Ṭabaqāt*, 8:339–49. Only three of them, namely Fāṭima bint ʿAlī b. Abī Ṭālib, Fāṭima bint al-Ḥusayn, and Sukayna bint al-Ḥusayn, are listed as transmitters in Ibn Ḥibbān's *Kitāb al-Thiqāt*, 2:217 and 2:436.

[69] Fāṭima bint al-Ḥusayn's network is broader than Fāṭima bint ʿAlī's. The few traditions that these women are credited with are included primarily in the *Musnad* of Ibn Ḥanbal, a less selective collection than the *Ṣaḥīḥ*s of al-Bukhārī and Muslim. Ibn Ḥanbal also devoted a separate work to selected transmissions of the *ahl al-bayt*: *Juz' fī-hi Musnad Ahl al-Bayt* (Beirut: Mu'assasat al-Kutub al-Thaqāfiyya, 1988).

[70] For further biographical information on Sukayna, see Sayyid Muḥsin al-Amīn al-ʿĀmilī, *Aʿyān al-Shīʿa*, 7:274. She is the subject of a historical biography by ʿĀ'isha ʿAbd al-Raḥmān (Bint al-Shāṭi') entitled *Sukayna bint al-Ḥusayn* (Cairo: Dār al-Hilāl, n.d.). Sukayna's prominence in the historical sources has attracted the attention of Western scholars as well. See, for example, Jean Claude Vadet, "Une personnalité féminine du Ḥiǧāz au Ier/VIIe siècle: Sukayna, petite-fille de ʿAlī," *Arabica* 4 (1957): 261–87. In a similar vein, the absence of Nafīsa bint al-Ḥasan (145–208/762–824) from the Sunnī *isnād*s is striking. She is extolled in Sunnī and Shīʿī literature for being a scholar and an ascetic. Her tomb in Cairo is a popular site of saint veneration and Ibn Khallikān records that she taught *ḥadīth* to al-Shāfiʿī. See Ibn Khallikān, *Wafayāt al-Aʿyān* (Beirut: Dār al-Thaqāfa, 1968) 5:423–24.

[71] For a more detailed analysis of the record of Shīʿī women's *ḥadīth* transmission, see my chapter, "Women in Imāmī Biographical Collections," in *Law and Tradition in Classical Islamic Thought*, ed. Michael Cook et al. The levels of women's *ḥadīth* transmission in Imāmism are even lower than those in Sunnism because of the differing emphases on *ḥadīth* learning in these sectarian milieux.

COMPARISON OF *ISNĀD* EVIDENCE WITH ADDITIONAL HISTORICAL SOURCES

Having extracted a bleak picture of the number of women represented in the *isnād*s in the post-Companion generations, we can ask if the selected Sunnī compilations accurately reflect historical patterns. That is, how can we ascertain that the *isnād* evidence does in fact portray more than merely the selection criteria of a few Sunnī compilers in the third/ninth and fourth/tenth centuries, and that women were actually not active on a larger scale? For example, as we have just seen, Sukayna is said to have relayed reports to Kūfan transmitters, but this activity is not represented in the major Sunnī collections. There are several avenues for exploring these questions.

Ibn Sa'd's *Ṭabaqāt* offers perhaps one of the strongest affirmations that our *isnād* evidence is not misleading. It is a particularly intriguing portrayal of female participation in *ḥadīth* transmission because it predates the compilation of most of the canonical and noncanonical collections. Ibn Sa'd was therefore uninfluenced by the relative contributions of his subjects to the compilations selected for this study, all of which were composed after his death. This is in contrast to the post-fourth-century biographers, who might have been affected by their subjects' status in the canonical Sunnī *ḥadīth* collections that they studied. Ibn Sa'd's biographical entries on women, focusing on the Companions and Successors, confirm the picture of largely incidental *ḥadīth* transmission. While some women, among them 'Amra bint 'Abd al-Raḥmān, Ṣafiyya bint Shayba, and Mu'ādha bint 'Abd Allāh, are described as knowledgeable with respect to 'Ā'isha's traditions, Ibn Sa'd provides no indication that women occupied themselves with the collection and dissemination of traditions at the level of luminaries such as 'Urwa b. al-Zubayr. Rather, he confirms that women's learning and teaching of *ḥadīth* was incidental and took place in contexts such as moralistic storytelling for popular audiences. Known as *quṣṣāṣ*, those engaged in such storytelling were popular preachers whose social stature varied greatly.[72] While some were noted for perspicacious sermons, others were condemned as charlatans. In this vein, Ibn Sa'd cites a report that Umm al-Ḥasan al-Baṣrī used to engage in storytelling to women, but he does not elaborate on her

[72] For an overview, see *EI*², s.v. "Ḳāṣṣ." For a more detailed study of popular preaching in classical Islam, see Jonathan Berkey, *Popular Preaching and Religious Authority in the Medieval Islamic Near East* (Seattle: University of Washington Press, 2001).

reputation in this regard.[73] In such contexts, Umm al-Ḥasan may well have incorporated Muḥammad's reports into her stories.

Historiographically, Ibn Sa'd's work is especially interesting for its apparent disregard for the *ḥadīth* contribution of several women who were praised by later historians and *ḥadīth* critics. As mentioned in Chapter 1, he is minimally interested in 'Ā'isha's contributions as a *muḥadditha* and dwells more on her relations with the co-wives. Likewise, Ibn Sa'd's frugal entries for most of the prolific female Successors discussed earlier give little indication that these women were respected *ḥadīth* transmitters. Umm al-Dardā', for example, is honored in post-fifth-century literature as a *faqīha* but is not even granted an entry in the volume of Ibn Sa'd's work that is devoted to women. Rather, she appears only in an *isnād* in the entry about her husband, Abū al-Dardā'.[74]

In all likelihood, Ibn Sa'd's attitude to the *ḥadīth* participation of his female subjects reflects an early-third-century perception of women's roles in *ḥadīth* transmission. His life (ca. 168–230/784–845) fell squarely within the period of decline in women's *ḥadīth* participation. Given the negligible participation of women in *ḥadīth* transmission in the world about him, Ibn Sa'd probably felt little reason to dwell on or glorify the accomplishments of early female narrators. This point is reinforced when we note that many post-fifth-century biographers and historians were more laudatory than Ibn Sa'd of female Companions' and Successors' contributions.[75] The shift in perspective is not coincidental but rather reflects changes in women's participation in *ḥadīth* transmission: the fifth/eleventh century marks the reentry of women into this domain of religious learning. From the fifth/eleventh century through the Mamlūk period, there is a marked increase in the ranks of celebrated female *ḥadīth* transmitters. Being cognizant of this evolution helps us understand the historical considerations that may have shaped Ibn Sa'd's relative silence on female narrators. His cursory treatment of female transmission, even as it suggests broad participation among

[73] Ibn Sa'd, *al-Ṭabaqāt*, 8:350. The report in Arabic employs the verb *qaṣṣa* (the mother of Usāma b. Zayd reports "*ra'aytu Umm al-Ḥasan taquṣṣu 'alā al-nisā'*"), thereby signaling Umm al-Ḥasan's engagement in the realm of popular preaching/storytelling.

[74] Ibn Sa'd, *al-Ṭabaqāt*, 7 (part 2):117–18.

[75] I have touched on this issue previously in Chapter 1 in my discussion of 'Ā'isha and other prominent female Companions. In this chapter too, I have noted that the reputations of Umm al-Dardā', Ḥafṣa bint Sīrīn, and Mu'ādha grow with time, a phenomenon partly attributable to the increasing circulation and importance of the canonical and noncanonical compilations.

the Companions, confirms the picture of decline thereafter as suggested by the *isnād* evidence.

In addition to historiographical analysis, we can consider data from the *rijāl* works, which do not always mirror the *isnād* evidence. Whereas some *rijāl* works are strictly concerned with transmitters in the canonical and noncanonical *ḥadīth* compilations, others have a broader scope.[76] Even al-Mizzī in his *Tahdhīb al-Kamāl* and Ibn Ḥajar in his *Taqrīb al-Tahdhīb*, for all that their stated focus is on the canonical collections, did not confine themselves exclusively to these works in gathering information on the teachers and students of narrators who merit biographical entries.[77] Additionally, *rijāl* works sometimes list women who do not appear at all in the *isnād*s of my data set. For example, Ibn Ḥajar's *Taqrīb al-Tahdhīb* lists three different women, all named 'Amra, as narrators from 'Ā'isha.[78] However, these three women are not credited with transmission in any of the major Sunnī compilations. Other such examples may be found in Ibn Ḥibbān's *Kitāb al-Thiqāt*, a *rijāl* work that does not focus on the canonical works as do al-Mizzī's and Ibn Ḥajar's works.

Though some discrepancies between the *isnād*s and *rijāl* collections emerge in the lists of female Companions and early Successors, the overall picture of decline in participation over the first three centuries remains

[76] The science of describing narrators and assessing their reliability (*'ilm al-rijāl*) formed an auxiliary branch of *ḥadīth* scholarship and produced a vast corpus of biographical literature. An introduction to the history and literature of this field is found in *EI*², s.v. "Ridjāl." In this article, Juynboll classifies many medieval biographical dictionaries, local histories, and chronicles under the general rubric of *rijāl* literature, given their authors' concern with *ḥadīth* transmitters. He thus includes in his description of *rijāl* literature such disparate works as the regional histories of al-Khaṭīb al-Baghdādī and Ibn 'Asākir as well as Ibn al-'Imād's chronicle *Shadharāt al-Dhahab*.

[77] Al-Mizzī's *Tahdhīb al-Kamāl*, for example, is a vastly expanded reworking of the still unpublished *al-Kamāl fī Ma'rifat al-Rijāl* of 'Abd al-Ghanī al-Maqdisī (d. 600/1203). In it, al-Mizzī gathers information not only from the six canonical Sunnī collections, but also from lesser works, some of which are not available to us today. For example, al-Mizzī cites Ḥafṣa as an authority for traditions from Khalīfa b. Ka'b, Rufay' Abū al-'Āliya al-Riyāḥī, and Umm al-Ḥasan al-Baṣrī. However, these people do not appear in her *isnād*s in the selected compilations. Also, al-Mizzī lists eleven men who are said to have transmitted from her. Only seven appear in the *isnād*s of the selected collections.

[78] Ibn Ḥajar, *Taqrīb*, 2:652, nos. 8689, 8690, and 8693. Another important work in this regard is Ibn Ḥajar's *al-Iṣāba*, which concerns itself only with Companions. Ibn Ḥajar's aim in this work was to record all Companions for whom he possessed some historical evidence. Throughout his volumes on women, we see evidence of broader participation on the part of female Companions than is recorded in the selected compilations. For example, Asmā' bint Sa'īd (*al-Iṣāba*, 12:112, #42) and Ḥayya bint Abī Ḥayya (*al-Iṣāba*, 12:209, #318) are both described as narrating from Muḥammad. However, their transmissions are not included in the *ḥadīth* compilations analyzed here.

the same. Ibn Ḥibbān's work, arranged according to *ṭabaqāt*, lists approximately 200 women in the Companion generation. In subsequent generations, the numbers drop as follows: eighty-six women in the Successor generation (*al-tābi'ūn*), ten women in the next generation (*atbā' al-tābi'īn*), and only two women in the following one (*man rawā 'an atbā' al-tābi'īn*).

Lastly, it is important to consider sources which offer broader perspectives on social, political, and intellectual culture than the biographical literature surveyed earlier. The picture that emerges from the *Ta'rīkh Dimashq* of Ibn 'Asākir is particularly instructive.[79] Ibn 'Asākir covers the history of Damascus from the rise of Islam up to his lifetime (i.e., the late sixth/twelfth century).[80] He includes approximately 125 entries for women whose claims to fame include kinship to the ruling elite, prominence as ascetics, *ḥadīth* transmission, and literary and poetic talents. In Ibn 'Asākir's biographies, female Companions and Successors, as *ḥadīth* transmitters, greatly outnumber their counterparts in subsequent generations up to the fifth/eleventh century. There are, moreover, details in the *Ta'rīkh Dimashq* that round out our view of female participation in the cultural and religious spheres. For example, Ibn 'Asākir chronicles second- and third-century poetesses and ascetics whose accomplishments reveal that women's declining participation in *ḥadīth* transmission was not mirrored in other arenas.[81]

79 The *Ta'rīkh Baghdād* of al-Khaṭīb al-Baghdādī, another local history, does not serve our purposes as well because it features biographical entries for only thirty-two women. Many of these women, moreover, lived after the fourth/tenth century, a period that is not the focus of this chapter.

80 There are also entries for various pre-Islamic personalities such as Eve, the wife of Ādam, and Bilqīs, the queen of Sheba, and for prominent early Muslims who are not known to have been residents of Damascus, among them the wives of Muḥammad.

81 Examples of poetesses in the *Ta'rīkh Dimashq* include Ḥubāba, 69:88–93, and Rayyā (the caretaker of Zayd b. Mu'āwiya's children), 69:158–61. Examples of ascetic women include Fāṭima bint Mujlī, 70:39–40, and Karīma bint al-Ḥasḥās al-Muzaniyya, who was a student of Umm al-Dardā', 70:49–53. While Ibn 'Asākir does not provide death dates for them, circumstantial evidence indicates that they lived in the late first/seventh and early second/eighth centuries. With respect to women of the post-Companion generations, Ibn 'Asākir, like Ibn Sa'd and Ibn Ḥajar, records the participation of several women who do not appear in the *isnāds* of the selected *ḥadīth* compilations. Among them is Zaynab bint Sulaymān b. 'Alī b. 'Abd Allāh b. 'Abbās (d. ca. mid-third/ninth century), who narrated from her father, Sulaymān b. 'Alī, to a number of other men including the 'Abbāsid caliph al-Ma'mūn (d. 218/833); see Ibn 'Asākir, *Ta'rīkh Dimashq*, 69:169–70. See also Nadwi, *al-Muḥaddithāt*, 252–54, for references to a few other women who transmitted traditions during this period of decline.

The salient points regarding female *ḥadīth* transmission among the generations of post-Companion women up to the early fourth/tenth century are as follows: the *isnād* data from the selected Sunnī collections indicate that women's transmission was recorded or incorporated primarily in the first two links of chains of transmission (ca. 11–95). To a greatly reduced extent, there are women who appear as the third and fourth links of these chains (ca. 95–180). There are no women who occur beyond the fourth link up to the time of the compilers of the selected collections (ca. 180–311). Thus, the *isnād* data strongly suggest that women's contributions to *ḥadīth* transmission diminished over the course of the first/seventh century and were negligible thereafter until the early fourth/tenth century. Additional historical sources corroborate *isnād* data and confirm a steep decline in the numbers of female *ḥadīth* transmitters from the end of the first/seventh century onward. Whereas the *isnād* data cover the period up to the early fourth/tenth century, biographical works, such as *Ta'rīkh Dimashq*, extend our purview and suggest minimal female participation into the early fifth/eleventh century.

EXPLAINING THE DECLINE

The rapid decline and disappearance of women's *ḥadīth* participation in early Islam is related to the following factors:

1. The evolution of *ḥadīth* transmission into a specialized field with higher standards for and greater scrutiny of the qualifications of *ḥadīth* transmitters.
2. The debate between the proponents of Prophetic traditions (*ahl al-ḥadīth*) and their opponents over the use of *ḥadīth* as a primary source of law and creed.
3. The proliferation of journeys to collect traditions (*riḥla fī ṭalab al-'ilm*) as a mainstay of *ḥadīth* transmission.

Each of these developments has been examined in previous scholarship with a view toward understanding the sciences of *ḥadīth*, Islamic theology, and the authenticity of *ḥadīth* literature. Extending the analysis to social history, I posit a correlation between the specified trends and the decline of women's *ḥadīth* participation. In doing so, I advance the central thesis of this book that evolving social uses of religious knowledge throughout Islamic history dramatically impacted women's roles, alternately promoting or inhibiting their religious participation in the public arena.

In the decades after Muḥammad's death, reports of his words and deeds served the general purposes of defining and promoting Islamic mores and piety. In addition to these traditions, the Qur'ān, Companion reports, and transmitted practices from the time of Muḥammad were authoritative in determining correct behavior. *Ḥadīth*, later defined technically as sayings from or about Muḥammad communicated via an *isnād*, had yet to establish their primacy as sources of law, creed, and ritual. Indeed, a number of prominent Companions were reluctant to record reports from Muḥammad in writing for fear of diverting attention and authority from the Qur'ān. Nonetheless, it is likely that Muslims were keen to extract as much information as possible about Muḥammad before the passing of the Companion generation. This was later termed the era of registering or documenting religious knowledge (*taqyīd al-'ilm*), and it was marked by little concern with whether the bearer of such information could analyze or interpret the conveyed text in legal or theological terms.[82] Given the rudimentary state of Islamic law, Qur'ānic exegesis, and other arenas in which Muḥammad's sayings would come to play a significant role, these reports themselves likely served ephemeral purposes by resolving disputes as they arose and guiding believers in moments of anxiety and uncertainty.[83]

Toward the end of the first century, the status of Prophetic traditions grew. Their social uses multiplied in proportion to their perceived utility. Scholars increasingly drew on this material to derive and support rulings on all manner of issues. The ruling elite, too, realized the potential of drawing on Muḥammad's legacy through his sayings to fortify their edicts and rights to power. Muḥammad b. Sīrīn's widely cited report succinctly captures the heightened caution that accompanied this proliferation of *ḥadīth* to advance a host of theological, sectarian, and political agendas. The report captures the transition from reporting Muḥammad's sayings without a concern for *isnād*s to a preoccupation with formal attribution to authorities who could claim Muḥammad himself as their ultimate source of knowledge:

They did not [customarily] ask about the *isnād* [of a *ḥadīth*]. When the *fitna* took place, they asked about it. They used to look at the adherents of the *sunna*, and their

[82] See Ṣubḥī al-Ṣāliḥ, *'Ulūm al-Ḥadīth wa-Muṣṭalaḥuhu* (Beirut: Dār al-'Ilm li'l-Malāyīn, 1991), 41–49, for his summary of different approaches to the writing of *ḥadīth* in this early period.

[83] See Donner, *Narratives*, chapter 2 (especially pp. 90–92) for his explanation of early Islamic piety and the function of Muḥammad's reports in this context.

ḥadīth were accepted, and at the innovators (*ahl al-bid'a*), and their *ḥadīth* were rejected.[84]

Scholars of the modern period have disagreed about the *fitna* (political upheaval) that is referred to in this tradition. The choices include events such as the assassination of 'Uthmān (35/656), the subsequent Battle of the Camel (35/656), and the revolt of 'Abd Allāh b. al-Zubayr (64–73/684–92).[85] Irrespective of whether the earlier or later *fitna* is being referred to in Ibn Sīrīn's report, there is evidence of ample political, theological, and sectarian strife in the second half of the first century.

Civil wars and ideological differences gave rise to propaganda in the form of fabricated Prophetic sayings. Storytellers (*quṣṣāṣ*) and popular preachers who saw no harm in buttressing their entertaining lore and moralistic teachings with false ascriptions to Muḥammad exacerbated this situation. Because these storytellers and preachers often performed for mass audiences, the impact of their forgeries was manifold as compared to forged *ḥadīth* circulating in limited partisan political or theological circles. The problem of forgery and the rising interest in *ḥadīth* for social, legal, and political regulation spurred a preoccupation with the qualifications of transmitters and with ascertaining their reliability and moral rectitude. This environment fostered the professionalization of *ḥadīth* transmission, a diffuse movement that scholars and members of the ruling elite encouraged. Their objectives were to promote rigorous standards for studying and transmitting *ḥadīth* and to detect and curtail fabrication in this arena.

Professionalization of *ḥadīth*, like many well-intentioned reforms, had its unintended victims because it introduced criteria that women had little hope of fulfilling. The following demands in particular were disproportionately burdensome: (1) that transmitters display legal acumen when conveying traditions; (2) that students learn *ḥadīth* through oral transmission and direct contact with their teachers (as opposed to written correspondence); and (3) that students unstintingly commit their resources and time to religious learning and acquire as many *ḥadīth* as possible in their lifetime.

Each criterion posed its own challenges for women. Legal training, for example, required not just familiarity with legal discourse and a growing

84 Muslim, *Ṣaḥīḥ*, 1:1:80.

85 For the modern debate over the dating of this tradition, see Schacht, *Origins*, 36–37; Azami, *Studies in Early Hadith Literature*, 212–18; and Juynboll, "The Date of the Great *Fitna*," *Arabica* 20 (1973): 142–59.

corpus of rulings but also knowledge of Arabic grammar, morphology, and rhetoric. Women, aside from a minority in the upper classes, often did not have the wherewithal or time free from domestic obligations to pursue such an education. The requirements of face-to-face meetings with teachers and oral transmission were intended as a safeguard against interpolations and erroneous recording of texts, which were typically copied in unvocalized Arabic, thereby increasing the possibility of mistakes in transmission. The teacher would read the text aloud, and the student would listen and review his own copy to ensure accurate transmission. The requirement of face-to-face pedagogy, however, collided with cultural and religious norms dictating against interaction between men and women who were not related to each other by marriage or within specified degrees of kinship (*maḥram*).[86] Furthermore, during the second/eighth and third/ninth centuries, scholars advocated that students begin studying *ḥadīth* (i.e., seeking traditions from different *ḥadīth* masters) only after demonstrating a good command of Arabic and the ability to memorize and convey texts accurately. According to the fourth-century *ḥadīth* scholar al-Rāmahurmuzī (d. ca. 360/970), Baṣrans encouraged the start of the study of *ḥadīth* around the age of ten, Kūfans around the age of twenty, and Syrians around the age of thirty.[87] Following these recommendations, girls or young women who wished to excel in this arena would have had to begin pursuing their studies around the onset of puberty and/or during their child-bearing years. The dominant culture of domesticity (in the premodern Muslim world and elsewhere) did not encourage such renunciation of familial obligations, nor did women typically enjoy the financial autonomy that would allow them such pursuits.

The following anecdote speaks clearly to the fate of women in the increasingly competitive arena of *ḥadīth* transmission. Ibn Sa‘d reports that al-Zuhrī compared ‘Amra bint ‘Abd al-Raḥmān to ‘Urwa, saying,

> When I heard the *ḥadīth* of ‘Urwa and then those of ‘Amra, I would put more stock by the *ḥadīth* of ‘Urwa. Although I could be sated with her [‘Amra's] *ḥadīth*, ‘Urwa was an inexhaustible sea [of knowledge].[88]

[86] The issue of *maḥram* bonds and the transmission of religious knowledge has been discussed in Chapter 1.

[87] Al-Rāmahurmuzī, *al-Muḥaddith al-Fāṣil*, 187. In Chapter 3, I discuss how the age requirements changed in the classical period (after the fourth/tenth century) so that female participation was again encouraged.

[88] Ibn Sa‘d, *al-Ṭabaqāt*, 5:134.

Whereas 'Amra built her reputation on transmission primarily from 'Ā'isha, 'Urwa assiduously collected *ḥadīth* from a range of male and female Companions and was recognized for his superior abilities. If 'Amra, a leading female *ḥadīth* transmitter, suffered in this way in al-Zuhrī's estimation, other women with lesser reputations must have fared even worse. Al-Zuhrī's view can be further contextualized in terms of his conversation with al-Hudhalī, cited at the beginning of this chapter, wherein he equates masculinity with the assiduous pursuit of *ḥadīth*. Al-Zuhrī's reported opinion of 'Amra, paired with his comments to al-Hudhalī, further supports the view that increasingly stringent demands help account for the decline of women's role in this domain. Furthermore, this gender association, which is strikingly discordant with the atmosphere that prevailed just a few decades earlier during the lifetimes of 'Ā'isha and Umm Salama, is first recorded from al-Zuhrī. This allows us to locate with more confidence shifting attitudes toward women's *ḥadīth* participation in the late first and early second century, the period spanning al-Zuhrī's lifetime.

Al-Zuhrī was not alone with respect to his standards. The trend of professionalization is widely attested throughout the second and third centuries.[89] The opinion of many scholars is reflected in Ibn Sīrīn's view that "this knowledge [i.e., reports concerning the Prophet] is religion, so investigate whomever you relate from."[90] A few second-century scholars who are identified with exacting standards in the study and critical evaluation of *ḥadīth* are 'Āmir b. Sharāḥīl al-Sha'bī (d. 103/721),[91] Muḥammad b. Sīrīn (d. 110/729), Abū Bakr b. Muḥammad b. Ḥazm (d. 120/738),[92] 'Amr b. Dīnār (d. 126/743),[93] al-Awzā'ī (d. 157/774),[94] and Sufyān al-Thawrī (d. 161/778).[95] In the third century, luminaries such as Yaḥyā b.

[89] The articulation of these standards was a precursor to the more formalized discipline of *isnād* criticism (i.e., *al-jarḥ wa'l-ta'dīl*). The works of al-Rāmahurmuzī (*al-Muḥaddith al-Fāṣil*) and al-Khaṭīb al-Baghdādī (*al-Kifāya fī 'Ilm al-Riwāya*) testify to developments in this field. Both contain detailed descriptions of the qualifications of narrators and the requirements they had to meet in order for their transmissions to be acceptable.

[90] Ibn Sa'd, *al-Ṭabaqāt*, 7 (part 1):141.

[91] Ibn Sa'd, *al-Ṭabaqāt*, 6:171–78; Ibn Ḥajar, *Tahdhīb*, 5:60–63.

[92] al-Dhahabī, *Siyar*, 5:313–14.

[93] Ibn Sa'd, *al-Ṭabaqāt*, 5:353–54; and Ibn Ḥajar, *Tahdhīb*, 8:25–26.

[94] Ibn Sa'd, *al-Ṭabaqāt*, 7 (part 2):185; Ibn Ḥajar, *Tahdhīb*, 6:215–18.

[95] Ibn Sa'd, *al-Ṭabaqāt*, 6:257–60; Ibn Ḥajar, *Tahdhīb*, 4:101–4. See Ṣiddīqī, *Ḥadīth Literature*, 6–7, and Ṣubḥī al-Ṣāliḥ, *'Ulūm al-Ḥadīth wa-Muṣṭalaḥuhu*, 41–49, for the view that these scholars were engaged in the project of regulating the use of *ḥadīth*. Scholars of the history of early Islam have not reached a consensus about the nature of

Maʿīn (d. 233/848),[96] ʿAlī b. al-Madīnī (d. 234/849),[97] Aḥmad b. Ḥanbal (d. 241/855),[98] Abū Zurʿa al-Dimashqī (d. 280/893),[99] and Abū Ḥātim al-Rāzī (d. 277/890)[100] set exacting critical standards for the study and transmission of *ḥadīth*. Exercising influence throughout major urban centers such as Mecca, Medina, Kūfa, Baṣra, Damascus, and Baghdad, none of these scholars is reputed to have studied *ḥadīth* with women nor are any women known to have been among their students. Biographical notices portray them as interacting with other male scholars in an environment marked by intense concern for the place of *ḥadīth* in regulating the articulation of Islamic law, ritual, and creed and for the qualifications of *ḥadīth* transmitters.

The evolving and varied social uses of *ḥadīth* during this period are further confirmed by Mālik b. Anas, the eponymous founder of the Mālikī juristic school, whose life spanned the second century. Mālik was one of several leading jurists advocating strict caution about accepting *ḥadīth* from those not known for legal discernment. In his report that follows, we clearly see the development of a more regulated, specialized engagement with Prophetic traditions.

> I have encountered people in Medina who, had they been asked to pray for rain, would have had their prayers answered. And [though] they have [also] heard much by way of knowledge and *ḥadīth*, I never transmitted [anything] from them. [This is] because they occupied themselves with fear of God and asceticism. This business, that is, teaching *ḥadīth* and pronouncing legal decisions, requires men who have awareness of God, moral scrupulousness, exactitude, knowledge, and understanding, so that they know what comes out of their heads and what the future results of it will be. As for the pious who are not possessed of this exactitude or knowledge, no benefit can be derived from them, nor can they provide valid legal proofs, nor should knowledge be taken from them.[101]

ḥadīth transmission in the first few decades, but there is agreement that this period is likely to have been characterized by informal and primarily oral exchanges of information about Muḥammad. See, for example, al-Ṣāliḥ, *ʿUlūm al-Ḥadīth wa-Muṣṭalaḥuhu*, 14–62, and Donner, *Narratives*, 275–80.

96 Ibn Ḥajar, *Tahdhīb*, 11:245–50.

97 al-Dhahabī, *Siyar*, 11:41–60.

98 al-Dhahabī, *Siyar*, 11:177–358.

99 Ibn Ḥajar, *Tahdhīb*, 6:214–15.

100 al-Dhahabī, *Siyar*, 13:247–63.

101 ʿAbd al-Raḥmān al-Suyūṭī (d. 911/1505), introduction to *Tanwīr al-Ḥawālik Sharḥ ʿalā Muwaṭṭaʾ Mālik wa-Yalīhi Kitāb Isʿāf al-Mubaṭṭaʾ bi-Rijāl al-Muwaṭṭaʾ* (Beirut: al-Maktaba al-Thaqāfiyya, 1973), 5. Al-Suyūṭī's brief introduction to his commentary on Mālik's *al-Muwaṭṭaʾ* is replete with such reports of Mālik's high standards in judging transmitters.

Mālik's advice provides strong evidence of the trend toward creating an elite scholarly corps who possessed an understanding of the role of *ḥadīth* in formulating legal and ritual norms. Such a development sets a markedly different tone from conditions in the decades just after Muḥammad's death, when women were more readily accepted as transmitters of his sayings. In this earlier period, contact or alleged contact with Muḥammad sufficed to confer credibility and authority on a man or woman who wished to transmit reports. From the late first century onward, one could no longer build a reputation simply through association with Muḥammad or someone who had seen him.

Even as Mālik affirms a tightening of standards among jurists, he also casts light on a different and more permissive social use of Prophetic traditions, namely the practice of *ḥadīth* recitation among ascetics and preachers who were not trained in the interpretation and legal application of traditions. Generating anxiety on the part of jurists such as Mālik, they used *ḥadīth* to shape popular understandings of Islam and were widely suspected of forging traditions to inculcate piety. Their motives may have been sound, but their traditions were often no more trusted than those of storytellers, mentioned earlier, and others discredited for fabricating *ḥadīth* to further sectarian agendas. Women likely relayed traditions in such unregulated forums throughout the second/eighth and third/ninth centuries when the compilations selected for this study reveal a decline in women's participation.[102] Yet such participation would not have been documented in the contexts of professionalized *ḥadīth* transmission, an area increasingly committed to the project of articulating Islamic law and creed.

My analysis thus far has examined the decline of women's *ḥadīth* activity as a coincidental, unintended outcome of increasing specialization in the field. A few of our sources also indicate an active resistance to women's *ḥadīth* participation. These can best be understood in the context of a broader debate about the use of *ḥadīth*. In the first and second centuries, traditionists (*ahl al-ḥadīth*) had not yet won widespread support for their view that *ḥadīth* were indeed a source of law secondary only to the Qur'ān. The professionalization of *ḥadīth* study occurred in the midst of a heated battle about the probative value of these reports in deriving Islamic law and theology. While modern scholarship has tended to focus on the Mu'tazilīs as opponents to the traditionists, the battle drew in a number of

102 As noted earlier in this chapter, Ibn Sa'd cites a report that Umm al-Ḥasan al-Baṣrī was seen preaching to women.

groups. Skepticism about the utility of *ḥadīth* is well attested among early Shī'īs, Ḥanafīs, Mālikīs, and Khārijīs.

The debate over *ḥadīth* was at its heart one about the validity of depending on the *isnād*, a tool highly susceptible to corruption, to ascertain the veracity of a report. A host of influential scholars pointed out that it was impossible to establish with complete certainty the accuracy of such transmissions, whether they were relayed by multiple transmitters or just a few of them. Al-Naẓẓām (d. ca. 230/845), an early Mu'tazilī leader, disavowed any source other than reason and Qur'ān.[103] Other scholars occupied different places on the spectrum with respect to accepting *ḥadīth* as a definitive source for law or theology.

Some scholars tried to accommodate the use of *ḥadīth* with the proviso that the transmitters be well-known, legally discerning ones. 'Īsā b. Abān (d. 221/836), an early Ḥanafī jurist, is among those known for articulating this position.[104] Women were disproportionately disadvantaged with respect to legal training, making the traditions they transmitted more susceptible to being rejected as proofs. This handicap contextualizes the report attributed to the Mu'tazilī scholar al-Balkhī, which was cited at the beginning of this chapter. In recording opposition to the use of *ḥadīth* among various early scholars, al-Balkhī gives the example of Mughīra b. Miqsam, a Kūfan authority, who noted that scholars were averse to the reports of women other than Muḥammad's wives.[105] This sentiment is found in non-Mu'tazilī works as well. For example, the fifth/eleventh-century jurist Ibn 'Abd al-Barr cites a similar report on the authority of Yaḥyā b. Dīnār (d. 122/740).[106] Al-Zarkashī relates that the great Iraqi jurist Abū Ḥanīfa reportedly did not accept traditions of women other than 'Ā'isha and Umm Salama in matters of religion.[107]

While discriminating on the basis of the legal discernment of transmitters satisfied some scholars, it only partially addressed the most contentious issue to arise in the battle between traditionists and their opponents, namely the validity of *ḥadīth* transmitted by only one or a few narrators in each

[103] Racha el-Omari, "Accommodation and Resistance: Classical Mu'tazilīs on Ḥadīth," *Journal of Near Eastern Studies* 71 (2012): 231–56.

[104] For a more detailed analysis of his views, see Murteza Bedir, "An Early Response to Shāfi'ī: 'Īsā b. Abān on the Prophetic Report (*Khabar*)," *Islamic Law and Society* 9, no. 3 (2002): 285–311.

[105] al-Balkhī, *Qabūl al-Akhbār wa-Ma'rifat al-Rijāl*, 1:51.

[106] Ibn 'Abd al-Barr, *Kitāb al-Istidhkār* (Cairo: Dār al-Wā'ī, 1993), 19:25.

[107] al-Zarkashī, *al-Baḥr al-Muḥīṭ fī Uṣūl al-Fiqh* (Beirut: Dār al-Kutub al-'Ilmiyya, 2000), 3:371.

generation (known as *khabar al-wāḥid*, pl. *akhbār al-āḥād*).[108] These constituted the vast majority of *ḥadīth*, and the opponents of the traditionists decisively rejected basing law and creed on such flimsy evidence. One scholar suggested that no less than twenty witnesses in each generation should have transmitted a tradition before it could be deemed valid.[109] Other scholars demanded that criteria used for testimony (*shahāda*) should also be applied to *ḥadīth* transmission (*riwāya*) to guard against forgeries and negligence. Based on a Qur'ānic verse (2:282), jurists equate the testimony of two women with that of one man in many cases. When applied to *ḥadīth* transmission, such criteria would diminish the probative value of traditions conveyed by single female transmitters. The cases of the Companions Fāṭima bint Qays and Busra bint Ṣafwān, which I have analyzed in a separate article, reveal how the conflation of the standards for testimony (*shahāda*) and *ḥadīth* transmission (*riwāya*) produced gender-based disparagement of women's transmission.[110]

The cumulative effect of such heightened scrutiny manifests itself in canonical *ḥadīth* collections, all authored by male scholars. Comparison of the incidence of female narrators in two works of comparable length and scope reinforces the earlier observations. Al-Bukhārī, reputed as one of the most stringent compilers, included approximately 7,395 *ḥadīth* in his *Ṣaḥīḥ*. Abū Dāwūd, on the other hand, who is not known to have been as strict as al-Bukhārī, included approximately 5,270 traditions in his *Sunan*.[111] Whereas al-Bukhārī's work features approximately 40 women as transmitters, Abū Dāwūd's contains close to 170. Similarly, there is a significant difference between these two works with respect to the numbers of women in the various links of their *isnād*s as shown in Figure 4.

In terms of the quality of the narrators themselves, the difference between al-Bukhārī's and Abū Dāwūd's implied selection criteria becomes pronounced primarily after the Companion generation. In the Companion generation, both compilers cite the *ḥadīth* of prominent and prolific female Companions, among them the wives of Muḥammad, as well as women

108 For an extensive discussion of such reports and a defense of their use in Islamic law, see Qāḍī Barhūn, *Khabar al-Wāḥid fī al-Tashrī' al-Islāmī wa-Ḥujjiyyatuhu* (Casablanca [?]: Maṭba'at al-Najāḥ al-Jadīda, 1995). In contrast to *āḥād* reports, those that are transmitted by numerous narrators in each generation are known as *mutawātir* reports. According to some scholars, there are only a handful of these reports.

109 el-Omari, "Accommodation and Resistance," 234.

110 See my article "Gender and Legal Authority."

111 The numbers given here do not account for repetitions of traditions or citations of similar variants in either collection.

	Al-Bukhārī, *Ṣaḥīḥ*	Abū Dāwūd, *Sunan*
Link #1	29	64
Link #2	13	89
Link #3	2[112]	12
Link #4	0	1

FIGURE 4: Comparison of Female Narrators in al-Bukhārī's *Ṣaḥīḥ* and Abū Dāwūd's *Sunan*

who are not as well known. Yet in the Successor generation and beyond, al-Bukhārī limits himself to the traditions of women known to have superior reputations as transmitters. These include Muʿādha al-ʿAdawiyya, ʿAmra bint ʿAbd al-Raḥmān, and Ḥafṣa bint Sīrīn. His selection criteria result in a decline of female representation of almost 50 percent between link one and link two (mainly corresponding to the Companion and Successor generations, respectively). As for link three, the only two women are Zaynab bint Abī Salama, who also narrates as links one and two in al-Bukhārī's *Ṣaḥīḥ*, and Muʿādha al-ʿAdawiyya, who also narrates as a link two. Thus, there are no women beyond the early Successor generation who are chosen as transmitters by al-Bukhārī.

In contrast to al-Bukhārī's choices of female Successors with established renown, Abū Dāwūd's female narrators range from the trustworthy (*thiqāt*) to the entirely unknown (*majhūlāt*). Further, many of Abū Dāwūd's female transmitters are not prolific, being credited with only one or two traditions. Abū Dāwūd's lower level of diligence in selecting narrators probably extended to male transmitters as well, yet it is relevant to this study because his standards result in greater female representation than those of al-Bukhārī. The fact that al-Bukhārī included any women at all reveals that he was not opposed to women's transmission as such. Rather, he was probably opposed to the transmission of those who were not deemed highly qualified. Similarly, Abū Dāwūd's greater inclusion of female narrators probably does not signal a more gender egalitarian perspective on his part, but rather less demanding criteria for judging narrators. In other words, Abū Dāwūd has not unearthed prolific and accomplished female transmitters whom al-Bukhārī overlooked.

112 Both of these women, namely Zaynab bint Abī Salama and Muʿādha bint ʿAbd Allāh, also narrate in the first or second link position.

Thus despite the fact that Abū Dāwūd includes nearly eight times as many women in the second link as al-Bukhārī, his compilation is not a testament to a high rate of female accomplishment in *ḥadīth* transmission that is otherwise concealed in al-Bukhārī's work. Rather, a comparison of the quality of female transmitters in both works reinforces the point that women were effectively excluded from meaningful participation in *ḥadīth* transmission from the end of the first/seventh century up to the early fourth/tenth century. Because of the variation in the standards of the compilers, the exclusion of women is more pronounced in the stricter collections.

RIḤLAS AND WOMEN'S TRAVEL

The aforementioned limitations were further exacerbated by the growing popularity of extensive travel in search of traditions, the final factor accounting for the decline of women's presence in this domain. The significant increase in journeys undertaken specifically to collect *ḥadīth* (*riḥla fī ṭalab al-'ilm*) marks a watershed in *ḥadīth* transmission history and is often dated to the mid-second/eighth century.[113] The *riḥla*s are viewed as instrumental in spreading traditions that had previously been circulated primarily within a few cities such as Baṣra, Kūfa, and Damascus.[114]

The observation that traveling to acquire religious knowledge was deemed critical for traditionists is borne out in reports on the accomplishments of numerous successful male *ḥadīth* scholars. One testament to the value attached to such travel is the work of the famed fifth/eleventh-century *ḥadīth* scholar and historian al-Khaṭīb al-Baghdādī. Entitled *Kitāb al-Riḥla fī Ṭalab al-Ḥadīth*, the work presents reports of men reputed to have undertaken arduous journeys in search of *ḥadīth*. Al-Khaṭīb also emphasizes the importance of *riḥla*s by linking them to the experience of prophets revered in Islam.[115]

Whereas the traditional Muslim view traces the *riḥla* to practices of the Companions during the lifetime of Muḥammad and immediately

113 al-Ṣāliḥ, *Muqaddima fī 'Ulūm al-Ḥadīth*, 50–62. Although Ṣubḥī al-Ṣāliḥ does not explicitly present a chronology for the shift from regionalism to a greater spread of *isnād*s, he does discuss the phenomenon more extensively than other modern *ḥadīth* scholars.

114 These developments are described in the following works: Schacht, *Origins*, 5; Juynboll, *Muslim Tradition*, 66; and Donner, *Narratives*, 280. See also Goldziher, *Muslim Studies*, vol. 2, chapter 6, "Ṭalab al-Ḥadīth."

115 For example, the story of Moses undertaking travels with Khiḍr is presented as the prime example of journeying for the sake of religious edification; see al-Khaṭīb al-Baghdādī, *Kitāb al-Riḥla fī Ṭalab al-Ḥadīth*, in Ṣubḥī al-Badrī al-Sāmarrā'ī, *Majmū'at Rasā'il fī 'Ulūm al-Ḥadīth* (Medina: al-Maktaba al-Salafiyya, 1969), 50–53.

thereafter, Juynboll argues that the spread of such *riḥla*s cannot have been earlier than the mid-second/eighth century.[116] Juynboll's hypothesis draws its support from a tradition claiming that the first *ḥadīth* transmitter to have undertaken extensive *riḥla*s purely for the sake of *ḥadīth* was Maʿmar b. Rāshid (d. 153/770).[117] Disagreement over the precise chronological origins of the *riḥla* aside, there is sufficient historical evidence that such journeys proliferated around the middle of the second/eighth century. Numerous *isnād*s reflect a period of regionalism (i.e., transmission within regional centers) for the first century and a half of transmission followed by the dissemination of these traditions to other centers of learning. This chronology places the increase in importance of the *riḥla* in the mid-second/eighth century, a period that coincides with the decline in the record of women's *ḥadīth* participation.

*Riḥla*s to disseminate *ḥadīth* were driven by the imperatives of preference for direct, oral transmission and the need to bolster one's reputation in the field, as well as the more ethereal promise of divine reward. Anecdotes about men traveling great distances to authenticate a single *ḥadīth* abound in Muslim tradition literature. The following account of a *riḥla* illustrates well the need to hear a report directly from the best available source:

> It is reported that Jābir b. ʿAbd Allāh said, "I heard of a man from among the Companions who narrated a *ḥadīth* that I had not heard from him [i.e., the Prophet] myself. I prepared for the journey and traveled to him [i.e., the man] for a month until I reached al-Shām, and there learned that he was ʿAbd Allāh b. Anīs al-Anṣārī. I sent an emissary to him to tell him that Jābir had come to call . . . I said to him [i.e., ʿAbd Allāh b. Anīs], "I have heard that there is a *ḥadīth* that you have heard from the Prophet on the topic of *maẓālim* that I have not heard. I was afraid that I would die or that you would die before I had a chance to hear it [directly from you].[118]

The corpus of such anecdotes confirms that traveling was deemed indispensable to the career of a transmitter. ʿAbd Allāh b. Aḥmad b. Ḥanbal reports that he asked his father, the renowned scholar and *ḥadīth* critic, whether it is better for a man who seeks knowledge to keep the constant company of one scholar and record what he knows or to travel to different places and hear from a number of scholars. Ibn Ḥanbal advised that it would be better for him to travel and record the knowledge of the Kūfans, the Baṣrans, the

[116] Juynboll, *Muslim Tradition*, 66–70.
[117] Reports such as these in the *awāʾil* ("firsts") genre of tradition literature form the backbone of Juynboll's chronology of early *ḥadīth* transmission.
[118] al-Baghdādī, *Riḥla*, 53–54.

Medinese, and the Meccans directly from their scholars.[119] Yaḥyā b. Maʿīn, a well-known and discriminating traditionist, considered a man who limits himself to local scholars and does not undertake *riḥla*s for *ḥadīth* among the four types of men from whom one cannot expect to garner religious knowledge.[120] In another anecdote, the critic Ibn ʿAdī encounters his dead colleague Ibn al-Mubārak in a dream. "What has God decreed for you?" asks Ibn ʿAdī. Ibn al-Mubārak responds, "He has forgiven me because of the travels I undertook in search of *ḥadīth*."[121]

The aforementioned account about Jābir b. ʿAbd Allāh exemplifies characteristics of the *riḥla* that put such an endeavor beyond the capacity of most women of early Islamic society. Jābir's story presupposes the wherewithal to undertake a month's journey alone, the possibility of unmediated contact between himself and ʿAbd Allāh b. Anīs, and independence from daily domestic obligations. While male *ḥadīth* transmitters with the requisite dedication could follow in Jābir's footsteps, women faced almost insurmountable hurdles. It is telling that many of the prolific female Successors were distinguished by their ties to prominent female Companions and flourished in the period before the *riḥla*s gained importance. Women such as ʿAmra bint ʿAbd al-Raḥmān and Zaynab bint Abī Salama were authorities mainly for the *ḥadīth* of female members of their own households, and their range was confined to Medina. Even Muʿādha al-ʿAdawiyya, who established her reputation in Baṣra as an authority for ʿĀ'isha's traditions (originating from Medina), is not known to have traveled to multiple Companions to seek out their traditions. Thus, the accomplished early female transmitters represent the localized reproduction of religious knowledge, precisely the type of transmission that the critic Yaḥyā b. Maʿīn deemed unworthy of "true" *ḥadīth* scholars.

The marginalization of women from the *riḥla* can be partly linked to religious constraints on women traveling alone. The Qur'ān does not explicitly prohibit women's travel. Rather, in the first two centuries of Islamic history, the period coinciding with the initial decline of women's *ḥadīth* participation, the restrictions on female travel can be traced to *ḥadīth* or to early legal opinions.[122] For example, in a tradition whose versions circulated in the Ḥijāzi and Iraqi regional centers, a woman is prohibited from traveling without her *maḥram* (husband, male guardian,

119 al-Baghdādī, *Riḥla*, 46–47.
120 al-Baghdādī, *Riḥla*, 47.
121 al-Baghdādī, *Riḥla*, 47.
122 See, for example, the traditions in Muslim, *Ṣaḥīḥ*, 5:1:87–95.

or a male relative whom she cannot legally wed). Textual variations in the tradition are primarily related to the amount of time specified for the journey (from half a day to three days) as well as to the context in which the travel may be undertaken. Whereas some of the traditions attributed to Muḥammad are clearly concerned with travel for the purposes of pilgrimage, others imply a more general prohibition. Collectively, the various versions of the traditions served to restrict almost all travel that women might have undertaken for economic, educational, personal, or religious reasons unless accompanied by *maḥram*.

Juristic opinions as reported in early legal sources reflect an overwhelming consensus on the issue of women's travel and do not depart from the general prohibition implied in the *ḥadīth* on the topic. The discouragement of women's solitary travel appears to have been so thorough that some jurists contemplated waiving the requirement of an accompanying *maḥram* only for the religious duty (*farḍ*) of Ḥajj. Jurists disagreed as to whether the obligation to perform the Ḥajj remained in effect for unmarried women who had no *maḥram*. Ibn Abī Shayba cites the agreement of a majority of jurists that if no *maḥram* was available for an unmarried woman, she was not obliged to perform Ḥajj.[123] He records only two opinions, those of Ibn Sīrīn and al-Ḥasan al-Baṣrī, to the effect that women in such situations may perform the Ḥajj in a company of women that guarantees their safety. Mālik b. Anas and al-Shāfiʿī express similar views in their own works.[124] Depending on how one interprets the opinion of ʿĀʾisha as cryptically reported by Ibn Abī Shayba, she may have been the lone voice of dissent on the *maḥram* issue.[125] When asked about the necessity of women traveling with a *maḥram*, ʿĀʾisha is said to have pointed out that not all women have one. The modern compiler of ʿĀʾisha's legal thought and her opinions (*fatwā*s) has interpreted this to mean that ʿĀʾisha supported the right of a woman to travel without a *maḥram* in all necessary circumstances, not just for the Ḥajj.[126]

ʿĀʾisha's possible dissent notwithstanding, there is little reason to doubt that the restrictions on solitary travel hindered women's ability to participate in *ḥadīth* transmission. It is true that women could and did accompany

[123] Ibn Abī Shayba, *Muṣannaf* (Beirut: Dār al-Tāj, 1989), 4:477–78. The following authorities are recorded as holding the opinion that the obligation of Ḥajj is voided for women who are unmarried and have no *maḥram*: al-Ḥasan al-Baṣrī; Ibrāhīm al-Nakhaʿī; ʿĀmir b. Sharāḥīl al-Shaʿbī; Ṭāwūs; ʿIkrima; and ʿUmar b. ʿAbd al-ʿAzīz.

[124] Mālik, *al-Muwaṭṭaʾ*, 1:569, and al-Shāfiʿī, *Kitāb al-Umm*, 2:164–72.

[125] Ibn Abī Shayba, *Muṣannaf*, 3:386.

[126] al-Dukhayyil, *Mawsūʿat Fiqh ʿĀʾisha*, 369.

men on their journeys for Ḥajj or trade and in the process learned traditions from various locales as indicated by biographies of women from the classical era. Yet a hallmark of the *riḥla*, as exemplified by Jābir b. ʿAbd Allāh's tradition mentioned earlier, was the ability to undertake journeys alone and unfettered by domestic or financial limitations. It is, therefore, not a coincidence that women's participation in *ḥadīth* shows a precipitous decline when the *riḥla* came into vogue. The *riḥla* movement was especially detrimental to women's participation from the mid-second/eighth century until approximately the fifth/eleventh century when developments such as the increased acceptance of written transmission mitigated the imperative for oral, face-to-face contact between teachers and students.

CONCLUSION

This chapter has presented empirical evidence of women's diminishing participation in *ḥadīth* transmission from the time of the Companions until the compilation of the major Sunnī *ḥadīth* collections. In the broadest sense, patterns of decline in women's role in *ḥadīth* transmission mirror trends previously observed in other historical studies on Muslim women. Several works have shown how women's range of activity, options, and freedoms suffered setbacks after the early decades of Islamic history. Most of these studies identify the transition of Muslim society from a tribal culture to an imperial one as the major catalyst for the reduction in women's status. This shift was accompanied by the absorption not only of elements of the more urbanized Byzantine and Sassanian cultures but also of patriarchal structures inherent in the neighboring religious traditions of Judaism, Christianity, and Zoroastrianism. The consensus in such studies is that foreign cultural and religious accretions, combined with elements of Arabian tribal patriarchy, were sanctified as Islamic religious norms and negatively affected Muslim women's roles from the beginnings of the Muslim imperial expansion up to the modern period.

This line of analysis is evident in Leila Ahmed's *Women and Gender in Islam*, which surveys Muslim women's history to extract patterns and a theory of Muslim gender relations. In this work, Ahmed asserts that the gender egalitarianism of Islam was undermined during the period of early imperial expansion and cultural assimilation. In her view, the effects of this process are evident from the time of the ʿAbbāsids up to our own times.[127]

127 See Leila Ahmed, *Women and Gender in Islam*, parts I and II, for her elaboration of the idea that women's liberties were limited by borrowings from Mesopotamian cultures that Muslim societies encountered in their early history.

A similar analysis characterizes works that focus on specific periods or areas of women's lives. Muḥammad Abū Shuqqa's *Taḥrīr al-Mar'a fī 'Aṣr al-Risāla* seeks to demonstrate the freedom and public participation of women during the lifetime of Muḥammad as compared to the restrictions placed on women in later times, and in particular, in the modern period.[128] Barbara Stowasser, in *Women in the Qur'ān, Traditions, and Interpretations*, attributes the elaboration of comparatively sparse, vague Qur'ānic references about women into more detailed and misogynistic exegeses to Islam's contact with Judeo-Christian and Zoroastrian patriarchal cultures.[129]

Such conclusions of previous studies, however, are not applicable in the arena of *ḥadīth* transmission. Damascus and Baṣra, urban areas with strong Christian influences, witnessed the extraordinary careers of Umm al-Dardā' al-Ṣughrā, Mu'ādha bint 'Abd Allāh, and Ḥafṣa bint Sīrīn, all prominent ascetics. As suggested by Rkia Cornell, ascetic Muslim women were probably influenced by their Christian counterparts in these cities, but this did not diminish their ability to participate in the transmission of religious knowledge. And it is in these very urban centers that we see the blossoming of the tradition of ascetic piety that would continue to provide a hospitable arena for women after their marginalization from *ḥadīth* transmission. In Medina and Mecca, on the other hand, 'Amra bint 'Abd al-Raḥmān, Fāṭima bint al-Mundhir, and Zaynab bint Abī Salama emerged as successful female transmitters primarily on the basis of their ties to prominent Companions rather than as independent critics or scholars of tradition. And the lone example of Ṣafiyya bint Shayba is the exception to the overall trend that centers in the Ḥijāz did not sustain an environment that fostered women's involvement.

Most importantly, the analysis in this chapter reveals that the contraction of opportunities for women was due to evolving standards in the field of *ḥadīth* as it concerned the derivation of Islamic law. These

[128] Muḥammad Abū Shuqqa, *Taḥrīr al-Mar'a fī 'Aṣr al-Risāla* (Cairo: Dār al-Qalam, 1999), 1:27–64. Abū Shuqqa states this objective clearly in his introduction, and his work is devoted to presenting evidence from the Qur'ān and *ḥadīth* that reveals women's independence and greater range of action under Prophet Muḥammad.

[129] This point is made in several places throughout Stowasser's work (see, in particular, Stowasser, *Women in the Qur'ān*, 22–24). The view that women's position suffered after the initial conquests and during the imperial expansion of Islam is apparent in a number of earlier, influential studies as well. These include Abbott, "Women and the State in Early Islam," *Journal of Near Eastern Studies* 1 (1942): 106–26; Abbott, *Aishah*; Lichtenstadter, *Women in the Aiyām al-'Arab*; and Gertrude Stern, *Marriage in Early Islam* (London: Royal Asiatic Society, 1939).

transformations include the growing emphasis on legal discernment, the correlated imperative of face-to-face transmission, and the growth of the *riḥla* movement. We cannot credibly link these developments to Byzantine or Sassanian influences but rather should see them as intrinsic to a tradition that was grappling with the place of *ḥadīth* in articulating communal identity and religious obligations.

CHAPTER 3

The Classical Revival

> The *shaykha*, the learned woman, possessed of excellent virtues, the one with the best *isnāds* (*al-musnida*), Umm al-Kirām, Karīma bint Aḥmad b. Muḥammad b. Ḥātim al-Marwaziyya, who lived in Mecca (*ḥaram Allāh*). [W]hen she transmitted *ḥadīth*, she would compare [whatever was being transmitted] with her own copy. She had understanding and knowledge and was virtuous and pious as well. She narrated the *Ṣaḥīḥ* [of al-Bukhārī] numerous times . . . Abū Bakr b. Manṣūr al-Sam'ānī said, "I heard my father mention Karīma, saying, 'Have you ever seen anyone like Karīma?'"[1]

In the second half of the fourth century, after a lag of nearly 250 years, women began to be incorporated anew as respected *ḥadīth* transmitters. This chapter focuses on the fourth/tenth and fifth/eleventh centuries, which were marked by a changing landscape in *ḥadīth* transmission and legal culture such that women's participation, heretofore marginalized, came to be extolled. Biographical dictionaries and chronicles evidence this shift in approximately the mid-fourth/tenth century. An overview from Ibn 'Asākir's *Ta'rīkh Dimashq* and al-Dhahabī's *Siyar A'lām al-Nubalā'* illustrates the point. Ibn 'Asākir's work provides the biographies of approximately fifty women commemorated as transmitters in the first two centuries, only two in the third and fourth centuries, and fifteen in the fifth and sixth centuries.[2] In al-Dhahabī's *Siyar*, there are approximately thirty-five women known for *ḥadīth* transmission in the Companion and Successor generations, only two women in the third and

[1] al-Dhahabī, *Siyar*, 18:233–35.

[2] Bulliet has also noted that there are more entries for women in dictionaries composed after the sixth/twelfth century (see "Women and the Urban Religious Elite," 68–69).

fourth centuries, fourteen in the fifth and sixth centuries, and ten in the seventh century.[3] Further, whereas it is rare to find female teachers mentioned in the biographies of second- and third-century scholars such as al-Awzāʿī, Sufyān al-Thawrī, and Yaḥyā b. Maʿīn, this is not the case for many post-fourth-century scholars. Al-Khaṭīb al-Baghdādī, Ibn ʿAsākir, and al-Dhahabī are but three leading scholars who collected *ḥadīth* from women. Al-Samʿānī (d. 562/1166) identifies sixty-nine female teachers from whom he transmitted *ḥadīth*.[4] Lists of teachers compiled by such scholars further substantiate women's growing influence in this field after the fourth/tenth century.

In addition to quantitative indicators, there is also a marked shift in the qualitative descriptions of women's *ḥadīth* participation. Most women before the third/ninth century merited historical attention for transmitting individual traditions, in many cases only one or two traditions. From the fourth/tenth century onward, in keeping with trends in the arena of *ḥadīth*, women were commemorated for transmitting collections of traditions.[5] In many instances, the activities of later women evince training and a critical sense for the meanings of the works narrated. As a reflection of this trend, the term *muḥadditha* (female transmitter of *ḥadīth* collections) as distinct from *rāwiya* (a woman who narrates a few traditions) is increasingly employed in the biographical literature of the classical period.[6]

[3] There are close to 100 entries on women in al-Dhahabī's *Siyar Aʿlām al-Nubalāʾ*. Approximately forty of these women are not included in this count because they are famed for skills other than *ḥadīth* transmission or are recognized because of their kinship or marital ties to prominent men. Also, this count includes only women who have their own biographical entries but does not account for women who are mentioned only in the course of someone else's biography.

[4] Al-Samʿānī, a *ḥadīth* scholar and biographer, is perhaps best known for his biographical work *al-Ansāb*. For a listing of his teachers, see his work *al-Taḥbīr fī al-Muʿjam al-Kabīr* (Beirut: Dār al-Kutub al-ʿIlmiyya, 1997).

[5] These include major authoritative collections such as the *Ṣaḥīḥ*s of al-Bukhārī and Muslim, minor collections such as the *Arbaʿīnāt* (compilations of forty *ḥadīth* on sundry topics), and also popular, edifying thematic works such as *Kitāb Shukr lillāh* and *Kitāb al-Qanāʿa waʾl-Taʿaffuf* by the third-century ascetic Ibn Abī al-Dunyā (d. 281/894).

[6] In the technical terminology of *ḥadīth* transmission, "*muḥaddith*" and "*muḥadditha*" designate a scholar with knowledge of *ḥadīth* as well as *ḥadīth* criticism (i.e., *man ishtaghala biʾl-ḥadīth riwāyatan wa-dirāyatan*). In reality, this term may have been applied indiscriminately to anyone who transmitted collections of *ḥadīth* extensively regardless of their critical knowledge of the sciences of *ḥadīth*. As I discuss in more detail later in the chapter, the extent to which individual women possessed critical and/or exegetical knowledge of their transmissions is not always clear from their biographies. For an introduction to the use of such titles in the classical period, see Muḥammad b. ʿAbd al-Raḥmān al-Sakhāwī (d. 902/1497), *al-Jawāhir waʾl-Durar fī Tarjamat Shaykh al-Islām Ibn Ḥajar* (Beirut: Dār Ibn Ḥazm, 1999), 1:65–84.

The purpose and practice of female *ḥadīth* transmission in the fourth/tenth century was different from what it had been in the first decades of Islam. Women of the Companion generation were unique in that they often narrated their own experiences and indeed inaugurated a novel tradition with respect to women's roles in religious learning. As discussed in Chapter 1, Companions were relaying traditions about Muḥammad and his community in informal, ad hoc settings as necessitated by the inquiries of early Muslims about rituals and beliefs. The concept of *ḥadīth* as a formalized saying attributed to Muḥammad and conveyed through a proper *isnād* had yet to take root. Additionally, a number of female Companions exercised a formative influence on legal and exegetical discourse through the narration of their reports. By contrast, the *muḥaddithas* of the classical period were trustworthy links in *isnāds*, which served as vehicles for authenticating not just individual traditions but books in their entirety. In this context, women's activities facilitated the blossoming of a book culture in classical Islam.[7] Even more broadly, these practices promoted Sunnī culture as it was coalescing in the fourth/tenth century and thereafter.

Despite the differences with the Companion generation, the revival of women's activities after the fourth/tenth century was anchored in and validated through reference to the remembered actions of female Companions. As discussed in the introduction, this creative borrowing is better understood through reference to Talal Asad's description of the Islamic discursive tradition as "a tradition of Muslim discourse that addresses itself to conceptions of the Islamic past and future, with reference to a particular Islamic practice in the present."[8] Such a tradition seeks to relate past practices, institutions, and social conditions to present ones, and to establish practices for future generations. In so doing, "traditional practices" do not seek to perfectly mimic previous generations. Rather, it is "the practitioners' conceptions of what is *apt performance*, and of how the past is related to present practices, that will be crucial for tradition, not the apparent repetition of an old form."[9] Applied to the fourth/tenth-century contexts of women's *ḥadīth* transmission, Asad's conceptualization elucidates that it was the rethinking and reimagining rather than blind imitation of the tradition of female Companions that enabled the reintegration of women in

[7] See Konrad Hirschler, *The Written Word in the Medieval Arabic Lands* (Edinburgh: Edinburgh University Press, 2012) for a detailed analysis of reading practices in classical Islam.

[8] Talal Asad, "The Idea of an Anthropology of Islam," 14.

[9] Asad, "Anthropology of Islam," 15.

this sphere. Indeed, a "perfect imitation" of the female Companions would likely not have been sustainable in classical Muslim communities.

In Chapter 2, I pointed out that Ibn Sa'd, writing during the period of decline of women's transmission, had little incentive to dwell on the *ḥadīth* transmission activities of female Companions, including 'Ā'isha bint Abī Bakr. By the fourth/tenth century, however, the *ḥadīth* sciences had come to occupy a different, and central, place in the culture of classical Sunnī Islam.[10] In this context, the selective emphasis on the *ḥadīth* transmission activity of female Companions helped legitimize and secure this practice for future generations. While the development is perceptible in the works of Abū Nu'aym al-Iṣbahānī (d. 430/1038) and Ibn 'Abd al-Barr (d. 463/1071), it becomes more pronounced in the later compilations of al-Mizzī (d. 742/1341), al-Dhahabī (d. 748/1348), and Ibn Ḥajar (d. 852/1449).[11] The emphasis that Ibn 'Abd al-Barr and Ibn Ḥajar placed on the *ḥadīth* transmission of female Companions rather than on other activities such as their service on the battlefront led Asma Afsaruddin to conclude that classical scholars constructed a restrictive model of feminine piety.[12] When we view the project of these classical scholars in light of prior centuries of women's marginalization in *ḥadīth* transmission, however, we can propose another explanation for their heightened attention to the *ḥadīth* transmission of the female Companions. Namely, their efforts helped validate the participation of women from the fourth/tenth century onward in this arena through reference to the early Islamic past and served to reintegrate women's activities into the circles of religious learning.

This chapter draws on the case studies of two prominent *muḥadditha*s, Karīma al-Marwaziyya (ca. 365–463/975–1070) and Fāṭima bint al-Ḥasan b. 'Alī al-Daqqāq (391–480/1000–88), to document how and why women reemerged as *ḥadīth* scholars beginning in the fourth/tenth century. In what

10 This complex evolution has been analyzed in greater depth in other studies. Lucas's *Constructive Critics* is the most thorough study to date of the history and place of the *ḥadīth* sciences in the sectarian development of Sunnism.

11 We have relatively less data from the late fourth/tenth century, which marks the reemergence of women in the historical records as trustworthy transmitters. However, the evidence from collections from the fifth/eleventh century onward, as cited earlier, is abundant.

12 Afsaruddin, "Reconstituting Women's Lives." In this article, Afsaruddin examines the representation of female Companions in Ibn Ḥajar's *Iṣāba* and Ibn 'Abd al-Barr's *Istī'āb* and compares this to Ibn Sa'd's portrayal in his *Ṭabaqāt*. She focuses in particular on the roles of female Companions in battle and demonstrates how such activities receive far less attention in later biographical compilations.

follows, I introduce three decisive trends and discuss them in detail in the course of this chapter.

REASONS FOR THE REVIVAL

1. In the last quarter of the third/ninth century, the growing acknowledgment of a *ḥadīth* canon, marked by the widespread acceptance of collections such as the *Ṣaḥīḥ*s of al-Bukhārī and Muslim, lent stability to the field of *ḥadīth* transmission.[13] This development effectively closed the "gates of *ḥadīth* discovery" and paradoxically opened the field to the participation of nonspecialists in the transmission of *ḥadīth* literature. Women, who were previously excluded due to rigorous standards for critical transmission, benefited from this more inclusive atmosphere.
2. Until the early second/eighth century, *ḥadīth* transmission was primarily oral, and writing served as an adjunct to memory. Between the second and third centuries, the relationship between oral and written transmission in *ḥadīth* learning evolved perceptibly.[14] By the fourth/tenth century, written transmission of *ḥadīth* was prevalent and writing and orality became complementary and often equivalent methods of safeguarding authoritative transmission. Though some scholars continued to insist on

[13] For a thorough analysis of the processes and impact of the canonization of *ḥadīth*, see Jonathan Brown, *The Canonization of al-Bukhārī and Muslim: The Formation and Function of the Sunnī Ḥadīth Canon* (Leiden: Brill, 2007). The *Ṣaḥīḥ* movement is also treated in a more summary fashion in the following works: Muḥammad Abdul Rauf, "*Ḥadīth* Literature – I: The Development of the Science of *Ḥadīth*," in *Arabic Literature to the End of the Umayyad Period*, ed. A. F. L. Beeston et al., 271–88 (New York: Cambridge University Press, 1983); Goldziher, *Muslim Studies*, 2:237–43; and Ṣiddīqī, *Ḥadīth Literature*, 43–75.

[14] For further analysis of this development, see Paul Heck, "The Epistemological Problem of Writing in Islamic Civilization," *Studia Islamica* 94 (2002): 85–114. Heck notes that prior to the stabilization of *ḥadīth* in the form of the six canonical collections (ca. mid-third century), writing was used in *ḥadīth* circles as an aid to memory and not in place of memorization as it evidently came to be within a century after the promulgation of the canonical six books. This does not preclude the written compilation and circulation of works such as *al-Jāmi' fi al-Ḥadīth* of Ibn Wahb (d. 197/813). Rather, the pedagogy of *ḥadīth* transmission focused more on accurate memorization to preserve the tradition rather than on writing (Heck, "Epistemological Problem of Writing," 98). See also Gregor Schoeler, *Genesis of Literature in Islam: From the Aural to the Read*, trans. Shawkat M. Toorawa (Edinburgh: Edinburgh University Press, 2009) and Hirschler, *Written World in the Medieval Arabic Lands* for more extensive analyses of the development of the cultures of reading and writing in early and classical Muslim societies.

the superiority of oral transmission, its primacy was essentially theoretical. In practice, the written text served on a par with oral transmission to perpetuate the authoritative transfer of knowledge from one generation to the next.[15] The increased incorporation of women into *ḥadīth* circles was an unintended consequence of this evolution in the form of transmission. Written transmission mitigated some of the requirements that had hindered women's access in the period of decline, namely the emphasis on legal acumen and training and the imperative for traveling (*riḥla*) to hear and learn directly from teachers.

3. The proliferation of *'ulamā'* kinship networks, correlated with the diffusion of 'Abbāsid political and military authority, also propelled women's reentry to *ḥadīth* transmission. Beginning in the third/ninth century, 'Abbāsid authority became increasingly fragmented, a process accelerated by the rise of semi-independent dynasties such as the Sāmānids (204–395/819–1005) and the Ghaznavids (367–583/977–1187). These developments transformed the political, military, and economic fabric of Muslim societies.[16] Among other shifts, they led to a strengthening of *'ulamā'* family networks that in turn could better withstand the fickleness of political and military arrangements under disparate governing dynasties and that helped safeguard the culture of the scholarly elite. Here, women's participation was not just about the transfer of *ḥadīth*. Their achievements became part of the cultural and social capital that enabled the survival and flourishing of the scholarly elite.[17] While

[15] Al-Khaṭīb al-Baghdādī's *Taqyīd al-'Ilm* is among the clearest testimonies to the scholarly effort to grapple with the relative value of written and oral transmissions. Also see al-Rāmahurmuzī, *al-Muḥaddith al-Fāṣil*, 363–402 and al-Ḥākim al-Naysābūrī, *Ma'rifat 'Ulūm al-Ḥadīth* (Beirut: Dār al-Kutub al-'Ilmiyya, 1977), 256–61, for their documentation of the debate over the uses of writing in *ḥadīth* transmission. See also Michael Cook, "The Opponents of the Writing of Tradition in Early Islam," *Arabica* 44 (1997): 437–530, for a thorough study of the debates over writing in early Islam.

[16] The second volume of Marshall Hodgson's *Venture of Islam* is devoted to analyzing these changes from the tenth to the sixteenth centuries.

[17] My use of the terms "cultural capital" and "social capital" draws on Pierre Bourdieu's articulation of these concepts. He divides cultural capital into the embodied state (e.g., accumulated habits, cultivation, and dispositions) and the objectified state (e.g., material cultural goods such as art, texts, and technology which represent the achievements of a particular class). Social capital consists of networks and relationships which can be converted into economic advantage for a class (Bourdieu, "The Forms of Capital"). A detailed application of Bourdieu's ideas regarding cultural and social capital is his landmark study of contemporary French society, *Distinction: A Social Critique of the*

> the educational practices of *'ulamā'* as an avenue for social survival have been studied in the context of sixth/twelfth-century Damascus, there has been little examination of the vital roles of women in this regard.[18] As women's education within kinship networks gained priority, the obstacles of legal and normative aversion to contact between non-*maḥram* men and women (discussed in Chapter 2) were partly overcome.

Chapters 1 and 2 highlighted the evolving social uses of *ḥadīth* over the first four centuries which alternately promoted and then inhibited women's participation. After the fourth century, the social function of religious knowledge evolved yet again, this time in a manner that led to women's contributions being welcomed anew. As women's educational achievements translated into social capital, their contributions were increasingly glorified in the *ṭabaqāt* and other historical literature. Successive generations of women drew inspiration from this literature, which helped model their own piety and learning. This feedback loop ultimately manifested itself as an extraordinary resurgence of women as *ḥadīth* transmitters.

The imprint of these three trends is clear in the careers of the two transmitters presented in this chapter. Karīma al-Marwaziyya's career illustrates the effects of canonization and the spread of written transmission on women's participation. Fāṭima bint al-Ḥasan's life demonstrates the positive impact of the evolving social organization of *'ulamā'* and their increased reliance on kin networks to assert, demarcate, and perpetuate *'ulamā'* identity.

KARĪMA AL-MARWAZIYYA (CA. 365–463/975–1070)

Karīma bint Aḥmad b. Muḥammad al-Marwaziyya commands attention as one of the first prominent female transmitters to appear in the historical record after the stark absence of women for more than two centuries.[19] Born in the second half of the fourth/tenth century, Karīma acquired a

Judgement of Taste, trans. Richard Nice (Cambridge, MA: Harvard University Press, 1984).

18 Michael Chamberlain, in *Knowledge and Social Practice in Medieval Damascus*, applies Bourdieu's theory of social and cultural capital to the *'ulamā'* of Damascus to show how they successfully leveraged practices associated with religious learning to ensure individual survival and success as well as their dynastic longevity.

19 Biographical notices for her are available in the following works: al-Ṣarīfīnī, *al-Muntakhab min al-Siyāq li-Ta'rīkh Naysābūr li-'Abd al-Ghāfir al-Fārisī* (Beirut: Dār al-Kutub al-'Ilmiyya, 1989), 427; al-Dhahabī, *Siyar*, 18:233–34; Kaḥḥāla, *A'lām al-Nisā'*, 1:240; and al-Ziriklī, *al-A'lām* (Beirut: Dār al-'Ilm li'l-Malāyīn, 1995), 5:225. The following

reputation as one of the most respected *muḥadditha*s of her time.[20] Sketches of Karīma's life reveal that her transmission of the *Ṣaḥīḥ* of al-Bukhārī distinguished her career and lent her a higher status than that of other contemporary female transmitters.

Karīma, also known as Umm al-Kirām al-Marwaziyya, is praised by 'Abd al-Ghāfir b. Ismā'īl al-Fārisī (451–529/1059–1135), her only contemporary biographer, as a chaste, virtuous, and well-known woman.[21] In a rather sparse notice, al-Fārisī reports the following about Karīma: that she narrated the *Ṣaḥīḥ* of al-Bukhārī on the authority of al-Kushmīhanī (d. 389/999);[22] that she heard *ḥadīth* from Abū 'Alī Zāhir b. Aḥmad al-Sarakhsī (d. 389/999)[23] and his generation of teachers; that she gave him (al-Fārisī) an *ijāza* for all of the works that she was known to have heard (*jamī' masmū'āti-hā*); and that Abū 'Abd Allāh al-Fārisī (d. 448/1056)[24] narrated *ḥadīth* on her authority. He also remarks that Karīma resided in Mecca for some time and died there. It is important to note here that al-Fārisī, Karīma's earliest biographer, does not mention the year of her birth or her death, and that this information is deduced by later biographers based on supplementary notes that they likely had. The lack of attention to birth and death dates speaks of an era in *ḥadīth* transmission history when the pursuit of short *isnād*s was not at its height. Among the twenty-six women to whom al-Fārisī devotes

biographical works list Karīma in the obituaries for the year 463 and provide a few details on her life: Ibn al-Jawzī, *al-Muntaẓam fī Ta'rīkh al-Mulūk wa'l-Umam* (Beirut: Dār al-Kutub al-'Ilmiyya, 1992), 16:135–36; Ibn al-Athīr, *al-Kāmil fī al-Ta'rīkh* (Beirut: Dār Ṣādir, 1966), 10:69; al-Yāfi'ī, *Mir'āt al-Jinān wa-'Ibrat al-Yaqẓān*, 3:89; and Ibn al-'Imād, *Shadharāt al-Dhahab*, 5:266. My citations for 'Abd al-Ghāfir al-Fārisī's *Siyāq* are primarily from al-Ṣarīfīnī's *Muntakhab*, which selectively reproduces biographies from al-Fārisī's *Siyāq*. It is important to note here that the manuscript of *al-Siyāq* on which al-Ṣarīfīnī relied is different in parts from the manuscript of *al-Siyāq* reproduced by Richard N. Frye in *The Histories of Nishapur* (Cambridge, MA: Harvard University Press, 1965). Thus, Karīma al-Marwaziyya's biography does not appear in the manuscript of *Siyāq* in Frye's edition.

20 With the exception of the modern biographical work, the *A'lām* of al-Ziriklī, sources on Karīma's life do not mention the year in which she was born. Al-Dhahabī asserts that she was approximately a hundred years old when she died. That would place her birth close to the year 365, the date that al-Ziriklī gives for her birth.

21 al-Ṣarīfīnī, *al-Muntakhab*, 427.

22 He is Abū al-Haytham Muḥammad b. Makkī al-Marwazī al-Kushmīhanī; see al-Dhahabī, *Siyar*, 16:491–92. Al-Sam'ānī vocalizes the *nisba* as Kushmīhanī while Yāqūt renders the place name as "Kushmayhan"; see al-Sam'ānī, *al-Ansāb* (Beirut: Dār al-Jinān, 1988), 5:76, and Yāqūt, *Mu'jam al-Buldān*, 4:526. Kushmīhan, known for its *ḥadīth* scholars, was a village near Marw.

23 al-Dhahabī, *Siyar*, 16:476–78.

24 This Abū 'Abd Allāh al-Fārisī is the grandfather of the biographer 'Abd al-Ghāfir al-Fārisī (al-Ṣarīfīnī, *al-Muntakhab*, 361–62).

biographical notices, there are only five for whom he provides information about birth and/or death years.[25] The picture changes considerably over the next two centuries during which birth and death years were more systematically recorded, a practice that in turn allowed *ḥadīth* transmitters to ascertain the quality of their *isnād*s and to compete in the accumulation of the shortest *isnād*s.

Following al-Fārisī, Karīma's biographers collectively praise her as an upright, learned woman. We also glean through other notices that she remained unmarried, devoted to religious study, and uncompromising in her standards of *ḥadīth* transmission.[26] In a particularly telling anecdote related by al-Dhahabī, the scholar Muḥammad b. 'Alī al-Narsī (d. 510/1116) tells of how Karīma brought out a copy of al-Bukhārī's *Ṣaḥīḥ* for him to read and transcribe.[27] He sat facing her and copied out seven pages and read them to her. When he wanted to compare his copy against hers by himself, she refused, insisting that she would review it with him.[28] In the same vein, al-Yāfi'ī remarks that she was precise, had correct understanding of her transmissions, and was eminent in *ḥadīth* circles (*dhāt ḍabṭ, fahm, wa-nabāha*). In addition to extolling Karīma, all of her biographers concur that her reputation in *ḥadīth* circles was grounded in her accurate transmission of the *Ṣaḥīḥ* of al-Bukhārī and in the fact that her authority could be traced to al-Kushmīhanī. Ibn al-Athīr remarks that she had the best *isnād*s for the *Ṣaḥīḥ* of al-Bukhārī and was not surpassed in this respect until the career of Abū al-Waqt (d. 553/1158).[29] A reconstruction of Karīma's network of students and teachers places her in the scholarly elite of Khurāsān, reveals her ties to *'ulamā'* of other major urban centers, and further clarifies her renown.

Biographers consistently name the following three *ḥadīth* scholars of Khurāsān as Karīma's teachers: Muḥammad b. Makkī al-Kushmīhanī, Zāhir b. Aḥmad al-Sarakhsī, and 'Abd Allāh b. Yūsuf b. Bāmawayh

[25] This is the count of women's biographies as recorded in al-Ṣarīfīnī's *Muntakhab* (an abridged version of al-Fārisī's *Siyāq*.)

[26] Al-Yāfi'ī, al-Dhahabī, and Ibn al-'Imād mention her unmarried status and her high standards for transmission.

[27] For a biography of Abū al-Ghanā'im Muḥammad b. 'Alī al-Narsī, see al-Dhahabī, *Siyar*, 19:274–76.

[28] al-Dhahabī, *Siyar*, 18:234. The term used to denote the type of transmission in which a student reads the text to his teacher and they review it for errors is *'arḍ*, more commonly known as *qirā'a*. See Ibn al-Ṣalāḥ, *Muqaddima*, 100. See also Ṣubḥī al-Ṣāliḥ, *'Ulūm al-Ḥadīth wa-Muṣṭalaḥu-hu*, 93–95.

[29] For his biography, see al-Dhahabī, *Siyar*, 20:303–11. (His name is given here as 'Īsā b. Shu'ayb al-Sijzī.)

(d. 409/1019).[30] If Karīma was indeed born around 365, she would have been in her late twenties and thirties at the death of these teachers. This chronology provides yet another significant detail regarding the evolution of the culture of *ḥadīth* transmission in the classical era. By the seventh/thirteenth century, the growing practice of bringing very young children to the assemblies of aged *shaykh*s nearing death enabled the shortening of *isnād*s, which were growing ever longer with the passage of time. Had Karīma lived in a later era, such as the Mamlūk period, her *isnād*s from these scholars would likely not have the same value. Ironically, the chronology of Karīma's career leaves open the possibility that she heard and learned the works of the scholars when she was old enough to actually assimilate the knowledge she would later transmit. Such a possibility is out of the question in later centuries in the cases of infants and toddlers who were granted certification to transmit compilations from aged *shaykh*s, an age structure that I discuss in greater detail in Chapter 4. The trajectory of Karīma's career when compared with that of later *muḥadditha*s sheds light on the pedagogical and social transformations in this arena of religious learning.

Al-Kushmīhanī receives special attention as Karīma's most noteworthy teacher because he narrated the *Ṣaḥīḥ* of al-Bukhārī accurately on the authority of the scholar Abū ʿAbd Allāh al-Firabrī (d. 320/932).[31] Al-Firabrī, in turn, had heard the *Ṣaḥīḥ* directly from al-Bukhārī himself twice. Thus, Karīma's reputation rested on her transmission of this major canonical work with only two intermediaries between her and the compiler himself. While her accurate transmission of the work no doubt formed her reputation initially, the fact that she outlived most other prominent, reliable transmitters who were students of al-Kushmīhanī accounts for her superlative rank.[32] According to al-Dhahabī, she died when she was nearly a hundred years old. Although Karīma was in her late twenties when

30 al-Dhahabī, *Siyar*, 17:239.

31 al-Dhahabī, *Siyar*, 15:10–13.

32 For example, Abū Dharr al-Harawī (ca. 355–434/965–1043), who was far more prominent than Karīma, also numbered among al-Kushmīhanī's students. However, he died thirty years before Karīma, and therefore, the *isnād* of the *Ṣaḥīḥ* via his authority had one more intermediary for later generations than did the *isnād* of Karīma. For his biography, see al-Dhahabī, *Siyar*, 17:554–63. According to al-Samʿānī, Muḥammad b. Mūsā b. ʿAbd Allāh al-Ṣaffār al-Marwazī (d. 471/1079) was the last to transmit from al-Kushmīhanī (al-Samʿānī, *Ansāb*, 5:76). However, al-Dhahabī cites widespread doubt as to the authenticity of Muḥammad b. Mūsā's audition of the *Ṣaḥīḥ* from al-Kushmīhanī, and he clearly did not acquire a reputation like Karīma's for this *isnād*. For his biography, see al-Dhahabī, *Siyar*, 18:382–84.

several of her well-known teachers died, her longevity still enabled her to function as a valued link between the old and young generations of scholars.

Karīma's biographies provide several clues that her reputation was well established and that she attracted numerous students to her assemblies. Luminaries of *ḥadīth* transmission, such as the Shāfi'ī scholar al-Khaṭīb al-Baghdādī and Manṣūr b. Muḥammad al-Sam'ānī (an erstwhile Ḥanafī) (d. 489/1096),[33] and Nūr al-Hudā al-Ḥusayn b. Muḥammad (d. 512/1118),[34] a leading Ḥanafī scholar of Baghdad, numbered among her students. Al-Khaṭīb and Nūr al-Hudā were likely among those who carried word of Karīma's reputation back to Baghdad. As with many scholars resident in Mecca, Karīma was sought out for her transmission authority by pilgrims. Her reputation attracted the Mālikī jurist Jumāhir b. 'Abd al-Raḥmān al-Ṭulayṭulī (of Toledo), who heard *ḥadīth* from her in 452/1061 when he undertook the Ḥajj.[35] Similarly, 'Alī b. al-Ḥusayn al-Mawṣilī and Muḥammad b. Barakāt heard *ḥadīth* from her in Mecca. Al-Dhahabī recounts an anecdote from Muḥammad b. 'Alī al-Hamadānī, who had set out for the Ḥajj in 463/1071 and received news of her death en route. He was thus unable to fulfill his wish to meet Karīma and obtain certification to transmit *ḥadīth* from her.[36] Karīma acquired an enviable reputation as a *muḥadditha* on the basis of her knowledge of more than just the *Ṣaḥīḥ*. Al-Fārisī, for example, remarks that she gave him permission (*ijāza*) to narrate all the works that she was known to have heard. Yet, after her death, her transmission of the *Ṣaḥīḥ* emerges as the outstanding feature of her career.

The fact that Karīma was a celebrated, trustworthy transmitter of al-Bukhārī's work is all the more striking when we recall that al-Bukhārī himself did not include any *ḥadīth* containing *isnād*s with female

33 For the biography of al-Khaṭīb, see al-Dhahabī, *Siyar*, 18:270–97. For that of al-Sam'ānī, see al-Dhahabī, *Siyar*, 19:114–19. He was the grandfather of the better-known scholar Abū Sa'd 'Abd al-Karīm b. Abī Bakr Muḥammad al-Sam'ānī (d. 562/1166). Manṣūr b. Muḥammad al-Sam'ānī created a stir by switching allegiance from Ḥanafism (the *madhhab* of his birth and in which he acquired the highest level of religious education) to Shāfi'ism. According to al-Dhahabī, this was made public in 467. Thus, he likely heard from Karīma while he was still a Ḥanafī (since she died in 463).

34 al-Dhahabī, *Siyar*, 19:353–55. Al-Dhahabī notes that he outlived all other students of Karīma who had heard the *Ṣaḥīḥ* of al-Bukhārī from her.

35 Abū Bakr Jumāhir b. 'Abd al-Raḥmān al-Ṭulayṭulī (d. 466/1073–74). His biography is found in al-Dhahabī, *Ta'rīkh al-Islām* (Beirut: Dār al-Kitāb al-'Arabī, 1994), 31:196.

36 al-Dhahabī, *Siyar*, 18:235. Here it is worth noting that Karīma attracted scholars of all *madhhab*s to her assemblies – a testament not just to her popularity but also to the power of *ḥadīth* transmission as a source of social cohesion, a point which will be taken up in Chapter 4.

transmitters after the generation of the Successors.[37] The canonization of *ḥadīth* literature is a major explanatory factor in this fundamental shift. Paradoxically, it was an unintended contribution of stringent scholars such as al-Bukhārī and Muslim that women were welcomed anew as *ḥadīth* transmitters beginning in the fourth/tenth century. The promulgation of authoritative compilations that could be reliably referenced in matters of creed, ritual, and law was a watershed in the history of *ḥadīth* transmission. The process was arguably initiated in the late second/eighth century with the widespread acceptance of Mālik's legal manual *al-Muwaṭṭa'*, which contains *ḥadīth* from Muḥammad in addition to traditions from the Companions that were deemed authentic by Mālik. It is important to clarify here that we cannot equate the appearance of any collection, be it the *Muwaṭṭa'* or the *Ṣaḥīḥ*s of al-Bukhārī and Muslim, with its acceptance as canonical. Rather, their canonical status was acquired only after scholars debated the authority and status of these works decades, and even centuries, after their initial appearance. In addition to the *Ṣaḥīḥ*s, the *Sunan* collections of Ibn Māja, Abū Dāwūd, and al-Nasā'ī as well as the *Jāmi'* of al-Tirmidhī were also eventually accorded a high status among Sunnī Muslims.[38]

In principle, it is inaccurate to describe the publication of the six major *ḥadīth* compilations and the widespread acceptance of their authority as the canonization of *ḥadīth* literature. The works of al-Bukhārī, Muslim, and other celebrated compilers are, in fact, open to criticism and revision. Several scholars undertook the task of examining the criteria of these compilers and their works and amending them.[39] None of these later works, however, acquired the status of the major compilations, and they had limited appeal even in scholarly circles. In view of the minimal success in amending the works of the compilers and in recognition of their

[37] As noted in Chapter 2, Ḥafṣa bint Sīrīn (d. after 100/718) is the last female transmitter to appear in al-Bukhārī's *isnād*s.

[38] Regarding the chronology of canonization, see Brown, *Canonization*, chapter 7.

[39] Examples of amendments to the *Ṣaḥīḥ* collections are al-Ḥākim al-Naysābūrī's *al-Mustadrak 'alā al-Ṣaḥīḥayn* (Cairo: Dār al-Ḥaramayn li'l-Ṭibā'a wa'l-Nashr wa'l-Tawzī', 1997), and al-Dāraquṭnī's *Kitāb al-Ilzāmāt wa'l-Tatabbu'* (Medina: al-Maktaba al-Salafiyya, 1978). For a more complete listing of works amending the canonical collections as well as works of "authentic" *ḥadīth* that did not achieve canonical status, see Muḥammad b. Ja'far al-Kattānī (d. 1345/1927), *al-Risāla al-Mustaṭrafa li-Bayān Mashhūr Kutub al-Sunna al-Musharrafa* (Damascus: Maṭba'at Dār al-Fikr, 1964), 23–32. For a recent analysis of al-Dāraquṭnī's amendments to al-Bukhārī's work, see Jonathan A. C. Brown, "Criticism of the Proto-*Ḥadīth* Canon: Al-Darāquṭnī's Adjustment of the *Ṣaḥīḥayn*," *Journal of Islamic Studies* 15 (2004): 1–37.

authority, the corollary principle that the *ḥadīth* canon was effectively closed after the compilation of the two *Ṣaḥīḥ* collections gained currency among *ḥadīth* scholars. Explicitly articulated in the seventh/thirteenth-century manual of Ibn al-Ṣalāḥ, the idea was resisted even then at a theoretical level, but practically speaking, it accurately described the reality of *ḥadīth* transmission in the classical period.[40] The acknowledgment of the authority of these collections in turn had implications for the transmitters of traditions. Among the many important consequences of the works of these six compilers, the ones most relevant to this analysis are (1) the effect of canonization on the social uses of *ḥadīth* and (2) *ḥadīth* learning gaining purchase as cultural and social capital.

During the pre-classical/formative period, prior to the collection of authoritative *ḥadīth* compilations, aspiring *ḥadīth* students had to meet criteria more stringent than those of the classical period. As discussed in Chapter 2, in this pre-classical milieu, comprehension of the legal application of *ḥadīth* and critical knowledge of traditionists (*ʻilm al-jarḥ wa'l-taʻdīl*) were necessary for accomplished *ḥadīth* transmitters. Before the acceptance of a *ḥadīth* canon, transmitters could more easily introduce previously unknown *ḥadīth* into the corpus of widely circulated traditions. By the late third/ninth century, however, the compilation and widespread dissemination of authoritative *ḥadīth* lent stability to the field, safeguarded against forgeries, and rendered it superfluous for transmitters of the works to be legal scholars and critical traditionists themselves. As Eerik Dickinson has astutely observed:

> When a later scholar transmitted an authentic *ḥadīth* also found in one of the great collections, the *authenticity* of the *ḥadīth* was entirely based on the declaration of the earlier compiler and not on the transmission of his more recent counterpart. Thus, the modern transmitters of *ḥadīth* were in such cases entirely removed from the equation.[41]

[40] Ibn al-Ṣalāḥ, *Muqaddima*, 19. Zayn al-Dīn al-ʻIrāqī (d. 806/1404) and Ibn Ḥajar al-ʻAsqalānī are among those who disagreed with Ibn al-Ṣalāḥ's assertion that it was no longer possible to add to the "canon." See Zayn al-Dīn al-ʻIrāqī, *al-Taqyīd wa'l-Iḍāḥ li-mā ʻUṭliqa wa-Ughliqa min Muqaddimat Ibn al-Ṣalāḥ* (Beirut: Mu'assasat al-Kutub al-Thaqāfiyya, 1991), 27–29, and Ibn Ḥajar al-ʻAsqalānī, *Nukat ʻalā Kitāb Ibn al-Ṣalāḥ* (Riyad: Dār al-Rāya, 1988), 1:270–72.

[41] Eerik Dickinson, "Ibn al-Ṣalāḥ al-Shahrazūrī and the Isnād," *Journal of the American Oriental Society* 122, no. 3 (2002): 481–505, at 488. It is important here to emphasize the distinction between ascertaining authenticity and upholding accuracy in transmission. Whereas determination of authenticity required specialized knowledge of the traditionists and the transmitted texts, accurate transmission hinged more on a person's reliable oral or written reproduction of a text, a task in which women excelled during the classical era.

In short, the achievement of scholars such as al-Bukhārī and Muslim was to diminish the imperative for each transmitter to critically evaluate *ḥadīth* and their *isnāds*. Over the course of the fourth/tenth century, the compilations opened the field of *ḥadīth* transmission to the participation of those who were not specialized in the critical evaluation of *isnāds* but who could nonetheless contribute by their faithful reproduction of selected works. *Ḥadīth* manuals aiming to distinguish the true practitioners of the craft from dilettantes continued to insist on legal acumen and knowledge of traditionists as prerequisites to transmission.[42] Alongside this insistence, however, there was the acknowledgment that traditionists did not need to understand the applications or nuanced meanings of their traditions but needed only to convey them in order to maintain the formality of transmission via an unbroken *isnād* that carried the smallest possible number of intermediaries (*isnād 'ālī*).

Ḥadīth manuals from the classical period testify to these profound changes in standards of transmission. For example, al-Khaṭīb al-Baghdādī's *al-Kifāya fī 'Ilm al-Riwāya* documents a period when *ḥadīth* transmission became more amenable to the participation of nonspecialists. In one particularly telling section of his work, al-Khaṭīb defines types of knowledge expected from commoners (*'āmmat al-nās*) and differentiates between that and what is limited to specialists of *ḥadīth* (*ahl al-'ilm*).[43] Commoners can be expected to have knowledge of financial transactions, the obligatory aspects of religious practice, and the avoidance of sin. *Ḥadīth* scholars, on the other hand, should master specialized knowledge of the precise, accurate transmission of *ḥadīth*, their legal implementation, and the conditions for accepting *ḥadīth*, and should exercise due caution about interpolations.

Having distinguished between these two types, al-Khaṭīb declares that it is acceptable to transmit from the *'āmma* because they merely serve to convey the words and not the specialized understanding of the text. His explicit assertion that the participation of women is acceptable in this

[42] The first extensive work of this type was al-Rāmahurmuzī's fourth-century compilation *al-Muḥaddith al-Fāṣil bayna al-Rāwī wa'l-Wā'ī*. See also al-Ḥākim al-Naysābūrī's *Ma'rifat 'Ulūm al-Ḥadīth*, which describes in detail fifty-two categories of knowledge necessary for students to be proficient transmitters.

[43] al-Khaṭīb al-Baghdādī, *al-Kifāya*, 92–94. A *ḥadīth* report allows that those who transmit religious knowledge may well transmit to those who are more proficient and knowledgeable than the bearer of the report(s). This was interpreted as license for broader, unrestricted participation in *ḥadīth* transmission. Al-Khaṭīb includes this report in his section on allowing nonspecialists to transmit traditions; see *al-Kifāya fī 'Ilm al-Riwāya* (Beirut: Dār al-Kutub al-'Ilmiyya, 1988), 93–94.

context is particularly revealing. Al-Khaṭīb observes that "[after all,] the early scholars (*'ulamā' al-salaf*) accepted the narrations of women, slaves, and those who were not known for their legal expertise even if they narrated merely one or two *ḥadīth*."[44] Al-Khaṭīb's categorical classification of women and slaves as nonspecialists (*'āmmat al-nās*) and his simultaneous justification for accepting their transmissions are a clear indicator of how the field of *ḥadīth* had developed a cautious yet accepting stance toward the participation of those who may not have had specialized knowledge of the science of *ḥadīth*.

Al-Khaṭīb's subsequent section on the similarities and differences between a *ḥadīth* transmitter (*muḥaddith*) and a legal witness (*shāhid*) provides further proof of developments in this arena and elucidates another aspect of the "liberalizing" effect of the canonization movement. In Chapter 2, I mentioned the ambiguities in the usage of the terms *riwāya* and *shahāda* in the formative period. As the controversies over the *ḥadīth* of Fāṭima bint Qays and Busra bint Ṣafwān show, conflation of the concepts of women's testimony (*shahāda*) and women's narration (*riwāya*) produced some negative assessments of women's *ḥadīth* participation. In practical terms, there could be little confusion between the two. But at the theoretical level, there was space for muddying the waters, thereby giving license to those who would discriminate against women's transmission on the basis of gender. The compilation of authoritative *ḥadīth* manuals served to define clearly the domains of testimony and *ḥadīth* transmission because, as observed by Eerik Dickinson earlier, the authenticity and legal authority of each tradition was established by the compilers and not by those who transmitted their works.[45] Al-Khaṭīb's discussion affirms that by the classical period, these ambiguities were resolved at the theoretical level. He states unequivocally that gender is not a consideration in *ḥadīth* transmission and that the narrations of women are accepted on a par with those of men. This is not so in cases of legal testimony where, he notes, the statement of a woman carries less weight than that of a man.[46]

It is in this light that we can understand how women such as Karīma could readily appear as transmitters *of* al-Bukhārī's *Ṣaḥīḥ* even though they do not figure as transmitters *in* it after the generation of the

44 al-Khaṭīb al-Baghdādī, *al-Kifāya*, 94.

45 All of the published *ḥadīth* manuals date from the period *after* the authority of the major canonical *ḥadīth* collections was established. They are all in agreement that a woman's *riwāya* is acceptable and is not the same as her *shahāda*. See my article "Gender and Legal Authority" for analysis of earlier discussions that conflate the two categories.

46 al-Khaṭīb al-Baghdādī, *al-Kifāya*, 94–95.

Successors. As suggested by al-Khaṭīb, who was Karīma's contemporary, the function of women was to reproduce *ḥadīth* knowledge, including collections such as the *Ṣaḥīḥ* of al-Bukhārī, and not to extract legal rulings on the basis of these texts. Their contributions consisted of authenticating their students' copies of *ḥadīth* works in one of three ways: through a public reading of their own authenticated copies; by listening to students read their copies aloud; or even more simply by certifying in writing that students were permitted to transmit specified works on their authority as long as their copies were free of error.

The importance of accurate reproduction of *ḥadīth* literature raises a second issue central to the success of female *ḥadīth* transmitters: the proliferation of written transmission. Notwithstanding the preference for direct transmission from Karīma, it is nonetheless apparent from her biographies that written transmission was prevalent and acceptable in her career. For example, al-Fārisī notes that he received permission (*ijāza*) to transmit everything she had heard.[47] Use of the term "*ijāza*" in *ḥadīth* transmission generally indicates purely written transmission without an accompanying oral rendition of the text.[48] The fact that al-Fārisī can boast of his *ijāza* from Karīma clearly indicates an acceptance of written transmission by his time. Such acceptance, however, was not widespread in the earliest period of *ḥadīth* history. As discussed in Chapter 2, the imperative to acquire *ḥadīth* through face-to-face, oral transmission, often entailing rigorous journeys in search of authoritative sources, raised the bar for women's participation and denied them access to this domain. Written transmission, by contrast, reinvigorated female *ḥadīth* transmission, compounding the positive effect that canonization had on their participation.

The unequivocal acceptance of written transmission in *ḥadīth* circles was accompanied by anxious hand-wringing on the part of leading scholars such as al-Rāmahurmuzī, al-Ḥākim al-Naysābūrī, Ibn ʿAbd al-Barr,

[47] al-Ṣarīfīnī, *al-Muntakhab*, 427.

[48] al-Khaṭīb, *al-Kifāya*, 311–53; Ibn al-Ṣalāḥ, *Muqaddima*, 106–11. A more detailed review of early and classical commentary on *ijāza*s is available in the work of Abū Ṭāhir Aḥmad b. Muḥammad al-Silafī (d. 576/1180), *al-Wajīz fī Dhikr al-Mujāz wa'l-Mujīz* (Beirut: Dār al-Gharb al-Islāmī, 1991). Contemporary analyses of the significance of *ijāza*s are available in the following studies: Aḥmad Ramaḍān Aḥmad, *al-Ijāzāt wa'l-Tawqīʿāt al-Makhṭūṭa fī al-ʿUlūm al-Naqliyya wa'l-ʿAqliyya* (Cairo: Wizārat al-Thaqāfa, 1986); ʿAbd Allāh al-Fayyāḍ, *al-Ijāzāt al-ʿIlmiyya ʿinda al-Muslimīn* (Baghdad: Maṭbaʿat al-Irshād, 1967); Hisham Nashabi, "The *Ijāza*: Academic Certification in Muslim Education," *Hamdard Islamicus* 8 (1985): 7–20; and Georges Vajda, "Un opuscule inédit d'as-Silafī," in *La transmission du savoir en Islam* (London: Ashgate Variorum, 1983).

and al-Khaṭīb al-Baghdādī.[49] Nevertheless, there is sufficient evidence to indicate that these same scholars were struggling to incorporate theoretically the de facto long-standing primacy of written transmission. Al-Khaṭīb, Karīma's contemporary, outlines different types of transmission in the period when women reemerged as *ḥadīth* transmitters. These modes included *samāʿ* (hearing the text directly from the author or transmitter), *qirāʾa* (reading one's copy to the author or transmitter), and *ijāza* (being granted permission to transmit a written text without an accompanying oral rendition of it).[50] The first two methods indicated oral transmission and were accordingly ranked superior to written transmission. *Ijāza*, on the other hand, came to have a ceremonial function in the period under discussion and served to uphold a semblance of the *isnād* system without signifying direct, oral contact. Although a sense of caution toward accepting written transmission is amply evidenced, al-Khaṭīb repeatedly favors accepting it whether or not there is an accompanying oral transmission.[51]

Written transmission enabled individuals who could not independently participate in the oral transmission of knowledge to have access to the arena of *ḥadīth* education. For example, fathers could obtain certification for young children who had not yet acquired the ability to speak, read, or write. In cases where infants and toddlers were brought to hear texts to maintain the façade of oral transmission, it was the written text and not the hearing of it by fledglings that ultimately assured the accurate transfer of knowledge. Due to the prevalent notion that the written text would guarantee for classical Muslims what orality and memory had guaranteed for the early generations of Muslims, some *shaykh*s were even known to have granted *ijāza*s to unborn children.[52] In a similar vein, men could obtain certification for female members of their household who could not

49 al-Rāmahurmuzī, *al-Muḥaddith al-Fāṣil*, 363–402; al-Ḥākim al-Naysābūrī, *Maʿrifat ʿUlūm al-Ḥadīth*, 256–61; Ibn ʿAbd al-Barr, *Ṣaḥīḥ Jāmiʿ Bayān al-ʿIlm wa-Faḍlihī* (Cairo: Maktabat Ibn Taymiyya, 1996), 59–78; al-Khaṭīb al-Baghdādī, *al-Kifāya*, 226–29.

50 al-Khaṭīb, *al-Kifāya*, 259–355.

51 al-Khaṭīb, *al-Kifāya*, 311–55. According to al-Khaṭīb, only the Ẓāhirīs classified *isnād*s in which transmission occurred by *ijāza* as *marāsīl* (interrupted chains of transmission) because they did not accept written transmission as equal to direct oral transmission (al-Khaṭīb, *al-Kifāya*, 311).

52 al-Khaṭīb al-Baghdādī, *al-Kifāya*, 325. Although al-Khaṭīb is reluctant to endorse such a practice, he concludes his discussion of this topic with the observation that some *shaykh*s gave *ijāza*s to children who had not been brought into their presence, and that by analogy other *shaykh*s felt it permissible to do the same with children who had not yet been born. In the seventh century, Ibn al-Ṣalāḥ does not endorse granting *ijāza*s to those who are not yet born but does permit *ijāza*s for very young children who may not be present for the granting of the certificate; Ibn al-Ṣalāḥ, *Muqaddima*, 108–9.

undertake *riḥla*s independently to collect *ḥadīth* and whose direct contact with men, even in the pursuit of religious knowledge, was curtailed. Scrutiny of the biographies of numerous women from the fourth/tenth century to the Mamlūk period reveals increasing use of the term *ijāza* to denote how women received and transferred much of their knowledge.[53]

Given the widespread use of written transmission, it is interesting to consider that women's literacy rates in the general population may also have risen, thereby enabling access to religious learning even on the part of women who did not belong to *'ulamā'* families. In previous chapters, I suggest that women flourished as *ḥadīth* transmitters in the earliest period of Islam when transmission was primarily oral precisely because literacy would not have been an issue. In the second phase of transmission history, as the use of writing grew in *ḥadīth* circles, women in the general population, who would not have enjoyed the same literacy rates as men, would have been at a disadvantage.[54] However, after this phase, and certainly by the fourth/tenth century, the relatively easy accessibility of paper and evolution in manuscript forms and writing technology is likely to have contributed to an overall increase in literacy rates in the Muslim world.[55] The increased use of the *ijāza* to certify written transmission among women serves as an important indicator of the spread of a more literate culture in classical Muslim societies among the general population enabling greater participation among a broader range of classes and among women and men beyond the *'ulamā'* elite.

Karīma's career demonstrates the impact of the canonical collections and written transmission on women's reemergence as *ḥadīth* transmitters. Fāṭima bint al-Ḥasan's life, analyzed in the next section, provides a lens to examine a third development: the emergence of *'ulamā'* kinship networks that relied on *ḥadīth* transmission to confirm and transmit status.

[53] Nearly 300 women in al-Sakhāwī's volume devoted to noteworthy women of the ninth century earned *ijāza*s or awarded them to their own students; al-Sakhāwī, *al-Ḍaw' al-Lāmi' li-Ahl al-Qarn al-Tāsi'* (Cairo: Maktabat al-Qudsī, 1936), vol. 12.

[54] For intriguing anecdotal information regarding literacy among the female slaves of the ruling elite as well as about female scribes in the fourth/tenth century, see Nadia Maria El-Cheikh, "Women's History: A Study of al-Tanūkhī," in *Writing the Feminine: Women in Arab Sources*, ed. Manuela Marin and Randi Deguilhem, 129–48 (New York: I. B. Tauris, 2002), 139–40.

[55] See Jonathan Bloom, *Paper Before Print: The History and Impact of Paper in the Islamic World* (New Haven: Yale University Press, 2001) for a detailed history of the introduction of paper in the Middle East and its impact on various fields of learning (see, in particular, pp. 90–123). See Hirschler, *Written Word*, chapter 3 for his analysis of evolution in children's education and the rise in literacy among children especially in Syria and Egypt beginning in the seventh/thirteenth century.

FĀṬIMA BINT AL-ḤASAN B. ʿALĪ AL-DAQQĀQ (391–480/1000–1088)

Whereas Karīma stands out as an exemplary authority on al-Bukhārī's *Ṣaḥīḥ*, Fāṭima, in the next generation of transmitters, is cast as a generalized model of female piety.[56] As the daughter of the Shāfiʿī-Ṣūfī leader al-Ḥasan b. ʿAlī al-Daqqāq (d. 405/1015) and the wife of the renowned Ṣūfī scholar Abū al-Qāsim al-Qushayrī (d. 465/1072), Fāṭima was located at the nucleus of one of the most influential scholarly families of Nishapur.[57] Her case exemplifies the ways in which female religious education depended on kinship networks to facilitate access and shows how women's accomplishments in turn bolstered the status of *ʿulamāʾ* families. The following interrelated points will be illustrated through an analysis of Fāṭima's profile:

1. Fathers (or other male guardians) were often crucial in forging connections at an early stage, and these connections would be a cornerstone for women's successes and reputations until their death.
2. Marriage of learned women to other scholars was an avenue for transmitting status and ensuring the continuity of the *ʿulamāʾ* culture of learning and piety.
3. *Ḥadīth* learning, as opposed to other religious sciences, evolved as the paramount arena for women's participation. Unlike the study of theology and law, it became a neutral arena that bound and demarcated Sunnī *ʿulamāʾ* irrespective of their other affiliations. Though there is a preponderance of Shāfiʿī and Ḥanbalī *muḥaddithas* in the early classical era (ca. fourth/tenth to sixth/twelfth centuries), by the late classical period, we can find records of *muḥaddithas* in each of the four major *madhhabs*.

Al-Fārisī, Fāṭima's grandson and earliest biographer, sings her praises, and his words offer an evocative introduction to her life.

> Fāṭima bint al-Ustādh Abī ʿAlī al-Daqqāq al-Ḥurra, the pride of women of her age. She was unique in her accomplishments in comparison with the women of ages past. She was raised by her father, who imparted to her religious knowledge, proper

[56] Her biographies are available in al-Ṣarīfīnī, *al-Muntakhab*, 419–20; al-Fārisī, *Kitāb al-Siyāq li-Taʾrīkh Nīsābūr*, in *The Histories of Nishapur*, ed. Richard Frye, fols. 76a, 77b; al-Dhahabī, *Siyar*, 18:479–80; and Kaḥḥāla, *Aʿlām al-Nisāʾ*, 4:42. She is listed in the obituaries for the year 480 in the works of al-Yāfiʿī, *Miʾrāt al-Jinān*, 3:132, and Ibn al-ʿImād, *Shadharāt al-Dhahab*, 5:348.

[57] For her father's biography, see al-Ṣarīfīnī, *al-Muntakhab*, 179. For that of her husband, see al-Ṣarīfīnī, *al-Muntakhab*, 334–35.

etiquette, and refinement, and instilled in her the correct beliefs, and the etiquette of the Ṣūfīs as well as concepts of theology (*kalimāt al-tawḥīd*). She had memorized the Qur'ān and would spend her days and nights reciting it, and she had [scholarly and mystical] knowledge of the Qur'ān (*'ārifa bi'l-kitāb*). Her father convened a *dhikr* assembly for her, and he had her memorize the material [recited] in assemblies because of his high opinion of her. At that time [i.e., when she was young], he did not have a son, so all his attention was devoted to this daughter. She was born in the year 391.[58] This was the same year in which he [i.e., her father] built the blessed *madrasa*. When she matured, he married her to Imām Zayn al-Islām after she had combined different types of virtues.

She heard [*ḥadīth*] from Abū Nu'aym al-Isfarāyīnī, al-Sayyid Abū al-Ḥasan al-'Alawī, al-Ḥākim Abī 'Abd Allāh al-Ḥāfiẓ, 'Abd Allāh b. Yūsuf, and Abū 'Alī al-Rūdhbārī [who heard] from Ibn Dāsa [who heard] from Abū Dāwūd al-Sijistānī. [She also heard] from Abū 'Abd al-Raḥmān al-Sulamī and the second generation [of scholars] such as al-Shaykh Abū 'Abd Allāh b. Bākawayh.[59] A *fawā'id* collection [compilation of her selected narrations] was prepared for her and many texts were read to her.

She was fully devoted (*bāligha*) to worship and exerted herself in this regard. She spent her time immersed in ritual purity and prayer and had six boys and [an unspecified number of] girls, who were unrivaled in their age.[60]

She lived in pious submission for ninety years not concerned with what she had inherited from her father or her mother and did not involve herself in matters of this world. Zayn al-Islām [her husband] exerted effort in taking care of her worldly affairs.

She died in the morning on Thursday the 13th day of Dhu'l-Qa'da in the year 480.[61]

Al-Fārisī's account provides fascinating glimpses into Fāṭima's father's role in her upbringing, her scholarly network, and her sectarian orientation within the intellectual culture of fourth/tenth- and fifth/eleventh-century Nishapur. Later biographers such as al-Dhahabī draw primarily on al-Fārisī, adding details that further clarify her reputation and activities. The value of al-Fārisī's description lies not just in its memorable portrait of Fāṭima. It is also a striking testament to the sea changes in the culture of the

[58] It is unusual that al-Fārisī provides the years of Fāṭima's birth and death. His knowledge and inclusion of this material indicates not just his closeness to Fāṭima (who was his grandmother) but also her status within an established *'ulamā'* network.

[59] In al-Fārisī's organizational scheme, the "second generation" consists of scholars whose death dates fall between ca. 425 and 460.

[60] Biographical sources do not clearly state how many daughters Fāṭima had. Through his research into the scholarly families of Nishapur, Bulliet has counted five daughters of al-Qushayrī. It is not clear how many of these are from his marriage to Fāṭima, although Bulliet surmises that Fāṭima was likely his only wife. See Bulliet, *Patricians of Nishapur*, 153.

[61] al-Ṣarīfīnī, *al-Muntakhab*, 419–20. Her biography as it appears in al-Fārisī's *Siyāq* reproduced by Richard Frye is slightly different from the version in *al-Muntakhab*.

scholarly elite. By Fāṭima's lifetime, this culture had not just reintegrated women's public religious participation but also extolled it in the annals of *ṭabaqāt* and chronicle literature, genres that functioned to identify and demarcate the *'ulamā'*.

Fāṭima's biographers paint a compelling portrait of a girl born in the final quarter of the fourth/tenth century who was doted on by her father with all the attention and care ordinarily reserved for sons. He took charge of her education, inculcating in her the ways of religious etiquette and Ṣūfī piety. He brought her to assemblies for hearing *ḥadīth* starting at the age of seven. Beyond that, he paved for her an exemplary path of religious learning such that she not only memorized the entire Qur'ān but was also proficient with respect to its interpretation. Given her father's background and her educational milieu, she is likely to have been well versed in Ṣūfī interpretations of the Qur'ān. Though Fāṭima was only fourteen when her father died, his efforts clearly set the trajectory for her life as a leading female religious scholar.

Abū 'Alī's connections gave Fāṭima access to an esteemed network of teachers and a scholarly lineage that was a cornerstone of her reputation. Fāṭima's biography and the biographies of other women active in the scholarly circles of Nishapur attest to the ways in which kinship networks mitigated restrictive norms with respect to contact between men and women, a factor that over the next few centuries would come to play an important role in female access to education. Kinship to Abū 'Alī was clearly critical to Fāṭima's early exposure to the scholarly elite of Nishapur. Without his mediation, she could not have acquired certifications from leading scholars at such a young age. Further, her father is the one who convened assemblies for her and taught her the material that would be recited there.

Fāṭima's attendance at the sessions of luminaries testifies to her father's awareness and astute calculation of the fact that her reputation as a *ḥadīth* transmitter would rest on a network constructed before she even reached puberty. Her first *ḥadīth* assembly for hearing traditions was at the age of seven in the presence of Abū al-Ḥasan al-'Alawī (d. 401/1011), a scholar who had attained the rank of *musnid* of Khurāsān.[62] Al-Dhahabī notes that out of piety and humility, al-'Alawī refused to transmit traditions until

[62] The term *musnid* was used with varying connotations in different periods of Islamic history. Generally, the term referred to someone who could transmit traditions or a collection with a reliable chain of transmission. An understanding of the legal implications and applications is not implied in the use of this term.

the end of his years. Finally, 1,000 *ḥadīth* were selected for him to relate, and at least a thousand ink-pots could be found at his assemblies, signaling the popularity of his sessions.[63] On the heels of her certification (*samā'a*) from al-'Alawī, Fāṭima was also brought to hear traditions from Abū Nu'aym al-Isfarāyīnī (d. 400/1009), Abū 'Alī al-Rūdhbārī (d. 403/1012), and Ibn Bāmawayh, all coveted teachers at the rank of *musnid* who were known for their narration of works such al-Bukhārī's *Ṣaḥīḥ* and Abū Dāwūd's *Sunan.*[64] Abū 'Alī would have also realized that, in keeping with the culture of *ḥadīth* transmission, Fāṭima's reputation for conveying traditions from these teachers would be magnified if she were to outlive the other students of these teachers.

Within the network of teachers mentioned by Fāṭima's biographers, two were especially influential. The first, al-Ḥākim al-Naysābūrī (d. 405/1014), was among the leading Shāfi'ī traditionists of Khurāsān and a prolific *ḥadīth* scholar and critic whose work *Ma'rifat 'Ulūm al-Ḥadīth* numbers among the earliest surviving systematic works on the science of *ḥadīth* transmission.[65] Her second illustrious teacher was al-Sulamī (d. 412/1021).[66] A Shāfi'ī-Ṣūfī leader, exegete, biographer, and *ḥadīth* transmitter, al-Sulamī claimed a considerable following in Nishapur and beyond. Al-Dhahabī reports that he was beloved among the elite and lay classes, among his opponents and his supporters, and among the rulers and the ruled not just in his own city but throughout the Muslim lands. Although al-Sulamī's views drew criticism, and he was faulted for not being a reliable transmitter, there is little doubt that he was overall a respected and popular scholar and Ṣūfī leader. Al-Sulamī's influence on Fāṭima may have been formative and enduring: he was an associate of her father's and later became her husband's mentor after her father's death. Fāṭima's long-term connection with al-Sulamī (in contrast to other more short-lived contacts she may have had with teachers in her youth) likely

63 al-Dhahabī, *Siyar*, 17:99.

64 Their biographies may be found in al-Dhahabī's *Siyar* as follows: al-Isfarāyīnī at 17:71–73; al-'Alawī at 17:98–99; al-Rūdhbārī at 17:219–20; and Ibn Bāmawayh at 17:239.

65 For his biography and comments on the controversies surrounding al-Naysābūrī, see *EI*^{2}, s.v. "al-Ḥākim al-Naysābūrī,"and al-Dhahabī, *Siyar*, 17:162–77. Fāṭima is not listed in al-Ḥākim's biography as someone who transmitted from him, although her husband Abū al-Qāsim al-Qushayrī is mentioned. The likely explanation for this omission is that he had far too many students for all to be listed and consequently only those who became leading scholars themselves were included in his list of students.

66 For his biography, see *EI*^{2}, s.v. "al-Sulamī," and al-Dhahabī, *Siyar*, 17:247–55. Al-Dhahabī provides a detailed exposition of his reputation in *ḥadīth* circles and among the Ṣūfīs of Nishapur.

influenced her own scholarly outlook on matters such as Qur'ānic interpretation and the correct practice of Ṣūfism.

Biographers consistently list Fāṭima's teachers, but there is little mention of what she actually heard and transmitted from these scholars. While this holds true for many biographical notices of both men and women, we cannot attribute these omissions simply to expediency. The inattention to the specific texts that Fāṭima heard at sessions with al-Sulamī and other scholars suggests that the value of these contacts went beyond the texts read in the assemblies. Rather, the contacts signaled Fāṭima's initiation into a Shāfi'ī-Ṣūfī culture of religious learning and piety. It was this culture that she was expected to embody and transmit to subsequent generations.

It is in this light that we can best understand her marriage to Zayn al-Islām al-Qushayrī, which, al-Fārisī points out, took place after her vita already comprised a number of virtues (*ba'da an istajma'at anwā' al-faḍā'il*).[67] Al-Qushayrī, fifteen years her senior, was one of her father's leading students and the one who inherited the leadership of his Ṣūfī circle. The marriage of al-Qushayrī to Abū 'Alī's highly accomplished daughter confirmed his standing as the most favored student of Abū 'Alī and as his heir apparent, who ultimately took over the leadership of his *madrasa*.[68] This relationship, binding a father, daughter, and son-in-law, emphasizes that in the *'ulamā'* culture of fourth/tenth- and fifth/eleventh-century Nishapur, the accomplishments of daughters could also transmit prestige and status within a kinship circle.[69]

A brief examination of al-Qushayrī's career enables us to appreciate further the significance of his marriage to Fāṭima. Al-Qushayrī came upon his career as an *'ālim* serendipitously. Unlike Fāṭima, it was only during his adult life that he assimilated the culture of the scholarly elite of Nishapur. Raised by his parents in the tradition of the landed aristocracy, al-Qushayrī learned horsemanship and the use of weaponry and was also

[67] His full name is Abū al-Qāsim 'Abd al-Karīm b. Hawāzin b. 'Abd al-Mālik b. Ṭalḥa al-Qushayrī. For his biography, see al-Ṣarīfīnī, *al-Muntakhab*, 334–35; Tāj al-Dīn al-Subkī (d. 771/1370), *Ṭabaqāt al-Shāfi'iyya al-Kubrā* (Cairo: Maṭba'at 'Īsā al-Bābī al-Ḥalabī, 1967), 5:153–62; and al-Dhahabī, *Siyar*, 18:227–33.

[68] I was unable to locate a definitive statement regarding the transfer of Abū 'Alī's *madrasa* to al-Qushayrī.

[69] Fāṭima did have a brother, Ismā'īl, about whom we know very little. Al-Fārisī's notice points out that during Fāṭima's early upbringing, Abū 'Alī did not have a son (al-Ṣarīfīnī, *al-Muntakhab*, 419). Bulliet notes that Ismā'īl and Fāṭima did not share the same mother, and that Ismā'īl's mother may have been of a more humble background. See Bulliet, *Patricians*, 153.

taught writing and Arabic.[70] During a trip to Nishapur to resolve a financial matter, he happened upon the circles of learning and Ṣūfī devotion led by Abū ʿAlī al-Daqqāq, who introduced him to other scholars of Nishapur, much as he had done for his own daughter Fāṭima. Not coincidentally, al-Qushayrī and Fāṭima share many of the same *ḥadīth* teachers. With the encouragement of his soon-to-be father-in-law, al-Qushayrī went on to excel in the study of law under the guidance of the Shāfiʿī jurist Abū Bakr Muḥammad b. Bakr al-Ṭūsī (d. 420/1029).[71] He studied Ashʿarī theology (*kalām*) with Ibn Fūrak (d. 406/1015f.)[72] and was also closely associated with (*lāzama*) Abū Isḥāq al-Isfarāyīnī (d. 418/1027). Upon his father-in-law's death, he came under the guidance of al-Sulamī, the aforementioned Ṣūfī leader and scholar who was also Fāṭima's teacher. By the time he was in his thirties, al-Qushayrī had clearly distinguished himself as a leader in the circles of Shāfiʿī-Ṣūfī-Ashʿarī learning in Nishapur. His copious writings include the *Tafsīr Laṭāʾif al-Ishārāt* and a treatise on and defense of Ṣūfī practices entitled *al-Risāla al-Qushayriyya*.[73] Though he himself did not descend from a family of scholars, aided by Fāṭima's father, he acquired the training and connections necessary to become one of the most influential Shāfiʿī leaders of Nishapur.

To nuance our understanding of women's religious education in Nishapur during this era, it is instructive to compare the biographies of Fāṭima and her husband, both of whom are portrayed as exemplary leaders in their community. The discrepancies between the standards for men and those for women are clear from the résumés compiled by Fāṭima and al-Qushayrī. Fāṭima's education in *ḥadīth* and Qurʾān receive the greatest attention in her biographies. While al-Fārisī does note that her father taught her theology (*kalimāt al-tawḥīd*), he does not expand on this information. Customarily, advanced training in theology necessitated close and long association (*mulāzama*) with scholars, tutelage that would have taken place when the student was mature and advanced in his/her studies. In Fāṭima's case, her father seems to have been the only one who taught her this subject. Given that he died when she was in her early teens, we can speculate that her training in this area was limited.

[70] al-Subkī, *Ṭabaqāt*, 5:155. Heinz Halm also notes that al-Qushayrī's father was of Arab descent and his mother from a *dihqān* (Persian land-owning elite) background. See *EI*[2], s.v. "al-Ḳushayrī."

[71] For al-Ṭūsī's biographical notice, see al-Ṣarīfīnī, *al-Muntakhab*, 22.

[72] For Ibn Fūrak's biography, see al-Dhahabī, *Siyar*, 17:214–16.

[73] Abū al-Qāsim al-Qushayrī, *Laṭāʾif al-Ishārāt* (Cairo: Dār al-Kātib al-ʿArabī, 1968) and al-Qushayrī, *al-Risāla al-Qushayriyya* (Cairo: Dār al-Kutub al-Ḥadītha, 1966). This work has also been translated as Abu'l-Qasim al-Qushayri, *Al-Qushayri's Epistle on Sufism*, trans. Alexander D. Knysh (London: Garnet Publishing, 2007).

Al-Qushayrī, on the other hand, pursued theological training through close association with Ibn Fūrak and al-Isfarāyīnī. His biographers note that he was deeply engaged with the theological disputes between the Ash'arīs and their opponents in Nishapur, a commitment that led to his brief imprisonment and his migration with his family first to Baghdad and then some years later to Ṭūs to escape persecution.

Al-Qushayrī also obtained systematic legal training, another area where Fāṭima's exposure was either comparatively limited or not noted by her biographers. Indeed, one of al-Qushayrī's noted accomplishments was the harmonizing of Ṣūfī doctrines with Shāfi'ī-'Ash'arī ones as attested in his *Risāla*. At the end of his career, al-Qushayrī was hailed as a unique, exemplary leader for Shāfi'ī-Ash'arī-Ṣūfīs everywhere. Al-Subkī, among his most admiring biographers, lavishly praises him, saying

> [He is] one of the leaders of [all] Muslims with respect to his knowledge and his deeds, and a pillar of the community in terms of his actions and his sayings. An *imām* of *imām*s, one who lights the darkness of the wayward; he is someone who sets an example with respect to the *sunna*, and the ways of Hellfire and Heaven become clear through his works. He is the *shaykh* of *shaykh*s and the teacher of the whole congregation, the one who is foremost in our group (*muqaddam al-ṭā'ifa*), and one who brings together many different types of knowledge.[74]

A final difference between the profiles of Fāṭima and al-Qushayrī is that the latter influenced the course of prevailing theological and sectarian discussions by authoring his own works of *tafsīr*, theology, and Ṣūfī doctrines and practices. If Fāṭima composed any works of her own, they are not noted by her biographers. Nevertheless, given her religious learning and exposure, it is difficult to imagine that Fāṭima was withdrawn from the theological and sectarian controversies that so profoundly affected her family's fortunes. While it is difficult to read the silence of her biographers on this matter, we can extrapolate that her involvement in such debates was not a matter to be extolled as was her *ḥadīth* transmission.

In addition to the strong focus on *ḥadīth* learning, adherence to a personal ethic of asceticism is also a prominent feature of Fāṭima's biographies, and she flourished in an atmosphere strongly influenced by Ṣūfism. Bulliet's research on Nishapur has shed light on the rapid growth of Ṣūfism, among those who were Shāfi'ī in their legal affiliation and Ash'arī in their theological outlook. Al-Sulamī was among the better-known scholars of this group of Ṣūfī-Shāfi'ī-Ash'arīs in Nishapur.[75]

[74] al-Subkī, *Ṭabaqāt*, 5:153.
[75] al-Ṣarīfīnī, *al-Muntakhab*, 419–20. See also Bulliet, *Patricians*, 43.

Al-Sulamī's outlook with respect to women's piety and religious participation is accessible in his noteworthy and pioneering biographical dictionary on female ascetics entitled *Dhikr al-Niswa al-Muta'abbidāt al-Ṣūfiyyāt*.[76] The significance of al-Sulamī's contribution is not merely that it describes women's religious engagement. Rather, it can be read as a normative tract that advocates a newly emergent Ṣūfī-Shāfi'ī vision of feminine piety and learning. *Dhikr al-Niswa* offers a rare testimony to the view that religiously devoted, pious women could in fact overcome social and cultural stigmas associated with the feminine. In her study of al-Sulamī's work, Rkia Cornell notes that "whatever limitations ordinary women may possess with respect to their religion and intellect, these have nothing to do with the spiritual and intellectual abilities of female Ṣūfī devotees." In this vein, al-Sulamī often describes the criticisms and advice given by female devotees to their male counterparts.[77] For example, Fāṭima of Nishapur (d. 223/837f.) was known to have guided two of the most prominent contemporary male Ṣūfīs, Dhū al-Nūn al-Miṣrī (d. 245/859) and Abū Yazīd al-Bisṭāmī (d. 261/875).[78] Al-Sulamī includes notices for twenty-one women who either lived in Nishapur or practiced their asceticism there.[79] These include highly respected and accomplished women such as 'Azīza al-Harawiyya (a contemporary of al-Sulamī), Umm 'Alī bint 'Abd Allāh b. Ḥamshādh, and Umm al-Ḥusayn al-Qurashiyya.[80] Al-Sulamī's brief biographical notices do not provide information on these women's legal affiliations. On the basis of Bulliet's research, which reveals strong connections between the Shāfi'īs and Ṣūfīs of Nishapur, we can surmise that these women were probably also Shāfi'ī and active in the Shāfi'ī circles of their city. These observations regarding the influence of Ṣūfism in Fāṭima's life square well with previous analyses

[76] This work has often been considered an appendix to al-Sulamī's *Ṭabaqāt al-Ṣūfiyyāt*. However, Rkia Cornell maintains that it was actually an independent work and not an addendum as are many other sections on women in classical Islamic biographical works. See Rkia Cornell, introduction to al-Sulamī, *Early Sufi Women*, 43–45.

[77] Cornell, introduction to al-Sulamī, *Early Sufi Women*, 54–60.

[78] al-Sulamī, *Early Sufi Women*, 142–45.

[79] Cornell, introduction to al-Sulamī, *Early Sufi Women*, 48. Cornell calculates that twenty-five of the eighty women documented by al-Sulamī were from Khurāsān. Iraq (in particular, the city of Baṣra) is the best-represented region in al-Sulamī's biographies on women, followed by Khurāsān.

[80] Biographical references for these three women in al-Sulamī's *Early Sufi Women* are as follows: 'Azīza al-Harawiyya at 242–43; Umm 'Alī bint 'Abd Allāh b. Ḥamshādh at 244–45; and Umm al-Ḥusayn al-Qurashiyya at 250. The death dates of these women are unknown, but Cornell has placed them in the second half of the fourth/tenth century based on evidence from their biographical notices.

that have correlated varieties of Ṣūfism with higher rates of women's religious participation in comparison with other strains of Muslim practice, particularly those that emphasize legalism and rationalism over spirituality and asceticism.[81]

Within this milieu that so clearly valued accomplishments in *ḥadīth* learning and asceticism, Fāṭima functioned as a linchpin in a kinship network distinguished by religious learning and piety. Al-Qushayrī's marriage to her was an initial step in the forging of a complex and influential dynasty spanning nearly two centuries. Fāṭima and al-Qushayrī had at least eight children; most of them are commemorated in the sources for their promotion of Ṣūfī devotion, *ḥadīth* studies, theology, and law. Among the better-known of these was ʿAbd al-Raḥīm Abū Naṣr (d. 514/1120), who followed in his father's footsteps not just in excelling in theology, law, and *taṣawwuf* but also with respect to his involvement in theological-sectarian strife. According to al-Subkī's biography of Abū Naṣr, his assemblies in Baghdad were implicated in the violent fighting between Ḥanbalīs and Shāfiʿīs.[82] To quell this strife, the Seljūq vizier Niẓām al-Mulk (d. 485/1092) ordered Abū Naṣr back to Nishapur, where he maintained a lower profile, devoting himself to religious studies, assemblies of *ḥadīth* and Ṣūfī devotion, and to giving *fatwā*s.[83]

The marriages of their children further extended the scholarly influence of the Qushayrī clan. Umm al-Raḥīm Karīma, one of their daughters, married a member of the Fārisī family, and it is this union that produced, among other scholars, the historian ʿAbd al-Ghāfir al-Fārisī. Another daughter married a member of the al-Fūrakī clan, descendants of the leading Ashʿarī-Shāfiʿī theologian and al-Qushayrī's teacher, Ibn Fūrak. Two granddaughters married into the al-Ṣaffār family, and a great-granddaughter married into the Shaḥḥāmī family. This grouping of five

[81] In Chapter 2, I noted that successful female Successors who were accomplished as *ḥadīth* transmitters, such as Umm al-Dardāʾ and Ḥafṣa bint Sīrīn, were often also acclaimed as ascetics. Studies that have examined the feminine in Ṣūfism include Annemarie Schimmel, *My Soul Is a Woman: The Feminine in Islam*, trans. Susan Ray (New York: Continuum, 1997); Sachiko Murata, *Tao of Islam* (Albany: SUNY Press, 1992); and sources mentioned in Chapter 2, footnote 24.

[82] al-Subkī, *Ṭabaqāt*, 7:161–62; al-Subkī's biography of Abū Naṣr is extensive and highly laudatory (see Subkī, 7:159–66). See also Ibn al-Jawzī, *al-Muntaẓam*, 17:190, for mention of this incident.

[83] Niẓām al-Mulk and his impact on Muslim political and intellectual history have been the subject of a number of studies. For a biographical overview and a bibliography, see *EI*^{2}, s.v. "Niẓām al-Mulk."

families over four generations produced scores of influential *ḥadīth* transmitters, jurists, and theologians. In his study of Nishapur, Bulliet charts the growth and interconnectedness of this complex of Shāfiʿī families and counts six major and several minor families in the network.[84] Over seven generations, nearly eighty of their members are noted for their learning or other pious contributions to Nishapur and surrounding areas.

The social significance of belonging to a household devoted to religious learning is clear in Fāṭima's biographies, which praise her in terms that recall Prophet Muḥammad's daughter Fāṭima. For example, al-Subkī's entry for ʿAbd al-Raḥmān, another of Fāṭima bint al-Ḥasan's sons, refers to her as *al-sayyida al-ṭāhira* (the pure *sayyida*, i.e., female exemplar), *al-sayyida al-khayra al-ṣāliḥa* (the good, virtuous *sayyida*), and *umm al-sādāt* (the mother of *sayyids*).[85] She is regularly mentioned as an authority in the biographies of her descendants who were brought to her to be inculcated in the tradition of piety characteristic of this household.[86] The cumulative impact of these notices impresses on us her tremendous status as the matriarch of a clan that exercised influence from Baghdad to Nishapur.

Fāṭima's network, replete with male and female *ḥadīth* scholars, casts into sharper relief the dramatic rise in the fortunes of female *ḥadīth* transmitters after a long period of decline. The eight female Successors examined in Chapter 2 were exceptions to the rule of marginalization characterizing female *ḥadīth* participation during their lifetimes. By contrast, Fāṭima's accomplishments were the product of a culture that exalted religious learning and piety among women as well as men. A number of Fāṭima's female descendants continued her tradition of transmitting religious knowledge in

84 Bulliet, *Patricians*, 149–91. Bulliet has distilled the complex web of these families' relations into genealogical charts in *Patricians of Nishapur*. See pp. 160–61 for his description of Abū Bakr Aḥmad al-Fūrakī, who married one of al-Qushayrī's daughters, and pp. 175–91 for the genealogical charts of the Qushayrī, Fūrakī, Ṣaffār, Fārisī, Shaḥḥāmī, and Furāwī clans.

85 al-Subkī, *Ṭabaqāt*, 5:105–6. In using the term *sādāt* for the children of Fāṭima and al-Qushayrī, al-Subkī emphasizes their lineage within the family of the Prophet.

86 See, for example, the biographical notices for her grandchildren Hibat al-Raḥmān b. ʿAbd al-Wāḥid b. ʿAbd al-Karīm and ʿAbd al-Razzāq b. ʿAbd Allāh in al-Samʿānī, *al-Taḥbīr fī Muʿjam al-Kabīr* (Beirut: Dār al-Kutub al-ʿIlmiyya, 1997), 2:212, #1091 (for Hibat al-Raḥmān), and 1:186, #399 (for ʿAbd al-Razzāq). It is difficult to ascertain the extent of Fāṭima's public presence as a teacher for students beyond her extensive family network. Al-Fārisī does not note the names of those who heard her *ḥadīth* within her own biography, although she is listed as an authority in the biographies of members of her extended family network. Al-Dhahabī lists Ibn al-Farāwī (d. 549/1155) and Zāhir al-Shaḥḥāmī (d. 533/1138) as Fāṭima's students in the course of her biography and notes that others also heard *ḥadīth* from her. For the biography of Ibn al-Farāwī, see al-Dhahabī, *Siyar*, 20:227–28, and for that of al-Shaḥḥāmī, see *Siyar*, 20:9–13.

the scholarly networks of Nishapur, and her daughter, Karīma, is described by the latter's son al-Fārisī in terms similar to those he used for Fāṭima in the entry cited earlier.[87] He praises her asceticism, saying that she never wore silk or indulged in material pleasures, and engaged in worldly matters only as necessary. Karīma acquired the tradition of piety and asceticism from Fāṭima, her mother, and Ṣūfī knowledge (*ṭarīq al-ma'rifa*) from Abū al-Qāsim al-Qushayrī, her father. Similarly, Fāṭima's granddaughters Amat al-Qāhir Jawhar (d. 530/1135f.), the daughter of 'Abd Allāh, and Amat Allāh Jalīla (d. 541/1146), the daughter of 'Abd al-Raḥīm, are praised for their pious conduct and their *ḥadīth* studies.[88]

Fāṭima's father was not alone in initiating his daughter into this culture of religious learning. Nearly every woman noted for piety and *ḥadīth* learning in al-Fārisī's history belonged to a prominent scholarly family.[89] Al-Ḥurra al-Bisṭāmiyya (d. in the 470s/1077f.), the daughter of Abū 'Umar Muḥammad b. al-Ḥusayn al-Bisṭāmī (d. 408/1018), who was a Shāfi'ī jurist and judge (*qāḍī*) of Nishapur, heard *ḥadīth* from a number of scholars. When she herself became a teacher, students would read to her while she sat listening behind a curtain.[90] Fāṭima al-Ṣābūniyya (death date unknown) acquired a special place within her scholarly family because of her superlative piety, learning, and generosity in spending all that she had on the poor and the Ṣūfīs (*al-mutaṣawwifa*). Al-Fārisī generously praises her as the pearl of the Ṣābūnī clan (*durrat ṣadaf al-ṣābūniyya*) and the pride of their eyes (*qurrat a'yuni-him*). He makes the striking comment that she was like a sister to her father (*kānat ka'l-ukht li-abī-hā*), thereby signaling their closeness and her special status within the family.[91]

Other such examples of scholarly, pious women leave little doubt that the tradition of educating women was firmly established among the

[87] al-Ṣarīfīnī, *al-Muntakhab*, 428–29.

[88] al-Sam'ānī, *Taḥbīr fī Mu'jam al-Kabīr*, 2:230–31 (for Amat al-Qāhir) and 2:231 (for Amat Allāh Jalīla).

[89] Bulliet has counted a total of thirty-six women belonging to the *'ulamā* families of Nishapur who merited mention in the following works: al-Ḥākim al-Naysābūrī's *Ta'rīkh Naysābūr* (three women), al-Fārisī's *Siyāq li-Ta'rīkh Naysābūr* (twenty-two women, one of them included in al-Ḥākim's work), and al-Sahmī's *Ta'rīkh Jurjān* (twelve women); Bulliet, "Women and the Urban Religious Elite," 68. See also Travis Zadeh , *The Vernacular Qur'ān: Translation and the Rise of Persian Exegesis* (New York: Oxford University Press, 2012), 346–49, for his observations on the involvement of women such as Fāṭima (the daughter of Abū 'Alī al-Daqqāq) in networks of learning in fifth/eleventh-century Nishapur. Zadeh also observes that women's religious learning is not exceptional for this period.

[90] al-Ṣarīfīnī, *al-Muntakhab*, 215.

[91] al-Ṣarīfīnī, *al-Muntakhab*, 230.

Nishapuri *'ulamā'*. Al-Fārisī also commemorates Khadīja al-Ṣābūniyya (d. 488/1095), one of Fāṭima al-Ṣābūniyya's sisters, and notes that her father and siblings took charge of her *ḥadīth* learning.[92] While she too acquired a reputation for piety, she did not attain the rank of her sister Fāṭima, described earlier in the chapter. The brief biographies of Fāṭima bint 'Alī b. al-Muẓaffar, who used to busy herself with teaching children, and Rūḥak (d. 491/1098), the daughter of the jurist Abū al-Qāsim al-Ṣaffār who attracted students because of her unusual name (which presumably would be featured in the students' *isnād*s after they heard *ḥadīth* from her), provide further windows onto the culture of *ḥadīth* learning.[93]

The publicizing of women's accomplishments through assemblies, *dhikr* sessions, individual classes, and genres such as biographical works, chronicles, and compilations devoted to women's learning and teaching (e.g., in the *fawā'id* and *mu'jam al-shuyūkh* genres) is significant not just as a marker of the revival of women's participation in *ḥadīth* learning. Such developments also reflect the evolving criteria of membership in the *'ulamā'* class and its increasingly visible constitution along the lines of kinship networks. Public assemblies and individualized teaching sessions wherein teaching and learning were conducted in formalized and hierarchical terms according to criteria of scholarly standing and seniority were important channels for the socialization of participants into the culture of the *'ulamā'*. Whereas lay people were welcome as students into such forums, generally only those properly qualified as *'ulamā'* could actually teach.

Biographical dictionaries and chronicles functioned not just as records of individuals and their actions, but equally importantly as documentation of occupational status and demarcation of the boundaries of the *'ulamā'* class. An individual's inclusion in biographical compilations, such as al-Dhahabī's *Siyar A'lām al-Nubalā'*, often commemorated his/her socialization into the scholarly class.[94] Rituals of initiation and belonging to the scholarly class and the texts that legitimized and glorified their accomplishments breathed

92 al-Ṣarīfīnī, *al-Muntakhab*, 219.

93 For their biographical notices, see al-Ṣarīfīnī, *al-Muntakhab*, 420 (Fāṭima bint 'Alī b. al-Muẓaffar) and 224 (Rūḥak).

94 Ahmed El Shamsy, citing the example of Umm Hāni' (1376–1454), a revered transmitter during the Mamlūk period, notes that women could not be properly socialized into the predominantly male discourse. The examples studied here reveal that women availed themselves of alternative avenues for socialization into the *'ulamā'* class. See El Shamsy, "The Social Construction of Orthodoxy," in *The Cambridge Companion to Classical Islamic Theology*, ed. Tim Winter, 97–117 (New York: Cambridge University Press, 2008), 103.

new spirit into older models of feminine piety, thereby establishing exemplars relevant to subsequent generations of women.

The activities of Fāṭima bint al-Ḥasan al-Daqqāq, Karīma al-Marwaziyya, and other women of the scholarly elite are part of a historical trend first observed in Khurāsān and spreading west toward Baghdad, Damascus, and Cairo.[95] The sociopolitical and economic contexts of this trend strongly suggest that women's increasing participation constituted an important element of the way in which Sunnī *'ulamā'* of the classical period developed as a social, political, and religious elite. This elite employed the culture of learning to acquire social and political power in a complex historical process profoundly influenced by the fragmentation of ʿAbbāsid central authority and the rise of autonomous regional dynasties. Nishapur was one of several major Eastern urban centers that experienced intense competition among those attempting to control it from the late third/ninth century until the early seventh/thirteenth century when the Mongols sacked the city (618/1221). As such, it illustrates how *'ulamā'* honed their strategies against a backdrop of political, socioeconomic, and military instability.

The history of Nishapur's *'ulamā'* is intimately bound up with the city's rise as a major urban center of Khurāsān under the Iranian Sāmānid dynasty (204–395/819–1005). By the early fourth century, Nishapur had a diversified, prosperous economy supporting a range of socioeconomic groups including the Sāmānid ruling elite, their military forces, and merchants, traders, craftsmen, and agriculturalists. Most importantly for our purposes, Nishapur was home to increasingly powerful coalitions of Shāfiʿī and Ḥanafī scholars. As Nishapur's prosperity and importance grew, so too did rivalry over its control. In the fourth and fifth centuries, the Sāmānids, Sīmjūrids, Ghaznavids, and Seljūqs deployed a range of military, political, and economic strategies to conquer this city and its environs.

The *'ulamā'* were central to the attempts of foreign dynasties to establish control. Their store of religious knowledge, authority to rule on matters relating to religious practice, and oftentimes charismatic leadership enabled them to command the loyalty of the local population in ways that the foreign ruling elite could not. While *'ulamā'* had always garnered a measure of control even in times of more centralized ʿAbbāsid rule, the ʿAbbāsid were also accorded their share of

[95] This westward trend of engagement with *ḥadīth* has been treated by Bulliet in *Islam: A View from the Edge*. Nadwi similarly notes this distinct geographic pattern specifically with respect to women's participation (see *al-Muhaddithat*, 254 and 257–58).

religious authority.[96] The foreign dynasties, on the other hand, being of non-Arab origin and often with shallow roots with respect to their acculturation to Islam, relied far more on *'ulamā'* to procure the allegiance and compliance of the ruled.

In spite of the power commanded by *'ulamā'*, they were vulnerable. The ruling elite could confiscate property, impose taxes, and imprison or exile *'ulamā'* who opposed their policies. In his analysis of social practices among the *'ulamā'* of Damascus (1190–1350 CE), Michael Chamberlain notes that medieval Muslim scholarly elites lacked the privileges and rights available to their counterparts in other parts of the world.[97] For example, European institutions such as hereditary charters, deeds, immunities, and titles of office, which could be used to ensure household survival, were absent from the medieval Muslim context. The fragmentation of 'Abbāsid authority and ensuing battles for regional control of competing dynasties exacerbated the vulnerability of the *'ulamā'*, exposing them even more to predatory practices.

With respect to the scholarly elite of Nishapur, Richard Bulliet details some of the ways in which the Sāmānids, Sīmjūrids, Ghaznavids, and Seljūqs alternately coerced and cajoled the Ḥanafī and Shāfi'ī *'ulamā'*, and how their policies exacerbated preexisting legal and theological tensions between these factions from the fourth/tenth to the sixth/twelfth century. The draconian policies of 'Amīd al-Mulk al-Kundurī, a vizier of the Seljūq leader Tughril Beg (d. 455/1063), illustrate how the ruling elite exerted pressure on the *'ulamā'* in the hopes of suppressing opposition. Al-Kundurī, favoring the Ḥanafī-Mu'tazilī leaders of Nishapur, ordered that their rivals, the Shāfi'ī-Ash'arīs, be condemned during Friday sermons. Additionally, Shāfi'ī-Ash'arīs were excluded from religious and educational posts, were subject to arrests and mob action, and came under pressure to leave Nishapur.[98] Fāṭima's husband, al-Qushayrī, was one of several *'ulamā'* leaders who faced imprisonment and exile during this period. His support of Ash'arī theology, which he expressed through his classes and writings, landed him in prison in 446/1054.[99] To secure his release, it took the intervention of his supporters who threatened civil

[96] See Muhammad Qasim Zaman, *Religion and Politics under the Early 'Abbāsids: The Emergence of the Proto-Sunnī Elite* (New York: Brill, 1997), for a detailed analysis of the division of religious authority between the 'Abbāsid caliphs and the *'ulamā'*.

[97] Chamberlain, *Knowledge and Social Practice*, 4.

[98] Bulliet, *Patricians*, 71–72.

[99] See, in particular, al-Qushayrī's work entitled *Shikāyat ahl al-sunna bi-mā nāla-hum min al-miḥna*, which is included in the following collection of his writings: *al-Rasā'il al-Qushayriyya* (Beirut: al-Maktaba al-'Aṣriyya, 1970), 1–49.

unrest and descended on the prison. Al-Qushayrī now found some respite teaching *ḥadīth* in Baghdad under the invitation of the ʿAbbāsid caliph al-Qā'im. His return to Nishapur only exposed him to further hostility, and he was compelled to emigrate to Ṭūs with his family to escape persecution. Only after Niẓām al-Mulk replaced al-Kundurī and inaugurated policies aimed at a more equitable balance of power between Ḥanafīs and Shāfiʿīs did al-Qushayrī feel comfortable returning to Nishapur with his family.[100]

In an environment characterized by the heightened use of state power to control the *'ulamā'* and by increased military and political instability, the *'ulamā'* elaborated on preexisting strategies of personal and group survival. These included collaboration with the ruling elite, competing with each other for teaching and judiciary posts in order to secure their financial futures, endowing charitable foundations to preserve property within a family, and using networks of learning to facilitate and perpetuate alliances. While such strategies have been recorded since the earliest periods of Islamic history, they were employed with far greater intensity and display greater sophistication in the post-ʿAbbāsid era as documented in case studies of the *'ulamā'* of Nishapur, Damascus, and Cairo.[101]

Another strategy through which *'ulamā'* could compete was to draw growing numbers of their family members into the orbit of religious learning, thereby increasing the status and competitive capacity of the family as a whole. It is in this context that we can better comprehend the significant increase in women's public participation that coincided with the rise of regional dynasties. The marshalling of women's contributions and their post fourth/tenth-century reentry into *ḥadīth* learning evolved as an important strategy in the interest of the social survival and perpetuation of *'ulamā'* culture. In part, our heretofore incomplete grasp of the chronology of women's *ḥadīth* participation has prevented an appreciation of how this chronology relates to the broader narrative of the history of the *'ulamā'* as a social class. Situating the fourth/tenth-century revival of women's *ḥadīth* transmission and, more specifically, the activities of Fāṭima bint al-Ḥasan and her female cohort within this sociopolitical context provides a more nuanced understanding of the development of the *'ulamā'* class.

100 A summary of the trials al-Qushayrī faced and the ways in which shifting political alliances affected his security may be found in al-Subkī, *Ṭabaqāt*, 5:157–58.

101 For Nishapur, see Bulliet, *Patricians*; for Damascus, see Chamberlain, *Knowledge and Social Practice*; and for Cairo, see Berkey, *Transmission of Knowledge*.

Women contributed to the efforts of *'ulamā'* families in a number of ways. One of these was the endowment of their own institutions and charitable contributions, which helped make property inalienable and less vulnerable to division, taxation, and confiscation by ruling authorities. Women were also central to scholarly networks. Their participation as students and as teachers cemented ties of religious learning. And their marriages created stronger bonds of kinship and forged dynasties of *'ulamā'*, which raised the chances of survival of a scholarly clan across generations. Fāṭima's family, which exercised pervasive influence for seven generations, is only one example of a dynasty wherein the efforts of women mitigated challenges confronted by *'ulamā'* families.[102]

Women were central to the survival of *'ulamā'* kinship networks in two other respects. As women, they were more sheltered from the political and factional violence that claimed the careers and lives of many male scholars.[103] Women could thus help preserve the tradition of *ḥadīth* transmission, which was critical to the culture of religious learning and piety that distinguished the *'ulamā'* class. Also, because of their natural longevity compared to men, they were more likely to perpetuate short chains of transmission – a point taken up further in Chapter 4.

Intriguingly, the women of Nishapur who appear in the historical records are for the most part Shāfi'ī, and there are no Ḥanafī women among the prominent *muḥaddithas*.[104] Yet *ḥadīth* learning and dissemination were integral to religious life in fourth- and fifth-century Nishapur for Ḥanafīs and Shāfi'īs alike. Indeed, al-Fārisī includes biographical notices for both Ḥanafī and Shāfi'ī male scholars. Valued by the rulers and the *'ulamā'*, *ḥadīth* transmission was perhaps the only activity that unified an

102 Studies of *'ulamā'* dynasties in different periods include Kamal Salibi, "Banū Jamā'a: A Dynasty of Shāfi'ī Jurists of the Mamluk Period," *Studia Islamica* 9 (1958): 97–109; William Brinner, "The Banū Ṣaṣrā: A Study on the Transmission of a Scholarly Tradition," *Arabica* 7 (May 1960): 167–95; Muḥammad b. 'Azzūz, *Buyūtāt al-Ḥadīth fī Dimashq* (Damascus: Dār al-Fikr, 2004); and Muḥammad Zayn al-'Ābidīn Rustam, *Buyūtāt al-'Ilm wa'l-Ḥadīth fi'l-Andalus* (Beirut: Dār Ibn Ḥazm li'l-Ṭibā'a wa'l-Nashr wa'l-Tawzī', 2009).

103 It is important to note that though women were not victims of political and sectarian violence as often as men were, they were nonetheless just as susceptible as men to other types of violence, such as that resulting from the Mongol invasions.

104 The following Ḥanafī biographical works do not contain entries for women: 'Abd al-Qādir b. Abī al-Wafā' al-Qurashī, *al-Jawāhir al-Muḍiyya fī al-Ṭabaqāt al-Ḥanafiyya* (Hyderabad: Maṭba'at Majlis Dā'irat al-Ma'ārif al-'Uthmāniyya, 1989); and al-Taqī al-Tamīmī, *al-Ṭabaqāt al-Saniyya fī Tarājim al-Ḥanafiyya* (Riyad: Dār al-Rifā'ī, 1983).

otherwise fractured city.[105] As Bulliet notes, in spite of the bitter, destructive strife perpetuated by these factions, they were united in their approach to religious learning. More specifically, it was the uniform approach to the system of the transmission of religious knowledge that maintained the fabric of Nishapuri society even as it was being torn apart by religio-political factionalism. Therefore, this discrepancy may only partly be explained by the fact that al-Fārisī, the main source for the women's biographies, was himself a Shāfi'ī.

Another possible explanation for the disparate rates of Ḥanafī and Shāfi'ī female participation arises from Bulliet's study of the *'ulamā'* elite of Nishapur. He describes the Ḥanafīs of fourth- and fifth-century Nishapur as the more conservative old guard, whose representatives in the *'ulamā'* class espoused rationalism over traditionalism in the derivation of Islamic law. The Shāfi'īs, on the other hand, represented the newly emergent religious elite, one that was more egalitarian in its approach to non-Arabs and more progressive in its social vision.[106] Bulliet hypothesizes that these differences manifested themselves in terms of social organization and an ethos uniquely associated with each of the *madhhabs*.[107] It may well be that the higher rate of women's *ḥadīth* participation among the Shāfi'ī families was due to a more gender-inclusive approach to religious learning espoused by leading Shāfi'ī *'ulamā'* as represented by Abū 'Alī al-Daqqāq and Abū al-Qāsim al-Qushayrī, Fāṭima's father and husband, respectively. In this respect, it is worth reiterating the prescriptive value of al-Sulamī's collection of women's biographies in his *Dhikr al-Niswa al-Muta'abbidāt*, a collection for which there is no Ḥanafī equivalent. The compilation itself may have been intended to legitimize and bolster the

105 For this reason, it would be a mistake to read the absence of Ḥanafī female transmitters as an extension of an overall Ḥanafī antipathy toward *ḥadīth* learning inherited from their Kūfan predecessors such that Ḥanafīs of Nishapur would not have inculcated a culture of *ḥadīth* transmission among their family members.

106 Bulliet, *Patricians*, 35–46. The growth of Ash'arism and the Shāfi'ī-Ash'arī alliance in Nishapur further fueled the animosity of the Ḥanafī-Mu'tazilī faction. Bulliet points out that the sectarian rivalries in Nishapur as well as in other cities of Khurāsān masked deeper social and political rivalries. Before the Shāfi'ī-Ḥanafī bifurcation in fourth- and fifth-century Nishapur, the ranks were split roughly along the Kūfan-Medinese legal divide. Bulliet, *Patricians*, 31–33.

107 Roy Mottahedeh in his review of *Patricians* adopts a more cautious stance regarding the impact of *'ulamā'* factionalism on local life, thereby highlighting that much research remains to be done before conclusive comment on dynamics between groups of *'ulamā'*. Mottahedeh, review of *Patricians of Nishapur: A Study in Medieval Islamic Social History*, by R. W. Bulliet, *Journal of the American Oriental Society* 95, no. 3 (1975): 491–95.

concerted effort of contemporary Shāfiʿī *ʿulamāʾ* to educate their daughters in the traditions of ascetic piety and *ḥadīth* learning. As such, al-Sulamī's compilation fits in a broader narrative of Shāfiʿī adaptation and survival in fourth- and fifth-century Nishapur. However, we must also be cautious about extending this line of analysis to suggest that Shāfiʿīs throughout the classical Muslim world espoused the same view. Indeed, in considering the rates of female religious learning in Damascus and its environs from the seventh/thirteenth to the ninth/fifteenth century, it appears that the Ḥanbalīs take the lead over the Shāfiʿīs in encouraging women's education. Thus, the explanation of social visions rooted in *madhhabs* remains to be tested in future research.

CONCLUSION

The careers of Karīma al-Marwaziyya and Fāṭima bint al-Ḥasan al-Daqqāq reveal how canonization, written transmission, and the evolution of the *ʿulamāʾ* as a social and religious elite positively impacted women's *ḥadīth* participation. The trend of women's *ḥadīth* participation continued for the next three centuries, producing numerous prolific and popular female transmitters. The next chapter traces this trend up to the early Ottoman period, when women's *ḥadīth* transmission waned yet again.

CHAPTER 4

A Culmination in Traditionalism

> It has not been transmitted on the authority of any scholar that he rejected the tradition of a woman on the basis that it was narrated by a woman.[1]
>
> Muḥammad b. ʻAlī al-Shawkānī (d. 1250/1834)

The trickle of women's *ḥadīth* participation that began in the mid-fourth century steadily gained momentum. Al-Fārisī, the sixth/twelfth-century historian of Nishapur, documented the lives of only twenty-two women active from the fourth/tenth to the sixth/twelfth century. By the ninth/fifteenth century, the Egyptian scholar Shams al-Dīn Muḥammad b. ʻAbd al-Raḥmān al-Sakhāwī (d. 902/1497) could devote an entire volume – more than a thousand entries – of his biographical compendium to women alone. Al-Sakhāwī's life was contemporaneous with the zenith of women's *ḥadīth* participation. His biographies therefore may not have captured the full extent of women's involvement in his time.[2]

[1] Muḥammad b. ʻAlī al-Shawkānī, *Nayl al-Awṭār: Sharḥ Muntaqā al-Akhbār min Aḥādīth Sayyid al-Akhyār* (Cairo: Maktabat al-Qāhira, 1978), 8:122.

[2] For an overview of the roles of women in this work, see Huda Lutfi, "Al-Sakhāwī's *Kitāb al-Nisā'* as a Source for the Social and Economic History of Muslim Women during the Fifteenth Century AD," *Muslim World* 71 (1981): 104–24. Nadwi also notes the tremendous rise in *ḥadīth* transmission activity in the eighth/fourteenth and ninth/fifteenth centuries, particularly in Syria, Egypt, Mecca, and Medina (*al-Muḥaddithāt*, 255–60). Contemporary research on female *ḥadīth* transmission tends to cluster around the Mamlūk period, reflecting the wealth of evidence for this period. See, for example, Abou-Bakr, "Teaching the Words of the Prophet"; Berkey, "Women and Islamic Education in the Mamluk Period," in *Women in Middle Eastern History*, ed. N. Keddie and B. Baron, 143–57 (New Haven: Yale University Press, 1991); and Roded, *Women in Islamic Biographical Collections*, 63–89.

The tenth/sixteenth century, however, witnessed a second dramatic decrease in women's *ḥadīth* transmission. One reason for this was that a de-emphasis on the narrative aspects of *ḥadīth* transmission (*riwāya*) in this period was accompanied by a renewed engagement with interpretive activity (*dirāya*). Simultaneously, women's religious involvement inclined more toward *ṭarīqa*-based Ṣūfism and increasingly found expression through Ṣūfī institutional frameworks such as *zāwiya*s and *khānqāh*s.[3] These trends help account for the drop in women's *ḥadīth* participation. Nonetheless, this was not a reenactment of the second/eighth-century saga of decline. Rather, women's resounding successes from the fourth/tenth to the ninth/fifteenth century had indisputably established the acceptability, even desirability, of women's *ḥadīth* transmission. Their contributions to this realm, though reduced, continued to garner praise.

The reshaping of historical memory as a by-product of these evolutions is evident in the words attributed to al-Shawkānī, the thirteenth/nineteenth-century jurist, cited at the beginning of this chapter. In asserting that scholars had not rejected traditions because they were narrated by women, al-Shawkānī shows no awareness of the ways in which gender-related variables had impacted women's fortunes from the late first/eighth to the early fourth/ninth century. By al-Shawkānī's time, the ambivalence about the value of women's traditions, including those of Companions such as Busra bint Ṣafwān and Fāṭima bint Qays, had been overlaid by unequivocal acceptance.

This chapter chronicles the resurgence and culmination of women's participation from the sixth/twelfth to the ninth/fifteenth century through a study of three extraordinary *muḥadditha*s: Shuhda al-Kātiba (482–574/1089–1178), Zaynab bint al-Kamāl (646–740/1248–1339), and 'Ā'isha bint Muḥammad b. 'Abd al-Hādī (723–816/1323–1413). The lives of these three women manifest parallels and continuities with those of women active in the fourth/tenth century such as Karīma al-Marwaziyya and Fāṭima bint al-Ḥasan, discussed in the previous chapter, and reflect the relatively stable model of feminine piety and learning that prevailed during the classical and late classical eras. Further, the collective portrait that emerges from their profiles illuminates hallmarks of classical Sunnī culture

[3] In the context of classical Ṣūfism, the terms *zāwiya*, *khānqāh*, and *ribāṭ* often refer to physical structures devoted to Ṣūfīs and to the provisioning of travelers. The functioning of individual institutions varied; each institution is best understood in its particular historical context. For introductions to the history and evolution of these institutions, see *EI*², s.v. "*ribāṭ*," "*khānḳāh*," and "*zāwiya*."

that enabled a greater mobilization of women as teachers and students of *ḥadīth* in urban centers west of Khurāsān (the regional focus of Chapter 3). Commonly labeled "traditionalism," this classical cultural matrix came to be equated with Sunnī orthodoxy across the central Islamic lands by about the sixth/twelfth century, once the sustained legal, theological, and sectarian disputes of previous centuries had run their course.[4] The profiles presented in this chapter enable us to identify common elements of women's traditionalist education across time and place, from fifth-century Baghdad to ninth-century Damascus. These features include a characteristic age structure in *ḥadīth* education; license for coeducational exchanges within socially accepted parameters; the persistence of noninstitutional education alongside *madrasa*s; and the proliferation of lesser, derivative compilations that formed the basis for a course of study in traditionalist circles. The chapter closes with a discussion of the decrease in women's participation in the early Ottoman period (tenth/sixteenth century) and some reasons for this change.

The reemergence of women as *ḥadīth* transmitters in the late fourth/tenth century, followed by a surge in their numbers from the sixth/twelfth to the ninth/fifteenth century, correlates with the articulation and maturation of traditionalism as a consensus-driven orthodoxy. Distinguished by a tendency to rely on the Qur'ān, the *ḥadīth* (as representative of the Prophet's actions), and the pious early generations (*al-salaf*) as the primary sources of religious guidance, traditionalism enabled its adherents to construct and validate their choices through creative and constant reference to the past.[5] The age of the Prophet was unanimously regarded as the golden age, with the corollary that subsequent generations represented a decline in terms of religious practice and morality. Connectedness to the

[4] See Roy Mottahedeh, *Loyalty and Leadership in an Early Islamic Society*, 2nd rev. ed. (New York: I. B. Tauris, 2001), 16–27, for a succinct, insightful commentary on the development of classical Sunnism and his understanding of the chronology of this historical process. The pre-classical debates and their resolutions, the subject of other detailed studies, are dealt with in this book only insofar as they help us understand the environment that cultivated women's *ḥadīth* participation at unprecedented levels.

[5] A number of studies have addressed the significance of traditionalism in Islam. These include Johann Fueck, "The Role of Traditionalism in Islam," in *Studies on Islam*, ed. Merlin L. Swartz, 99–122 (New York: Oxford University Press, 1981); Makdisi, "The Sunni Revival"; and Graham, "Traditionalism in Islam." See also Lucas, *Constructive Critics* for an extensive study of the development of Sunnī Islam and its emphasis on traditionalism. Classical Sunnī traditionalism is distinct from modern traditionalist thought, associated with figures such as Martin Lings, Frithjof Schuon, and Sayyid Hossein Nasr. For an introduction to the modern trends, see Mark Sedgwick, *Against the Modern World: Traditionalism and the Secret Intellectual History of the Twentieth Century* (New York: Oxford University Press, 2004).

time of the Prophet was acquired by practicing a personal ethic of ascetic piety and implementing the vision of ideal religious practice as advocated by the consensus of the *'ulamā'* of the major schools of law. Rationalist theologies were generally shunned.[6] However, it is important to emphasize here that I do not use "traditionalism" to signify only a dogmatic Ḥanbalism that rejected all rationalist theologies. Rather, as stated in the introduction, I intend to evoke the worldview that inclined toward allowing a diversity of theological and legal inclinations as acceptable expressions of Islamic ideals.

Traditionalism's success as the expression of mainstream Sunnī Islam can be attributed in part to its ability to draw together diverse factions in the rapidly expanding and evolving Muslim empire. With its previously stated foci on the ideal past, ascetic individual piety, and submission to the consensual authority of the *'ulamā'*, traditionalism was a banner under which the caliph, regional dynasts, and the myriad local populations could find common cause. Different regions of the Islamic empire experienced the growth and eventual domination of Sunnī traditionalism through disparate circumstances. In Baghdad, traditionalism prevailed in the maneuvering between the 'Abbāsid caliphs and the Sunnī Seljūq dynasts, who ruled in the caliphs' name after seizing power from the Shī'ī Būyids. Damascus and Cairo witnessed the establishment of traditionalism through the rule of the Ayyūbids and the Mamlūks, who espoused this ideology to counter Shī'ī-Fāṭimid propaganda and to legitimize their own rule as foreign dynasties.

Irrespective of specific, disparate dynastic histories, the major vehicle for promoting traditionalism was *ḥadīth*. The study and dissemination of *ḥadīth*, unlike other religious sciences, was easily accessible to lay classes and lent itself to political purposes as well. Rulers garnered mass support through public displays of piety, which included frequenting *ḥadīth* assemblies, endowing mosques and *madrasas* that were in turn arenas for the study of *ḥadīth*, and financially supporting scholars who propagated traditionalist Islam.[7] Participation in *ḥadīth* transmission provided

[6] George Makdisi's *Ibn 'Aqil: Religion and Culture in Classical Islam* (Edinburgh: Edinburgh University Press, 1991) provides a detailed analysis of conflicts between traditionalists and rationalists in fifth/eleventh-century Baghdad.

[7] The Seljūq, Ayyūbid, and Mamlūk periods, in particular, marked the dominance of Sunnī traditionalism in Baghdad, Damascus, and Cairo, respectively, and are notable for the increase in the numbers of *ḥadīth* schools (*dūr al-ḥadīth*). Al-Nu'aymī's work offers ample evidence of the prolific architectural activity of the Ayyūbid, Seljūq, and Mamlūk ruling elite, which in turn contributed to the entrenchment of traditionalist values in cities such as Damascus. See 'Abd al-Qādir b. Muḥammad al-Nu'aymī (d. 927/1521), *al-Dāris fī*

an entry point into *isnād*s: a channel for instant pedigree and universally valued "lineage" that connected transmitters to the time of the Prophet and his community. The devotion of the Seljūq vizier Niẓām al-Mulk to this pursuit attests to the appeal of *ḥadīth* transmission for nonspecialists. Niẓām al-Mulk transmitted *ḥadīth* in Marw, Nishapur, Rayy, Isfahan, and Baghdad and held dictation sessions in Jāmiʿ al-Mahdī as well as in his own *madrasa* in Baghdad. Acknowledging his limitations as well as his motivations, he stated, "I know that I am not well suited for *riwāya*, but I want to bind myself to the caravan of the *ḥadīth* of the Prophet of God (*lākinnī urīdu an arbuṭa nafsī ʿalā qiṭār al-naql li-ḥadīth rasūl Allāh*)."[8] *Ḥadīth* transmission was thus compelling to diverse sectors of society: Arabs and non-Arabs, recent converts and lifelong Muslims, and the rulers and the ruled.

It appears an unremarkable truism that women's *ḥadīth* participation flourished as a result of the triumph of traditionalism as orthodoxy. Yet the fact that women did participate and excel in a traditionalist milieu was not historically inevitable. Another likely scenario might have been the further marginalization of women in the conservative social environments often associated with the formation of orthodoxies across religious traditions. It is a paradox, then, that traditionalism can be credited with the reenlistment of women as religious scholars in the classical Muslim world.

Examining the selected *muḥadditha*s within their political, social, and religious contexts elucidates how traditionalism supported women's *ḥadīth* participation. I first consider the impact of this ideology in the case of Shuhda and present a reconstruction of her scholarly career in Baghdad in the late fifth/eleventh and sixth/twelfth centuries. I then transition to Damascus, where Zaynab bint al-Kamāl and ʿĀʾisha bint Muḥammad flourished in the eighth/fourteenth and ninth/fifteenth centuries. Their careers are largely archetypal, and I focus on different aspects of their accomplishments. In so doing, I aim to fashion a collective portrait that illuminates the histories of numerous other female *ḥadīth* scholars and also to convey some of the exceptionality of each of these women.

Taʾrīkh al-Madāris, 2 vols. (Beirut: Dār al-Kutub al-ʿIlmiyya, 1990). See also Stephen Humphreys, "The Expressive Intent of the Mamlūk Architecture of Cairo: A Preliminary Essay," *Studia Islamica* 35 (1972): 69–119. For further analyses of urban elites' support for traditionalism through *ḥadīth* transmission, see Berkey, *Transmission of Knowledge in Medieval Cairo*, and Chamberlain, *Knowledge and Social Practice in Medieval Damascus*.

8 Ibn al-Jawzī, *al-Muntaẓam*, 16:304.

SHUHDA AL-KĀTIBA (482–574/1089–1178)

Political and religious turmoil in Baghdad framed the endeavors of Shuhda al-Kātiba, the first case study.[9] The Seljūq conquest (447/1055), which vanquished the Shīʿī Būyid dynasty, was at best a qualified victory for the Sunnī ʿAbbāsid caliphate and the inhabitants of this city. The Seljūqs were ideologically and economically invested in Sunnism. Yet their ostensible patronage and loyalty to the ʿAbbāsid caliphate did little to mask their aspirations for political and military dominance, and their very presence bespoke caliphal impotence. Unlike Nishapur, which the ʿAbbāsid caliph could hope to control only through dynasties loyal to him, Baghdad was the heart of Sunnī caliphal authority and as such became the arena for the fiercest political struggles.[10] The seven caliphs who ruled during Shuhda's life struggled to reestablish ʿAbbāsid control in the capital and its environs. Several of them, including al-Muqtadī (r. 467–87/1075–94) and al-Mustaẓhir (r. 487–512/1094–1118), were generally ineffective in channeling Seljūq rivalries and politics to their advantage. Others, such as al-Muqtafī (r. 530–55/1136–60) and al-Mustanjid (r. 555–66/1160–70), more successfully asserted political and military control.[11] Al-Muqtafī, for example, exploited Seljūq infighting and extended his control over Wāsiṭ and Ḥilla. Al-Mustanjid continued to carve out autonomous territory for the ʿAbbāsids, though his efforts and achievements waned toward the end of his reign.

The inhabitants of Baghdad were vulnerable during these struggles for political and military dominance. Seljūq efforts to regain areas claimed by the caliph necessitated garrisoning Turkish troops, who settled awkwardly in the predominantly Arab urban quarters of Baghdad. Their presence

9 Biographical notices for her can be found in the following works: al-Dhahabī, *Siyar*, 20:542–43; Ibn al-Jawzī, *al-Muntaẓam*, 17:254; al-Ṣafadī, *al-Wāfī*, 16:111–12; and Kaḥḥāla, *Aʿlām al-Nisāʾ*, 2:309–12.

10 For an analysis of elite women's roles in these political struggles, see Eric Hanne, "Women, Power, and the Eleventh and Twelfth Century Abbasid Court," *Hawwa* 3, no. 1 (2005): 80–110.

11 The seven caliphs are as follows: al-Muqtadī (r. 467–87/1075–94); al-Mustaẓhir (r. 487–512/1094–1118); al-Mustarshid (r. 512–29/1118–35); al-Rāshid (r. 529–30/1135–36); al-Muqtafī (r. 530–55/1136–60); al-Mustanjid (r. 555–66/1160–70); and al-Mustaḍīʾ bi-Amr Allāh (r. 566–75/1170–80). Summaries of the lives of each of these caliphs are available in *EI*[2]. Ibn al-Jawzī's *Muntaẓam* also chronicles the major events marking their reigns and describes the struggles for power between the caliphs and the Seljūq sultans. Eric Hanne, in *Putting the Caliph in His Place* (Madison, NJ: Fairleigh Dickinson University Press, 2007), analyzes the power struggles marking the late ʿAbbāsid caliphate in the fifth/eleventh and sixth/twelfth centuries from the perspective of the caliphs themselves.

should have signaled the authority of the Seljūqs and maintained security. Instead, their looting sprees heightened anxiety and underscored the inefficacy of both the Seljūqs and the ʿAbbāsids.

Sectarian strife was yet another element in the volatile mix of life in Baghdad. In the year of Shuhda's birth (482 AH), protracted fighting between Sunnīs and Shīʿīs in the predominantly Shīʿī quarter of al-Karkh resulted in widespread destruction of property and high casualties.[12] Ibn al-Jawzī's vivid description of these incidents powerfully evokes the material and psychological costs of such strife:

> I cite from the writing of Abū al-Wafāʾ b. ʿAqīl, who said, "The ongoing *fitna* between the Sunnīs and the people of al-Karkh [i.e. Shīʿīs] was terrible. Nearly 200 hundred people were killed during this time. It went on for months during the year 482, and it overwhelmed the Seljūq military governor (*shiḥna*), and the Sultan was shaken (*ittaḥasha*). The common people began pursuing each other on the roads and in boats. The strong were killing the weak and taking their property. The youth were growing out their hair [in the style known as *jumam* to indicate their Shīʿī affiliation and rebellion], carrying weapons, fashioning armor, and shooting with all manner of arrows. The people of al-Karkh were insulting the Companions and the Wives of the Prophet from their rooftops, and they even insulted the Prophet himself. There was not a single inhabitant of al-Karkh from among the jurists and those who were known for their sound religion who were moved to anger or were even troubled by living in close quarters with them. Al-Muqtadī, the Imam of the Age, sent a group to apprehend these people, and he made the Turks ride [into battle], and the troops donned their weapons. He had [the youth] shave their heads, and [cut their] long hair (*kalālajāt*) and whipped them and imprisoned them in homes [forbidding them from going up on the rooftops]. It was the month of Āb. There was plenty of talk against the Sultan. The people said, "The religion (*dīn*) has been destroyed; the *sunna* is dead. And innovation has risen. We see that God gives victory only to the Rāfiḍīs (Shīʿīs) so we will leave Islam [i.e., become apostates].[13]

The perceived threat of Shīʿism extended beyond the chaos detailed by Ibn al-Jawzī. The annual public commemorations of Shīʿī rituals, which had been strongly promoted by the Shīʿī Būyids, persisted as points of friction. Sunnī counter-ceremonies fomented further confrontation. At a different level, increasing intellectual cohesion and scholarly production in the areas of Imāmī Shīʿī law and theology posed a new set of challenges for the Sunnī scholarly elite.[14] And just beyond the boundaries of the

[12] See EI^2, s.v. "al-Karkh," for a summary of the history of sectarian rivalries in al-Karkh and the surrounding quarters.

[13] Ibn al-Jawzī, *al-Muntaẓam*, 16:283. I thank Andras Hamori and Yasir Ibrahim for their insights on this passage.

[14] The writings of scholars such as Ibn Bābawayh (d. 381/991), Ibn al-Muʿallim Shaykh al-Mufīd (d. 413/1022), and Abū al-Qāsim b. al-Ḥusayn al-Mūsawī (Sharīf al-Murtaḍā)

Sunnī-Seljūq-'Abbāsid domains, the Fāṭimid counter-caliphate in Egypt and the military provocations of the Nizārīs (a branch of the Ismā'īlī Shī'īs) were perceived as existential challenges to the 'Abbāsid caliphate.[15]

In 492/1099, when Shuhda was ten, news of the Crusader occupation of Jerusalem circulated throughout the central Islamic lands. The reports of these attacks registered only dimly at first with the 'Abbāsid caliph al-Mustaẓhir, but they could not be ignored for long. Ibn al-Jawzī chronicles the horror that Muslims experienced in that year, as the Crusaders massacred more than 70,000 Muslims in Jerusalem and pillaged the Dome of the Rock.[16] Firsthand accounts from refugees fleeing to cities such as Baghdad made the alarm palpable in areas far removed from the Crusaders' battlefields. Further, the loss of Jerusalem, a sacred center, had a profound psychological impact throughout the Muslim world, and the occupation of cities along vital trade routes undermined the economic stability of the entire region. Such factors, in turn, exacerbated the apprehension pervading Baghdad during Shuhda's life.

Inter-Sunnī rivalries precluded a unified response to these crises. Competition between the 'Abbāsid caliphs and the Seljūq sultans created political and military fissures. Theological disputes, often manifested along *madhhab* lines, fueled bitter animosity among leading scholars. Theological feuding was not confined to verbal exchanges between members of the intellectual elite. Rather, seemingly arcane disputes mobilized lay followers of preacher-theologians to violent action. In 469/1077, the sermons of Ibn al-Qushayrī, the Shāfi'ī-'Ash'arī scholar (and a son of Fāṭima bint al-Ḥasan, whom we encountered in Chapter 3), had precipitated bloody rioting between his supporters (Shāfi'ī-'Ash'arīs) and detractors (Ḥanbalīs). The conflict was resolved only when the Seljūq vizier Niẓām al-Mulk advised Ibn al-Qushayrī to affirm his support for the views of his opponents and desist from his preaching in Baghdad. This was but one of such violent disputes marking the decade before Shuhda's birth.

Amidst these internal and external challenges and threats, traditionalism evolved to emphasize points of consensus among Sunnīs and ultimately prevailed as a classical Muslim orthodoxy. As discussed in the

(d. 436/1044) are but a few of the indicators of the increased cohesion and intellectual strength of Imāmī Shī'ism.

15 Fāṭimid expansionism was limited during Shuhda's lifetime in comparison with previous decades. In 450/1058, the military leader al-Basāsīrī, acting on behalf of the Fāṭimids, routed the 'Abbāsid caliph in Baghdad itself. Signaling a military and psychological victory, he had the *khuṭba* in Baghdad recited in name of al-Mustanṣir, the Fāṭimid caliph. For a summary of al-Basāsīrī's life and military career, see EI^2, s.v. "al-Basāsīrī."

16 Ibn al-Jawzī, *al-Muntaẓam*, 17:47.

introduction, Talal Asad's conceptualization of orthodoxy as relationships of power is useful for understanding how traditionalism fostered women's *ḥadīth* participation. To reiterate here, Asad asserts that with respect to Islam, "wherever Muslims have the power to regulate, uphold, require, or adjust *correct* practices, and to condemn, exclude, undermine, or replace *incorrect* ones, there is the domain of orthodoxy."[17] The principal arena of exchange among traditionalists, that of *ḥadīth* transmission, drew together scholars irrespective of their theological, *madhhab*, and even sectarian affiliations, men and women, young and old, and rulers and ruled in the common pursuit of piety and hope of eternal reward. By way of contrast, Mu'tazilism, a rationalist theology, was premised on dialectic and intense intellectual rivalry amongst a highly educated elite and was associated with a more exclusivist culture.[18]

The profiles of the *muḥadditha*s selected here affirm that certain practices of intellectual exchange and modes of manifesting inclusion in traditionalist culture were particularly amenable to the participation of women. Indeed, two primary signifiers of status, namely the *isnād 'ālī* (a short chain of transmission) and *ijāza*s (in this case, certifications for *ḥadīth* transmission), were gender-blind. These mechanisms (*isnād 'ālī* and *ijāza*s) supported the impulse to propagate traditionalist literature and also helped create "textual communities" that were independent of institutional affiliations and thereby vital to women's successes. This female participation in the central task of preserving the memories of the Prophet and earlier generations without regard to their gender, *madhhab* affiliation, or age (as I explain later, women's natural longevity was perceived as an advantage) ultimately strengthened the traditionalists' cause. Women's centrality to the domestic sphere meant that their mobilization in the service of this orthodoxy enabled it to permeate both the public and private domains of its adherents.

The career of Shuhda al-Kātiba, beginning in her youth, is a template for the ideal traditionalist woman. Her father, Abū Naṣr Aḥmad b. al-Faraj al-Ibrī (d. 506/1112), was an essential agent in her success. He himself had migrated from Dīnawar to Baghdad and established his reputation there as a Shāfi'ī *muḥaddith* affiliated with the ruling elite.[19] Al-Sam'ānī counts

[17] Talal Asad, "Anthropology of Islam," 15.

[18] See Ahmed El Shamsy, "Social Construction of Orthodoxy," 105–6, for a similar description of the cultures of the traditionalists and the theologians (especially the Mu'tazilīs). See also Mottahedeh, *Loyalty and Leadership*, 20, for his characterization of the inclusiveness of the "consensus-minded Muslims" (those to whom I refer as "traditionalists").

[19] For his biography, see al-Sam'ānī, *Ansāb*, 1:73–74; Ibn al-Jawzī, *al-Muntaẓam*, 17:129; and Ibn al-Athīr, *al-Kāmil*, 10:494. While the *nisba* "al-Ibrī" generally denotes the

him among the famous men of Baghdad and notes that he narrated from prominent *'ulamā'*, including the Ḥanbalī Abū Ya'lā b. al-Farrā' (d. 458/1066) and the Shāfi'ī al-Khaṭīb al-Baghdādī. Aḥmad b. al-Faraj's training and connections, in turn, enabled and facilitated Shuhda's education. Her appreciation for him is voiced in a rare personal comment inserted in a collection of her *ḥadīth*, entitled *al-'Umda min Fawā'id wa'l-Athār al-Ṣiḥāḥ wa'l-Gharā'ib fī Mashyakhat Shuhda*. Here she narrates a tradition that she heard from her father in the year 490/1096f. and states, "all of this [i.e., her accomplishments] is due to his blessings and his invocations on my behalf."[20]

Through her father's efforts, Shuhda, by the age of eight, had been initiated into a network of *'ulamā'* with ties to the ruling elite. One of her first teachers, Ṭirād b. Muḥammad al-Zaynabī (d. 491/1098), was a Ḥanafī *naqīb* for the 'Abbāsids in Baṣra and Baghdad.[21] In spite of al-Zaynabī's involvement in political circles and embroilment in theological and inter-*madhhab* disputes, his *ḥadīth* assemblies were extremely popular and were well attended by jurists and *ḥadīth* scholars alike.[22] His association with Shuhda and other students, occurring in the protected, neutral zone of *ḥadīth* assemblies, ultimately buttressed the cause of forging a traditionalist culture across *madhhab* lines. Shuhda narrated several works on his authority including the *Amwāl*, a *fiqh* manual by Abū 'Ubayd b. Sallām

occupation of needle merchant, in Aḥmad b. al-Faraj's case, it likely refers to a defunct family trade. With respect to his provenance from Dīnawar, Yāqūt mentions that many men of letters (*ahl al-adab*) as well as *ḥadīth* scholars had their origins in this province, which is located to the northeast of Baghdad (*Mu'jam al-Buldān*, 2:616).

20 Shuhda, *al-'Umda*, 155.

21 For his biographical notices, see al-Dhahabī, *Siyar*, 19:37–39; al-Ṣafadī, *al-Wāfī*, 16:240–41; and Ibn al-Jawzī, *al-Muntaẓam*, 17:44. Consistent with standards established for the field of *ḥadīth* transmission, Shuhda's biographers use different terms to describe how she received certification or transmission authority. Thus, *uḥḍirat 'alā* is employed for instances in which she was physically brought into the presence of a particular scholar. *Ajāza(t) la-hā* is used for permission granted in writing either through a direct meeting with the granter of the certificate or by correspondence, and *sami'at min* describes occasions in which she was brought to an assembly or meeting in which a specific work was read out loud. These terms were not always applied consistently and usage of them was not regulated by any strict conventions. Nonetheless, in Shuhda's case, the fact that a discriminating *ḥadīth* scholar such as al-Dhahabī uses these terms as well as the ages at which Shuhda is likely to have engaged in the different types of interactions suggest that the terms connote the meanings indicated in this footnote. For further elucidation of *ḥadīth* terminology related to types of transmission, see Ibn al-Ṣalāḥ, *Muqaddima*, 96–118.

22 al-Dhahabī, *Siyar*, 19:38, and Ibn al-Jawzī, *al-Muntaẓam*, 17:44. Ibn al-Jawzī and al-Dhahabī note that he was prolific in his transmissions, that students traveled to him from all regions, and that he was close to the political elite. Ibn al-Jawzī adds that some people were wary of transmitting from al-Zaynabī because of his intimacy with the rulers (*salāṭīn*).

(d. 224/838).[23] There were at least two other women who narrated *ḥadīth* on al-Zaynabī's authority: Kamāl bint Abī Muḥammad al-Samarqandī (d. 558/1163f.) and Tajannā al-Wahbāniyya (d. 575/1180).[24] Neither, however, attained the fame that Shuhda claimed toward the end of her life.

Shuhda's transmissions from Ja'far b. Aḥmad al-Sarrāj (d. 500/1106), an acclaimed Ḥanbalī *ḥadīth* transmitter, poet, and jurist, were also vital to her reputation. A prolific author, he was praised by al-Dhahabī for his profound knowledge and expertise in a range of subjects, especially grammar, Qur'ānic readings, and poetry.[25] Given his death in the year 500, Shuhda would have been taken to him by the time she was eighteen. Toward the end of her life, Shuhda served as the last living connection to al-Sarrāj. As Ibn al-Jawzī reports, "the last one to transmit from him was Shuhda bint al-Ibrī. I read his [al-Sarrāj's] book, the one called *Maṣāri' al-'Ushshāq*, to her by virtue of her having heard it directly from him."[26] The fact that Ibn al-Jawzī viewed her as a reliable authority for this work (even though she received the certification for it at a young age) signals that she must have learned the compilation later in life. This strategy of a priori certification, counterintuitive by our modern standards, was a salient characteristic of classical *ḥadīth* transmission and appears to have been promoted with greater frequency during the Mamlūk period.

Another of Shuhda's prominent *shaykhs* was Abū Bakr al-Shāshī (d. 507/1114), a leading jurist of the Shāfi'ī *madhhab* and a successor to Abū Ḥāmid al-Ghazzālī's (d. 505/1111) post in the prestigious Niẓāmiyya *madrasa*. Shuhda's association with him commands our attention at multiple levels.[27] In identifying her as someone who transmits from al-Shāshī, al-Dhahabī distinguishes her with the honorific (*laqab*) "the pride of all women" (*fakhr al-nisā'*). Indeed, the mere mention of her name in this context is remarkable; the practice of naming only the most prominent students in the biographical notices of leading authorities such as al-Shāshī often resulted in the omission of women from these lists. Second, since Shuhda likely acquired certification from al-Shāshī in the context of his appointment to the Niẓāmiyya in Baghdad, their relationship exemplifies

[23] Shuhda's name occurs in the *isnād* of a published edition of *al-Amwāl*; see Ibn Sallām, *Kitāb al-Amwāl* (Cairo: Dār al-Fikr, 1975), 10.

[24] For Kamāl's biography, see al-Dhahabī, *Siyar*, 20:420 and for Tajannā's, see *Siyar*, 20:550–51.

[25] al-Dhahabī, *Siyar*, 19:228–31.

[26] Ibn al-Jawzī mentions this in the context of his obituary of al-Sarrāj; see *al-Muntaẓam*, 17:103.

[27] For al-Shāshī's biography, see al-Dhahabī, *Siyar*, 19:393–94.

the ways in which the proliferation of *madrasas* beginning in Shuhda's lifetime could have benefited women even though they were not known to have acquired posts or stipends in such institutions. The increased endowment of *madrasas* prompted greater scholarly traffic and in the process augmented opportunities for women to engage with teachers and students. Finally, al-Shāshī's role as the author of *al-Ḥilya* (also known as *al-Mustaẓhirī* because it was produced for the 'Abbāsid caliph al-Mustaẓhir) casts light on the multiple avenues for promoting traditionalism that characterize Shuhda's context. A work dedicated to examining the differences (*ikhtilāf*) of reasoning among the *madhhabs*, the *Ḥilya* was reportedly commissioned to help overcome divisions amongst the adherents of different *madhhabs*, thereby promoting the traditionalist ethos. Al-Shāshī's efforts on behalf of the 'Abbāsid caliph underscore the collaboration of scholars and rulers in forging a consensus-based Sunnī orthodoxy.

While Shuhda's affiliations with the ruling and scholarly elite are a prominent thread in her career, the tapestry can be better appreciated when we consider her less prominent teachers as well. A study of al-Ḥusayn b. Aḥmad al-Ni'ālī reveals how *ḥadīth* transmission united Muslims of disparate backgrounds and how women's activities criss-crossed the divides.[28] Al-Dhahabī notes that al-Ni'ālī bore the honorific "*al-ḥāfiẓ*," which in his case meant that he took care of clothes in a public bath (*ḥammām*) and guarded its proceeds. This is but one indication that al-Ni'ālī did not belong to the scholarly elite. Al-Dhahabī proceeds to cite other reports that al-Ni'ālī was not a trusted transmitter. A blind man who had heard *ḥadīth* presumably in his youth, al-Ni'ālī descended from a family versed in religious knowledge.[29] However, he himself did not follow this path perhaps due to his disability. Rather, he was employed in a *ḥammām* in the predominantly Shī'ī al-Karkh quarter of Baghdad. Abū 'Āmir al-'Abdarī, one of his critics, brands him as utterly unreliable: "he was a commoner, blind, and a Rāfiḍī [i.e., Shī'ī]. It is not permitted to transmit a single letter on his authority. He had no idea of what was read to him."[30] And yet, as al-Dhahabī notes, many people transmitted from him. His popularity was likely attributable to his short chains of transmission

28 For his biographical notice, see al-Dhahabī, *Siyar*, 19:101–3.

29 See al-Sam'ānī, *Ansāb*, 5:508, for brief biographies of other members of this family. Though some of them are known to have transmitted *ḥadīth*, none acquired a high reputation in this arena. Al-Ni'ālī's grandfather, Abū al-Ḥasan Muḥammad b. Ṭalḥa (d. 413/1022), is also criticized for his weak transmission and labeled as a Rāfiḍī.

30 al-Dhahabī, *Siyar*, 19:102.

(*isnād ʿālī*), which drew *ḥadīth* seekers to him irrespective of his sectarian inclinations or qualifications.

Al-Niʿālī's association with female students is particularly intriguing in the context of our study; he is credited with transmitting to more women than any of Shuhda's other teachers who were tracked for this study. Four women, aside from Shuhda, are listed among his students.[31] The teaching contexts in which a non-scholar, such as al-Niʿālī, functioned were likely more open to the public, and the standards for certification less stringent. In collecting *ḥadīth* from al-Niʿālī, the women could have augmented their storehouse of transmissions with relative ease and would have been able to pass these on to future generations provided they themselves became recognized transmitters.

Al-Niʿālī's certification of Shuhda and other women exposes the broad spectrum of *ḥadīth* transmission in fifth/eleventh- and sixth/twelfth-century Baghdad as well as evolutions in the culture of *ḥadīth* transmission by the classical period. In Chapter 2, I cited Mālik's opinion that there were many pious *shaykh*s whose transmissions he did not trust in spite of their piety. I also noted that women's transmission, when it occurred in less professionalized contexts, was not recorded. By Shuhda's lifetime, however, the *ḥadīth* transmission of women, irrespective of the legal acumen of the participants, was more likely to enter the historical record because it was a form of social capital that was recognized and valued across the social spectrum. In this vein, her certification from cloth merchants and traders and even from a chamberlain (*ḥājib*) of the ʿAbbāsid caliph is duly noted by scholars of the caliber of al-Dhahabī.[32] These records are valuable testaments to the porous boundaries of *ḥadīth* transmission in classical Islam.

The network of Shuhda's teachers described earlier gives us one window into the diverse sectarian, occupational, and legal affiliations claimed by *ḥadīth* transmitters; her renown among students from remote areas of the Muslim world further confirms this impression. The frequency with which she is cited as a teacher in the biographies of sixth/twelfth-century scholars who either lived in Baghdad or journeyed there to study is striking

[31] They are Kamāl bint Abī Muḥammad, Tajannā al Wahbāniyya (both are also mentioned as al-Zaynabī's students), Tarkānz bint ʿAbd Allāh al-Dāmaghānī, and Nafīsa al-Bazzāza. See al-Dhahabī, *Siyar*, 19:101–2.

[32] Shuhda's teachers include Ibn Ayyūb (d. 492/1099), Ibn al-Baṭir (d. 494/1101), and Ibn Ḥiyd (d. 494/1101). For their biographies, see the following references in al-Dhahabī's *Siyar*: Ibn Ayyūb, 19:145–46; Ibn Baṭir, 19:46–49; Ibn Ḥiyd, 19:181–82. The *ḥājib* was Ibn al-ʿAllāf (see *Siyar*, 19:242–43).

and leaves no doubt about her extraordinary perpetuation not just of *ḥadīth* literature but also of the culture of traditionalist Sunnī Islam. Nājiya Ibrāhīm, author of a modern biography of Shuhda, gleaned the names of 168 students from the sources available to him; 162 of these were men, the remainder women.[33] Of these, Ibn al-Jawzī, the Ḥanbalī jurist and historian; Ibn Qudāma (d. 620/1223), the Ḥanbalī jurist and author of the legal compendium *al-Mughnī*; and al-Samʿānī, the Shāfiʿī historian and biographer, are among the most accomplished. Several members of the Damascene family of Banū Qudāma went to hear *ḥadīth* from Shuhda during their scholarly travels to Baghdad. It is likely no coincidence that these same Ḥanbalī scholars were later active in promoting women's education in the Ṣāliḥiyya suburb of Damascus, which witnessed an extraordinarily high rate of women's *ḥadīth* participation in the subsequent century. Scholarly peregrinations led to cross-pollination across urban centers and help account for the replication of patterns of women's participation throughout the Muslim world.

Two additional characteristics of Shuhda's *ḥadīth* transmission will be mentioned here but discussed later as they recur in the lives of Zaynab bint al-Kamāl and ʿĀ'isha bint Muḥammad, the other case studies in this chapter. First, an analysis of the life span of many of Shuhda's students reveals that the majority of them were born after 550 – that is, when Shuhda was approximately sixty-eight years old. Thus her reputation was greatest in the last few decades of her life, and she attracted many young students during this time. Ibn Khallikān and al-Dhahabī note that Shuhda's seniority allowed her to perpetuate better *isnād*s by connecting the oldest and youngest generations of her time.[34] Second, Shuhda's "curriculum" provides rich clues as to her niche in the scholarly culture of Baghdad. The compilations with which she is associated were quintessentially traditionalist. She is mentioned as a key transmitter of the works of the noted third/ninth-century ascetic Ibn Abī al-Dunyā, including *al-Faraj baʿda al-Shidda* (Relief after the Trial), *Kitāb al-Shukr lillāh* (Book of Gratitude to God), and *Kitāb Dhamm al-Muskir* (Book on Censure of Intoxicants). Shuhda also transmitted works of Sunnī law, including the *Muwaṭṭa'* of Mālik b. Anas and the *Kitāb al-Amwāl* of Ibn Sallām, a comprehensive work devoted to the *fiqh* of a range of financial questions.

Shuhda's renown extended beyond her *ḥadīth* transmission. She also ranked as one of the great calligraphers of Baghdad. Her father was likely

33 Nājiya Ibrāhīm, *Musnidat al-ʿIrāq*, 59.
34 Ibn Khallikān, *Wafayāt*, 2:172; al-Dhahabī, *Siyar*, 20:543.

responsible for her initial exposure to masters of this trade as well. Yāqūt asserts that there was no one in that age who could write like Shuhda, and notes that she wrote in the style of another female calligrapher, Bint al-Aqra' (d. 480/1087).[35] Al-Ṣafadī, in quoting a poem attributed to Shuhda, adds that she probably did not compose it. It was nevertheless ascribed to her because it was written with an elegant hand.[36] Shuhda was a master of the school of Ibn al-Bawwāb (d. 413/1022), the renowned calligrapher of the Būyid period whose illuminated reproduction of the Qur'ān continues to elicit widespread admiration. In a discussion of the role of female calligraphers, Annemarie Schimmel notes that Shuhda was among those who formed a link between Ibn al-Bawwāb and Yāqūt al-Musta'ṣimī (d. 698/1298).[37] The latter was a calligrapher at the court of the last 'Abbāsid caliph, al-Musta'ṣim, and his talents earned him the title "*qiblat al-kuttāb*," that is, the *qibla* for all calligraphers.[38] Shuhda's skills had aesthetic as well as practical value. Al-Khaṭīb al-Baghdādī devotes a section to the improvement of handwriting in his *al-Jāmi' li-Akhlāq al-Rāwī wa-Adab al-Sāmi'*, an etiquette manual for aspiring *ḥadīth* students. Here he cites traditions from the Companions and Successors regarding the importance of clear, legible handwriting, which is indispensable for accurate *ḥadīth* transmission. It is likely that Shuhda's talents drew the approbation of her contemporaries across the fields of Islamic learning.

A final aspect of Shuhda's life further nuances our understanding of her unusual career. Her husband, 'Alī b. Muḥammad b. Yaḥyā (d. 549/1154f.), was her father's protégé and was also associated with the ruling class of Baghdad, a connection that probably gave Shuhda greater access to this social class.[39] According to Ibn al-Athīr, Shuhda's father, Aḥmad b. al-Faraj, took charge of 'Alī b. Muḥammad's upbringing (*rabbāhu*), such that the latter eventually came to be called Ibn al-Ibrī.[40] Eventually, Abū Naṣr married 'Alī b. Muḥammad to his daughter Shuhda. Al-Sam'ānī

[35] Yāqūt, *Mu'jam al-Udabā'*, 3:1422–23. The full name of Bint al-Aqra' is Fāṭima bint al-Ḥasan al-Baghdādiyya; for her biography, see al-Dhahabī, *Siyar*, 18:480–81.

[36] al-Ṣafadī, *al-Wāfī*, 16:111–12.

[37] Annemarie Schimmel, *Calligraphy and Islamic Culture* (New York: New York University Press, 1984), 47.

[38] J. Sourdel-Thomine, "Ibn al-Bawwāb," in *EI*², and David Rice, *L'Unique manuscrit d'Ibn al-Bawwāb à la Chester Beatty Library* (Paris: Club du Livre, 1981). See also Schimmel, *Calligraphy and Islamic Culture*, 21.

[39] His biography is available in Ibn al-Jawzī, *al-Muntaẓam*, 18:100, Ibn al-Athīr, *al-Kāmil*, 11:200, and al-Ṣafadī, *al-Wāfī*, 22:96–97.

[40] Ibn al-Athīr, *Kāmil*, 11:200.

records that after this union, 'Alī b. Muḥammad's fortunes rose, and he entered into the service of the caliph al-Muqtafī li-Amr Allāh (d. 555/1160). It is probably in this capacity that he acquired the honorific "Thiqat al-Dawla" (i.e., one who is trusted in the caliphal domains). Like his wife and father-in-law, 'Alī b. Muḥammad studied *ḥadīth* with some of the prominent *ḥadīth* scholars of Baghdad, and his teachers are among Shuhda's *shaykh*s as well.[41] However, 'Alī b. Muḥammad lagged behind his wife as a *ḥadīth* transmitter. Al-Ṣafadī is the only biographer who even mentions that 'Alī b. Muḥammad studied *ḥadīth*. In this notice, we learn that he also composed poetry and endowed a Shāfi'ī *madrasa* and a Ṣūfī *ribāṭ* in Baghdad.[42] Through such philanthropy, he promoted the flourishing of institutional education in this period.

Shuhda lived into her early nineties, and at the time of her death she was held in great esteem. Ibn al-Jawzī, her student, reports that her funeral prayers were conducted in Jāmi' al-Qaṣr, one of the large congregational mosques of Baghdad. He notes that the screens (presumably of the women's section) were lifted during her funeral – a practice that would have allowed women to view her before her burial from their section of the mosque.[43] A number of Shuhda's female contemporaries were also praised in the historical sources, but there appear to be none who approximate her fame or her range of talents. She looms large in the chronicles as a woman who fully availed herself of a variety of educational avenues available to Muslim women of the classical period.

WOMEN AND *ḤADĪTH* TRANSMISSION IN MAMLŪK DAMASCUS

Shuhda's extraordinary career is better understood as part of a broader trend when we turn to Zaynab bint al-Kamāl (646–740/1248–1339) and 'Ā'isha bint Muḥammad (723–816/1323–1413), two *muḥaddītha*s who thrived in the suburbs of Damascus. The seventy-two years between Shuhda's death and Zaynab's birth were marked by radical transformations in the political order of the central Middle East. In 567/1171, the Ayyūbid sultan Ṣalāḥ al-Dīn (d. 589/1193) decisively defeated the Fāṭimids, bringing Egypt back into the Sunnī fold and under the nominal

[41] These include al-Zaynabī, al-Ni'ālī, and Ibn al-Baṭir.

[42] al-Ṣafadī, *al-Wāfī*, 22:96; Ibn al-Athīr, *al-Kāmil*, 11:200; and Ibn al-Jawzī, *al-Muntaẓam*, 18:100.

[43] Ibn al-Jawzī, *al-Muntaẓam*, 18:254.

control of the ʿAbbāsid caliphate. This victory was soon followed by the reconquest of Acre and Jerusalem from the Crusaders. These triumphs were offset by continuing military engagements with the Crusaders and with the more menacing and destructive Mongol invaders from Central Asia, who not only decimated armies in their path but also annihilated settled populations and urban infrastructures in their westward advance. Ultimately, a force led by the Mongol conqueror Hülegü sacked Baghdad and terminated even the semblance of ʿAbbāsid control in this area. The advance of the Mongols was checked in 658/1260 by Baybars, the leader of the Mamlūks, a dynasty that had come to power a decade earlier first supplanting the Ayyūbids in Cairo and then expanding to other areas of the central Middle East. Yet the lives of our two Mamlūk *muḥadditha*s reveal little, if any, negative impact on their participation due to the Mongols or the Crusades. Rather, over the course of Shuhda's life and thereafter, traditionalist culture had become entrenched as a means of unifying Sunnīs across the socioeconomic, legal, and theological spectrum and was embraced by Ayyūbids and Mamlūks as well. The success of traditionalism in turn led to the remarkable culmination of women's *ḥadīth* education during the late classical period.

The Mamlūks conquered Damascus, the provenance of Zaynab and ʿĀʾisha, in 659/1261. By the eighth/fourteenth century, the city was fully incorporated into their domain as a crucial economic and administrative center.[44] In the mid-eighth/fourteenth century, the decline of the Mongol threat and the victories against the Crusaders led to the transfer of military activity farther north to Aleppo, a development that consolidated the civilian functions of Damascus.[45] Reorganization of state finances and investment in urban infrastructure increased regional economic stability, which in turn created a hospitable environment for intellectual endeavors. In the tradition of their Seljūq and Ayyūbid predecessors, the Mamlūks continued to endorse

[44] The social history of Damascus under the Mamlūks is explored in greater detail in the following sources: *EI*^{2}, s.v. "Dimashq;" Chamberlain, *Knowledge and Social Practice in Medieval Damascus, 1190–1350*; and Ira Lapidus, *Muslim Cities in the Later Middle Ages* (Cambridge, MA: Harvard University Press, 1967).

[45] Lapidus, *Muslim Cities*, 20. Adding to the prosperity of Damascus, Tankiz, the Mamlūk governor of Damascus (711–39/1311–38), initiated a period of "unequaled splendor and expansion" by endowing schools, mosques, and other institutions. Approximately forty institutions were constructed or renovated under his rule (Lapidus, *Muslim Cities*, 22). See also Joan E. Gilbert, "Institutionalization of Muslim Scholarship and Professionalization of the *'Ulamā'* in Medieval Damascus," *Studia Islamica* 52 (1980): 106–7, for a discussion of the expansion and rise of Damascus as an educational center in the centuries preceding Zaynab bint al-Kamāl's life (468–658/1075–1260).

Sunnī traditionalism through the endowment of *madrasas*, *dūr al-ḥadīth*, and other institutions focused on the preservation and dissemination of Sunnī thought.[46] These developments created favorable conditions for the careers of Zaynab bint al-Kamāl and 'Ā'isha bint Muḥammad.

The relative economic and social stability in Damascus during the eighth/fourteenth and ninth/fifteenth centuries contributed to the prosperity of several of its suburbs. Among these was al-Ṣāliḥiyya to the northwest of Damascus, where both Zaynab bint al-Kamāl and 'Ā'isha bint Muḥammad lived. The growth of this suburb is credited to a community of Ḥanbalīs who, fleeing from the Crusaders, had migrated from Nablus to Damascus in the mid-sixth/twelfth century.[47] The majority of these scholars were from the Banū Qudāma, an influential clan of Ḥanbalī *'ulamā'*.

Al-Ṣāliḥiyya is an unusual example of a Muslim suburb that flourished foremost as a center of religious learning. Muḥammad b. Ṭūlūn's (d. 953/1546) history of al-Ṣāliḥiyya lists numerous educational institutions, including congregational mosques, *dūr al-Qur'ān*, *dūr al-ḥadīth*, *madrasas*, and *zāwiyas*.[48] Ibn Faḍl Allāh al-'Umarī (d. 749/1349), a Damascene historian, described al-Ṣāliḥiyya as a prosperous area that exhibited signs of a thriving city, such as "gardens, *madrasas*, *ribāṭs*, important cemeteries, lofty buildings, hospitals, and busy markets filled with dry goods and other materials."[49] Ibn Baṭṭūṭa (d. 779/1377), another

46 Berkey, *Transmission of Knowledge*, 7–9. The Sunnī inclinations of these dynasties and their patronage of Sunnī institutions and scholars have been well documented. For a brief introduction, see P. M. Holt, *The Age of the Crusades* (New York: Longman, 1986), 77–81. A more extensive discussion may be found in Humphreys, "Expressive Intent."

47 These Ḥanbalīs from Palestine ultimately did not feel welcome in the predominantly Shāfi'ī milieu of Damascus, which prompted their move to al-Ṣāliḥiyya. The migration of this community has been studied by Joseph Drory, "Ḥanbalīs of the Nablus Region in the Eleventh and Twelfth Centuries," *Asian and African Studies* 22 (1988): 93–112; and Daniella T. Heller, "The Shaykh and the Community: Popular Hanbalite Islam in the 12th–13th Century Jabal Nablus and Jabal Qasyūn," *Studia Islamica* 79 (1994): 103–20. Drory explains that the Ḥanbalī refugees were often called *maqādisa* (plural of *maqdisī*) either because of their origins from Nablus, adjacent to Jerusalem (*al-bayt al-muqaddas*), or because they were from a vaguely defined territory termed *al-arḍ al-muqaddasa* in the Qur'ān; Drory, "Ḥanbalīs of the Nablus Region," 98. The Ḥanbalīs of Damascus are also the subject of a chapter in Michael Cook's *Commanding Right and Forbidding Wrong in Islamic Thought* (New York: Cambridge University Press, 2000), chapter 7.

48 Muḥammad b. Ṭūlūn, *al-Qalā'id al-Jawhariyya fī Ta'rīkh al-Ṣāliḥiyya*, ed. Muḥammad Duhmān (Damascus: Maktabat al-Dirāsāt al-Islāmiyya, 1949), 49–211. See also Shākir Muṣṭafā, *Madīnat al-'Ilm: Āl Qudāma wa'l-Ṣāliḥiyya* (Damascus: Dār Ṭalās, 1997).

49 Ibn Faḍl Allāh al-'Umarī al-Dimashqī, "Masālik al-Abṣār," manuscript excerpted in *Madīnat Dimashq 'inda al-Jughrāfiyyīn wa'l-Raḥḥālīn al-Muslimīn*, ed. Ṣalāḥ al-Dīn al-Munajjid (Beirut: Dār al-Kitāb al-Jadīd, 1967), 226.

admirer of al-Ṣāliḥiyya, enumerated its divine blessings. Among its virtues (*faḍā'il*) was its reputation not only as the possible birthplace of Abraham, but also as the burial site (between Bāb al-Farādīs and the Qāsiyūn mosque) of some 700 prophets.[50] Owing to its religious legends, socioeconomic prosperity, and the presence of resident scholars, al-Ṣāliḥiyya was an ideal haven for itinerant students.

Women shared in the educational life of al-Ṣāliḥiyya in a number of ways. A well-documented contribution of elite women throughout much of Islamic history was the endowment of *madrasa*s, mosques, and *ribāṭ*s as expressions of piety and charity.[51] Their activities in Damascus and its environs were no exception. One example is the Madrasat al-Ṣāḥiba, a prominent Ḥanbalī school, endowed by Rabī'a Khātūn (d. 643/1245), a sister of the Ayyūbid sultan Ṣalāḥ al-Dīn.[52] Women were not usually appointed to endowed posts for teaching nor did they benefit from assigned stipends for studying at these institutions. Nevertheless, educational endowments transformed urban areas and positively impacted women's endeavors.

Scholarly traffic in the region of al-Ṣāliḥiyya increased as a result of investments in education and was a boon to women's participation in spite of the fact that women did not themselves undertake *riḥla*s as much as men did. Contact with scholars who sojourned in the cities of their residence allowed women to acquire and disseminate *ḥadīth*. Itinerant scholars would obtain certification from *muḥadditha*s of various locales and subsequently convey word of these women's reputations to other areas of the Muslim world. The suburb of al-Ṣāliḥiyya, in particular, witnessed substantial female *ḥadīth* participation due to its development as a religious center. The modern editor of Ibn Ṭūlūn's history of al-Ṣāliḥiyya notes that women were encouraged to attend religious circles (*ḥalaqāt al-'ilm*) and assemblies for *ḥadīth* (*majālis al-ḥadīth*). He characterizes this activity as the beginnings of a Damascene feminist cultural movement, in which the majority of women were Ḥanbalī.[53] This reference to feminism in the Mamlūk period, albeit anachronistic, impresses on us the high level of women's involvement in the field of

[50] Ibn Baṭṭūṭa, *Riḥlat Ibn Baṭṭūṭa* (Cairo: al-Maktaba al-Tijāriyya al-Kubrā, 1964), 1:61–62.

[51] Berkey, *Transmission of Knowledge*, 162–65, and Carl Petry, "A Paradox of Patronage," *Muslim World* 73 (1983): 195–201.

[52] Ibn Ṭūlūn, *al-Qalā'id*, 156–57; see also the descriptions of al-Madrasa al-Mārdāniyya, founded by Azīzat al-Dīn Ukhshāh Khātūn (at p. 61), and al-Madrasa al-Atābakiyya, endowed by Tarkān Khātūn (at p. 102).

[53] Muḥammad Duhmān, introduction to Ibn Ṭūlūn, *al-Qalā'id*, 5.

religious learning and contextualizes the lives of the two women examined in greater detail in the sections that follow.

ZAYNAB BINT AL-KAMĀL (646–740/1248–1339)

Zaynab bint al-Kamāl elicits curiosity on account of the numerous *ijāza*s that she accumulated. Ibn Ḥajar al-ʿAsqalānī reports that by the time she died, she possessed a camel-load of *ijāza*s.[54] Zaynab had an even earlier start to her career than Shuhda. At the age of one, she received an *ijāza* to transmit *ḥadīth* from ʿAbd al-Khāliq al-Nishtibrī (537–649/1142f.–1252), a famed Shāfiʿī jurist and *muḥaddith*. Al-Nishtibrī sent this *ijāza* for Zaynab in 647/1249f., two years before his death.[55] Although biographers do not record the work(s) that this *ijāza* qualified her to transmit, they affirm that Zaynab's reputation rested partly on her link to al-Nishtibrī. Al-Dhahabī wrote, "[T]hose who wanted the unmatched prestige [of this *isnād*] would go to hear her; if the student traveled a month to hear even one part of this [work], his journey would not be in vain."[56] Also in the first year of her life, Zaynab received two other *ijāza*s: from ʿAjība al-Bāqadriyya (d. 647/1249) and Ibn al-Sayyidī (d. 647/1249f.), both prominent *ḥadīth* scholars resident in Baghdad. At the age of two, Zaynab obtained additional certification after being brought into the presence of (*uḥḍirat ʿalā*) Ḥabība bint Abī ʿUmar (d. 648/1250f.).[57] In the same year, she received another *ijāza* from Baghdad, this time from Ibrāhīm b. Maḥmūd b. al-Khayr (d. 648/1250). By the time Zaynab was

[54] Her full name is Zaynab bint Aḥmad b. ʿAbd al-Raḥīm b. ʿAbd al-Wāḥid b. Aḥmad al-Maqdisiyya. Her biography is available in the following works: al-Dhahabī, *Muʿjam al-Shuyūkh al-Dhahabī* (Beirut: Dār al-Kutub al-ʿIlmiyya, 1990), 199; al-Dhahabī, *Kitāb Duwal al-Islām* (Hyderabad: Dāʾirat al-Maʿārif al-Niẓāmiyya, 1918), 1:190; al-Dhahabī and al-Ḥusaynī (d. 765/1364), *Min Dhuyūl al-ʿIbar* (Kuwait: Maṭbaʿat Ḥukūmat al-Kuwayt, n.d.), 213; al-Ṣafadī, *al-Wāfī*, 15:43; al-Yāfiʿī, *Mirʾāt al-Jinān*, 4:305; Ibn Ḥajar, *al-Durar*, 2:209–10; Ibn al-ʿImād, *Shadharāt al-Dhahab*, 8:221; Kaḥḥāla, *Aʿlām al-Nisāʾ*, 2:46–51; and al-Ziriklī, *al-Aʿlām*, 3:65. Though Zaynab's biographers do not state her *madhhab*, the editor of *al-Durr al-Munaḍḍad fī Dhikr Aṣḥāb al-Imām Aḥmad* awards her a brief biography in his footnotes indicating her Ḥanbalī affiliations. See ʿAbd al-Raḥmān b. Muḥammad al-ʿUlaymī, *Al-Durr al-Munaḍḍad* (Cairo: Maṭbaʿat al-Madanī, 1992), 2:501. Further, her *nisba* of al-Maqdisiyya suggests that she descended from the aforementioned community of Palestinian Ḥanbalīs, who had settled in Damascus and its environs in the twelfth century. Zaynab's prodigious collection of *ijāza*s also attracted Goldziher's attention (see *Muslim Studies*, 2:367).

[55] For the biography of al-Nishtibrī, see al-Dhahabī, *Siyar*, 23:239–48. In this notice, al-Dhahabī mentions 647 as the year in which he sent this *ijāza* to Zaynab (*Siyar* 23:243).

[56] al-Dhahabī, *Siyar*, 23:243.

[57] Ibn Ḥajar, *al-Durar*, 2:209.

six years old, prominent scholars from Aleppo, Ḥarrān, Alexandria, Cairo, and al-Shām had sent her written permission to transmit specific works. Between the ages of three and twelve, Zaynab was brought to several assemblies or individual meetings in which she heard (*sami'at min*) scholars read works aloud. The encounters were duly recorded and endowed her with authority to transmit the works she had heard.[58] In passing their authority to the young Zaynab, these scholars were no doubt invested in the hope that she would eventually master and accurately transmit the works specified in the certificates.

Since Zaynab's acquisition of *ijāzā*s began unusually early, we can infer that as with the women previously studied, there was a family member facilitating her first steps. However, Zaynab's case is unusual because biographers do not mention her father's role in this regard.[59] The various biographical dictionaries and chronicles that cover the seventh/thirteenth and eighth/fourteenth centuries yield no clues about Aḥmad Kamāl al-Dīn al-Maqdisī, Zaynab's father, which suggests that he did not acquire a reputation as a religious scholar.[60] However, Zaynab had at least one prominent uncle who excelled in *ḥadīth* transmission, and it is possible that she received lessons from him.[61] Though her prominence as a *muḥadditha* was not built on her father's reputation in the field, he nonetheless may have brought Zaynab to *ḥadīth* assemblies before the age of five and solicited the *ijāza*s conferred on her.

Aside from kinship networks and paternal support, several practical factors impacted a woman's success as a scholar. Ibn Ḥajar informs us that Zaynab never married and that she suffered from ophthalmia

[58] Ibn Ḥajar, *al-Durar*, 2:209–10. Zaynab's biographies yield the names of a total of twenty-four teachers from cities such as Baghdad, Aleppo, Damascus, Alexandria, Ḥarrān, and Cairo. These *shaykhs* and *shaykha*s either sent the certification to Zaynab without meeting her or granted it to her when she was brought into their presence at a young age. See footnote 21 (in this chapter), which clarifies the terminology used to indicate how the certification took place.

[59] For observations regarding the importance of paternal connections in the Mamlūk period, see Berkey, *Transmission of Knowledge*, 169–71; Lutfi, "Al-Sakhāwī's *Kitāb al-Nisā'*," 123–24; and Roded, *Women in Islamic Biographical Collections*, 76.

[60] Given the cultural norms encouraging silence on the issue of maternal descent or mothers in general, it is not surprising that we are told nothing about Zaynab's mother and her possible contributions to her daughter's education.

[61] He was Shams al-Dīn Muḥammad b. 'Abd al-Raḥīm al-Maqdisī (d. 688/1289). His accomplishments earned him a teaching post in al-Madrasa al-Ḍiyā'iyya. See Ibn Ṭūlūn, *al-Qalā'id*, 80–81. His daughter, Zaynab's paternal cousin, Asmā' bint Muḥammad (d. 723/1323), also acquired a reputation as a *ḥadīth* transmitter (Ibn Ḥajar, *al-Durar*, 1:385). Asmā' heard *ḥadīth* from her father and is listed among al-Dhahabī's authorities (*Mu'jam al-Shuyūkh*, 150).

(*ramad*).[62] He does not elaborate on whether her illness hampered her efforts as a *muḥadditha* (or her marriage prospects). However, her superlative reputation indicates that she prevailed over her eye trouble. In addition, remaining single may have eased her domestic burdens, allowing her uninterrupted time for her studies.

Zaynab's biographers are most interested in the certifications she acquired in the earliest years of her life and in her teaching career between the age of sixty and her death at the age of ninety-four. The intervening years have left few traces in the published sources. Her later career as a teacher suggests that, between the ages of ten and sixty, she must have continued her studies, in part by studying the works for which she had received early certification. For example, she had received an *ijāza* to narrate the *Kitāb al-Ṣamt* of Ibn Abī al-Dunyā from Ibn al-Sayyidī.[63] Ibn al-Sayyidī died in 647, a year after Zaynab was born, so she obviously did not have a chance to study the work with him. Since the *Kitāb al-Ṣamt* was a work that Zaynab transmitted in a *ḥadīth* assembly (*sumiʿa ʿalayhā*), she must have learned the compilation after the death of Ibn al-Sayyidī and subsequently transmitted it on the authority of the *ijāza* he granted to her. The same chronology of certification followed by learning applies to other works for which she received early *ijāza*s and which she later transmitted to her own students.

Zaynab bint al-Kamāl's renown also rested on her narration of a wide variety of works. Her biographers confirm that she was a reliable authority for compilations of diverse genres. Among the works that she transmitted are major *ḥadīth* collections including the *Ṣaḥīḥ*s of al-Bukhārī and Muslim, the *Sunan* of Abū Dāwūd, and the *Muwaṭṭaʾ* of Mālik.[64] Additionally, she acquired certification for numerous lesser compilations. Al-Dhahabī lists ten works that she narrated through an *ijāza* from Ibrāhīm b. al-Khayr, another Ḥanbalī *muḥaddith*.[65] This list includes works promoting ascetic piety, such as the *Kitāb al-Shukr lillāh* and *al-Qanāʿa* of Ibn Abī al-Dunyā. Zaynab also transmitted *mashyakha*s, extensive lists of a scholar's *shaykh*s and the works related on their authority.[66] A final testament to her repertoire comes from Ibn Ḥajar's *al-Muʿjam al-Mufahras*, a collection of *isnād*s through which Ibn

62 Ibn Ḥajar, *al-Durar*, 2:210.
63 Kaḥḥāla, *Aʿlām al-Nisāʾ*, 2:49.
64 This information is culled from the various biographies for Zaynab cited earlier.
65 al-Dhahabī, *Siyar*, 23:236.
66 She is listed as transmitting eight *mashyakha*s to Ibn Ḥajar. See Ibn Ḥajar, *al-Muʿjam al-Mufahras* (Beirut: Muʾassasat al-Risāla, 1998), nos. 801, 802, 816, 817, 818, 838, 866,

Ḥajar acquired authority to transmit specific works. Zaynab appears (with an intermediary) in 139 of his *isnāds*, signifying that she acquired permission to narrate at least that many works.[67] These were primarily collections of *ḥadīth* on specific subjects including early Muslim history, the sciences of Qur'ān and *ḥadīth* (*'ulūm al-Qur'ān* and *'ulūm al-ḥadīth*), and legal rulings in specific branches of Islamic law (*al-aḥkām al-furū'iyya*).

The roster of Zaynab's students also confirms her rank as a respected *muḥadditha*. Prominent eighth/fourteenth-century scholars number among them, revealing that she was well connected within the intellectual circles of her time. Al-Dhahabī, al-Ṣafadī, and al-Subkī are among the more accomplished men who received *ijāza*s from her.[68] Ibn Baṭṭūṭa refers to her as "a traveler of the world" and lists her among those who granted him an *ijāza* during his visit to Damascus in 726/1325f.[69] Shams al-Mulūk al-Dimashqī (d. 803/1401) and 'Ā'isha bint Muḥammad (d. 816/1413), two respected *muḥadditha*s, also received certification from her.[70] Since *ḥadīth* transmission was accessible to all classes of society, many laypeople also counted among her students. Remarking on her popularity, Ibn Ḥajar wrote that students crowded around her to read to her for most of the day.[71]

In addition to information drawn from published biographical works and chronicles, archival evidence in the form of *samā'āt* (certificates of oral transmission, lit. of "hearing" a text) is crucial to understanding the activities of *ḥadīth* transmitters. These *samā'āt* were often issued at a *majlis al-samā'* (assembly for hearing *ḥadīth* compilations and other works in different fields of religious learning), the primary function of which was to verify the accuracy of the text being read. In such forums, participants would not actually study or discuss the text extensively in terms of its meaning or exegesis. The role of those presiding over these assemblies was to either listen to or read the specific texts; the students would examine their own

and 885. Among these were the *mashyakhas* of al-Ḥasan b. Shādhān (d. 425/1034) (for his biography, see al-Dhahabī, *Siyar*, 17:415–18), Shuhda al-Kātiba, and Ibn al-Jawzī.

67 Ibn Ḥajar did not narrate directly from Zaynab; he had not been born during her lifetime, so there would have been an intermediary between them in these *isnāds*. Ibn Ḥajar, *al-Mu'jam al-Mufahras*, 672.

68 For references to these scholars' associations with Zaynab, see, respectively, al-Dhahabī, *Mu'jam al-Shuyūkh*, 199; al-Ṣafadī, *al-Wāfī*, 15:43; and Ibn al-'Irāqī (d. 826/1423), *Dhayl 'alā al-'Ibar fī Khabar man 'Abar* (Beirut: Mu'assasat al-Risāla, 1989), 2:304.

69 Ibn Baṭṭūṭa, *Riḥla*, 67. Ibn Baṭṭūṭa does not elaborate on his reference to Zaynab's travels, so we cannot know whether she did indeed travel extensively.

70 For Shams al-Mulūk's biography, see Kaḥḥāla, *A'lām al-Nisā'*, 2:304. 'Ā'isha bint Muḥammad is the final case study of this chapter.

71 Ibn Ḥajar, *al-Durar*, 2:210.

copies to ensure that these were identical with the text being read. In the centuries before the advent of the printing press, the *majlis al-samāʿ* was one way to ensure the accuracy of handwritten texts. Often students would attend multiple sessions for the same text, thereby raising the probability that the copy in their possession was faithful to the original.[72]

An overview of several *samāʿāt* in which Zaynab is mentioned suggests that the richest documentary evidence for women's educational participation in classical Muslim society has yet to be explored. In the index compilation of Damascene certificates, *Muʿjam al-Samāʿāt al-Dimashqiyya*, thirty-four certificates name Zaynab as a presiding authority, either alone or in conjunction with other teachers, over a *majlis al-samāʿ*.[73] A typical certificate that served as a record of the assembly contains the following elements: the name of the presiding *shaykh*(s) or *shaykha*(s); the name of the text being read or studied; the place and date of the meeting; the name of the reader of the text (in cases where the reader is not the presiding teacher); the name of the writer of the *samāʿ*; and the number of students present for the occasion. Hirschler concludes that the practice of recording the names of all attendees became more widespread starting around the sixth/twelfth century, a trend indicative of shifts in the culture of reading among the scholarly elite as well as those who pursued a range of other full-time occupations.[74]

Samāʿāt are invaluable because they offer concrete details concerning the routines of students and teachers. In addition, their precise dating allows a fuller reconstruction of scholars' careers. All of the certificates in which Zaynab is mentioned as a teacher were awarded between the years 713 and 739, when she was between seventy-seven and ninety years old. She held these assemblies in a variety of locations, including her home and the homes of the readers of the texts.[75] Once, she presided over a small

[72] For example, Ibn Ḥajar, in his *al-Muʿjam al-Mufahras*, lists the names of everyone from whom he transmitted texts, either by reading the text(s) out loud or by hearing them in an assembly. See, for example, his *isnād*s for the *Ṣaḥīḥ* of Muslim, where it is clear that he heard the work from a number of *shaykh*s and *shaykha*s, at times in its entirety and at times in parts; *al-Muʿjam al-Mufahras*, 27–29.

[73] Stefan Leder et al. (eds.), *Muʿjam al-Samāʿāt al-Dimashqiyya* (Damascus: al-Maʿhad al-Faransī li'l-Dirāsāt al-ʿArabiyya, 1996), 311–12.

[74] Hirschler, *Written Word in the Medieval Arabic Lands*, 60–70.

[75] Examples of assemblies in her home can be found in *Muʿjam al-Samāʿāt*, p. 30, ms. 955, *risāla* 9, *samāʿa* 4; p. 58, ms. 1137, *risāla* 1, *samāʿa* 18; and p. 59, ms. 1137, *risāla* 1, *samāʿa* 22; for assemblies held in the home of the reader of the text, see p. 31, ms. 955, *risāla* 9, *samāʿa* 8; and p. 41, ms. 1039, *risāla* 7, *samāʿa* 4.

session in the garden of a certain Amīn al-Dīn.[76] Zaynab also held classes comprised of male and female students in al-Madrasa al-Ḍiyā'iyya, where her uncle Shams al-Dīn held a post, and in the *ribāṭ* of Ibn al-Qalānisī.[77] Another certificate describes an assembly of a little more than 100 students in the large congregational mosque, al-Jāmi' al-Muẓaffarī, in 721/1321. Zaynab was among ten other authorities, most of them male, presiding over this assembly.[78] She would have been seventy-five years old at the time. Yet another *samā'* reveals that Zaynab convened a class in her home after a Friday congregational prayer.[79] Twenty-one students, male and female, were present at this assembly.[80] The date of the certificate, 738/1337, places her in her early nineties at the time. Taken at face value, these *samā'āt* depict Zaynab as active and thriving at an age well beyond the reasonable life expectancy in the Mamlūk period.[81]

More broadly, the chronology of Zaynab's career recalls the issue of age differentials between scholars and their students in the field of *ḥadīth* transmission as a whole, a feature that is also prominent in Shuhda's life. As previously noted, before the age of five, Zaynab was granted *ijāza*s by teachers who were in the final years of their lives. By the time Zaynab was twelve, most of the teachers named in her biographies had died. She is famed precisely for the *ijāza*s she received from these men and women, and her prominence derives partly from being among their last surviving students. Al-Dhahabī

[76] *Mu'jam al-Samā'āt*, p. 41, ms. 1039, *risāla* 7, *samā'a* 5. Four students were present in this *majlis* for the reading of a work entitled *Karāmāt al-Awliyā'* by al-Ḥasan b. Muḥammad al-Khallāl (d. 439/1047).

[77] A description of these institutions can be found in Ibn Ṭūlūn, *al-Qalā'id*: for al-Madrasa al-Ḍiyā'iyya, see 76–84, and for Ribāṭ al-Qalānisī, see 85–87. Ibn Ṭūlūn has listed both of these as *dūr al-ḥadīth*, indicating that the functions of different educational institutions often overlapped. In addition, his section on al-Madrasa al-Ḍiyā'iyya includes a brief description of the post that Zaynab's uncle, the aforementioned Shams al-Dīn, held in this *madrasa*.

[78] *Mu'jam al-Samā'āt*, p. 89, ms. 3757, *risāla* 10, *samā'a* 11; the text heard at this assembly was entitled *Juz' fī-hi ḥadīth wāḥid 'an Ādam b. Abī Iyās 'Abd al-Raḥmān b. Muḥammad b. Shu'ayb al-Khurāsānī al-'Asqalānī* (d. 220/835).

[79] *Mu'jam al-Samā'āt*, p. 30, ms. 955, *risāla* 9, *samā'a* 4.

[80] *Mu'jam al-Samā'āt*, p. 39, ms. 955, *risāla* 9, *samā'a* 80 (with editorial designation "*mukarrar*").

[81] In a study of women as custodians of property in the Mamlūk period, Carl Petry has suggested that Mamlūk women enjoyed lower rates of mortality as they were sheltered from the political violence and instability that characterized this era. This made them more attractive as candidates for inheriting property and managing it within individual Mamlūk clans. A similar principle may have applied to civilian women's roles as *ḥadīth* transmitters in the Mamlūk period. See Carl Petry, "Class Solidarity versus Gender Gain: Women as Custodians of Property in Later Medieval Egypt," in *Women in Middle Eastern History*, eds. Nikki R. Keddie and Beth Baron, 122–42 (New Haven: Yale University Press, 1991).

reaffirms her value in this respect, for he notes that Zaynab was distinguished with respect to her certificates (*tafarradat bi'l-ijāza*) from 'Ajība al-Bāqadriyya, Ibrāhīm b. al-Khayr, Ibn al-'Ulayq, and 'Abd al-Khāliq al-Nishtibrī because, in her seniority, she came to be the only living link to them.[82] She was also the last to narrate from Sibṭ al-Silafī (d. 651/1253).[83]

This scenario of the very old transmitting authority to the very young is replayed in Zaynab's life as a teacher. She granted *ijāza*s to her students between 713/1313 and her death in 740/1339, when she was between the ages of sixty-seven and ninety-four. Students such as 'Ā'isha bint Muḥammad (723–816/1323–1413), Tāj al-Dīn al-Subkī (727–71/1327–70), and Muḥammad b. 'Alī b. Sa'īd al-Anṣārī (734–74/1333–72) encountered her in their youth.[84] 'Ā'isha bint Muḥammad, the eldest of these three, would have been seventeen when Zaynab died.

By the end of her life, Zaynab's prodigious accomplishments as a *ḥadīth* transmitter earned her the honorific *musnidat al-Shām*.[85] She died at the age of ninety-four. Biographers consistently praise her as a pious, chaste, and generous woman. As with Shuhda, her reliability as a transmitter combined with her longevity enabled her to connect the "young with the old" in the continuous transfer of religious knowledge. Furthermore, she likely inspired those women who acquired transmission authority from her. One such example is that of 'Ā'isha bint Muḥammad, the subject of the final case study.

'Ā'ISHA BINT MUḤAMMAD (723–816/1323–1413)

'Ā'isha bint Muḥammad b. 'Abd al-Hādī belonged to the Banū Qudāma, one of the most prominent Ḥanbalī families in the Ṣāliḥiyya

82 al-Dhahabī, *Siyar*, 23:233, 236, 241, and 243. "*Tafarradat bi'l-ijāza*" indicates that she was the only surviving student who held an *ijāza* to narrate on the authority of the referenced scholar.

83 al-Ziriklī, *al-A'lām*, 3:65; for Sibṭ al-Silafī's biography, see al-Dhahabī, *Siyar*, 23:278–80.

84 For mention of connections with al-Subkī and al-Ansārī, see Ibn al-'Irāqī, *Dhayl 'alā al-'Ibar*, 2:304 and 2:357, respectively. Zaynab's certification of 'Ā'isha will be discussed later in this chapter.

85 The term *musnid* as used by *ḥadīth* scholars in this period referred to someone who could faithfully transmit traditions or collections with a reliable chain of transmission. Critical understanding of the traditions or of the science of *isnād* criticism (*'ilm al-rijāl*) was not necessary for one to be deemed a *musnid*. Al-Sakhāwī ranks a *musnid* below a *muḥaddith* in terms of the former's proficiency as a *ḥadīth* scholar. See al-Sakhāwī, *al-Jawāhir wa'l-Durar*, 70, for his citation of an opinion that a *musnid* does not rise to the level of a *muḥaddith*. The use of such terminology, however, is not consistent in the chronicles and biographical dictionaries. It would, therefore, be inappropriate to conclude that Zaynab bint al-Kamāl's skills were limited only to rote transmission without critical knowledge of the sciences of *ḥadīth* transmission.

district.[86] As mentioned earlier, the influence of the Banū Qudāma in this area can be traced to their migration from Nablus to Damascus in the sixth/twelfth century and to their subsequent decision to settle in the Damascene suburb of al-Ṣāliḥiyya. The prominence of the Banū Qudāma and their prodigious scholarly output contributed to the spread of the Ḥanbalī *madhhab* from al-Ṣāliḥiyya to its environs.[87] ʻĀ'isha's kinship to this network no doubt facilitated her access to teachers.

The tradition of being educated by women and of educating them was not foreign to the Banū Qudāma. Ibn Qudāma (d. 620/1223), the most prominent jurist and scholar of this clan, heard *ḥadīth* from three well-known women during his travels to Baghdad: Khadīja al-Nahrawāniyya (d. 570/1175), Nafīsa al-Bazzāza (d. 563/1168), and Shuhda al-Kātiba.[88] Two other members of the Banū Qudāma likewise heard *ḥadīth* from Shuhda al-Kātiba.[89] Several of the Banū Qudāma also taught *ḥadīth* to women. Zaynab bint al-Wāsiṭī is listed as one of Ibn Qudāma's students.[90]

Although ʻĀ'isha bint Muḥammad could clearly claim a distinguished lineage in and access to the intellectual circles of al-Ṣāliḥiyya, her own father, Muḥammad b. ʻAbd al-Hādī (680–749/1281–1348), was not a prominent scholar. Rather, he earned his living as a market inspector (*muḥtasib*) in al-Ṣāliḥiyya, a position that granted him access to the

[86] Her full name is ʻĀ'isha bint Muḥammad b. ʻAbd al-Hādī b. ʻAbd al-Ḥamīd b. Yūsuf b. Muḥammad b. Qudāma b. Miqdām. The following sources contain biographical entries for her: Ibn Ḥajar, *Inbā' al-Ghumr bi- Anbā' al-ʻUmr* (Cairo: al-Majlis al-Aʻlā li'l-Shu'ūn al-Islāmiyya, 1971), 3:25; al-Sakhāwī, *al-Ḍaw' al-Lāmiʻ*, 12:81; Ibn Ṭūlūn, *al-Qalā'id*, 287–88; Ibn al-ʻImād, *Shadharāt al-Dhahab*, 9:178–79; al-Ziriklī, *al-Aʻlām*, 3:241; and Kaḥḥāla, *Aʻlām al-Nisā'*, 3:187–88.

[87] Muḥammad Duhmān, introduction to Ibn Ṭūlūn's *al-Qalā'id*, 4–5. The contributions of various members of the Banū Qudāma are apparent in chronicles and biographical dictionaries, where they are commemorated as *ḥadīth* transmitters, jurists, and judges. These works include al-Ṣafadī's *Kitāb al-Wāfī bi'l-Wafayāt*, Ibn Ḥajar al-ʻAsqalānī's *al-Durar al-Kāmina*, and al-Sakhāwī's *al-Ḍaw' al-Lāmiʻ*. Also, Ibn Ṭūlūn's history of al-Ṣāliḥiyya contains many biographies of members of the Banū Qudāma.

[88] Ibn Qudāma was mentioned earlier in the context of Shuhda's case study as one of her students. For the biography of Khadīja al-Nahrawāniyya, see al-Dhahabī, *Siyar*, 20:551–52, and for that of Nafīsa al-Bazzāza, see al-Dhahabī, *Siyar*, 20:489.

[89] They are Ibrāhīm b. al-Waḥīd al-Maqdisī (d. 614/1218; see Ibn Ṭūlūn, *al-Qalā'id*, 335–39) and Muḥammad b. ʻAbd al-Hādī (d. 658/1260; see al-Dhahabī, *Siyar*, 23:342–43). Zaynab bint al-Kamāl also narrated on the authority of this same Muḥammad b. ʻAbd al-Hādī, who incidentally is not the father of ʻĀ'isha bint Muḥammad.

[90] al-Dhahabī, *Siyar*, 22:167. Other similar examples may be found in Ibn Ṭūlūn's *al-Qalā'id*; see, for example, Ibn Ṭūlūn's biographies for Ibrāhīm b. Aḥmad (p. 304), Aḥmad b. Abī Bakr (p. 334–35), ʻAbd al-Raḥmān b. ʻAlī (p. 308), and ʻUmar b. Muḥammad b. Aḥmad (p. 287).

'ulamā' of Damascus.[91] Whatever he knew of *ḥadīth* would have been communicated to his daughter in the initial phase of her studies. In this regard, Ibn Ṭūlūn notes that 'Ā'isha heard traditions from her father along with other *ḥadīth* transmitters of her period.[92] His commitment to educating his daughters is evident in the fact that 'Ā'isha's older sister, Fāṭima bint Muḥammad (719–803/1319–1401), was also a *muḥadditha* who studied and taught *ḥadīth* alongside 'Ā'isha.[93]

As with Shuhda and Zaynab, discussed earlier, 'Ā'isha's acquisition of *ḥadīth* began at a strikingly early age. When she was four, 'Ā'isha was brought into the presence of the well-known *ḥadīth* authority al-Ḥajjār (d. 730/1329).[94] Through this meeting, she acquired an *ijāza* to narrate the *Ṣaḥīḥ* of al-Bukhārī on his authority. Al-Ḥajjār himself was a sought-after source as he had heard the *Ṣaḥīḥ* from Ibn al-Zabīdī (d. 649/1251), another prominent *muḥaddith*.[95] Al-Ḥajjār's repute was such that he narrated the *Ṣaḥīḥ* no less than seventy times in Damascus, al-Ṣāliḥiyya, Cairo, Miṣr, Ḥamāh, Ba'labakk, Ḥims, Kafr Baṭnā, and the surrounding regions.[96] Since 'Ā'isha outlived all others who transmitted al-Bukhārī's *Ṣaḥīḥ* from al-Ḥajjār, she became a coveted authority for those seeking to have his name in their chain of transmission.[97]

Aside from al-Ḥajjār, seventeen of 'Ā'isha's teachers are named in her biographies. Of these, biographical information can be found for nine, all of whom had died by the time she was eighteen. Four of the teachers mentioned by 'Ā'isha's biographers are women. Not surprisingly, three of them are well-known *muḥadditha*s of Damascus: Sitt al-Fuqahā' bint Ibrāhīm (d. 726/1326), Zaynab bint Yaḥyā (d. 735/1335), and Zaynab

91 Ibn Ṭūlūn, *al-Qalā'id*, 271. See also Ṣāliḥ 'Abbās, "Min Rijāl al-Ḥisba fī al-Qarnayn al-Sābi' wa'l-Thāmin," in *Dirāsāt fī al-Ḥisba wa'l-Muḥtasib 'inda al-'Arab* (Baghdad: Markaz Iḥyā' al-Turāth al-'Ilmī al-'Arabī, 1988), 201, #49. Lapidus defines the position of market inspector as a "prominent *'ulamā'* office" along with the post of chief *qāḍī*, the head of the public treasury, and army judges (*Muslim Cities*, 108–9).

92 Ibn Ṭūlūn, *al-Qalā'id*, 287.

93 Fāṭima's biography occurs in al-Sakhāwī's *al-Ḍaw' al-Lāmi'*, 12:103. See also Kaḥḥāla, A'lām al-Nisā', 4:133.

94 For his biography, see Ibn Kathīr, *al-Bidāya wa'l-Nihāya fī al-Ta'rīkh* (Cairo: Dār al-Fikr al-'Arabī, n.d.), 14:150.

95 This is noted in the following biographies: al-Dhahabī, *Dhuyūl al-'Ibar* (Beirut: Mu'assasat al-Risāla, 1985), 4:88; Ibn Kathīr, *al-Bidāya*, 14:150; Ibn Ḥajar, *al-Durar*, 1:152–53; Ibn Ṭūlūn, *al-Qalā'id*, 298–99; and Ibn al-Qāḍī, *Dhayl Wafayāt al-A'yān* (Cairo: Dār al-Turāth, n.d.), 1:28; and Ibn al-'Imād, *Shadharāt al-Dhahab*, 8:162. For Ibn al-Zabīdī's biography, see al-Dhahabī, *Siyar*, 23:251–52.

96 Ibn Ḥajar, *al-Durar*, 1:152.

97 All of her biographers note that she was the last one who could relate the *Ṣaḥīḥ* of al-Bukhārī on the authority of al-Ḥajjār.

bint al-Kamāl (d. 740/1339).[98] The fourth is ʿĀʾisha bint Muḥammad b. al-Muslim of Ḥarrān (d. 736/1336).[99] The death dates of these women indicate that ʿĀʾisha's contact with them must have occurred when she was very young: Sitt al-Fuqahāʾ died when ʿĀʾisha was four, Zaynab bint Yaḥyā when she was eleven, Zaynab bint al-Kamāl when she was seventeen, and ʿĀʾisha bint Muḥammad b. al-Muslim when she was fourteen. A similar age relationship is evident in her association with the six male teachers for whom we have death dates.[100] All of them had died by the time she was fifteen.

The certificates that ʿĀʾisha acquired during her early years authorized her to transmit a number of works. These included the *Ṣaḥīḥ* collections of both al-Bukhārī and Muslim,[101] the *Sīra* of Ibn Hishām,[102] the *Arbaʿīn* collection of al-Ṭāʾī,[103] a minor *ḥadīth* compilation (*juzʾ*) of Abū al-Jahm, and a portion of the *Dhamm al-Kalām* of al-Harawī.[104] Ibn Ḥajar cites her as his authority for fourteen additional works not mentioned by her biographers.[105] Ibn al-ʿImād states admiringly that at the end of her life, she had the best *isnād*s from among her contemporaries and was prolific in terms of both the number of works that she had heard and the number of *shaykh*s that she could claim as her teachers ("*kānat fī ākhir ʿumri-hā asnada ahli zamānihā mukthiratan samāʿan wa-shuyūkhan*").[106] Additionally, Kaḥḥāla refers to an alphabetically

[98] For Sitt al-Fuqahāʾ's biography, see Ibn Ḥajar, *al-Durar*, 2:221; for Zaynab bint Yaḥyā's, see Ibn Ḥajar, *al-Durar*, 2:215.

[99] Ibn Ḥajar, *al-Durar*, 2:342.

[100] The following are the six male teachers for whom biographical data was found: Ibrāhīm b. Ṣāliḥ al-Ḥalabī (d. 731/1331, see Ibn Ḥajar's *al-Durar*, 1:28–29); Aḥmad b. Abī Ṭālib al-Ḥajjār (d. 730/1329, see *al-Durar*, 1:152–53); Abū Bakr b. Muḥammad al-Maqdisī (d. 738/1338, see *al-Durar*, 1:491); ʿAbd Allāh b. al-Ḥusayn al-Maqdisī (d. 732/1332, see *al-Durar*, 2:361–62); ʿAbd Allāh b. al-Ḥusayn al-Anṣārī (d. 735/1334, see *al-Durar*, 2:362–63); Yaḥyā b. Faḍl Allāh al-ʿAdawī (d. 738/1338, see *al-Durar*, 5:199–200).

[101] al-Sakhāwī, *al-Ḍawʾ al-Lāmiʿ*, 12:81.

[102] al-Sakhāwī, *al-Ḍawʾ al-Lāmiʿ*, 12:81.

[103] Ibn Ḥajar, *Inbāʾ al-Ghumr*, 3:25. The work is identified in Ḥājjī Khalīfa Kātip Çelebi (d. 1067/1657), *Kashf al-Ẓunūn ʿan Asāmī al-Kutub waʾl-Funūn* (Beirut: Dār Iḥyāʾ al-Turāth al-ʿArabī, 1990), 1:56.

[104] Kaḥḥāla, *Aʿlām al-Nisāʾ*, 3:188. For the *juzʾ* of Abū al-Jahm, see Ḥājjī Khalīfa, *Kashf*, 1:584. The *Dhamm al-Kalām* is a published work that presents a Ḥanbalī critique of theology.

[105] Ibn Ḥajar, *al-Muʿjam al-Mufahras*, 669. Two of these works are in the genre of *ḥadīth* compilations known as *Arbaʿīnāt* (collections of forty *ḥadīth* usually on a particular subject), and the remaining twelve fall in the category of *fawāʾid* (a collection of *ḥadīth* narrated by a particular *shaykh*, often on disparate topics).

[106] Ibn al-ʿImād, *Shadharāt al-Dhahab*, 9:178.

arranged index of 'Ā'isha's authorities, which was compiled by a certain Ḥāfiẓ Najm al-Dīn.[107]

'Ā'isha bint Muḥammad's students underscore her distinction as a *muḥadditha*. Ibn Ḥajar al-'Asqalānī is perhaps her best-known student. His accomplishments in the field of *ḥadīth* criticism are exemplified in his monumental work *Fatḥ al-Bārī bi-Sharḥ Ṣaḥīḥ al-Bukhārī*, an extensive and authoritative commentary on the traditions contained in the *Ṣaḥīḥ* of al-Bukhārī, which he was authorized to transmit on 'Ā'isha's authority.[108] While the extent to which he studied the *Ṣaḥīḥ* with her is unclear, having her name in his *isnād* likely boosted his reputation for the transmission of this work. As mentioned above, Ibn Ḥajar cites her in his *isnād*s for fifteen works. Interestingly, he records, in each case, that he read the specified work or verified it in the presence of both 'Ā'isha and her sister Fāṭima.[109] Ibn Ḥajar's concurrent citation of both of them was likely intended to underscore the accuracy of his transmission. In addition to Ibn Ḥajar, several Mamlūk notables numbered among 'Ā'isha's male students, highlighting yet again the unifying force of traditionalism during this period.[110] Al-Sakhāwī remarks that "many learned men (*a'imma*), particularly travelers [in search of religious knowledge], went to her and narrated profusely from her," thereby confirming that her reputation was well established in Damascus and its environs.[111]

[107] Kaḥḥāla, *A'lām al-Nisā'*, 3:187. In addition, the index of *Mu'jam al-Samā'āt al-Dimashqiyya*, 349, references a certificate for an assembly that she attended at the age of eleven. The assembly was for transmitting the text *Majlis al-Biṭāqa min Amālī Ḥamza al-Kinānī* (d. 357/968); see *Mu'jam al-Samā'āt*, p. 30, ms. 955, *risāla* 9, *samā'a* 1. Given that this work catalogs certificates recorded between the years 550/1155 and 750/1349, it cannot be used as a source for *samā'āt* that 'Ā'isha granted.

[108] Kaḥḥāla, *A'lām al-Nisā'*, 3:188.

[109] Ibn Ḥajar, *al-Mu'jam al-Mufahras*, 669. For simultaneous mention of 'Ā'isha and Fāṭima, see the following entries in Ibn Ḥajar, *al-Mu'jam al-Mufahras*: nos. 905, 927, 973, 1014, 1022, 1106, 1117, 1160, 1276, 1394, 1400, 1414, 1520, 1611, and 1615.

[110] The following are the Mamlūks named as 'Ā'isha's students: Aḥmad b. Qāḍī al-Quḍāt Burhān al-Dīn (800–876/1398–1471; for his biography, see 'Alī b. Dāwūd b. al-Ṣayrafī [d. 900/1495], *Inbā' al-Haṣr bi-Abnā' al-'Aṣr* [Cairo: Dār al-Fikr al-'Arabī, 1970], 345–48); Aḥmad b. Ibrāhīm b. Naṣr Allāh (800–876/1398–1472; for his biography, see Ibn al-Ṣayrafī, *Inbā' al-Haṣr*, 450–54); and Muḥammad b. al-Qāḍī Nāṣir al-Dīn (796–856/1393–1452; for his biography, see Ibn Taghrībirdī [d. 874/1470], *Nujūm al-Ẓāhira fī Mulūk Miṣr wa'l-Qāhira* [Cairo: al-Hay'a al-Miṣriyya al-'Āmma li'l-Kutub, 1972], 16:13–14). Two articles that explore the subject of intellectual culture among the Mamlūks are Ulrich Haarmann, "Arabic in Speech, Turkish in Lineage: Mamluks and their Sons in the Intellectual Life of Fourteenth Century Egypt and Syria," *Journal of Semitic Studies* 33 (1988): 81–114, and Jonathan Berkey, "'Silver Threads among the Coal': A Well-Educated Mamlūk of the Ninth/Fifteenth Century," *Studia Islamica* 73 (1991): 109–25.

[111] al-Sakhāwī, *al-Ḍaw' al-Lāmi'*, 12:81.

'Ā'isha bint Muḥammad served as an authority not only for the men mentioned earlier, but also for many women. Al-Sakhāwī provides entries for thirty-one of 'Ā'isha's female students.[112] Most of these entries follow his standard pattern of providing birth dates, names of spouses and children, and names of a few prominent authorities from whom the women narrated. In only one case, that of Zaynab bint 'Alī b. Muḥammad b. 'Abd al-Bar'am, do we learn the name of the work that she heard from 'Ā'isha (the *Ṣaḥīḥ* of al-Bukhārī).[113]

The biographical data at our disposal permit a few important observations regarding 'Ā'isha's contact with both male and female students. The four male students for whom we have names were born sometime after her fiftieth birthday. More precisely, Ibn Ḥajar was born when she was fifty, Kamāl al-Dīn Muḥammad when she was seventy-three, and the remaining two, 'Izz al-Dīn Aḥmad and Aḥmad b. Ibrāhīm, when she was seventy-seven. Her female students similarly had contact with her late in her life. Al-Sakhāwī provides a combination of birth dates and *ijāza* dates for twenty-seven of these women. Only one of these students, Fāṭima bint 'Alī b. Manṣūr (b. ca. 770/1368), was born by the time 'Ā'isha bint Muḥammad had reached the age of forty-seven. The remaining birth date data show that two students were born when she was in her seventies and eight of them when she was past the age of eighty. As for the *ijāza* dates, one woman obtained her *ijāza* from 'Ā'isha when the latter was in her sixties, eleven of them when she was in her eighties, and six of them when she was in her early nineties.

A final comment pertains to the geographical extent of 'Ā'isha's reputation. Al-Sakhāwī mentions the provenance of twenty-six of her female students as follows: twenty-one were from Mecca, two were from Aleppo, one from Cairo, and one from Būlāq. We do not know whether the students actually went to see 'Ā'isha in al-Ṣāliḥiyya or if she encountered them in the cities of their origin. It may well be that the *ijāza*s were granted in absentia, a practice that appears to have proliferated during 'Ā'isha's lifetime. Irrespective of the particulars of how the *ijāza*s were granted, the provenance of her students allows us to map the spread of her reputation to urban areas distant from her own home.

[112] For 'Ā'isha's female students, see the following numbered entries in al-Sakhāwī's *al-Ḍaw' al-Lāmi'*, volume 12: 46, 47, 60, 103, 145, 156, 169, 231, 232, 258, 339, 346, 409, 488, 593, 609, 694, 741, 806, 843, 860, 919, 946, 975, 978, 983, 984, 987, 999, 1002, and 1004.

[113] al-Sakhāwī, *al-Ḍaw' al-Lāmi'*, 12:44, #258.

Ā'isha bint Muḥammad lived to the age of ninety-three; at the time of her death, her reputation matched those of the foremost *ḥadīth* transmitters in the region of al-Ṣāliḥiyya. Her funeral prayers were held in one of the large Damascene congregational mosques, al-Jāmi' al-Muẓaffarī. Describing the occasion, Ibn Ṭūlūn notes that "many people came from all regions on the occasion of her death."[114] Her accomplishments as a student and a teacher earned her an enviable reputation as an exemplary and revered *muḥadditha*.

A COLLECTIVE PORTRAIT

The lives of Shuhda, Zaynab, and 'Ā'isha span three and a half centuries (482–816/1089–1413). Yet as the biographical accounts in this chapter indicate, the system of *ḥadīth* transmission was relatively stable, and the careers of these women overlap in many ways. Features common to all of their lives can be extracted and extrapolated toward a collective portrait of female *ḥadīth* transmitters in classical and late classical Islam. One similarity emerges in the age structure of their relationships with their teachers as well as their students. A second parallel is the interaction between men and women as illustrated in their careers. Third, their successes highlight the persistence of education outside the *madrasa* system; it is this phenomenon that helps explain the accomplishments of *muḥadditha*s in spite of their general exclusion from endowed, salaried posts in educational institutions. Fourth, the women were authorities primarily for compilations of *ḥadīth* and less commonly for works of *fiqh*, grammar, theology, and poetry.

Each woman's profile indicates that her most widely appreciated *ḥadīth* acquisitions occurred between the ages of one and twelve. In our modern context, this would be roughly analogous to basing our scholarly reputations on who our teachers were between preschool and elementary school. Yet in the classical Muslim context of *ḥadīth* transmission, this practice was a means for preserving the authenticity of the religious tradition transmitted from Muḥammad and his Companions to each subsequent generation. Guarding against corruption of the original often meant seeking the shortest *isnād*s narrated by reliable authorities (*isnād 'ālī*). Prominent *ḥadīth* scholars such as al-Khaṭīb al-Baghdādī and Ibn al-Ṣalāḥ al-Shahrazūrī agreed that awarding *ijāza*s to young children was acceptable so long as the material was learned later in life and transmitted accurately.[115] Aside from the *muḥadditha*s studied here, many other women whose lives are recorded in

[114] Ibn Ṭūlūn, *al-Qalā'id*, 288.
[115] al-Khaṭīb al-Baghdādī, *al-Kifāya*, 76–77; and Ibn al-Ṣalāḥ, *Muqaddima*, 108–9.

Ibn Ḥajar's *al-Durar al-Kāmina* and in al-Sakhāwī's *al-Ḍaw' al-Lāmi'* were awarded *ijāzas* before the age of five.[116]

The phenomenon of transmission authority passing from the very old to the very young has been observed in other regions of the Muslim empire. Richard Bulliet's study of tenth/sixteenth- and eleventh/seventeenth-century Nishapur assessed the significance of age in male teacher-student relationships and noted similar patterns.[117] Using a sample of 200 teachers in Nishapur, Bulliet notes a trend among *ḥadīth* teachers to have young students, particularly in their final years of teaching. *Ḥadīth* study often began as early as age four with fathers or uncles taking notes for children in these "classes." The teachers that *ḥadīth* students had at a young age appear frequently in their biographies.[118] The practice of granting *ijāzas* for *ḥadīth* transmission to the young appears to have intensified beginning in the fifth/eleventh century and peaked around the tenth/sixteenth century. The increased passion over these centuries for acquiring the shortest possible chain of transmission either back to Muḥammad or to the compiler of a given work helps account for the rise in *ijāzas*, which, as discussed in Chapter 3, did not require face-to-face transmission and came to be associated with less stringent standards. Ultimately, the quest for the *isnād 'ālī* proved to be a boon for women's participation in this arena.

That the very old transmitted to the very young is understandable in light of the preference for short *isnāds*. That many of the transmitters, among them our three case studies, lived to ages rarely seen in the classical period prompts scrutiny. There are reasons to believe that reports of such ages do not fall in the realm of myth-making. The practice of recording birth and death dates had become more commonplace by the Mamlūk period and may well have been linked to the popular quest for *isnād 'ālī*. Also, many of our records for this era are primary sources that record the birth and death dates of women and men who were more short-lived as well as those blessed with longevity. However, the process of "natural selection" that occurred in the quest for the shortest chains of transmission meant that biographical

116 This is readily observed through a perusal of these two dictionaries as well as Kaḥḥāla's compendium, *A'lām al-Nisā'*. Roded has made similar observations in her study *Women in Islamic Biographical Collections*, 70–71.

117 Richard Bulliet, "The Age Structure of Medieval Education," *Studia Islamica* 57 (1983): 105–17.

118 Berkey, although he did not conduct the same type of quantitative analysis as Bulliet, draws a similar conclusion regarding age structures in educational relationships during the Mamlūk period (see *Transmission of Knowledge*, 177).

dictionaries tended to extol the accomplishments of transmitters who surpassed average life expectancy. These statistical outliers would be then disproportionately represented in the historical records.

The acquisition of *ḥadīth*, however, likely extended beyond perfunctory exchanges between children and their *shaykh*(*a*)s. As Bulliet notes, though students would continue their study of *ḥadīth* beyond their youth, it would not be as useful to formally record their attendance at sessions.[119] In this vein, the teachers that Shuhda, Zaynab, and ʿĀʾisha encountered before the age of fourteen predominate in their biographies and the three *muḥaddithas*, in turn, appear frequently in the biographies of students they had in their advanced years. Thus biographical sources show similar age structures for male and female *ḥadīth* transmission. These dictionaries, however, do not provide information for women that would allow conclusive comment on the period between youth and seniority.[120] Normative constraints on women's public participation during their marriageable years make it less likely that coeducational involvement would be recorded by biographers and chroniclers.

Though the period between puberty and menopause is not well documented in women's biographies, we can imagine the following probable scenarios for these intervening years. The first possibility is that women, in conformity with religious norms prescribing strict seclusion for women of marriageable age, ceased attending public, coeducational *ḥadīth* sessions. Instead, they devoted themselves primarily to the private study of collections for which they had received certification in their early childhood. Once they reached an advanced enough age that their public presence did not threaten social order, they would convene classes for male and female students.

A second scenario, which finds greater support, is that women's careers in this domain largely paralleled those of their male counterparts. That is, they may have continued their education in study circles open to both men and women rather than in cloistered or segregated settings. Anecdotal evidence suggests that women participated as auditors in public

119 Bulliet, "Age Structure," 114–15.

120 Elizabeth Sartain, while researching the biography of Jalāl al-Dīn al-Suyūṭī, also found a "surprisingly large" number of women commemorated as *ḥadīth* transmitters in the ninth/fifteenth century. She notes that cultural norms prohibiting mixing between men and women of marriageable age left girls up to the age of sexual maturity (ca. ten to thirteen years old) free to attend coeducational classes. Likewise, old women, past the age of sexual attraction, were accepted as teachers of boys and men. See Sartain, *Jalāl al-Dīn al-Suyūṭī: Biography and Background* (New York: Cambridge University Press, 1975), 125–27.

educational forums even at ages when we would expect more rigorous seclusion. The Mālikī scholar Ibn al-Ḥājj al-ʿAbdarī (d. 737/1336), for example, describes an undesirable scenario in which women attended *ḥadīth* assemblies held in mosques and in the company of men. The women would sit facing men in these assemblies, and in their excitement, would get up and sit down in ways that manifested their *ʿawrāt* (i.e., parts of a woman's body that should not be seen by a man to whom she is not married or related).[121]

It is interesting that Ibn al-Ḥājj, whose views on women's public presence are extremely conservative, does not protest the participation of women in such gatherings.[122] Rather, he is opposed to aspects of their comportment that caused disturbances. In fact, Ibn al-Ḥājj insists on a woman's right to a religious education. He maintains that if her husband cannot educate her properly, he should allow her to go out and learn from others who are more knowledgeable. If the husband denies her permission, Ibn al-Ḥājj encourages the wife to seek legal redress.[123] While he does not specify whether women in such instances should learn exclusively from other women, he does not appear opposed, in principle, to women learning from men. Commentary such as Ibn al-Ḥājj's suggests that in spite of overarching prescriptions limiting contact between the sexes at certain ages, exceptions may have been made for religious forums.

Another common thread in the careers of these *muḥaddithas* is their success outside the framework of *madrasas*. There is no evidence that any of these women ever officially enrolled in a *madrasa*, let alone held an endowed teaching post.[124] However, different modes of classical Muslim education were not mutually exclusive, and the proliferation of *madrasas* under the Seljūqs, Ayyūbids, and Mamlūks did not diminish the importance of other, informal channels of learning. Salaried teachers from

[121] Ibn al-Ḥājj al-ʿAbdarī, *Madkhal al-Sharʿ al-Sharīf* (Cairo: al-Maṭbaʿa al-Miṣriyya biʾl-Azhar, 1929), 2:219. Berkey, in his analysis of female education in Mamlūk Cairo, concludes on the basis of such anecdotal evidence that gender barriers were permeable in the world of *ḥadīth* transmission; Berkey, *Transmission of Knowledge*, 177.

[122] Ibn al-Ḥājj prescribes severe restrictions for women's public presence throughout his work. See, in particular, *Madkhal*, 1:245–72 on women going out for various needs and occasions.

[123] Ibn al-Ḥājj, *Madkhal*, 1:276–77. Ibn al-Ḥājj states that a woman should take her case to a *ḥākim* (a judge overseeing social regulations) and that this officer should force her husband to grant her religious rights just as he is forced to in cases of material, worldly rights. See also *Madkhal*, 1:209–10 for further discussion of a man's duty to teach his wife her religious obligations.

[124] Although Zaynab's *samāʿāt* record her assemblies in al-Madrasa al-Ḍiyāʾiyya, it is not clear that she held a salaried teaching position there.

madrasas tutored individual students and presided over classes in mosques and private homes. Generally, women participated as teachers and students of *ḥadīth* through study circles in private homes or mosques.[125] As Berkey notes, throughout Islamic history, "education remained fundamentally informal, flexible, and tied to persons rather than institutions."[126] This informality and the persistence of the educational process in diverse locations such as private homes, libraries, and literary salons clarifies how women studied and taught in spite of their formal exclusion from institutions such as *madrasas*. In light of these alternative modes of education, it is not unusual that the *muḥaddithas* discussed here were granted numerous *ijāzas* and that they disseminated this knowledge to other *ḥadīth* students. Ibn Ḥajar notes that Zaynab collected *ijāzas* from scholars of Aleppo, Damascus, Baghdad, Jericho, Ḥarrān, Alexandria, and Cairo, and that students crowded around her to read great works with her.[127] Similarly, the reputations of Shuhda and 'Ā'isha attracted itinerant students to their study circles.

A final characteristic of this collective portrait pertains to the works studied and transmitted. As previously noted, these works are primarily compilations of *ḥadīth* on particular topics of Muslim ritual and ascetic piety as well as some of the major canonical collections. Legal commentaries, theological tracts, and Qur'ānic exegeses are listed less frequently. There are several possible explanations for the apparent preponderance of the field of *ḥadīth* in the scholarly activity of women. Among them is that learning and then teaching works of *fiqh*, theology, or Qur'ānic exegesis required prolonged and uninterrupted years of study (*mulāzama*), often with one or more *shaykhs*.[128] Such contact between men and women who were not married to each other was not condoned. Further, demands placed on women by marriage and child-rearing may have rendered such devotion to education difficult. Our evidence on this issue is uneven. Zaynab did not marry and attained remarkable success. Shuhda and Fāṭima bint al-Ḥasan (discussed in Chapter 3), on the other hand, were supported by their husbands in their endeavors. In addition to the time demanded by the study of law or theology, the fact that such subjects were commonly studied and taught under the auspices of *madrasas*, facilitated

125 Berkey, *Transmission of Knowledge*, 171; and Roded, *Women in Islamic Biographical Collections*, 76–78, 85.
126 Berkey, *Transmission of Knowledge*, 18.
127 Ibn Ḥajar, *al-Durar*, 2:210.
128 Makdisi, *The Rise of Colleges* (Edinburgh: Edinburgh University Press, 1981), 128–29, and Berkey, *Transmission of Knowledge*, 179–80.

by endowed stipends and salaries, may have hampered women's access to this type of education.

The profiles of Shuhda, Zaynab, and 'Ā'isha accord with traditionalism as it was promoted in Baghdad and Damascus, where the study, memorization, and incorporation of *ḥadīth* into daily life paved the way to salvation. In keeping with traditionalist norms, compilations of the ascetic Ibn Abī al-Dunyā, with titles such as *Kitāb al-Shukr lillāh* (Book of Gratitude to God), and *al-Qanā'a* (Contentment [with God and Divine Will]), recur among these women's transmissions. It is also not surprising that 'Ā'isha was authorized to transmit the *Dhamm al-Kalām wa-Ahlihi* (Reproof of Theology and Its Practitioners) of the Ḥanbalī scholar al-Harawī. Compilations such as the *Karāmāt al-Awliyā'* of al-Khallāl (d. 439/1047), in the *faḍā'il* category, promoted contemplation of the virtues of pious ancestors. The dissemination of such works in these communities supports observations in previous studies that traditionalism went hand in hand with ascetic piety. Organized Ṣūfism, however, does not appear to have exercised a strong influence on the careers of Shuhda, Zaynab, or 'Ā'isha.[129]

THE OTTOMAN DECLINE

The final evolution in women's *ḥadīth* participation that falls within the purview of this study is a marked decline that coincided with Ottoman expansion into Egypt and Syria beginning in the early tenth/sixteenth century. This early Ottoman trend, much like the precipitous decline in women's participation in the second/eighth and third/ninth centuries, has gone unnoticed save for M. A. Nadwi's mention of it.[130] Given the Ottoman focus on Islamic law and especially on the Ḥanafī juristic tradition, and given that the second/eighth-century decline of women occurred in the context of the project of articulating Islamic law, we may be inclined to view this trend as a repetition of a past pattern. Yet data from tenth/sixteenth-century biographies do not suggest an overall diminution of women's roles in religious education.

[129] Heller has made a similar observation regarding "popular Islam" among the Ḥanbalīs of al-Ṣāliḥiyya as a whole; Heller, "Shaykh and Community," 117–20. George Makdisi has pointed out that Ḥanbalism was not inimical to organized Ṣūfism as a whole but rather was opposed to particular types of Ṣūfism; Makdisi, "The Ḥanbalī School and Ṣūfism," *Boletín de la Asociación Española de Orientalistas* 15 (1979): 115–26.

[130] Nadwi, *al-Muḥaddithāt*, 260–63. Nadwi states that this decline is not unique to women and is symptomatic of the overall deterioration of all areas of Islamic learning.

Ibn al-'Imād's *Shadharāt al-Dhahab*, encompassing the first ten centuries of Islamic history, offers a view of this development affirming patterns noted in earlier chapters of this book and also attesting the drop-off in women's participation beginning in the tenth/sixteenth century. Whereas there are notices for thirty-eight women, most of them *ḥadīth* transmitters, in each of the seventh/thirteenth and eighth/fourteenth centuries (seventy-six in total), only twenty-one women are commemorated as *ḥadīth* transmitters in the ninth/fifteenth century. In the tenth/sixteenth century, a mere seven are granted obituary notices. Of those seven, only two are noted primarily for their skills as *ḥadīth* transmitters. Of these two, Amat al-Khāliq bint al-Khayr (d. 902/1496f.) appears to have attained fame as the last transmitter of the *Ṣaḥīḥ* of al-Bukhārī on the authority of the companions of al-Ḥajjār.[131] Umm al-Hanā' bint Muḥammad al-Miṣriyya (d. 911/1505) is the other woman known primarily for her *ḥadīth* activity.[132] However, Ibn al-'Imād provides few details of her accomplishments, suggesting that her renown was limited.

The five women who are not primarily transmitters stand out because their entries either hint at or explicitly reveal a broader range of women's educational engagement beginning in the tenth/sixteenth century. Ibn al-'Imād praises Khadīja bint Muḥammad (d. 930/1524) as a pious *shaykha* learned in *fiqh* (*mutafaqqiha*).[133] Her legal reasoning is evident in her choice of the Ḥanafī *madhhab* for herself, even though her father and brothers were Shāfi'ī. According to Ibn al-'Imād, she favored the Ḥanafī interpretation on a matter related to her marriage and had memorized a legal work on these issues. Zaynab bint Muḥammad (d. 980/1572) also extended her learning beyond *ḥadīth* transmission to poetry and calligraphy. Ibn al-'Imād accords high praise to her poetry (*fī ghāyat al-riqqa wa'l-matāna*).[134] Fāṭima bint Yūsuf al-Tādafī (d. 925/1519f.) is the final example of a woman who attracts attention for achievements other than learning *ḥadīth*.[135] Ibn al-'Imād notes that she performed the Ḥajj twice and decided to "give up the dress of women of the world." She donned a robe (presumably one in keeping with her ascetic

131 In her obituary, Ibn al-'Imād laments that after her death, the transmission of the *Ṣaḥīḥ al-Bukhārī* diminished by a degree since she was the last to transmit from the companions of al-Ḥajjār (*nazala ahl al-arḍ darajatan fī riwāyat al-Bukhārī bi-mawtihā*). See Ibn al-'Imād, *Shadharāt al-Dhahab*, 10:21. Amat al-Khāliq heard the *Ṣaḥīḥ* on the authority of 'Ā'isha bint Muḥammad. As noted in 'Ā'isha's biography, she was the last to transmit the *Ṣaḥīḥ* on al-Ḥajjār's authority.

132 Ibn al-'Imād, *Shadharāt al-Dhahab*, 10:73.

133 Ibn al-'Imād, *Shadharāt al-Dhahab*, 10:239.

134 Ibn al-'Imād, *Shadharāt al-Dhahab*, 10:574.

135 Ibn al-'Imād, *Shadharāt al-Dhahab*, 10:190.

life) and undertook pilgrimage to Jerusalem and a third Ḥajj. She then settled in Mecca and died there. Fāṭima's choice to withdraw from the world, while not necessarily signaling religious learning, nonetheless highlights yet another avenue of pietistic engagement available to women of the late Mamlūk and early Ottoman eras.

The unusual cases of 'Ā'isha bint Yūsuf al-Bā'ūniyya (d. 922/1516) and Fāṭima bint 'Abd al-Qādir (a.k.a. Bint al-Qarimzān, d. 966/1558) reveal additional prospects for women's religious education. 'Ā'isha al-Bā'ūniyya ranks as one of the most prodigious women of late classical Islam.[136] Born in Damascus in the mid-ninth/fifteenth century, 'Ā'isha belonged to a well-established *'ulamā'* family that had produced generations of preachers, jurists, Qur'ān scholars, and literary figures.[137] Ibn al-'Imād introduces her in superlative terms, highlighting her uniqueness as a literary figure, scholar, poet, and one who exhibited exemplary piety and virtue.[138] In addition to acquiring the requisite training in Qur'ān and *ḥadīth*, to which she would have been entitled in accordance with her lineage, 'Ā'isha surpassed her peers by being granted *ijāza*s for issuing legal edicts and teaching law (*ujīzat bi'l-iftā' wa'l-tadrīs*) and by composing numerous works of poetry and prose, most of them infused with Ṣūfī themes such as longing for the Prophet, praise for Ṣūfī masters, and mastering the practice of ascetic piety.[139] While her intellectual genealogy is similar to that of Zaynab bint al-Kamāl and 'Ā'isha bint Muḥammad b.'Abd al-Hādī, she was more accomplished and attained a superlative reputation as a Ṣūfī writer and poetess. A study of her life suggests that she was elaborating and building on the legacies of prior generations of female religious scholars.

The second woman, Fāṭima bint 'Abd al-Qādir b. Muḥammad, was a Ḥanafī *shaykha* who, though less accomplished than 'Ā'isha al-Bā'ūniyya, attracts attention for attaining the rank of *shaykha* of two Ṣūfī institutions, the Khānqāh al-'Ādiliyya and the Khānqāh al-Dajjājiyya.[140] Further

[136] She has been the subject of several studies by Th. Emil Homerin. See his "Living Love: The Mystical Writings of 'Ā'ishah al-Bā'ūniyah," *Mamlūk Studies Review* 7 (2003): 211–34; "Writing Sufi Biography: The Case of 'Ā'ishah al-Bā'ūnīyah (d. 922/1571)," *Muslim World* 96, no. 3 (2006): 389–99; and *Emanations of Grace: Mystical Poems by 'Ā'ishah al-Bā'ūnīyah*, ed., trans., and introd. Th. Emil Homerin (Louisville: Fons Vitae, 2011).

[137] For an overview, see EI^2, s.v. "al-Bā'ūnī."

[138] Ibn al-'Imād, *Shadharāt al-Dhahab*, 10:157.

[139] See Homerin, "Living Love," for a more detailed treatment of 'Ā'isha's mystical writings.

[140] Ibn al-'Imād, *Shadharāt al-Dhahab*, 10:506. For an analysis of the role of the *khānqāh* in the Mamlūk period, see Th. Emil Homerin, "Saving Muslim Souls: The *Khānqāh* and the Sufi Duty in Mamlūk Lands," *Mamlūk Studies Review* 3 (1999): 59–83.

research on women's positions in these and other Ṣūfī institutions is necessary to determine whether this practice was widespread and what women's duties were for such positions. With respect to Fāṭima's religious learning, Ibn al-'Imād notes that she had beautiful calligraphy, copied out many books, and was well-spoken, pious, and devoted to prayer even in times of illness. Further, he notes that Fāṭima credited her religious education to her husband, Muḥammad b. Mīr al-Ardabīlī. Her remark about her husband's role suggests a different educational trajectory from that of many others, who launched their careers through paternal support.

A survey of Ibn al-'Imād's biographical notices over the ninth/fifteenth and tenth/sixteenth centuries sheds further light on the nature of the decline in women's participation. Patterns in terminology describing the educational endeavors of male and female scholars show that engagement with *ḥadīth* shifted away from preoccupation with narration to hermeneutics – that is, away from *riwāya* to *dirāya*. Ibn al-'Imād's notices for countless scholars at the beginning of the ninth/fifteenth century employ specialized terms such as *qara'a 'alā* (he read to), *ajāza lahu* (he granted a certificate to him), and *ḥaddatha 'an* (he narrated from) to describe the exchanges between scholars and their students: these are terms indicating a continuity of the culture of *ḥadīth* transmission as practiced in previous centuries. Entries from the late ninth/fifteenth and early tenth/sixteenth centuries, however, evoke a different milieu. The aforementioned terms become rarer and are replaced with increasing references to the legal and Qur'ānic learning of scholars. Additionally, scholars' affiliations with Ṣūfī *ṭarīqa*s and their achievements in this area are noted with greater frequency, indicating that organized Ṣūfism came to play a greater role in this period.[141] Ibn al-'Imād's work is a valuable testament to the impact of ninth/fifteenth- and tenth/sixteenth-century evolutions in the social uses of religious knowledge on the prevalence and practice of *ḥadīth* transmission among both men and women. This late classical trend is qualitatively different from what occurred in the second/eighth century, a period that witnessed the severe marginalization of women from the profession of *ḥadīth* transmission even as men continued their robust engagement in this arena.

The evidence presented in this chapter accords with what we know of the intellectual and religious milieu of the early Ottoman period. An

[141] Further research is necessary before we can decisively conclude that Ṣūfī *ṭarīqa*-based piety edged out individualistic, *ḥadīth*-based, ascetic piety. See Christopher Melchert's "Piety of the *Ḥadīth* Folk," *IJMES* 34, no. 3 (2002): 425–39, for his analysis of the characteristics of early (up to the tenth century) asceticism and piety.

emphasis on the legal training of scholars, especially those within the imperial educational hierarchy, along with the proliferation of organized Ṣūfism are dominant characteristics of the early Ottoman era. However, we know little about the specific evolution of *ḥadīth* transmission as a distinct field of religious learning in the early Ottoman period.[142] It is, therefore, not clear how Ottoman reforms impacted curricula of study for those within the state-sanctioned Ottoman *madrasa*s or those outside this framework, as many female scholars would have been.

Our comprehension of the social impact of Ottoman education would be greatly advanced not just through closer studies of the curricula of Ottoman institutions but also through an analysis of the shifting pedagogical uses of classical texts. One rare study on the content of an Ottoman curriculum revealed that there were twelve works of *fiqh* and twelve of *ḥadīth* in addition to several Qur'ān commentaries on a list of required books at an imperial *madrasa* in the mid-sixteenth century.[143] While these numbers at first suggest equivalent treatment of both law and *ḥadīth*, a closer examination of the titles shows that the focus of the *ḥadīth* curriculum is on the *Ṣaḥīḥ* collections and their commentaries, indicating a more legally oriented approach to *ḥadīth*. Derivative collections such as the ones that our Mamlūk *muḥadditha*s were transmitting have no place in this imperial syllabus. While such collections may have continued to circulate in other settings, it is also quite possible that values from the imperial *madrasa*s guided and shaped the curricula in less formal settings as well. Referring again to Talal Asad's understanding of "orthodoxy," we can hypothesize that just as the articulation of *ḥadīth*-oriented traditionalist orthodoxy positively impacted women's *ḥadīth* education, the promotion of a new Ottoman orthodoxy with its increased emphasis on law and Ṣūfism generated new criteria and new dynamics of inclusion and exclusion of women in the practice and perpetuation of this orthodoxy.

CONCLUSION

The period covered in this chapter witnessed a dramatic flourishing of women's *ḥadīth* participation as the culmination of currents set in motion

[142] The *Turkish Encyclopedia of Islam* does not provide much information on *ḥadīth* study under the Ottomans or about the endowment of institutions for *ḥadīth* study (*dūr al-ḥadīth*), further confirming that the field was marginalized and viewed as secondary to other educational pursuits. I thank Susan Gunasti for her observations in this regard.

[143] Shahab Ahmed and Nenand Filipovic, "The Sultan's Syllabus," *Studia Islamica* 98/99 (2004): 183–218.

during the fourth/tenth and fifth/eleventh centuries. A host of factors correlate with this development: the canonization of *ḥadīth*, the widespread acceptance of written transmission, the rise of family-based *'ulamā'* networks, and the promotion of traditionalism as classical Sunnī orthodoxy through mechanisms such as an unusual age structure for pedagogy, *ijāza*s, and preference for the shortest possible chains of transmission (*isnād 'ālī*). While the confluence of these factors clearly resulted in environments that welcomed and extolled women's contributions, none of these variables were expressly intended to promote women's educational mobilization. The coincidental nature of women's revival and resurgence make this an all the more intriguing phenomenon. In the same light, the developments of the late Mamlūk and early Ottoman era, which resulted yet again in women's diminished *ḥadīth* participation, merit closer examination in future studies as heralding yet another unexpected turn in the history of Muslim women's religious education.

Conclusions

This book has explored the tradition of women's *ḥadīth* transmission and its evolution over nearly ten centuries in the central Islamic lands. The first century and a half of Islamic history witnessed significant rates of female participation, followed by negligible activity for close to two and a half centuries. Around the mid-fourth/tenth century and thereafter, women reemerged as extolled transmitters of *ḥadīth*. During the Seljūq, Ayyūbid, and Mamlūk periods (fifth/eleventh to tenth/sixteenth centuries), numerous women achieved superlative reputations, and their transmission authority was coveted by both male and female students throughout the Muslim world. The early Ottoman period (ca. mid-tenth/sixteenth century) is marked by yet another sharp reduction in the numbers of female *ḥadīth* transmitters. My analysis contextualizes this striking chronology in terms of concurrent developments in Muslim intellectual, political, and social history and highlights the evolving social uses of religious knowledge that help explain these trends.

Among the Companions, both well-known and obscure women shared reports about Muḥammad and the earliest Muslims. Representing 12 percent of all Companion-Narrators in the major Sunnī collections, the female Companions are overall more prolific than women of immediately subsequent generations. They vary tremendously with respect to the quantity and quality of their participation. For example, ʿĀ'isha and Umm Salama, the most prominent wives of Muḥammad, narrated more extensively than other women on various aspects of the Prophet's *sunna*. They are also among the few women who regularly display an understanding of the legal import and application of traditions. In this respect, they resemble leading male Companions, such as ʿUmar b. al-Khaṭṭāb or ʿAbd Allāh

b. 'Abbās, who relayed reports on a broad range of issues and who authoritatively derived the legal significance of Muḥammad's injunctions. Other female Companion-Narrators enter the *ḥadīth* compilations in different capacities: as his female kin, as fighters in battles, or as *fatwā*-seekers on sundry topics. These women's reports are conveyed as syncopated, cryptic accounts of their encounters with Muḥammad or as more elaborate testimonials that at times influence disputes on a host of ritual, legal, and doctrinal issues. In general, biographers portray female Companions as respected and devout women central to the perpetuation of the legacy of Muḥammad and his community.

The roles and level of participation of women shifted considerably after the Companions. From the time of the Successors up to the compilers of the major Sunnī collections (i.e., from the final quarter of the first/seventh century to the beginning of the fourth/tenth century), the quantity and quality of women's transmission fell dramatically. In this period, which encompasses close to eleven generations of transmitters, there are approximately 235 women who were credited with reports.[1] By contrast, in the first generation alone there are 112 female narrators. In addition to this overall decline in the numbers of women recorded in the collections, the transmission activity of individual women of the post-Companion generations is diminished. Only eight women are credited with more than ten traditions, and these eight attained varying levels of renown as transmitters of Muḥammad's reports. Moreover, the reputations of these eight women, all of whom died by the end of the first century, are grounded either in their relationship to a prominent female Companion through kinship or in their accomplishments as ascetics. None of the remaining 227 women are commemorated as traditionists who assiduously collected and disseminated *ḥadīth* in the manner of prominent male Successors such as 'Urwa b. al-Zubayr and Ibn Shihāb al-Zuhrī. With a few exceptions, such as 'Amra bint 'Abd al-Raḥmān and Umm al-Dardā', there is little indication that women were deemed qualified to assess the legal significance of the reports they transmitted. Rather, much like female Companions other than 'Ā'isha and Umm Salama, the participation of women of subsequent generations is incidental, arising from contacts made during the Ḥajj or ad hoc questioning on miscellaneous issues to determine correct religious practice. The vast majority of these women are credited with only one tradition each, reinforcing the picture of the decline in the quality and

[1] In Chapter 2, I note that there are 276 women who narrate as links 2–4. Of these 276, 41 are Companions, and the remaining 235 women are from the subsequent generations.

quantity of women's roles. Finally, most women who are credited with traditions after the time of the Companions had died by 150 AH, which suggests that in early Islam, what little there was of women's *ḥadīth* participation was limited to the first century and a half. There are a handful of obscure women credited with transmission in the final quarter of the second century. Thereafter, no women appear in the *isnād*s of the selected compilations.

Multiple sources substantiate and nuance this picture of stark decline that emerges from the *isnād* evidence. Chronicles and biographical dictionaries drawing on a broader array of sources round out the picture. For example, both the *Ṭabaqāt* of Ibn Sa'd and the *Ta'rīkh Dimashq* of Ibn 'Asākir contain entries for female transmitters who do not appear in the *isnād*s of the selected compilations. However, most of these women are again from the generations of the Companions or early Successors. Similarly, none of the biographical dictionaries and chronicles consulted for this research indicates significant levels of women's participation from the second/eighth to the mid-fourth/tenth century. Thus these works confirm simultaneously the selectivity inherent in the *ḥadīth* compilations chosen for this study as well as the historicity of the patterns of decline observed in the *isnād* data.

In making sense of this marked decline, we might at first suspect explicit discrimination against women. A few discussions recorded in second/eighth-century legal manuals such as the *Kitāb al-Ḥujja* of al-Shaybānī do show that the sex of the narrator, regardless of whether she was a Companion or not, could diminish the value of a tradition in legal discussions. Thus, some women's narrations, particularly on highly contested issues, were stigmatized on the basis of gender. Yet such references are scattered and do not fully account for the pervasive and profound marginalization of women over two and a half centuries.

Several other impediments derailed women's participation. The early second/eighth century witnessed the beginnings of the "professionalization" of *ḥadīth* transmission in the course of which rigorous criteria came to be applied to judge the quality of an individual's transmission. This development placed a high bar on entry to the field, favoring those who demonstrated legal acumen and who acquired training through extensive individual tutelage with other leading scholars. Cultural and religious norms curtailing women's interactions with non-*maḥram* men hampered women's acquisition of the requisite training. Around the same time, undertaking strenuous journeys to collect *ḥadīth* (*riḥla*s) became critical for the success of a *ḥadīth* scholar. Women's limited mobility, again dictated by cultural and religious norms, further constrained their participation. The confluence of these factors resulted in the precipitous decline in women's *ḥadīth* transmission as evidenced in their minimal representation in the sources during this period.

The noteworthy pattern of initially widespread transmission on the part of women followed by a sharp decline has significant implications for the dating of traditions ascribed to women. Notwithstanding my assertion (in the introduction) that it is impossible to conclusively confirm or deny the historicity of individual *isnād*s that feature early women, my data make a strong argument for the early dating of traditions ascribed to women. As I have shown in Chapter 2, female participation in *ḥadīth* transmission fell into disfavor, and women began to be increasingly marginalized around the end of the first century. In this context, it is important to emphasize that the *ḥadīth* studied here have doctrinal, ritual, and legal significance for Muslims.[2] Therefore, forgers would logically select narrators who could in fact claim authority in the milieu in which they were operating. In the second/eighth and third/ninth centuries, women's presence was so marginalized that there would be little incentive to forge an *isnād* with a female authority during that period. Only ʿĀ'isha and Umm Salama, the most prominent wives of Muḥammad, appear to have claimed enough narrative authority to override the effects of women's marginalization as *ḥadīth* transmitters.[3] Although it is possible that many *ḥadīth* on the authority of ʿĀ'isha and Umm Salama originated in the second/eighth century or thereafter, it is less likely that other women served as a desirable locus for forgeries in the second/eighth and third/ninth centuries.[4]

It is important, however, to differentiate between the *dating* and *authenticity* of traditions ascribed to female Companions and Successors. The

2 This is with the exception of traditions in the categories of eschatology and the virtues and vices of Companions, which are deemed suspect genres even by the standards of many traditional Muslim scholars.

3 Although the other wives of Muḥammad may have claimed a level of prestige similar to that of ʿĀ'isha and Umm Salama, their low level of participation as compared to these two wives reveals that they were not remembered as prolific transmitters of Muḥammad's practices.

4 In this vein, it should be mentioned here that the doctrine that confers collective immunity from error on all the Companions in their narration of *ḥadīth* (*taʿdīl al-ṣaḥāba*) was not articulated in the sources before approximately the late third century. It can thus be eliminated as a possible explanation for the interpolation of female Companions in *isnād*s forged in the second and third centuries. My statement about the early dating of women's traditions is not intended to entirely exclude the possibility of second-century or later forgeries in the name of women. Rather, I intend to highlight a general principle that false attribution of *ḥadīth* to women after the first century was far less likely.

dence presented here does not establish that the female Companions or Successors to whom these traditions are attributed are actually the ones who uttered them. Rather, it indicates that any fabrications that may have occurred are likely to have taken place in the earliest phases of *ḥadīth* transmission in a milieu in which women's participation was still readily accepted and not closely regulated. In this atmosphere, forging a *ḥadīth* with a woman in the *isnād* would not have undermined the authority of the *ḥadīth* itself. I thus conclude that *ḥadīth* credited to women other than ʿĀ'isha and Umm Salama are likely to have originated in the first century. As such, these traditions can be valuable in the reconstruction of the earliest period of Islamic social, political, and legal history, an era for which our sources are notoriously scarce. Ultimately, traditions must be evaluated on a case-by-case basis as to their authenticity and dating.[5] However, the hypothesis presented earlier may well serve as a starting point from which to test individual traditions narrated by women.

Returning to the chronology analyzed in this book, the prolonged absence of women from the field of *ḥadīth* studies beginning in the second century makes it difficult to imagine that women would ever reclaim authority in this domain. Yet in the late fourth/tenth century, we see increasing references to revered and accomplished women who were accepted as authoritative transmitters of various *ḥadīth* compilations. The impediments that had earlier curtailed women's activities were mitigated not by women's agency but by happenstance. The compilation of the canonical collections, the rise in written transmission, and the triumph of Sunnī traditionalism generated alternative uses for religious knowledge, which in turn favored women's reentry into this domain.

The activities of *muḥadditha*s in the post-fourth/tenth-century revival were qualitatively different from those of female Companions. The latter are depicted as composing *ḥadīth* narratives, and some of them interpret the legal significance of their reports for contemporary seekers of knowledge. Indeed, Companions (both male and female) are endowed with a creative influence that did not extend to later generations of men and

[5] Here it is worth noting that Harald Motzki, using a different methodology, convincingly dates the tradition of Fāṭima bint Qays (on her divorce) to the earliest decades of Islam. His quantitative analysis is one method that helps identify *ḥadīth* that are likely to have originated in the first century and that can in turn serve as historical sources to nuance our understanding of a variety of issues. See Harald Motzki, *Origins of Islamic Jurisprudence: Meccan Fiqh before the Classical Schools*, trans. Marion Katz (Leiden: Brill, 2002), 157–67.

women in their capacities as reproducers of these texts.[6] In this limited capacity, around the mid-fourth/tenth century, prominent female transmitters acquired superlative reputations, and knowledge seekers throughout the Muslim world sought to include their narrative authority in their own *isnāds*. These *muḥaddithas*, in turn, helped perpetuate the traditionalist ethos that emphasized ascetic piety and devotion to the legacy of Muḥammad and the early Muslim exemplars. In this context, women were acclaimed for embodying the virtues promoted by classical Sunnī traditionalism and for propagating traditionalist literature via short *isnāds*. Their participation waned again by the beginning of the Ottoman era as a result of a decreased emphasis on *ḥadīth* narration and a concurrent focus on studying *ḥadīth* as an auxiliary to law.

This history of women as *ḥadīth* transmitters leads to a reconsideration of two well-promoted positions in Muslim women's studies. The first concerns the impact of traditionalist Sunnī Islam on women's public participation. Several recent analyses have advanced the view that this brand of Islam has restricted women's mobility and active participation in the public sphere.[7] Yet this book shows that it was precisely this strain of Islam that successfully mobilized numerous women in Sunnī circles after the fourth/tenth century and engaged them in the public arena of *ḥadīth* transmission.

A second misconception is that women's range of mobility and status were highest during the first century of Islam and suffered irreversible decline thereafter due to imperial expansion, the absorption of women-demeaning patriarchal values from neighboring Byzantine and Sassanian cultures, and the legal codification of these misogynistic values.[8] Accordingly, women's activities and influence came to be largely restricted to the domestic realm throughout the early and classical periods. It was only in the nineteenth century that Western discourse about women's rights, coincident with European imperialism, infiltrated the Muslim

6 Other enterprises in the field of *ḥadīth* study did permit creativity and individual authorship. These included the tasks of composing commentaries on *ḥadīth*, exploring their legal significance, and compiling authoritative collections of traditions. Male scholars of the post-Companion generations immersed themselves in these labors, but we have no evidence that women followed suit in significant numbers.

7 See, for example, Leila Ahmed, *Women and Gender*; Fatima Mernissi, *Women's Rebellion and Islamic Memory* (Atlantic Highlands, NJ: Zed Books, 1996); and Asma Afsaruddin, "Reconstituting Women's Lives."

8 A range of studies have advanced this position. They include the early works of Lichtenstadter and Stern as well as the more recent studies of Leila Ahmed and Barbara Stowasser.

world, destabilized the status quo, and sparked the gradual reclamation of public space by Muslim women. However, as I show here, women did suffer setbacks after the first/seventh century in the domain of *ḥadīth* transmission but were able to reenter the field in the mid-fourth/tenth century and attain enviable reputations as prominent, trustworthy *ḥadīth* transmitters. Zaynab bint al-Kamāl, for example, convened popular assemblies in public arenas, interacted with male and female students who coveted her name in their *isnād*s, and clearly achieved a high level of prominence on a par with contemporary male traditionists. This level of activity and the acclaim bestowed on women like her is particularly remarkable given the prior prolonged absence of women. In light of women's fluctuating fortunes in *ḥadīth* transmission, it is important to reevaluate our understanding of the fate of women's status and mobility from the rise of Islam to the eve of the modern period.

My research on these ten centuries of Muslim women's education took me on compelling detours and produced many as yet unanswered questions. I present a few of those here in the hopes of sparking future research that builds on my macroscopic analysis. First, I found myself lingering on the lives of a number of early and classical Muslim women. Women are generally awarded brief, fragmentary biographical entries and obituaries in chronicles. The exceptions to this rule, however, are presented in enticingly richer detail and give us windows onto otherwise inaccessible worlds. Aside from offering opportunities for more detailed historical reconstruction of women's lives, such studies can illuminate the intellectual milieus with which these women were associated. For example, the lives of Ḥafṣa bint Sīrīn, ʿAmra bint ʿAbd al-Raḥmān, and ʿĀʾisha bint Ṭalḥa have much to tell us about early Islamic asceticism, the early Medinese legal and historical tradition, and Umayyad literary circles and court culture, respectively. Further, the ascetic and devotional practices of women such as Ḥafṣa, Umm al-Dardāʾ, and Muʿādha bint ʿAbd Allāh find parallels with their Christian counterparts and can shed light on inter-religious exchanges in this early period. As for women of the post-Successor generations, the richest documentary evidence dates from the Seljūq, Ayyūbid, and Mamlūk periods. The published sources along with archival material including *samāʿāt* and *ijāzāt* can be used to produce microstudies of *muḥaddithas* and fill lacunae with respect to women's history in early and classical Islam. The utility of such research extends beyond women's studies to enhancing our understanding of broader issues in the social, political, and intellectual history of these eras. Women who attained expertise in other areas of religious learning such as law and Qur'ānic exegesis also merit attention, as do female practitioners of Ṣūfism.[9] Finally, research on women in the other sects, such as the Imāmī, Zaydī, Ismā'īlī, and Ibāḍī ones, and their participation in various fields of religious studies is necessary to appreciate the extent of women's religious education as well as the many variables that impacted their engagement.

From a comparative religions perspective, I was struck by similarities and contrasts between Muslim women's experiences and those of women in other traditions. Feminist scholars have highlighted a pattern of higher initial female participation in the founding history of several world religions. This early, often public, engagement is followed by women's marginalization, correlating with factors such as institutionalization of religious authority and practice, and the emergence of orthodoxies. For example, the early successes of an order of Buddhist nuns in India (from the third century BC to the third century AD) were followed by a precipitous decline in their fortunes.[10] Similarly, the marginalization of Brahmanic women after the Vedic period is a familiar theme in Hindu women's studies.[11] And for the Jewish and Christian traditions, the early public religious participation of women was curtailed by factors such as the canonization of texts inimical to women's interests and the emergence of male-dominated central institutions of religious authority.[12] Viewed through a comparative lens, the early demise of female *ḥadīth* transmitters is entirely predictable.

Yet just as the narrative of Muslim women's participation does not end with their disappearance from the scene of religious learning, the religious participation of women in other traditions can be seen to adapt

[9] A recently published edition of Sitt al-'Ajam bint al-Nafīs's commentary on the writings of Ibn al-'Arabī exemplifies the rich resources that can be used to understand women's contributions to Ṣūfism. Sitt al-'Ajam was a seventh/thirteenth-century woman who herself could not write but whose thoughts on Ibn al-'Arabī (d. 638/1240) were conveyed by her husband. See Sitt al-'Ajam bint al-Nafīs, *Sharḥ al-Mashāhid al-Qudsiyya*, ed. Bakr 'Alā' al-Dīn and Su'ād al-Ḥakīm (Damascus: al-Ma'had al-Faransī li'l-Sharq al-Adnā, 2004).

[10] Nancy Auer Falk, "The Case of the Vanishing Nuns: The Fruits of Ambivalence in Ancient Indian Buddhism," in *Unspoken Worlds: Women's Religious Lives*, ed. Nancy Auer Falk and Rita Gross, 196–206 (Belmont, CA: Wadsworth, 1989).

[11] See, for example, Mary McGee, "Ritual Rights: The Gender Implications of *Adhikāra*," in *Jewels of Authority*, ed. Laurie Patton, 32–50 (New York: Oxford, 2002).

[12] Jewish women's leadership roles in the synagogue have been examined by Bernadette Brooten in *Women Leaders in the Ancient Synagogue* (Chico, CA: Scholars Press, 1982). For Christian women's studies, this position has been forcefully articulated by several Christian feminists. See, for example, Rosemary Ruether (ed.), *Womanguides: Readings toward a Feminist Theology* (Boston: Beacon Press, 1996), preface.

to evolving circumstances. In the Christian case, for example, Herbert Grundmann highlights the pious engagement of European women from the late twelfth to the early fourteenth centuries. He correlates a rise in such activity with Pope Innocent III's reforms, which redrew boundaries between orthodox and heterodox movements in an attempt to bring new, popular religious movements (many of which incorporated women) into the Church's orbit.[13] Talal Asad's model of discursive tradition and orthodoxy sensitizes us to the strategies of medieval Europeans who validated women's engagement by recasting "tradition" in order to effectively respond to their unique cultural and historical contexts.

This model may also prove fruitful for understanding Jewish women's evolving engagement with the Torah and Talmud. Although premodern Rabbinic Judaism proscribed women's scriptural learning and teaching, some Jewish women excelled as religious authorities, mastering both the Torah and the Talmudic traditions.[14] Their strategies for rationalizing their education within the discursive traditions of Rabbinic Judaism allow us to see similarities in Jewish and Muslim women's religious education as well as contrasts between them.

My final concluding point concerns the relevance of this history for contemporary concerns about Muslim women's educational access. Widespread news reports about the denial of such rights by extremists unfortunately mask the reality that Muslim women's religious education is flourishing and attracting women across the socioeconomic spectrum in diverse global contexts. Yet the forms and purposes of such education have been molded to local exigencies such that the early and classical lineages, as presented in this book, are unacknowledged or barely recognizable. An example from contemporary Syria illustrates this disjuncture.

In 2001, the Madrasat al-Ḥadīth al-Nūriyya for women enrolled its first students. Situated in the Old City of Damascus, this institution's walls adjoin the Umayyad mosque, where 'Ā'isha bint Muḥammad b. 'Abd al-Hādī held her *ḥadīth* assemblies in the ninth/fifteenth century. And a few streets away, in the mosque where Umm al-Dardā' is said to have taught in the

[13] Herbert Grundmann, *Religious Movements in the Middle Ages*, trans. Steven Rowan (Notre Dame: University of Notre Dame Press, 1995). Caroline Bynum has devoted her landmark *Holy Feast and Holy Fast* to uncovering the significance of food for pious, ascetic women during this period, which witnessed greater opportunities for women's religious participation.

[14] See, for example, the discussions on Jewish women's engagement with the Torah in Avraham Grossman, *Pious and Rebellious: Jewish Women in Medieval Europe*, trans. Jonathan Chipman (Waltham: Brandeis University Press, 2004), chapters 7 and 8.

second/eighth century, women continue to congregate to pursue religious learning. My own quest to understand modern manifestations of women's *ḥadīth* transmission brought me to the Madrasat al-Ḥadīth al-Nūriyya in 2010.[15] Even before visiting the school, I had heard about the feats of its graduates, a few of whom had memorized the *Ṣaḥīḥ* of al-Bukhārī as well as other well-known compilations. I was certain that I had happened upon a contemporary reincarnation of classical women's *ḥadīth* education, which might enlighten me further about my historical subject.

My expectations were misplaced. The Madrasat al-Ḥadīth al-Nūriyya is, in some respects, the first of its kind. Indeed, this should not be surprising given the diverse iterations of women's *ḥadīth* participation across ten centuries. The only constant, perhaps, is the reference to the practice of leading early exemplars such as ʿĀʾisha bint Abī Bakr.

A number of obvious differences between this twenty-first-century institution and its early and classical antecedents bring the historical rupture into sharper focus. First, this is an institution strictly and solely dedicated to female *ḥadīth* education. The building itself contains classrooms, an assembly hall, a library and computer center, and a cafeteria. All teachers and students are women, though leading male scholars such as Nūr al-Dīn ʿItr serve on its founding and advisory board. By contrast, the assemblies of a number of early and classical female scholars were coeducational and took place in diverse locales. The purposes of *ḥadīth* study have likewise evolved. The teachers and students of *ḥadīth* at the Madrasat al-Ḥadīth al-Nūriyya are not charged with the accurate reproduction of texts such as *al-Faraj baʿd al-Shidda* or *Dhamm al-Muskir*. Rather, there are two primary courses of study: (1) *ḥadīth* sciences (*ʿulūm al-ḥadīth wa-muṣṭalaḥuhu*) and (2) study and memorization of seven Qurʾānic readings. The curricula require advanced proficiency in Arabic since students focus on close readings and discussions of a few widely circulated texts, among them al-Nawawī's (d. 676/1277) *Riyāḍ al-Ṣāliḥīn*. Through such engagement, the institution aims to revive the centrality of *ḥadīth* study as an integral aspect of the religious education of women.

A third disjuncture is that perpetuating the *isnād ʿālī* is not a priority at this institution. At the Madrasat al-Ḥadīth al-Nūriyya, students are

[15] My remarks on this *madrasa* are based on my own visit to the institution in early 2010. During my visit, I obtained some of the material that is distributed to students about the curricula of the school. I have not conducted a detailed study of the institution (though it certainly merits such a study). Therefore, my observations here are tentative.

permitted to enroll only after reaching the age of sixteen and only after acquiring an elementary education at a minimum. By contrast, many of the classical-era *muḥadditha*s were brought in their infancy to acquire certification from aged teachers, and their environments were saturated with the culture of traditionalism from childhood to old age. The modern age structure (especially in comparison with classical precedents) and the altered pedagogical routines have profound implications for the role of religious education in identity formation. These implications intersect with modern discourses about nation-building, religious resurgence, and the role of gender politics in these processes. Many of the students at the Madrasat al-Ḥadīth al-Nūriyya would have been exposed to the Syrian school curriculum before enrolling in the *madrasa*. Along with imparting literacy in a number of core subjects, the Syrian curriculum inculcates nationalism and the ideals of Syrian citizenship, which in themselves are secularly oriented. In these modern contexts, the curricula and pedagogical environment of the Syrian *madrasa* indicate a social purpose for *ḥadīth* learning that is altered from its classical iteration. Here, *ḥadīth* learning provides a safe arena for asserting contemporary conservative visions of Islamic practice that may otherwise not find secure institutional harbor in the broader society.

The case of the Madrasat al-Ḥadīth al-Nūriyya is but one example of how the deep-rooted tradition of Muslim women's religious education has starkly different manifestations across time and place. Other contemporary examples include women's hermeneutical engagement with the Qur'ān in Indonesia and the state-sponsored legal training of Moroccan female jurists (*murshidāt*).[16] Each case of women's education, however, is rationalized as upholding and securing a historically valid precedent of women's education and religious engagement that dates back to the era of Muḥammad. Thus, the Syrian members of the Madrasat al-Ḥadīth al-Nūriyya, the Indonesian female Qur'ān scholars,

[16] See Pieternella van Doorn-Harder, *Women Shaping Islam: Reading the Qur'an in Indonesia* (Chicago: University of Illinois Press, 2006), for a detailed study of the Indonesian case. The *murshidāt* program in Morocco was launched by King Muhammad VI, and its first graduates began their work in 2006. The initiative has been the subject of recent articles and documentaries. See, for example, the documentary film *Class of 2006: Morocco's Female Religious Leaders* (New York: Films Media Group, 2006). See also Richard Hamilton, "Islam's Pioneering Women Preachers," *BBC News*, February 25, 2007 (http://news.bbc.co.uk/go/pr/fr/-/2/hi/africa/6392531.stm), and Sally Williams, "Mourchidat: Morocco's Female Muslim Clerics," *The Telegraph*, April 26, 2008 (http://www.telegraph.co.uk/culture/3672924/Mourchidat-Moroccos-female-Muslim-clerics.html).

and the Moroccan *murshidāt*, irrespective of their divergent goals and forms of practice, see themselves in line with the template fashioned long ago by 'Ā'isha bint Abī Bakr and her cohort. And indeed, this template is efficacious not because it enables exact replication of the practices of female Companions but because it meets historical exigencies and facilitates change as demonstrated by the dynamic history of women's *ḥadīth* transmission.

Bibliography

'Abbās, Ṣāliḥ. "Min Rijāl al-Ḥisba fī al-Qarnayn al-Sābi' wa'l-Thāmin." In *Dirāsāt fī al-Ḥisba wa'l-Muḥtasib 'inda al-'Arab*. Baghdad: Markaz Iḥyā' al-Turāth al-'Ilmī al-'Arabī, 1988.

Abbott, Nabia. *'Ā'ishah, the Beloved of Muhammad*. Chicago: University of Chicago Press, 1942. Reprint, London: al-Saqi Books, 1985.

Studies in Arabic Literary Papyri. vol. 1, *Historical Texts*. Chicago: University of Chicago Press, 1957.

"Women and the State in Early Islam." *Journal of Near Eastern Studies* 1 (1942): 106–26.

'Abd al-Raḥmān, 'Ā'isha [Bint al-Shāṭi']. *Sukayna bint al-Ḥasan*. Cairo: Dār al-Hilāl, n.d.

al-'Abdarī, Ibn al-Ḥājj. *Madkhal al-Shar 'al-Sharīf*. Cairo: al-Maṭba'a al-Miṣriyya bi'l-Azhar, 1929.

Abdul Rauf, Muḥammad. "*Ḥadīth* Literature – I: The Development of the Science of *Ḥadīth*." In *Arabic Literature to the End of the Umayyad Period*, edited by A. F. L. Beeston et al., 271–88. New York: Cambridge University Press, 1983.

Abou-Bakr, Omaima. "Teaching the Words of the Prophet: Women Instructors of the *Ḥadīth* (Fourteenth and Fifteenth Centuries)." *Hawwa* 1, no. 3 (2003): 306–28.

Abrahamov, Binyamin. *Islamic Theology: Traditionalism and Rationalism*. Edinburgh: Edinburgh University Press, 1998.

Abū Dāwūd, Sulaymān b. al-Ash'ath. *Sunan*. Beirut: al-Maktaba al-'Aṣriyya, n.d.

Abū Shuqqa, Muḥammad. *Taḥrīr al-Mar'a fī 'Aṣr al-Risāla*. Cairo: Dār al-Qalam, 1999.

Afsaruddin, Asma. "Reconstituting Women's Lives: Gender and the Poetics of Narrative in Medieval Biographical Collections." *Muslim World* 92, no. 3/4 (2002): 461–80.

Aḥmad, Aḥmad Ramaḍān. *al-Ijāzāt wa'l-Tawqī'āt al-Makhṭūṭa fī al-'Ulūm al-Naqliyya wa'l-'Aqliyya*. Cairo: Wizārat al-Thaqāfa, 1986.

Ahmed, Leila. *Women and Gender in Islam: Historical Roots of a Modern Debate.* New Haven: Yale University Press, 1992.

Ahmed, Shahab. "The Satanic Verses Incident in the Memory of the Early Muslim Community: An Analysis of the Early *Riwāyah*s and their *Isnād*s." PhD diss., Princeton University, 1999.

Ahmed, Shahab, and Nenand Filipovic. "The Sultan's Syllabus." *Studia Islamica* 98/99 (2004): 183–218.

'Ā'ishah al-Bā'ūniyya. *Emanations of Grace: Mystical Poems by 'Ā'ishah al-Bā'ūnīyah*. Edited and translated with an introduction by Th. Emil Homerin. Louisville: Fons Vitae, 2011.

al-'Āmilī, Sayyid Muḥsin al-Amīn. *A'yān al-Shī'a.* Beirut: Dār al-Ta'āruf, 1986.

Amin, Yasmin. "Umm Salama and Her *Ḥadīth*." Master's thesis, American University in Cairo, 2011.

Andrae, Tor. *In the Garden of Myrtles*. Translated by Brigitta Sharpe. Binghamton: SUNY Press, 1987.

al-Anṣārī, Muḥammad Riḍā 'Abd al-Amīr. *Wafā' al-Imā'*. Beirut: Majma' al-Buḥūth al-Islāmiyya,1996.

Asad, Talal. "The Idea of an Anthropology of Islam." *Occasional Papers Series*. Center for Contemporary Arab Studies, Georgetown University (1986).

Azami, Muhammad Mustafa. *Studies in Early Ḥadīth Literature*. Indianapolis: American Trust Publications, 1992.

al-Balkhī, Abū al-Qāsim 'Abd Allāh b. Aḥmad. *Qabūl al-Akhbār wa-Ma'rifat al-Rijāl*. Beirut: Dār al-Kutub al-'Ilmiyya, 2000.

Barhūn, Qāḍī. *Khabar al-Wāḥid fī al-Tashrī' al-Islāmī wa-Ḥujjiyyatuhu*. Casablanca [?] Maṭba'at al-Najāḥ al-Jadīda, 1995.

Bedir, Murteza. "An Early Response to Shāfi'ī: 'Īsā b. Abān on the Prophetic Report (*Khabar*)." *Islamic Law and Society* 9, no. 3 (2002): 285–311.

Berg, Herbert. *The Development of Exegesis in Early Islam: The Authenticity of Muslim Literature from the Formative Period*. Richmond: Curzon, 2000.

Berkey, Jonathan. *The Formation of Islam*. New York: Cambridge University Press, 2003.

Popular Preaching and Religious Authority in the Medieval Islamic Near East. Seattle: University of Washington Press, 2001.

"'Silver Threads among the Coal': A Well-Educated Mamlūk of the Ninth/Fifteenth Century." *Studia Islamica* 73 (1991): 109–25.

The Transmission of Knowledge in Medieval Cairo. Princeton: Princeton University Press, 1992.

"Women and Islamic Education in the Mamluk Period." In *Women in Middle Eastern History*, edited by Nikki Keddie and Beth Baron, 143–57. New Haven: Yale University Press, 1991.

Bībā bint 'Abd al-Ṣamad. *Juz' Bībā bint 'Abd al-Ṣamad al-Harthamiyya*. Kuwait: Maktabat al-Khulafā', 198–.

Bloom, Jonathan. *Paper before Print: The History and Impact of Paper in the Islamic World*. New Haven: Yale University Press, 2001.

Bourdieu, Pierre. *Distinction: A Social Critique of the Judgement of Taste*. Translated by Richard Nice. Cambridge, MA: Harvard University Press, 1984.

"The Forms of Capital," translated by Richard Nice. In *Handbook of Theory and Research for the Sociology of Education*, edited by John G. Richardson, 241–58. New York: Greenwood Press, 1986.
Brinner, William. "The Banū Ṣaṣrā: A Study on the Transmission of a Scholarly Tradition." *Arabica* 7 (May 1960): 167–95.
Brock, Sebastian, and Susan Harvey, trans. *Holy Women of Syrian Orient*. Berkeley: University of California Press, 1987.
Brooten, Bernadette. *Women Leaders in the Ancient Synagogue*. Chico, CA: Scholars Press, 1982.
Brown, Jonathan. *Canonization of al-Bukhārī and Muslim*. Boston: Brill, 2007.
"Criticism of the Proto-*Ḥadīth* Canon: Al-Dāraquṭnī's Adjustment of the *Ṣaḥīḥayn*." *Journal of Islamic Studies* 15 (2004): 1–37.
Hadith: Muhammad's Legacy in the Medieval and Modern World. Oxford: Oneworld, 2009.
Brown, Peter. *Body and Society: Men, Women, and Sexual Renunciation in Early Christianity*. New York: Columbia University Press, 1988.
al-Bukhārī, Muḥammad b. Ismā'īl. *Ṣaḥīḥ*. Beirut: Dār al-Qalam, 1987.
Bulliet, Richard. "The Age Structure of Medieval Education." *Studia Islamica* 57 (1983): 105–17.
Patricians of Nishapur. Cambridge, MA: Harvard University Press, 1972.
View from the Edge. New York: Columbia University Press, 1994.
"Women and the Urban Religious Elite in the Pre-Mongol Period." In *Women in Iran from the Rise of Islam to 1800*, edited by Guity Nashat and Lois Beck, 68–79. Urbana: University of Illinois Press, 2003.
Burke, Jeffrey. "Education." In *Islamic World*, edited by Andrew Rippin, 305–17. New York: Routledge, 2008.
Burton, John. *Introduction to the Ḥadīth*. Edinburgh: Edinburgh University Press, 1994.
Bynum, Caroline. *Holy Feast and Holy Fast*. Los Angeles: University of California Press, 1987.
Calamawy, Suhair. "The Narrative Element in *Ḥadīth* Literature." In *Arabic Literature to the End of the Umayyad Period*, edited by A. F. L. Beeston et al., 308–16. New York: Cambridge University Press, 1983.
Chamberlain, Michael. *Knowledge and Social Practice in Medieval Damascus, 1190–1350*. New York: Cambridge University Press, 1994.
El-Cheikh, Nadia Maria. "Women's History: A Study of al-Tanūkhī." In *Writing the Feminine: Women in Arab Sources*, edited by Manuela Marin and Randi Deguilhem, 129–48. New York: I. B. Tauris, 2002.
Cook, Michael. *Commanding Right and Forbidding Wrong in Islamic Thought*. New York: Cambridge University Press, 2000.
"Eschatology and the Dating of Traditions." *Princeton Papers in Near Eastern Studies* 1 (1992): 23–47.
"The Opponents of the Writing of Tradition in Early Islam." *Arabica* 44 (1997): 437–530.
Cooperson, Michael. *Classical Arabic Biography: The Heirs of the Prophets in the Age of al-Ma'mūn*. New York: Cambridge University Press, 2000.

Dakake, Maria. "'Guest of the Inmost Heart': Conceptions of the Divine Beloved among Early Sufi Women." *Comparative Islamic Studies* 3, no. 1 (2007): 72–97.

al-Dāraquṭnī, 'Alī b. 'Umar. *Kitāb al-Ilzāmāt wa'l-Tatabbu'*. Medina: al-Maktaba al-Salafiyya, 1978.

al-Dhahabī, Muḥammad Shams al-Dīn. *Dhuyūl al-'Ibar*. Beirut: Mu'assasat al-Risāla, 1985.

Kitāb Duwal al-Islām. Hyderabad: Dā'irat al-Ma'ārifal-Niẓāmiyya, 1918.

Mu'jam al-Shuyūkh. Beirut: Dār al-Kutub al-'Ilmiyya, 1990.

Siyar A'lām al-Nubalā'. Beirut: Mu'assasat al-Risāla, 1981.

Tadhkirat al-Ḥuffāẓ. Beirut: Dār al-Kutub al-'Ilmiyya, 1998.

al-Dhahabī and al-Ḥusaynī. *Min Dhuyūl al-'Ibar*. Kuwait: Maṭba'at Ḥukūmat al-Kuwayt, n.d.

Dickinson, Eerik. "Ibn al-Ṣalāḥ al-Shahrazūrī and the *Isnād*." *Journal of the American Oriental Society* 122, no. 3 (2002): 481–505.

Donner, Fred. *Narratives of Islamic Origins: The Beginnings of Islamic Historical Writing*. Princeton: Princeton University Press, 1998.

Drory, Joseph. "Ḥanbalīs of the Nablus Region in the Eleventh and Twelfth Centuries." *Asian and African Studies* 22 (1988): 93–112.

Dukhayyil, Sa'īd Fāyiz. *Mawsū'at Fiqh 'Ā'isha Umm al-Mu'minīn: Ḥayātuhā wa-Fiqhuhā*. Beirut: Dār al-Nafā'is, 1989.

Elias, Jamal. "The *Ḥadīth* Traditions of 'Ā'isha as Prototypes of Self-Narrative." *Edebiyât* 7 (1997): 215–33.

Fadel, Mohammad. "Two Women, One Man: Knowledge, Power, and Gender in Medieval Sunni Legal Thought." *International Journal of Middle East Studies* 29 (1997): 185–204.

Falk, Nancy Auer. "The Case of the Vanishing Nuns: The Fruits of Ambivalence in Ancient Indian Buddhism." In *Unspoken Worlds: Women's Religious Lives*, edited by Nancy Auer Falk and Rita Gross, 196–206. Belmont, CA: Wadsworth, 1989.

al-Fayyāḍ, 'Abd Allāh. *al-Ijāzāt al-'Ilmiyya 'inda al-Muslimīn*. Baghdad: Maṭba'at al-Irshād, 1967.

Frye, Richard, ed. *The Histories of Nishapur*. Cambridge, MA: Harvard University Press, 1965.

Fueck, J. "The Role of Traditionalism in Islam." In *Studies on Islam*, edited by Merlin L. Swartz, 99–122. New York: Oxford University Press, 1981.

Giladi, Avner. *Infants, Parents, and Wet Nurses: Medieval Islamic Views on Breastfeeding and Their Social Implications*. Leiden: E. J. Brill, 1999.

Gilbert, Joan E. "Institutionalization of Muslim Scholarship and Professionalization of the *'Ulamā'* in Medieval Damascus." *Studia Islamica* 52 (1980): 105–34.

Goldziher, Ignaz. *Muslim Studies*. Translated by C. R. Barber and S. M. Stern. Chicago: Aldine, 1968.

Graham, William A. "Traditionalism in Islam: An Essay in Interpretation." *Journal of Interdisciplinary History* 23, no. 3 (1993): 495–522.

Grossman, Avraham. *Pious and Rebellious: Jewish Women in Medieval Europe*. Translated by Jonathan Chipman. Waltham: Brandeis University Press, 2004.

Grundmann, Herbert. *Religious Movements in the Middle Ages*. Translated by Steven Rowan. Notre Dame: University of Notre Dame Press, 1995.

Günther, Sebastian. "Be Masters in that You Teach and Continue to Learn." In *Islam and Education*, edited by Wadad Kadi and Victor Billeh, 61–82. Chicago: University of Chicago Press, 2007.

Haarmann, Ulrich. "Arabic in Speech, Turkish in Lineage: Mamluks and Their Sons in the Intellectual Life of Fourteenth Century Egypt and Syria." *Journal of Semitic Studies* 33, no. 1 (1988): 81–114.

Hafsi, Ibrahim. "Recherches sur le genre *ṭabaqāt*." *Arabica* 23 (1976): 227–65; and *Arabica* 24 (1977): 1–41, 150–86.

Ḥājjī Khalīfa Kātip Çelebi. *Kashf al-Ẓunūn ʿan Asāmī al-Kutub wa'l-Funūn*. Beirut: Dār Iḥyā' al-Turāth al-ʿArabī, 1990.

Hallaq, Wael. "Authenticity of Prophetic *Ḥadīth*: A Pseudo-Problem." *Studia Islamica* 89 (1999): 75–90.

al-Ḥamawī, Yāqūt b. ʿAbd Allāh. *Muʿjam al-Buldān*. Beirut: Dār al-Kutub al-ʿIlmiyya, 1990.

Hamilton, Richard. "Islam's Pioneering Women Preachers." *BBC News*, February 25, 2007 (http://news.bbc.co.uk/go/pr/fr/-/2/hi/africa/6392531.stm).

Hanne, Eric. *Putting the Caliph in His Place*. Madison, NJ: Fairleigh Dickinson University Press, 2007.

"Women, Power, and the Eleventh and Twelfth Century Abbasid Court." *Hawwa* 3, no. 1 (2005): 80–110.

al-Ḥasanī, Amīna Amziyān. *Umm Salama Umm al-Mu'minīn*. Rabat: Wizārat al-Awqāf wa'l-Shu'ūn al-Islāmiyya, 1998.

Hawting, G. R. "The Role of the Qur'ān and *Ḥadīth* in the Legal Controversy about the Rights of a Divorced Woman during Her 'Waiting Period' (*ʿIdda*)." *Bulletin of the School of Oriental and African Studies* 52 (1989): 430–45.

Heck, Paul. "The Epistemological Problem of Writing in Islamic Civilization." *Studia Islamica* 94 (2002): 85–114.

Heller, Daniella T. "The Shaykh and the Community: Popular Hanbalite Islam in the 12th-13th Century Jabal Nablus and Jabal Qasyūn." *Studia Islamica* 79 (1994): 103–20.

Hirschler, Konrad. *The Written Word in the Medieval Arabic Lands*. Edinburgh: Edinburgh University Press, 2012.

Hodgson, Marshall. *The Venture of Islam*. Chicago: University of Chicago Press, 1974.

Holt, P. M. *The Age of the Crusades*. New York: Longman, 1986.

Homerin, Th. Emil. "Living Love: The Mystical Writings of ʿĀ'ishah al-Bāʿūnīyah." *Mamlūk Studies Review* 7 (2003): 211–34.

"Saving Muslim Souls: The *Khānqāh* and the Sufi Duty in Mamlūk Lands." *Mamlūk Studies Review* 3 (1999): 59–83.

"Writing Sufi Biography: The Case of ʿĀ'ishah al-Bāʿūnīyah (d. 922/1571)." *Muslim World* 96, no 3 (2006): 389–99.

Humphreys, Stephen. "The Expressive Intent of the Mamluk Architecture of Cairo: A Preliminary Essay." *Studia Islamica* 35 (1972): 69–119.

al-Ḥusaynī, Muḥammad b. ʿAlī al-ʿAlawī. *Kitāb al-Tadhkira bi-Maʿrifat Rijāl al-Kutub al-ʿAshara*. Cairo: Maṭbaʿat al-Madanī, 1997.

Ibn ʿAbd al-Barr, Yūsuf b. ʿAbd Allāh. *al-Istīʿāb fī Maʿrifat al-Aṣḥāb*. Cairo: Maktabat Nahḍat Miṣr, 196-.

Kitāb al-Istidhkār. Cairo: Dār al-Wā'ī, 1993.
Ṣaḥīḥ Jāmi' Bayān al-'Ilm wa-Faḍlihi. Cairo: Maktabat Ibn Taymiyya, 1996.
Ibn Abī Shayba, 'Abd Allāh b. Muḥammad. *Muṣannaf*. Beirut: Dār al-Tāj, 1989.
Ibn Abī Ṭāhir al-Ṭayfūr. *Balāghat al-Nisā'*. Beirut: Dār al-Aḍwā', 1999.
Ibn 'Asākir, 'Alī b. Abī Muḥammad. *Ta'rīkh Dimashq*. Beirut: Dār al-Fikr, 1995.
Ibn al-Athīr, 'Izz al-Dīn Alī b. Muḥammad b. 'Abd al-Karīm. *al-Kāmil fī al-Ta'rīkh*. Beirut: Dār Ṣādir, 1966.
Usd al-Ghāba fī Ma'rifat al-Ṣaḥāba. Tehran: al-Maktaba al-Islāmiyya, 1958.
Ibn 'Azzūz, Muḥammad. *Buyūtāt al-Ḥadīth fī Dimashq*. Damascus: Dār al-Fikr, 2004.
Ibn Baṭṭūṭa, Muḥammad b. 'Abd Allāh. *Riḥlat Ibn Baṭṭūṭa*. Cairo: al-Maktaba al-Tijāriyya al-Kubrā, 1964.
Ibn Faḍl Allāh al-'Umarī al-Dimashqī. "Masālik al-Abṣār." MS. Excerpted in *Madīnat Dimashq 'inda al-Jughrāfiyyīn wa'l-Raḥḥālīn al-Muslimīn*, edited by Ṣalāḥ al-Dīn al-Munajjid. Beirut: Dār al-Kitāb al-Jadīd, 1967.
Ibn Ḥajar al-'Asqalānī, Aḥmad b. 'Alī. *al-Durar al-Kāmina fī A'yān al-Mi'a al-Thāmina*. Cairo: Dār al-Kutub al-Ḥadītha, 1966.
Inbā' al-Ghumr bi-Anbā' al-'Umr. Cairo: al-Majlis al-A'lā li'l-Shu'ūn al-Islāmiyya, 1971.
al-Iṣāba fī Tamyīz al-Ṣaḥāba. Cairo: Maktabat al-Kulliyyāt al-Azharīyya, 1977.
al-Mu'jam al-Mufahras. Beirut: Mu'assasat al-Risāla, 1998.
Nukat 'alā Kitāb Ibn al-Ṣalāḥ. Riyad: Dār al-Rāya, 1988.
Tahdhīb al-Tahdhīb. Beirut: Dār al-Kutub al-'Ilmiyya, 1994.
Ta'jīl al-Manfa'a bi-Zawā'id Rijāl al-A'imma al-Arba'a. Beirut: Dār al-Kutub al-'Ilmiyya, 1996.
Taqrīb al-Tahdhīb. Beirut: Dār al-Kutub al-'Ilmiyya, 1993.
Ibn Ḥanbal, Aḥmad b. Muḥammad. *Juz' fī-hi Musnad Ahl al-Bayt*. Beirut: Mu'assasat al-Kutub al-Thaqāfiyya, 1988.
Musnad. Beirut: al-Maktab al-Islāmī, 1993.
Ibn Ḥazm, 'Alī b. Aḥmad. *al-Muḥallā bi'l-Āthār*. Beirut: Dār al-Kutub al-'Ilmiyya, 1988.
Ibn Ḥibbān, Muḥammad. *Kitāb al-Thiqāt*. Beirut: Dār al-Kutub al-'Ilmiyya, 1998.
Ibn Hishām, 'Abd al-Malik. *al-Sīra al-Nabawiyya*. Beirut: al-Maktaba al-'Aṣriyya, 1994.
Ibn al-'Imād, 'Abd al-Ḥayy b. Aḥmad. *Shadharāt al-Dhahab*. Beirut: Dār Ibn Kathīr, 1986.
Ibn al-'Irāqī, Aḥmad b. 'Abd al-Raḥīm. *Dhayl 'alā al-'Ibar fī Khabar man 'Abar*. Beirut: Mu'assasat al-Risāla, 1989.
Ibn al-Jawzī, 'Abd al-Raḥmān b. 'Alī. *al-Muntaẓam fī Ta'rīkh al-Mulūk wa'l-Umam*. Beirut: Dār al-Kutub al-'Ilmiyya, 1992.
Ṣifat al-Ṣafwa. Beirut: Dār al-Kutub al-'Ilmiyya, 1989.
Ibn Kathīr, 'Imād al-Dīn. *al-Bidāya wa'l-Nihāya fī al-Ta'rīkh*. Cairo: Dār al-Fikr al-'Arabī, n.d.
Ibn Khallikān, Aḥmad b. Muḥammad b. Ibrāhīm. *Wafayāt al-A'yān*. Beirut: Dār al-Thaqāfa, 1968.

Ibn Māja, Muḥammad b. Yazīd. *Sunan*. Cairo: Dār al-Ḥadīth, 1994.
Ibn al-Qāḍī, Aḥmad b. Muḥammad. *Dhayl Wafayāt al-A'yān*. Cairo: Dār al-Turāth, n.d.
Ibn Qudāma, 'Abd Allāh b. Aḥmad. *al-Mughnī*. Beirut: Dār al-Kutub al-'Ilmiyya, 1996.
Ibn Sa'd, Muḥammad. *Kitāb al-Ṭabaqāt al-Kabīr*. Leiden: E. J. Brill, 1904–18.
Ibn al-Ṣalāḥ al-Shahrazūrī, 'Uthmān b. 'Abd al-Raḥmān. *Muqaddima fī 'Ulūm al-Ḥadīth*. Beirut: Dār al-Kutub al-'Ilmiyya, 1995.
Ibn Sallām, Abū 'Ubayd al-Qāsim. *Kitāb al-Amwāl*. Cairo: Dār al-Fikr, 1975.
Ibn al-Ṣayrafī, 'Alī b. Dāwūd. *Inbā' al-Haṣr bi-Abnā' al-'Aṣr*. Cairo: Dār al-Fikr al-'Arabī, 1970.
Ibn Taghrībirdī, Yūsuf. *Nujūm al-Ẓāhira fī Mulūk Miṣr wa'l-Qāhira*. Cairo: al-Hay'a al-Miṣriyya al-'Āmma li'l-Kutub, 1972.
Ibn Ṭūlūn, Muḥammad. *al-Qalā'id al-Jawhariyya fī Ta'rīkh al-Ṣāliḥiyya*. Edited by Muḥammad Duhmān. Damascus: Maktabat al-Dirāsāt al-Islāmiyya, 1949.
Ibrāhīm, Nājiya. *al-Juhūd al-'Ilmiyya li'l-Mar'a khilāl al-Qarnayn al-Khāmis wa'l-Sādis al-Hijriyyayn*. Amman: Mu'assasat al-Balsam, 1996.
Musnidat al-'Irāq: Shuhda al-Kātiba. Amman: Mu'assasat al-Balsam, 1996.
al-'Irāqī, Zayn al-Dīn. *al-Taqyīd wa'l-Iḍāḥ li-mā 'Uṭliqa wa-Ughliqa min Muqaddimat Ibn al-Ṣalāḥ*. Beirut: Mu'assasat al-Kutub al-Thaqāfiyya, 1991.
al-Iṣbahānī, Abū al-Faraj. *Kitāb al-Aghānī*. Beirut: Dār al-Thaqāfa, 1990.
al-Iṣbahānī, Abū Nu'aym. *Ḥilyat al-Awliyā'*. Cairo: Maktabat al-Khānjī, 1932.
Ma'rifat al-Ṣaḥāba. Edited by 'Ādil b. Yūsuf al-'Azāzī. Riyad: Dār al-Waṭan li'l-Nashr, 1998.
Islam, Sarah. "Qubaysiyyāt: Growth of an International Muslim Women's Revivalist Movement in Syria and the United States, 1960–2008." Master's thesis, Princeton University, 2010.
Jamāl al-Dīn Muḥammad, Amīna. *al-Nisā' al-Muḥaddithāt fī al-'Aṣr al-Mamlūkī wa-dawruhunna fī al-Ḥayāt al-Adabiyya wa'l-Thaqāfiyya*. Cairo: Dār al-Hidāya, 2003.
Juynboll, G. H. A. "The Date of the Great *Fitna*." *Arabica* 20 (1973): 142–59.
"Dyeing the Hair and Beard in Early Islam: A Ḥadīth-Analytical Study." *Arabica* 33 (1986): 49–75.
"Early Islamic Society as Reflected in Its Use of *Isnāds*." In *Studies on the Origins and Uses of Islamic Ḥadīth*. Brookfield: Variorum, 1996.
Muslim Tradition: Studies in Chronology, Provenance, and Authorship of Early Ḥadīth. New York: Cambridge, 1983.
"The Role of the *Mu'ammarūn* in the Early Development of the *Isnād*." In *Studies on the Origins and Uses of Islamic Ḥadīth*. Brookfield: Variorum, 1996.
Kaḥḥāla, 'Umar Riḍā. *A'lām al-Nisā'*. Damascus: al-Maṭba'a al-Hāshimiyya, 1959.
al-Kattānī, Muḥammad b. Ja'far. *al-Risāla al-Mustaṭrafa li-Bayān Mashhūr Kutub al-Sunna al-Musharrafa*. Damascus: Maṭba'at Dār al-Fikr, 1964.
Katz, Marion. *Body of Text*. Albany: SUNY Press, 2002.
Khalidi, Tarif. *Arabic Historical Thought in the Classical Period*. New York: Cambridge University Press, 1994.
al-Kharrāṭ, Amīna 'Umar. *Umm 'Imāra*. Damascus: Dār al-Qalam, 1998.

al-Khaṭīb al-Baghdādī, Aḥmad b. ʻAlī. *al-Kifāya fi ʻIlm al-Riwāya*. Beirut: Dār al-Kutub al-ʻIlmiyya, 1988.

Kitāb al-Riḥla fi Ṭalab al-Ḥadīth. In *Majmūʻat Rasāʼil fi ʻUlūm al-Ḥadīth*, edited by Ṣubḥī al-Badrī al-Sāmarrāʼī. Medina: al-Maktaba al-Salafiyya, 1969.

Sharaf Aṣḥāb al-Ḥadīth. Ankara[?]: Dār Iḥyāʼ al-Sunna al-Nabawiyya, 1972.

Taqyīd al-ʻIlm. n.p: Dār Iḥyāʼ al-Sunna al-Nabawiyya, 1974.

Künkler, Mirjam, and Roja Fazaeli. "The Life of Two *Mujtahidahs*: Female Religious Authority in 20th Century Iran." In *Women, Leadership and Mosques: Contemporary Islamic Authority*, edited by Masooda Bano and Hilary Kalmbach, 127-60. Leiden: Brill, 2011.

Lapidus, Ira. *Muslim Cities in the Later Middle Ages*. Cambridge, MA: Harvard University Press, 1967.

Leder, Stefan, Yāsīn Muḥammad al-Sawwās, and Māʼmūn al-Ṣāgharjī, eds. *Muʻjam al-Samāʻāt al-Dimashqiyya*. Damascus: al-Maʻhad al-Faransī liʻl-Dirāsāt al-ʻArabiyya, 1996.

Librande, Leonard. "The Categories of High and Low as Reflections on the *Riḥla* and *Kitāba* in Islām." *Der Islam* 55, no. 2 (1978): 267–80.

Lichtenstadter, Ilse. *Women in the Aiyām al-ʻArab: A Study of Female Life during Warfare in Pre-Islamic Arabia*. London: Royal Asiatic Society, 1935.

Lucas, Scott. *Constructive Critics, Ḥadīth Literature, and the Articulation of Sunnī Islām*. Leiden: Brill, 2004.

"Divorce, *Ḥadīth*-Scholar Style: From al-Dārimī to al-Tirmidhī." *Journal of Islamic Studies* 19, no. 3 (2008): 325–68.

Lutfi, Huda. "Al-Sakhāwī's *Kitāb al-Nisāʼ* as a Source for the Social and Economic History of Muslim Women during the Fifteenth Century AD." *Muslim World* 71 (1981): 104–24.

MacIntyre, Alasdair. *After Virtue*. Notre Dame: University of Notre Dame Press, 1984.

Whose Justice? Which Rationality? Notre Dame: University of Notre Dame Press, 1988.

Mahmood, Saba. *Politics of Piety: The Islamic Revival and the Feminist Subject*. Princeton: Princeton University Press, 2005.

Makdisi, George. "Ashʻarī and the Ashʻarites in Islamic Religious History I." *Studia Islamica* 17 (1962): 37–80; and "Ashʻarī and the Ashʻarites in Islamic Religious History II." *Studia Islamica* 18 (1963): 19–39.

"The Ḥanbalī School and Ṣūfism." *Boletín de la Asociación Española de Orientalistas* 15 (1979): 115–26.

Ibn ʻAqil: Religion and Culture in Classical Islam. Edinburgh: Edinburgh University Press, 1997.

The Rise of Colleges. Edinburgh: Edinburgh University Press, 1981.

"The Sunni Revival." Reprinted in *History and Politics in Eleventh Century Baghdad*. Aldershot: Ashgate Variorum, 1991.

Mālik b. Anas. *al-Muwaṭṭaʼ*. Beirut: Dār al-Gharb al-Islāmī, 1996.

Martin, Richard, and Mark Woodward. *Defenders of Reason in Islam*. Oxford: Oneworld, 1997.

Maʻrūf, Bashshār ʻAwwād et al., compilers. *al-Musnad al-Jāmiʻ*. Beirut: Dār al-Jīl, 1993.

Ma'tūq, Ṣāliḥ. *Juhūd al-Mar'a fī Riwāyat al-Ḥadīth: al-Qarn al-Thāmin al-Hijrī.* Beirut: Dār al-Bashā'ir al-Islāmiyya, 1997.

McGee, Mary. "Ritual Rights: The Gender Implications of *Adhikāra*." In *Jewels of Authority*, edited by Laurie Patton, 32–50. New York: Oxford, 2002.

Meisami, Julie Scott. "Writing Medieval Women: Representations and Misrepresentations." In *Writing and Representation in Medieval Islam*, edited by Julia Bray, 47–87. New York: Routledge, 2006.

Meja, Volker, and Nico Stehr, eds. *The Sociology of Knowledge*. Northampton: Edward Elgar, 1999.

Melchert, Christopher. "Bukhārī and Early *Ḥadīth* Criticism." *Journal of the American Oriental Society* 121, no. 1 (2001): 7–19.

"Piety of the *Ḥadīth* Folk." *International Journal of Middle East Studies* 34, no. 3 (2002): 425–39.

Mernissi, Fatima. *Women's Rebellion and Islamic Memory*. Atlantic Highlands, NJ: Zed Books, 1996.

al-Mizzī, Yūsuf b. 'Abd al-Raḥmān b. Yūsuf. *Tahdhīb al-Kamāl fī Asmā' al-Rijāl*. Beirut: Mu'assasat al-Risāla, 1992.

Tuḥfat al-Ashrāf bi-Ma'rifat al-Aṭrāf. vols. Beirut: Dār al-Gharb al-Islāmī, 1999.

Modarressi, Hossein. *Tradition and Survival*. Oxford: Oneworld, 2003.

Mottahedeh, Roy. *Loyalty and Leadership in an Early Islamic Society*. 2nd ed. New York: I. B. Tauris, 2001.

Review of *Patricians of Nishapur: A Study in Medieval Islamic Social History*, by R. W. Bulliet." *Journal of the American Oriental Society* 95, no. 3 (1975): 491–95.

Motzki, Harald. ed. *Ḥadīth: Origins and Developments*. Burlington: Ashgate Variorum, 2004.

"*Muṣannaf* of 'Abd al-Razzāq al-Ṣan'ānī as a Source of Authentic *Aḥādīth* of the First Century A.H." *Journal of Near Eastern Studies* 50, no. 1 (1990): 1–21.

Origins of Islamic Jurisprudence: Meccan Fiqh before the Classical Schools. Translated by Marion Katz. Leiden: Brill, 2002.

"The Prophet and the Cat: On Dating Mālik's *Muwaṭṭa'* and Legal Traditions." *Jerusalem Studies in Arabic and Islam* 22 (1998): 18–83.

Murata, Sachiko. *Tao of Islam*. Albany: SUNY Press, 1992.

Musa, Aisha. *Ḥadīth as Scripture*. New York: Palgrave, 2008.

Muslim b. al-Ḥajjāj al-Qushayrī. *Ṣaḥīḥ*. With commentary of Yaḥyā b. Sharaf al-Nawawī. Beirut: Dār al-Fikr, 1995.

Muṣṭafā, Shākir. *Madīnat al-'Ilm: Āl Qudāma wa'l-Ṣāliḥiyya*. Damascus: Dār Ṭalās, 1997.

Nadwi, Mohammad Akram. *al-Muhaddithat: The Women Scholars in Islam*. London: Interface, 2007.

al-Nasā'ī, Aḥmad b. Shu'ayb. *al-Sunan*. Beirut: Dār al-Kutub al-'Ilmiyya, n.d.

al-Sunan al-Kubrā. Beirut: Mu'assasat al-Risāla, 2001.

Nashabi, Hisham. "The *Ijāza*: Academic Certification in Muslim Education." *Hamdard Islamicus* 8 (1985): 7–20.

al-Naysābūrī, al-Ḥākim. *Kitāb Ma'rifat 'Ulūm al-Ḥadīth*. Beirut: Dār al-Kutub al-'Ilmiyya, 1977.

al-Mustadrak 'alā al-Ṣaḥīḥayn. Cairo: Dār al-Ḥaramayn li'l-Ṭibā'a wa'l-Nashr wa'l-Tawzī', 1997.
al-Nu'aymī, 'Abd al-Qādir b. Muḥammad. *al-Dāris fī Ta'rīkh al-Madāris*. Beirut: Dār al-Kutub al-'Ilmiyya, 1990.
El-Omari, Racha. "Accommodation and Resistance: Classical Mu'tazilites on Ḥadīth. *Journal of Near Eastern Studies* 71 (2012): 231–56.
Petry, Carl. "Class Solidarity versus Gender Gain: Women as Custodians of Property in Later Medieval Egypt." In *Women in Middle Eastern History*, edited by Nikki R. Keddie and Beth Baron, 122–42. New Haven: Yale University Press, 1991.
"A Paradox of Patronage." *Muslim World* 73 (1983): 182–207.
Powers, Carla. "A Secret History." *New York Times*, February 25, 2007 (http://www.nytimes.com/2007/02/25/magazine/25wwlnEssay.t.html).
al-Qurashī, 'Abd al-Qādir b. Abī al-Wafā'. *al-Jawāhir al-Muḍiyya fī Ṭabaqāt al-Ḥanafiyya*. Hyderabad: Maṭba'at Majlis Dā'irat al-Ma'ārif al-'Uthmāniyya, 1989.
al-Qushayrī, Abū al-Qāsim. *Laṭā'if al-Ishārāt*. Cairo: Dār al-Kātib al-'Arabī, 1968.
al-Rasā'il al-Qushayriyya. Beirut: al-Maktaba al-'Aṣriyya, 1970. Reprint of 1964 Pakistani edition.
al-Risāla al-Qushayriyya. Cairo: Dār al-Kutub al-Ḥadītha, 1966.
al-Rāmahurmuzī, al-Ḥasan b. 'Abd al-Raḥmān. *al-Muḥaddith al-Fāṣil bayna al-Rāwī wa'l-Wā'ī*. Beirut: Dār al-Fikr, 1971.
Rapoport, Yossef. *Marriage, Money and Divorce in Medieval Islamic Society*. New York: Cambridge University Press, 2005.
Rice, David. *L'Unique manuscrit d'Ibn al-Bawwāb à la Chester Beatty Library*. Paris: Club du Livre, 1981.
Robinson, Chase. *Islamic Historiography*. New York: Cambridge University Press, 2003.
Roded, Ruth. *Women in Islamic Biographical Collections*. Boulder: Lynne Rienner Publishers, 1994.
Rosenthal, Franz. "Muslim Social Values and Literary Criticism: Reflections on the *Ḥadīth* of Umm Zar'." *Oriens* 34 (1994): 31–56.
Ruether, Rosemary, ed. *Womanguides: Readings toward a Feminist Theology*. Boston: Beacon Press, 1996.
Rustam, Muḥammad Zayn al-'Ābidīn. *Buyūtāt al-'Ilm wa'l-Ḥadīth fi'l-Andalus*. Beirut: Dār Ibn Ḥazm li'l-Ṭibā'a wa'l-Nashr wa'l-Tawzī', 2009.
Sadovnik, Alan R., ed. *Sociology of Education*. New York: Routledge, 2007.
al-Ṣafadī, Khalīl b. Aybak. *Kitāb al-Wāfī bi'l-Wafayāt*. Beirut: Dār Iḥyā' al-Turāth al-'Arabī, 2000.
al-Sahmī, Abū al-Qāsim Ḥamza b. Yūsuf. *Ta'rīkh Jurjān*. Hyderabad: Maṭba'at Majlis Dā'irat al-Ma'ārif al-'Uthmāniyya, 1950.
al-Sakhāwī, Muḥammad b. 'Abd al-Raḥmān. *al-Ḍaw' al-Lāmi' li-Ahl al-Qarn al-Tāsi'*. Cairo: Maktaba al-Qudsī, 1936.
al-Jawāhir wa'l-Durar fī Tarjamat Shaykh al-Islām Ibn Ḥajar. Beirut: Dār Ibn Ḥazm, 1999.
Salibi, Kamal. "Banū Jamā'a: A Dynasty of Shāfi'ī Jurists of the Mamluk Period." *Studia Islamica* 9 (1958): 97–109.

al-Ṣāliḥ, Ṣubḥī. *'Ulūm al-Ḥadīth wa-Muṣṭalaḥuhu*. Beirut: Dār al-'Ilm li'l-Malāyīn, 1991.
Salmān, Mashhūr b. Ḥasan. *'Ināyat al-Nisā' bi'l-Ḥadīth al-Nabawī, Ṣafaḥāt, Muḍī'a min Ḥayāt al-Muḥaddithāt ḥattā al-Qarn al-Thālith 'Ashar al-Hijrī* Beirut: Dār Ibn Ḥazm, 1994.
al-Sam'ānī, 'Abd al-Karīm b. Muḥammad. *al-Ansāb*. Beirut: Dār al-Jinān, 1988.
al-Taḥbīr fī al-Mu'jam al-Kabīr. Beirut: Dār al-Kutub al-'Ilmiyya, 1997.
Samāra, Muḥammad Salīm Ibrāhīm et al., eds. *Fihris Aḥādīth wa-Āthār al-Muṣannaf li'l-Ḥāfiẓ al-Kabīr Abī Bakr 'Abd al-Razzāq b. Hammām al-Ṣan'ānī*. Beirut: 'Ālam al-Kutub, 1988.
Fihris Aḥādīth wa-Āthār al-Muṣannaf li'l-Imām al-Ḥāfiẓ 'Abd Allāh b. Muḥammad b. Abī Shayba. Beirut: 'Ālam al-Kutub, 1989.
al-Ṣarīfīnī, Ibrāhīm b. Muḥammad. *al-Muntakhab min al-Siyāq li-Tārīkh Naysābūr li-'Abd al-Ghāfir al-Fārisī*. Beirut: Dār al-Kutub al-'Ilmiyya, 1989.
Sartain, Elizabeth. *Jalāl al-Dīn al-Suyūṭī: Biography and Background*. New York: Cambridge University Press, 1975.
Sayeed, Asma. "Gender and Legal Authority: An Examination of Early Juristic Opposition to Women's *Ḥadīth* Transmission." *Islamic Law and Society* 16, no. 2 (2009): 115–50.
"Shifting Fortunes: Women and *Ḥadīth* Transmission in Islamic History." PhD diss., Princeton University, 2005.
"Women in Imāmī Biographical Collections." In *Law and Tradition in Classical Islamic Thought*, eds. Michael Cook et al. New York: Palgrave, 2013.
Sayyid al-Ahl, 'Abd al-'Azīz. *Ṭabaqāt al-Nisā' al-Muḥaddithāt: Min al-Ṭabaqa al-Ūlā ilā al-Ṭabaqa al-Sādisa*. Cairo: Maṭba'at al-Ahrām al-Tijāriyya, 1981.
Schacht, Joseph. *Origins of Muḥammadan Jurisprudence*. Oxford: Clarendon, 1950.
Schimmel, Annemarie. *Calligraphy and Islamic Culture*. New York: New York University Press, 1984.
My Soul Is a Woman: The Feminine in Islam. Translated by Susan Ray. New York: Continuum, 1997.
Schoeler, Gregor. *The Genesis of Literature in Islam: From the Aural to the Read*. Translated by Shawkat M. Toorawa. Edinburgh: Edinburgh University Press, 2009.
Scott, Joan. "Gender: A Useful Category for Historical Analysis." *American Historical Review* 91, no. 5 (1986): 1053–75.
Sedgwick, Mark. *Against the Modern World: Traditionalism and the Secret Intellectual History of the Twentieth Century*. New York: Oxford University Press, 2004.
Sezgin, Fuat. *Ta'rīkh al-Turāth al-'Arabī*. Riyad: Wizārat al-Ta'līm al-'Ālī, 1991.
al-Shāfi'ī, Muḥammad b. Idrīs. *Kitāb al-Umm*. Beirut: Dār al-Kutub al-'Ilmiyya, 1993.
al-Risāla. Beirut: Dār al-Nafā'is, 1999.

Shaikh, Khanum. "New Expressions of Religiosity: Al-Huda International and the Expansion of Islamic Education for Pakistani Muslim Women." In *Women and Islam*, edited by Zayn Qassam, 163–84. Santa Barbara: Praeger, 2010.

Shalabī, Ahmad. *Ta'rīkh al-Tarbiya al-Islāmiyya*. Cairo: Maktabat al-Nahḍa al-Miṣriyya, 1966.

El Shamsy, Ahmed. "The Social Construction of Orthodoxy." In *The Cambridge Companion to Classical Islamic Theology*, edited by Tim Winter, 97–117. New York: Cambridge University Press, 2008.

Shaukat, Jamila. "A Critical Edition, with Introduction, of Tradition Recounted by 'Ā'isha, Extracted from the *Musnad* of Isḥāq b. Rāhawayh." PhD diss., Cambridge University, 1984.

al-Shawkānī, Muḥammad b. 'Alī. *Nayl al-Awṭār Sharḥ Muntaqā al-Akhbār min Aḥādīth Sayyid al-Akhyār*. Cairo: Maktabat al-Qāhira, 1978.

Shuhda bint Aḥmad. *al-'Umda min al-Fawā'id wa'l-Āthār al-Ṣiḥāḥ wa'l-Gharā'ib fī Mashyakhat Shuhda*. Cairo: Maktabat al-Khānjī, 1994.

Ṣiddīqī, M. Z. *Ḥadīth Literature*. Revised and edited by Abdul Hakim Murad. Cambridge: Islamic Texts Society, 1993.

al-Silafī, Abū Ṭāhir Aḥmad b. Muḥammad. *Mu'jam al-Safar*. Beirut: Dār al-Fikr, 1993.

al-Wajīz fī Dhikr al-Mujāz wa'l-Mujīz. Beirut: Dār al-Gharb al-Islāmī, 1991.

Silvers, Laury. "'God Loves Me': The Theological Content and Context of Early Pious and Sufi Women's Sayings on Love." *Journal for Islamic Studies* 30 (2010): 33–59.

Sitt al-'Ajam bint al-Nafīs. *Sharḥ al-Mashāhid al-Qudsiyya*. Edited by Bakr 'Alā' al-Dīn and Su'ād al-Ḥakīm. Damascus: al-Ma'had al-Faransī li'l-Sharq al-Adnā, 2004.

Slackman, Michael. "A Compass That Can Clash with Modern Life." *New York Times*, June 12, 2007 (http://query.nytimes.com/gst/fullpage.html?res=F20D10F83C5B0C718DDDAF0894DF404482).

Smith, Margaret. *Rabi'a, the Life and Works of Rabi'a and Other Women Mystics in Islam*. Cambridge: Cambridge University Press, 1928. Reprinted with an introduction by Annemarie Schimmel, New York: Cambridge University Press, 1984.

Soufi, Denise. "The Image of Fāṭima in Classical Muslim Thought." PhD diss., Princeton University, 1997.

Spellberg, Denise. *Politics, Gender, and the Islamic Past*. New York: Columbia University Press, 1994.

Stern, Gertrude. *Marriage in Early Islam*. London: Royal Asiatic Society, 1939.

Stowasser, Barbara. *Women in the Qur'an, Traditions, and Interpretation*. New York: Oxford University Press, 1994.

al-Subkī, Tāj al-Dīn. *Ṭabaqāt al-Shāfi'īyya al-Kubrā*. Cairo: Maṭba'at 'Īsā al-Bābī al-Ḥalabī, 1964–76.

al-Sulamī, Abū 'Abd al-Raḥmān. *Dhikr al-Niswa al-Muta'abbidāt al-Ṣūfiyyāt*. Translated and edited by Rkia Cornell. Louisville: Fons Vitae, 1999.

al-Suyūṭī, 'Abd al-Raḥmān b. Abī Bakr b. Muḥammad. *Musnad Fāṭima al-Zahrā'*. Beirut: Mu'assasat al-Kutub al-Thaqāfiyya, 1993.

Tanwīr al-Ḥawālik Sharḥ 'alā Muwaṭṭa' Mālik wa-Yalīhi Kitāb Is'āf al-Mubaṭṭa' bi-Rijāl al-Muwaṭṭa'. Beirut: al-Maktaba al-Thaqāfiyya, 1973.

al-Ṭabarī, Muḥammad b. Jarīr. *Jāmi' al-Bayān 'an Tafsīr al-Qur'ān*. Beirut: Dār al-Shāmiyya, 1997.

al-Tamīmi, Taqī al-Dīn b. 'Abd al-Qādir. *al-Ṭabaqāt al-Saniyya fī Tarājim al-Ḥanafiyya*. Riyad: Dār al-Rifā'ī, 1983.

al-Tirmidhī, Muḥammad b. 'Īsā. *Sunan*. Beirut: Dār al-Fikr, 1994.

al-'Ulaymī, 'Abd al-Raḥmān b. Muḥammad. *al-Durr al-Munaḍḍad*. Cairo: Maṭba'at al-Madanī, 1992.

Vadet, Jean Claude. "Une personnalité féminine du Ḥiğāz au Ier/VIIe siècle: Sukayna, petite-fille de 'Alī." *Arabica* 4 (1957): 261–87.

Vajda, Georges. "Un opuscule inedit d'as-Silafī." In *La transmission du savoir en Islam*. London: Variorum, 1983.

van Doorn-Harder, Pieternella. *Women Shaping Islam: Reading the Qur'an in Indonesia*. Chicago: University of Illinois Press, 2006.

Williams, Sally. "Mourchidat: Morocco's Female Muslim Clerics." *The Telegraph*, April 26, 2008 (http://www.telegraph.co.uk/culture/3672924/Mourchidat-Moroccos-female-Muslim-clerics.html).

al-Yāfi'ī, 'Abd Allāh b. As'ad. *Mir'āt al-Jinān wa-'Ibrat al-Yaqẓān*. Beirut: Mu'assasat al-A'lamī lil-Maṭbū'āt, 1970.

Zadeh, Travis. *Vernacular Qur'ān: Translation and the Rise of Persian Exegesis*. New York: Oxford University Press, 2012.

al-Zamakhsharī, Maḥmūd b. 'Umar. *al-Kashshāf*. Cairo: Maktabat al-Bābī al-Ḥalabī, 1966.

Zaman, Muhammad Qasim. *Religion and Politics under the Early 'Abbāsids: The Emergence of the Proto-Sunnī Elite*. New York: Brill, 1997.

'Ulamā' in Contemporary Islam: Custodians of Change. Princeton: Princeton University Press, 2002.

al-Zarkashī, Muḥammad b. Bahādur. *al-Baḥr al-Muḥīṭ fī Uṣūl al-Fiqh*. Beirut: Dār al-Kutub al-'Ilmiyya, 2000.

al-Ijāba li-Īrād mā Istadrakathu 'Ā'isha 'alā al-Ṣaḥāba. Beirut: al-Maktab al-Islāmī, 1970.

Zaydān, 'Abd al-Karīm. *Mufaṣṣal fī Aḥkām al-Mar'a wa'l-Bayt Muslim*. Beirut: Mu'assasat al-Risāla, 1994.

al-Ziriklī, Khayr al-Dīn. *al-A'lām*. Beirut: Dār al-'Ilm li'l-Malāyīn, 1986.

Zoepf, Katherine. "Islamic Revival in Syria Is Led by Women." *New York Times*, August 29, 2006 (http://www.nytimes.com/ref/world/middleeast/29syria.html).

Index

Titles in the series

Popular Culture in Medieval Cairo Boaz Shoshan
Early Philosophical Shiism: The Ismaili Neoplatonism of Abū Ya'qūb Al-Sijistānī Paul E. Walker
Indian Merchants and Eurasian Trade, 1600–1750 Stephen Frederic Dale
Palestinian Peasants and Ottoman Officials: Rural Administration around Sixteenth-Century Jerusalem Amy Singer
Arabic Historical Thought in the Classical Period Tarif Khalidi
Mongols and Mamluks: The Mamluk – Īlkhānid War, 1260–1281 Reuven Amitai-Preiss
Hierarchy and Egalitarianism in Islamic Thought Louise Marlow
The Politics of Households in Ottoman Egypt: The Rise of the Qazdağlis Jane Hathaway
Commodity and Exchange in the Mongol Empire: A Cultural History of Islamic Textiles Thomas T. Allsen
State and Provincial Society in the Ottoman Empire: Mosul, 1540–1834 Dina Rizk Khoury
The Mamluks in Egyptian Politics and Society Thomas Philipp *and* Ulrich Haarmann *(eds.)*
The Delhi Sultanate: A Political and Military History Peter Jackson
European and Islamic Trade in the Early Ottoman State: The Merchants of Genoa and Turkey Kate Fleet
Reinterpreting Islamic Historiography: Hārūn Al-Rashīd and the Narrative of the 'Abbāsid Caliphate Tayeb El-Hibri
The Ottoman City between East and West: Aleppo, Izmir, and Istanbul Edhem Eldem, Daniel Goffman, *and* Bruce Masters
A Monetary History of the Ottoman Empire Şevket Pamuk
The Politics of Trade in Safavid Iran: Silk for Silver, 1600–1730 Rudolph P. Matthee
The Idea of Idolatry and the Emergence of Islam: From Polemic to History G. R. Hawting
Classical Arabic Biography: The Heirs of the Prophets in the Age of al-Ma'mūn Michael Cooperson
Empire and Elites after the Muslim Conquest: The Transformation of Northern Mesopotamia Chase F. Robinson
Poverty and Charity in Medieval Islam: Mamluk Egypt, 1250–1517 Adam Sabra
Christians and Jews in the Ottoman Arab World: The Roots of Sectarianism Bruce Masters
Culture and Conquest in Mongol Eurasia Thomas T. Allsen
Revival and Reform in Islam: The Legacy of Muhammad al-Shawkani Bernard Haykel
Tolerance and Coercion in Islam: Interfaith Relations in the Muslim Tradition Yohanan Friedmann
Guns for the Sultan: Military Power and the Weapons Industry in the Ottoman Empire Gábor Ágoston
Marriage, Money and Divorce in Medieval Islamic Society Yossef Rapoport
The Empire of the Qara Khitai in Eurasian History: Between China and the Islamic World Michal Biran
Domesticity and Power in the Early Mughal World Ruby Lal

Power, Politics and Religion in Timurid Iran Beatrice Forbes Manz
Postal Systems in the Pre-Modern Islamic World Adam J. Silverstein
Kingship and Ideology in the Islamic and Mongol Worlds Anne F. Broadbridge
Justice, Punishment and the Medieval Muslim Imagination Christian Lange
The Shiites of Lebanon under Ottoman Rule, 1516–1788 Stefan Winter
Women and Slavery in the Late Ottoman Empire Madeline Zilfi
The Second Ottoman Empire: Political and Social Transformation in the Early Modern World Baki Tezcan
Non-Muslims in the Early Islamic Empire: From Surrender to Coexistence Milka Levy-Rubin
The Legendary Biographies of Tamerlane: Islam and Heroic Apocrypha in Central Asia Ron Sela
Ritual and Piety in Medieval Islamic Law Megan Reid
The Origins of the Shīʿa: Identity, Ritual, and Sacred Space in Eighth-Century Kufa Najam Haider
Politics, Law, and Community in Islamic Thought: The Taymiyyan Moment Ovamir Anjum
The Power of Oratory in the Medieval Muslim World Linda G. Jones
Animals in the Qu'ran Sarra Tlili
The Logic of Law-Making in Islam: Women and Prayer in the Legal Tradition Behnam Sadeghi
Empire and Power in the Reign of Süleyman Kaya Şahin
Women and the Transmission of Religious Knowledge in Islam Asma Sayeed